NIKON® DATA

BY PAUL COMON AND ART EVANS

This is an independent publication by Photo Data Research. Photo Data Research is not connected with the Nikon Corporation or Nikon Inc. in any way. The cooperation of the Nikon Corporation and Nikon Inc., however is acknowledged. All information contained in this book is correct to the best knowledge of the authors and the publisher. The use of this information, however, is beyond the control of the authors and the publisher; all liability is expressly disclaimed.

Library of Congress Catalog Card Number 90-81643
ISBN 0-9626508-0-3

Published by Photo Data Research
800 S. Pacific Coast Highway, Suite 8332, Redondo Beach, California 90277
Phone (213) 540-8068 FAX 213-540-2607

Manufactured in the United States of America

Cover design by Monica Craig

OCTOBER 1954

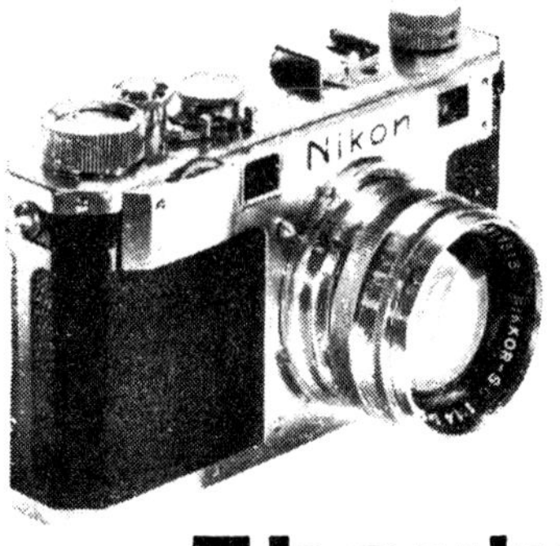

Within just a few years, the names Nikon and Nikkor have rocketed from relative obscurity to first place prominence.

They've <u>got</u> to be good

From the very moment they were introduced, NIKON CAMERAS and NIKKOR LENSES became the talk of the nation. Rave comments were heard everywhere, and feature articles appeared in widely read national publications extolling the virtues of these new products born of the new Japanese optical industry. In very short order, they were adopted and put to work by America's most critical users; names that read like the 'who's who' of journalistic photographers.

Nikon
35mm
CAMERAS

Nikkor
LENSES

The Reasons Are Clear:

1 NIKON CAMERAS embody every important advance developed to date . . . every feature regarded as useful and desirable in miniature camera design. Shutter, Rangefinder, Lens Mount, Film Transport . . . all operate and perform with an ease and smoothness that can only result from superior materials and faultless workmanship.

2 NIKKOR LENSES are, without doubt, the finest known to optical science. Only complete devotion to infinite detail, and rigid quality control practices account for their performance. Nikkor lenses have created some of the greatest pictures of our time, and at this very moment, are covering the world's most important events.

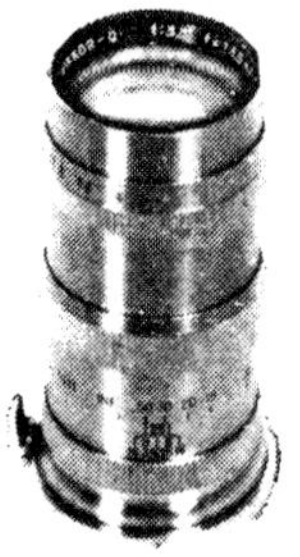

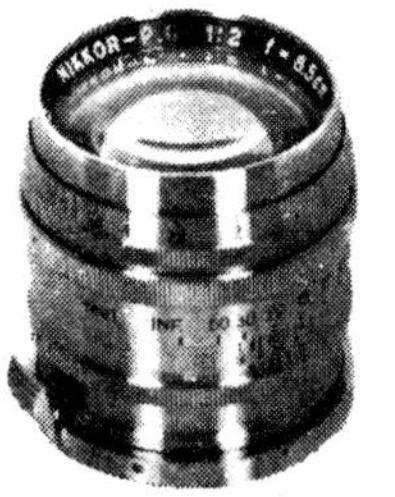

NIKON CAMERA with Coated 50mm f2 NIKKOR Lens is priced at $269 list.

NIKKOR LENSES are also available in mounts to fit Leica, Contax, Canon, and Exakta Cameras.

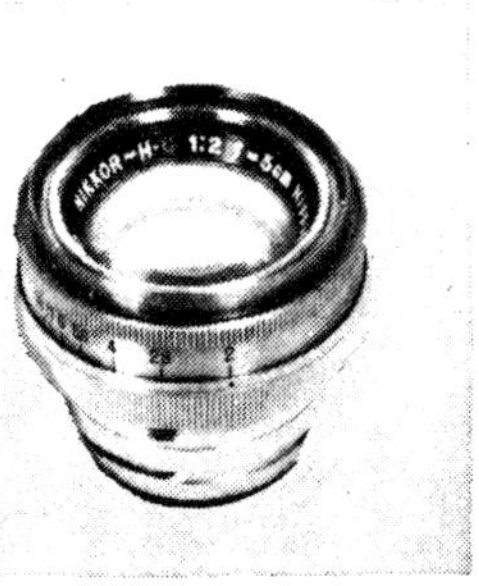

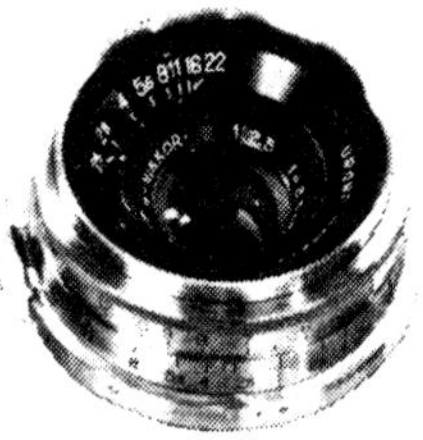

Nikon Cameras and Nikkor Lenses are made by Nippon Kogaku, Tokyo, Japan

See your dealer or write to Dept. BK-2, NIKON INCORPORATED, 277 Fifth Avenue, New York 16, N. Y.

TABLE OF CONTENTS

PREFACE

This book contains a great deal of data and information. Even with careful proof reading, with such an amount of material to compile, it is inevitable there might be errors. The authors are very desirous that future editions of the book be as accurate as possible; therefore, each reader is enlisted to help. Please write to us with any comments, suggestions or corrections. When you do, please keep in mind that all of the data and information in this book is based on either documentation or direct physical evidence. If you have a correction, deletion or addition to suggest, we would very much appreciate it if you would send along evidence to support your contribution. Please write us in care of the publisher whose name and address is listed on the title page of this book.

Since there will be future editions of this book, this presents an opportunity to improve the contents. The authors have a number of ideas for additions which may appear in the next edition. And there are very probably things which should be in this edition. The authors believed, however, that it would be more useful to publish this present edition in a timely manner rather than delay its publication in order to include more material.

The authors are interested in hearing from you regarding the contents and usefulness of this book. Please write us with your comments.

This book is not an official publication of the Nikon Corporation, Nikon Inc. or any other organization connected with the company. While the authors gratefully acknowledge the vast amount of assistance provided by the company, many of its officers and employees, this book is entirely an independent effort.

A number of people helped in the preparation of the manuscript. Among them were Lisa Hughes, Jay Jeszenka, Roger Newsham, Ginny Dixon, Susann Cellier, Chuck Gorton and Peter Hubert, Shirley Comon and David Evans.

Joe Strear and others at Strear, David & Mitchell, Inc., the Nikon Inc. public relations agency were very helpful.

Thanks are due Nikon Inc. for the many photographs, charts and tables. Among those who helped at Nikon Inc. were John Clouse, Richard LoPinto, Don Crown (retired), Glen Miyoda, Steve Jarmon, Suzanne Freeman, Bill Giordano and particularly David Sears.

Important contributions were received from Robert Rotoloni, author of *Nikon Rangefinder Cameras* and the foremost Nikon historian.

Special thanks are due to Willi Winzelberg of Authorized Camera Service, and Graham Ashford, without whose help this book would not have been possible.

In spite of all the very valuable assistance the authors have received from the individuals listed above, it is inevitable that errors have been made. In these instances, the fault lies solely with the authors, not with any of the consultants or contributors.

An interesting part of this book is the reprints of advertisements. On the inside front cover there are two ads. The ad for a Nikon rangefinder camera is the first one the authors could find which was printed in the US.

The other ad on the title page is for Nikon's newest professional camera, the F4s. The two ads, together, symbolize the contents of this book: data and information about Nikon photographic products since the introduction of Nikon's first camera to the present.

The advertisments are identified by the date they appeared in a magazine. The date is printed inside a rectangle:

MONTH, YEAR

Over the years, Paul Comon has compiled a collection of printed materials from which selections were made. In future editions, the authors intend to include different ads. If any reader has any interesting or significant ads, please mail them to the publisher.

Thanks is due to Scali, McCabe, Stoves, Inc. (the current Nikon Inc. advertising agency) and Brooks Elder. Credit is due to Jerry Friedman who photographed the ads on pages 38 and 130 and Dennis Manarchy who photographed the ad on page 86.

INTRODUCTION

This book is intended for those who buy, sell, use or collect Nikon photographic equipment. The authors are hopeful it will be useful to both professional and amateur photographers as well as those who deal in photographic equipment.

Nikon cameras and accessories are among the very best available. The proof of this is their popularity among those who depend on cameras for their living. For professionals, the most important characteristic about equipment is reliability. A pro can do without "bells and whistles" just so long as the equipment works every time.

Another important characteristic is flexibility. Most Nikon cameras, lenses and accessories are interchangeable to the extent that a camera system can be customized for particular uses. And this brings up one of the reasons for this book. What works with what?

Every year, Nikon introduces new equipment and discontinues some items that are past their prime. In some instances, parts for certain items become unavailable. For many of those concerned with Nikon products, knowledge pertaining to availability is important. This book attempts to address that subject.

As changes warrant it, a new edition of *Nikon Data* will be published. The date of publication will depend on the availability of new data and information. Sometime each year, Nikon Inc. publishes a new price list. The list not only reflects any price changes, but also additions or deletions. Additionally, the Photo Marketing Association usually has its annual meeting sometime during the first quarter of each year. Many manufacturers, Nikon included, often use this occasion to introduce new products.

Each new edition of *Nikon Data* will reflect those items added to the line since the previous edition plus changes in prices, items withdrawn, parts no longer available as well as other new and additional information.

It is important that the readers of these pages understand that this book is intended for those who buy and/or sell Nikon photographic products. It should not be utilized as a user's manual. The first and best source of user information is the printed instructional materials packaged with each Nikon product. When you purchase a new Nikon product, be sure it is accompanied by appropriate printed instructions. Many used products are offered without instructions. In this instance, printed materials on all current and many discontinued items can be obtained from Nikon. For the most convenient Nikon location refer to the first chapter in this book.

Before using any product, you should read the instructions very carefully. **In some instances, mismatching items can result in damage.** The instructions should be a part of your kit until you know them by heart.

In addition to the manufacturer's printed instructions, there are a number of books about using various Nikon products which may be of value. It is certainly less expensive, as well as much less traumatic, to learn from books rather than by trial and error. And often, printed information in such magazines as *Shutterbug* can be of great value.

This book should also be useful to collectors. Nikon rangefinder cameras have become very valuable, particularly those in mint condition. And recently, more and more collectors are interested in later Nikon products. The best source for further rangefinder information is *Nikon Rangefinder Cameras* by Robert Rotoloni. See pages 17 and 152.

A revised edition of *Nikon Data* is already in the planning stage. The first copies will be delivered to those who have placed prepublication orders. In order to do so, send in the form at the back of this book.

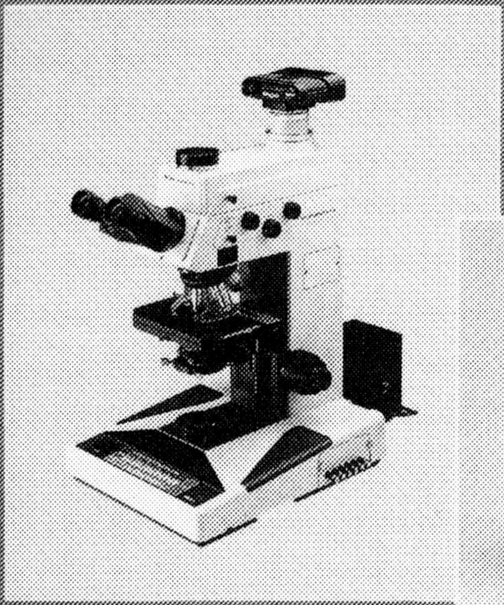

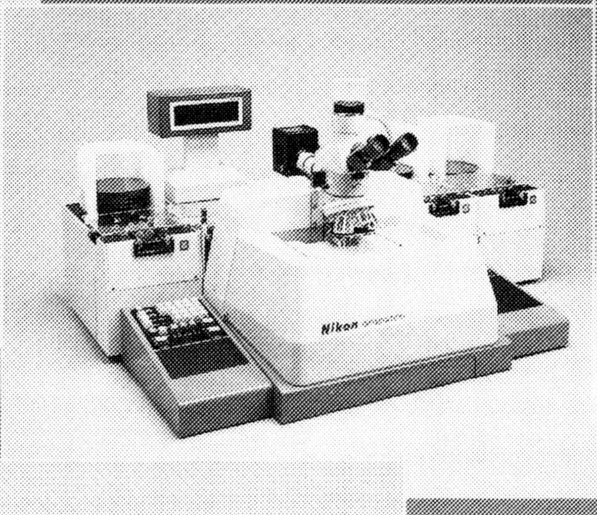

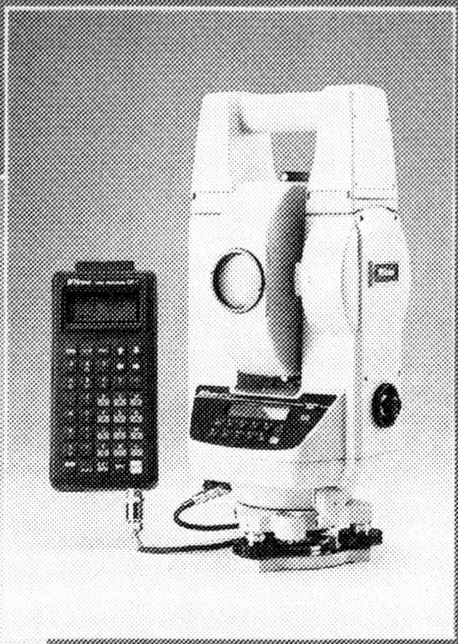

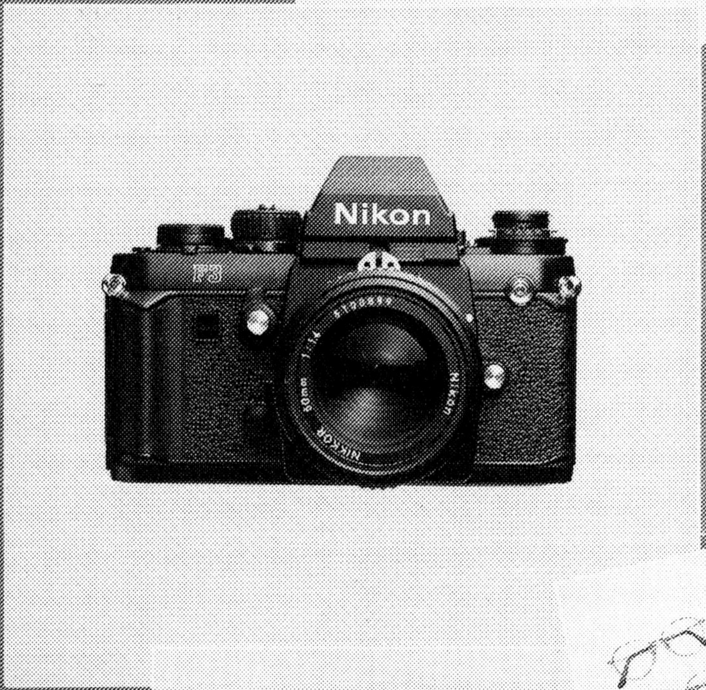
Nikon

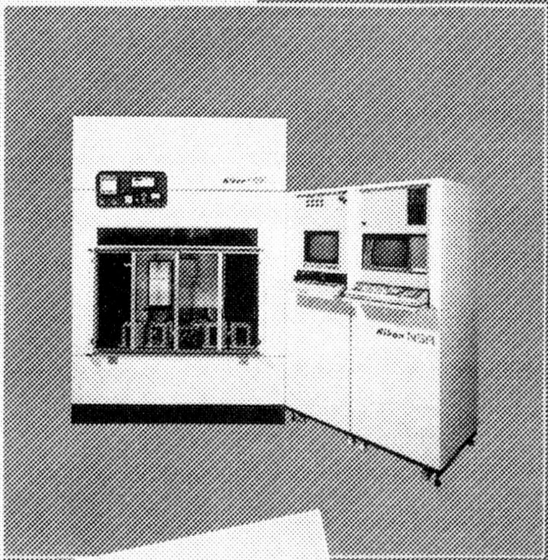

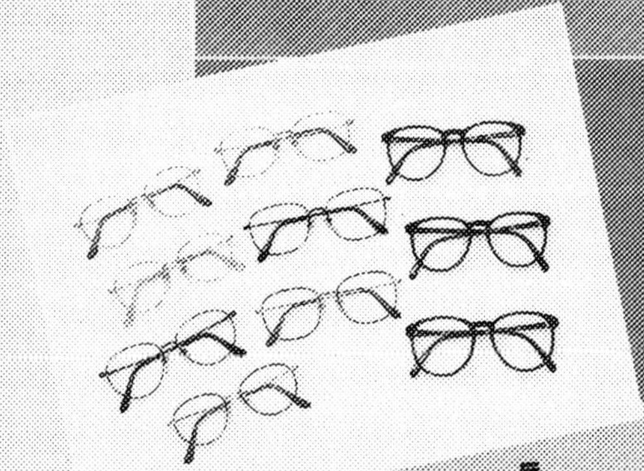

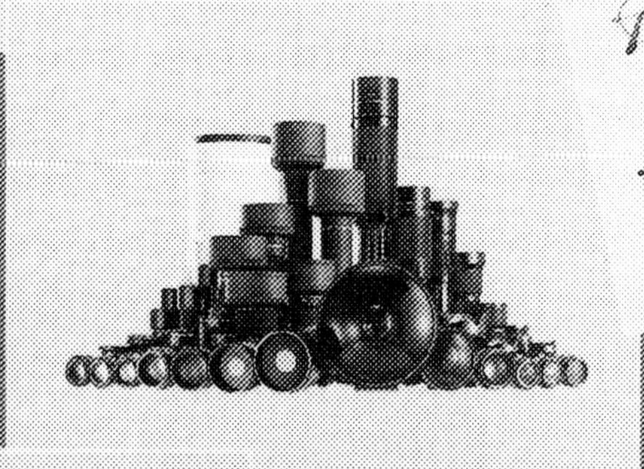

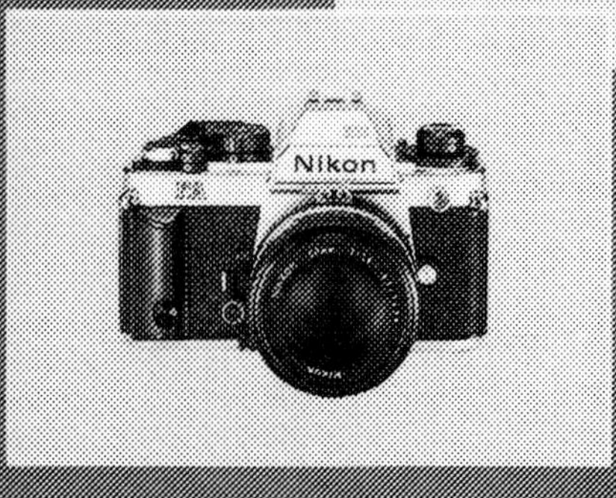
Nikon

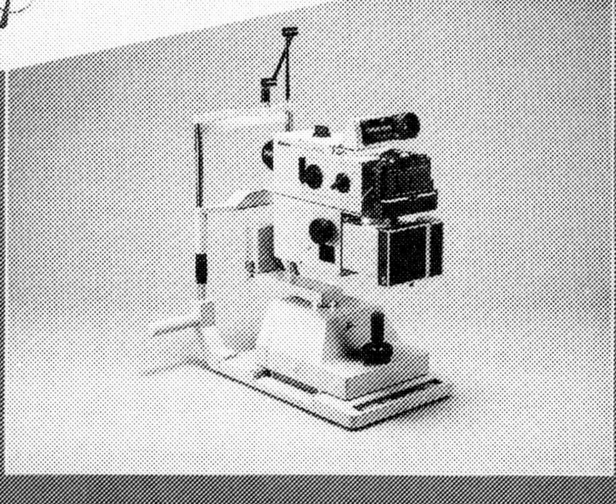

CHAPTER ONE

THE NIKON ORGANIZATION AND HISTORY

Nikon is a world-wide organization. The company is based in Japan. The official name of the company is The Nikon Corporation. The original name of the company was Nippon Kogaku (which means Japan Optical). The name, Nikon, comes from the first two letters of the company name: NIppon KOgaku. Most manufacturing takes place in Japan. In the United States, Nikon is represented by Nikon Inc., which is incorporated in the United States and wholly owned by The Nikon Corporation.

NIKON DIVISIONS

- Photo Products Division
  - Nikon 35mm SLR and leaf-shutter cameras
  - Nikonos all-weather cameras
  - Nikkor and Nikon interchangeable lenses
  - Nikon system accessories
  - Large format Nikkor lenses
- Electronic Image Engineering Division
  - Nikon video camcorders
  - Nikon lenses for TV cameras
  - Nikon still video system
  - Nikon 35mm film direct telephoto transmitter
  - El-Nikkor
  - APO-Nikkor
  - Printing-Nikkor
- Instruments Division
  - Microscopes
  - Optical Measuring Instruments
  - Surveying Instruments
- Ophthalmic Division
  - Binoculars, riflescopes, telescopes
  - Ophthalmic instruments
  - Ophthalmic lenses
  - Frames and sunglasses
- Industrial Supplies and Equipment Division
  - IC manufacturing and inspection instrument
  - Nikon step and repeat system, NSR Series
  - Laser interferometric X-Y measuring machine
  - Incident-light micro-pattern analyzer lamps
  - Mask comparator, micro-pattern analyzer
  - Particle monitor, reticle cleaner

NIKON PLANTS AND FACILITIES

The Nikon Corporation

Head Office

Fuji Building, 2-3, 3-Chome, Marunouchi, Chiyoda-Ku, Tokyo 100
Phone: (03) 214-5311; Telex: J22601 Nikon A; Fax: 03-201-5856

Industrial Supplies and Equipment Division

Tokiokaijo Building, Shinkan, 2-1, 1-Chome, Marunouchi, Chiyoda-Ku, Tokyo 100, Japan
Phone: (03) 216-1030; Fax: 03-214-0619 or 03-214-2920

Ohi Plant

6-3, 1-Chome, Nishiohi, Shinagawa-Ku, Tokyo 140, Japan
Phone: (03) 773-1111

Yokohama Plant

471, Nagaodai-Machi, Sakai-ku, Yokohama, Kanagawa 244, Japan
Phone: (045) 852-2111

Sagamihara Plant

1773, Asamizodai, Sagamihara, Kanagawa 288, Japan
Phone: (0427) 45-3311

Kumagaya Plant

201-9, Miizugahara, Kumagaya, Saitama 360, Japan
Phone: (0485) 33-2111

Ginza Service Center

B1, Yuraku Food Cntr, Higashikan 2-2, Ginzanishi, Chou-Ku, Tokyo 104, Japan
Phone: (03) 561-0888

Shinjuku Service Center

B1, Shinjuku-Center Bldg., 25-1, 1-Chome, Nishi-Shinjuku, Tokyo 160, Japan
Phone: (03) 349-0701

NIKON OVERSEAS SUBSIDIARIES

Nikon Inc.

New York Headquarters

623 Stewart Ave., Garden City, NY 11530, USA
Phone: (516) 222-0200; Telex: 967806 NIKON GRCY; Fax: 516-222-2823

IMPORTANT NOTICE

In June 1990, Nikon Inc. Headquarters will move to:
1300 Walt Whitman Road, Melville, NY 11746; Call Information for phone #

Los Angeles Branch

19601 Hamilton St., Torrance, CA 90502, USA
Phone: (213) 516-7124; Fax: 213-516-7751

Chicago Branch

7550 N. Oak Park Ave., Niles, IL 60648, USA
Phone: (312) 647-1075; Fax 312-647-7854

San Francisco Branch (photo only)

501 Folsom St., San Francisco, CA 94105, USA
Phone: (415) 541-7406, (415) 541-7414; Fax 415-541-0110

Atlanta Branch

5355 Oakbrook Parkway, Norcross, GA 30093, USA
Phone: (404) 564-2156, (404) 564-2401; Fax 404-921-4359

Dallas Branch

1600 Corparate Court, Colinas Business Park, Irvine, TX 75038, USA
Phone: (214) 550-0046; Fax: 214-0144

Washington, DC Office (photo only)

655 15th St., NW, Suite 220, Washington, DC 20005, USA
Phone: (202) 393-0253

Nikon Precision Inc.
San Bruno Head Office
1176 Cherry Ave., San Bruno, CA 94066, USA
Phone: (415) 952-8188; Fax: 415-878-0124
Dallas Office
1600 Corporate Court, Colinas Business Park, Irvine, TX 75038, USA
Phone: (214) 550-0046; Fax: 214-550-0144
Nikon Canada Inc.
Toronto Office
1366 Aerowood Dr., Mississauga, Ontario L4W1C1, Canada
Phone: (416) 625-9910; Telex: 06960231 NIKONCANMSGA
Montreal Office
3300 Chemin Cote Vertu Road, Montreal, Quebec H4R2B7, Canada
Phone: (514) 332-5681; Fax: 514-332-3305
Vancouver Office
Nunber 5, 13511 Crestwood Place, Richmond, BC V6V2E9, Canada
Phone: (604) 276-0531; Fax 604-0873
Nikon Europe B.V.
Bldg. 72, PO Box 7609 1117 ZJ Schiphol-oost, The Netherlands
Phone: 020) 414-831; Telex: 11328 NIKONNL; Fax 020-43-73-95
Nikon AG
Kaspar Fenner-Strasse 6, 8700 Kusnacht/ZH, Switzerland
Phone: (01) 910-92-62; Telex: 825709 NIKONCH; Fax: 01-910-61-38
Nikon GMBH
Tiefenbroicher Weg 25, 4000 Dusseldorf 30, West Germany
Phone: (0211) 4157-0; Telex: 8584019 NIKOD; Fax: 0211-4157-590
Nikon UK Ltd.
380 Richmond Rd., Kingston, Surrey KT2 5PR, United Kingdom
Phone: (01) 541-4440; Telex: 923044 NIKONG; Fax 01-541-4584
Nikon UK Ltd., Instruments Department
Haybrook Halesfield 9, Telford, Shropshire TF7 4EW, United Kingdom
Phone: (0952) 587-444; Telex: 35509 NIKONG; Fax 0952-588-009
Nikon France SA
16, Rue de la Cerisaie, B.P. 33, 94222, Charenton-Le Pont, France
Phone: (1) 43-75-97-55; Telex: NIKONFR 262546F; Fax 1-43-78-53-97
Nikon Hong Kong Ltd.
Room 1202-3, 12th Floor, Admiralty Center, Tower II,
18 Harcourt Road, Central, Hong Kong
Phone: (5) 861-0028; Fax: 5-295-914

NIKON SHOWROOM AND GALLERY
Nikon House
620 Fifth Avenue at Rockfeller Center, NY, NY 10020, USA
Phone: (212) 586-3907
Nikon Live Gallerie
Schoffelgasse 3, (Beim Rudenplatz) 8001 Zurich, Switzerland
Phone: (01) 251-2407

NIKON USA AUTHORIZED SERVICE STATIONS
Alabama
Bush and Millimaki Services, Inc.
902 Bob Wallace Ave. SE; Huntsville, AL 35801; (205) 533-9274
Arizona
Phoenix Camera Repair, Inc.
3232 N. Sixteenth St.; Phoenix, AZ 85016; (602) 277-1811

Tucson Camera Repair
742 W. Limberlost; Tucson, AZ 85705; (602) 887-1841
California
Nikon Inc.
501 Folsom St.; San Francisco, CA 94105; (415) 541-1700
Nikon Inc.
19601 Hamilton Ave.; Torrance, CA 90502; (213) 516-7124
Authorized Camera Service
12918 Riverside Dr.; Sherman Oaks, CA 91423; (818) 788-0404
Camera Service Center
4355 S. Sepulveda Blvd.; Culver City, CA 90203; (213) 397-0072
International Camera Technicans
914 West El Camino Real; Mountain View, CA 94040; (415) 961-5825
Kurt's Camera Repair, Inc.
7805 Mission Gorge Road; San Diego, CA 92120; (714) 286-1810
Mel Pierce Camera
5645 Hollywood Blvd.: Hollywood, CA 90028; (213) 465-2191
Metro Camera Service, Inc.
150 Fifth Street North; San Francisco, CA 94102; (415) 421-3551
California Precision Service, Inc.
1714 28th St.; Sacramento, CA 95816; (916) 451-1330
Pro Camera Service
3166 Thousand Oaks Blvd.; Thousand Oaks, CA; (805) 497-7240
Colorado
Metro Camera Service, Inc.
1470 S. Federal Blvd.; Denver, CO 80219; (303) 934-2471
Rocky Mountain Camera Repair
240 Broadway; Denver, CO 80203; (303) 744-3459
District of Columbia
Strauss Photo-Tech Service, Inc.
1240 Mt. Olivet Road, N.E.; Washington, DC 20002; (202) 529-3200
Florida
Dan's Camera Clinic, Inc.
5142 Biscayne Blvd.; Miami, FL 33137; (305) 759-2541
So Photo-Tech Service, Inc.
3241 Beach Blvd.; Jacksonville, FL 32207; (904) 398-7577
So Photo-Tech Service, Inc.
14352 Biscayne Blvd.; Miami, FL 33181; (305) 947-2470
So Photo-Tech Service, Inc.
1201 N. Mills Ave.; Orlando, FL 32803; (305) 896-0233
So Photo-Tech Service, Inc.
2630 Jefferson Highway; St. Petersburg, FL 33713; (813) 896-6141
Georgia
Nikon Inc. Atlanta
5355 Oakbrook Parkway; Norcross, GA 30093; (404) 564-2394
Camera Service Company
4391 Atlanta Road; Smyrna, GA 30080; (404) 432-4257
Hawaii
Photocine Servicenter, Inc.
1585 Kapiolani Blvd., Suite 722; Honolulu, HI 96814; (808) 941-4133
Illinois
Nikon Inc. Illinois
7550 N. Oak Park Ave.; Niles, IL 60648; (312) 647-0343

International Camera Corporation
321 S. Jefferson St.; Chicago IL 60608; (312) 876-1530
Kansas
Photo-Tech Service Center
110 North Main Street; Heston, KS 67062; (316) 327-2190
Kentucky
Camera Service Inc.
216 S. Selby St.; Louisville, KY 40202; (502) 583-5385
Louisiana
So Photo-Tech Service Inc.
2630 Jefferson Highway; Jefferson, LA 70121; (504) 853-3379
Massachusetts
Precision Camera Repair, Inc.
43 Sheridan St.; Chicopee Falls, MA 01020; (413) 598-8005
Sanford Camera and Projector Repair
1054 Massachusetts Ave.; Arlington, MA 02174; (617) 648-2505
S. K. Grimes
23 Drydock Ave.; Boston, MA 02210
Michigan
Midwest Camera
318 Oak St.; Wyandotte, MI 48192; (313) 285-2220
Minnesota
Marquette Camcra Repair
903 Marquette Ave.; Minncapolis, MN 55402; (612) 333-5787
Northwest Camera Repair Co.
529 South Seventh St.; Minneapolis, MN 55415; (612) 333-4125
Custom Camera
823 W. Lake St.; Minneapolis, MN 55408
Missouri
CPI Camera Repair Center
7935 Clayton Road; St. Louis, MO 63117; (314) 725-5649
Nevada
Lamb's Camera Repair
4229 W. Sahara; Las Vegas, NV 89102; (702) 876-0968
New Jersey
Mack Camera Service
200 Morris Ave.; Springfield, NJ 07081; (201)467-2291
New York
Nikon Inc.
623 Stewart Ave.; Garden City, NY 11530; (516) 222-0978
Hudson Valley Camera Repair
233 West Route 59; Nanuet, NY 10954; (914) 623-8057
Kipling's Camera, Inc.
19 Morris Ave.; Rockville Centre, NY 11570; (516) 678-7760
Photo-Tech Repair Service Inc.
132 Fourth Ave.; New York, NY 10003; (212) 673-8400
Professional Camera Service
37 West 47th St.; New York, NY 10036; (212) 382-0550
Russo Camera Repair
941-5 North Salina St.; Syracuse, NY 13208; (315) 471-5825
North Carolina
So Photo-Tech Service, Inc.
2610 South Blvd.; Charlotte, NC 28209; (704) 532-0012 or 532-0013
Ohio
Camera Service and Repair Company
18 W. Seventh St.; Cincinnati, OH 45202; (513) 241-8100

Camtronics
4345 N. High St.; Columbus, OH 43214; (614) 262-2784

Oklahoma

Photo Products Repair Inc.
3109 Classen Blvd.; Oklahoma City, OK 73118; (405) 521-8022

Oregon

Associated Camera Repair
3333 N.E. Sandy Blvd.; Portland, OR 97232; (503) 232-5625

Pennsylvania

Comet Camera Repair Shop Inc.
1223 Arch St.; Philadelphia, PA 19107; (215_569-2822

Texas

Archinal Camera Repair
3100 Commerce St.; Dallas, TX 75226; (214) 748-6637

Havel Camera Service
1102 Basse Road; San Antonio, TX 78212; (512) 735-7412

Camera Services Inc.
3407 South Shephard St.; Houston, TX 77098; (713) 528-6652

Virginia

Strauss Photo-Tech Service Inc.
434 West 21st St.; Norfolk, VA 23517; (804) 625-5341

Washington

Yakima Camera Repair
406 S. Third St.; Yakima, WA 98901; (509) 575-1539

Wisconsin

BDC Enterprises, Inc.
133 West Johnson St.; Madison, WI 53703; (608) 257-5315

Wyoming

Photo-Electronics
145 S. Washington St.; Casper, WY 82601; (307) 234-8282

NIKON WORLDWIDE SERVICE FACILITIES

Argentina

Eduardo Udenio y Cia. S.A.C.I.F.I.
Ayacucho 1235; Buenos Aires; 425-538

Australia

Maxwell Optical Industries Pty. Ltd.
Unit 5, Level B, 100 Harris St.; Pymont 2009, N.S.W.; (02) 660-7088

Austria

Prihoda & Beck Ges m.b.H.
Schottenfeldgasse 14, 1072 Wien, 0222-931-521 or 931-523

Barbados

Louis L. Bayley & Son Ltd.
33Brood St., Bridgetown, 65-651

Brazil

T. Tanaka & Cia. Ltda.
Rua Martim Francisco, 438 (Sta Cecilia) Sao Paulo, 825-2255

Canada

Nikon Canada Inc.
3300 Chemin Cote Verfu Rd., Montreal, Quebec H4R 2B7, (514) 332-5681

Nikon Canada Inc.
1366 Aerowood Drive, Mississauga, Ontario L4W 1C1, (416) 625-9910

Nikon Canada Inc.
Unit 5, 13551 Crestwood Place, Richmond, B.C. V6V 2E9 (604) 276-0531

Chile
Reifschneider Foto S.A.C.I.
Agustinas 1451-1161, Santiago, 225-4004
Cyprus
K. H. Papasian Ltd.
240 Ledra Street, Nicosia, 63-795
Denmark
Dansk Fotoagentur A/S
Produktionsvej 23B, DK 2600 Glostrup, 02-94-70-22
Finland
Suomen I.C.I Oy
Nuijamiestentie, 1-3, A, SF-00400, Helsinki40, 90-585-550
France
Nikon France S.A.
16 Rue de la Cerisaie, 94220 Charenton-le-Pont, 1-43-75-97-55
Greece
D & J Damkalids S.A.
7 Karageorgi Servais St., Athens 126, 32-48-391-4
West Germany
Nikon GmbH
Tiefenbroicher Weg 25, 4 Dusseldorf 30, (0211) 4157-0
Hong Kong
Shriro (H>K>) Ltd.
2d Floor, Hutchson House, 10 Harcourt Road, 5-245031-8
Ireland
Somerton Foto Ltd.
12 Grafton St., Dublin 2, (01) 773-173
Israel
Hadar Photo Supply Agencies Ltd.
PO Box 1686, Tel-Aviv 61016, 03-623-407/8
Italy
Konos S.p.A.
Via Ticino 12-14, Osmannoro, Firenze, (055) 372-381
Kuwait
Ashraf & Co., Ltd.
Safat P. Code 13036-Safat, 531-2960
Malaysia
Shriro (Malaysia) SDN-BHD
No. 9 Jalan Dua, Off Jalan, Chan Sow Lin, Kuala Lumpur, 07-01
Mexico
Mayoristas Fotograficos, S.A.
Dr. Jimenez 159, Mexico 7, D.F., 588-7011
Netherlands
INCA B.V.
Rutherfordstraat 7, Haarlem, 023-249181
New Caledonia
Phocidis
B.P. 2359, Noumea, 721-70
New Zealand
T. A. Macalister Limited
Private Bag Auckland, 65-73 Parnell Rise Parnell, Auckland, 34-334
Norway
Interfoto A.S.
O.H. Bangsvel 51, 1322 Hovik, (02) 53-49-90

Reunion
  Dimaciphot S.A.
    5-7 rue Amiral Lacaze, B.P., 288, 974467, Saint-Denis Cedex, 21-78-51
Saudi Arabia
  Ahmed Abdulwahed Abdullah Trading Establishment
    Hail Commercial Centre, 3rd Floor, Hail Road, Jeddah, 642-5333
Singapore
  Shriro (Singapore) Pte. Ltd.
    Orchard Shopping Centre, 08-07 Orchard Road, 284-0058
South Africa
  Frank & Hirsch (Pty.) Ltd.
    350 Bree Street, Johannesburg 2001, (011) 28-3020
Spain
  Finicon S.A.
    Calle Laforja 95, Barcelona 21, (93) 200-1744
  Finicon S.A.
    Calle Reina Mercedes 7, Madrid 20, (91) 253-9392
Sweden
  Nordic Camera AB
    Pyramidvagen 7, Solna, 08-734-0090
Switzerland
  Nikon AG
    Kaspar-Fenner Strasse 6, 8700 Kusnacht/Zurich, 01-910-9262
United Kingdom
  Nikon U.K. Ltd.
    380 Richmond Road, Kingston, Surrey KT2 5PR, 01-541-4440
Uruguay
  Micro S.C.
    Avenida 18 de Julio 1202, Montevideo, 982-639
USA
  Nikon Inc.
    623 Stewart Ave., Garden City, New York 12530, (516) 222-0200

IMPORTANT NOTICE

In June 1990, Nikon Inc. Headquarters will move to
1300 Walt Whitman Rd., Melville, NY 11746, call information for phone number.

Japan
  Nikon Corporation Ohmori Service Department
    6-19-22 Ohmorikita, Ohta-ku, Tokyo 143, (03) 764-2605
  Nikon Corporation Sapporo Branch Office
    Ohdori Bldg., 1-12 Ohdorinishi, Chou-ku, Sapporo 060, (011) 231-7896
  Nikon Corporation Shinjuku Service Center
    1-25-1 Nishi-Shinjuku, Shinjuku-ku, Tokyo (02) 349-0701
  Nikon Corporation Ginza Service Center
    2-2 Ginzanishi, Chou-ku, Tokyo (02) 561-0888
  Nikon Corporation Yokahama Branch Office
    5-15 Kitasaiwai 2-chome, Nishi-ku, Yokohama 220, (045) 312-1101
  Nikon Corporation Nagoya Service Station
    3-28-12 Meieki, Nakamura-ku, Nagoya 450, (052) 562-2881
  Nikon Corporation Osaka Branch Office
    2-11-20 Minamisenba, Minami-ku, Osaka 542, (06) 251-7024
  Nikon Corporation Osaka Umeda Service Station
    1-4-17 Shibata, Kita-ku, Osaka 530, (06) 372-3385
  Nikon Corporation Fukuoaka Branch Office
    2-12-1 Tenjin, Chou-ku, Fukuoaka 810, (092) 721-3561
  Nikon Corporation Okinawa Nikon Service Station
    1-1-9 Kume, Naha, (0988) 68-7651

DECEMBER 1970

家

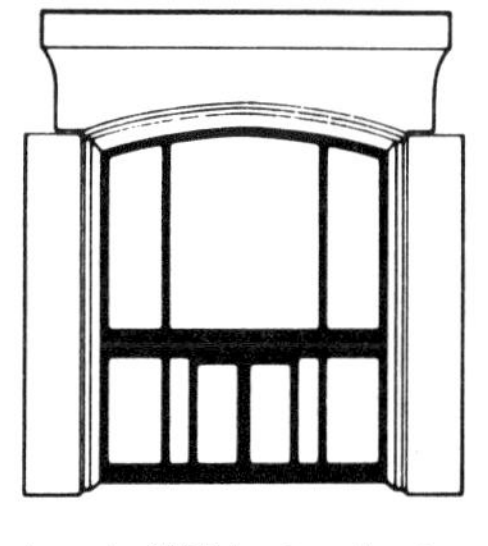

We are pleased to tell you of our new house. Nikon House. A place to see all the things we make. Cameras, yes. And lenses and microscopes. And other things, which may surprise you. A place to touch them and try them before you buy. With technical experts to answer questions. A place to see fine photographs. Watch motion pictures. Slide shows. A place to spend a quiet hour. We should be most pleased if you thought of our home as your home in New York City. Nikon House. Grand opening October 20, 1970. Open 10AM to 6 PM Monday through Saturday. First exhibition: 1969 Nikon Photo Contest International winners.

Nikon House, 437 Madison Avenue at 50th Street New York 10017. International showcase for Nippon Kogaku K.K., Tokyo, manufacturers of Nikon products. Marketed in the U.S.A. by Nikon Inc.

家 This is the Japanese symbol for "house." Please think of it as your invitation to visit our's.

NIKON HOUSE

THE NIKON STORY

The first Nikon cameras were created in an environment few can comprehend. Try to imagine the emotions of the average person in early post-war Japan. The war had been lost, unconditional articles of surrender had been signed, the economy was nonexistent, virtually everyone was in worse financial condition than during the devastating depression of the thirties and the country was being run by an army of occupation, people who until months ago were the enemy.

This was the situation for everyone in the Japan of 1945. But there were additional problems for the people at Nippon Kogaku (Japan Optical). Manufacturers must make and sell products or go out of business. During the thirties and until the end of the conflict, Japan Optical was oriented towards the production of military optical ordnance . . . bomb sights, gun sights, gun cameras, binoculars and the like, but General MacArthur's occupation administration limited Japanese firms to the manufacture of peacetime products.

Years would pass before the Japanese economy would improve sufficiently to provide a domestic market for the products made by Japan Optical. Before its conversion to military manufacturing, the company was Japan's leading producer of microscopes, telescopes and optical measuring devices as well as lenses for photography.

Of course there was a market outside Japan, but export was virtually impossible. Worldwide, Japan Optical was unknown. To build name recognition and develop lines of distribution would take more time and capital than the company had. So what could they do?

If the company was to survive, it had to make and sell something within Japan. Events in their past dictated a direction to pursue.

Nippon Kogaku Kogyo Kaisha was formed on July 25, 1917 by the merger of three small optical firms, the oldest of which was founded in 1881. In 1918, Nippon Kogaku opened its Ohi Plant in the Shinagawa section of Tokyo. In 1921, they placed their 5cm, 7.5cm and 10cm refractor telescopes on the market. In 1923 a research laboratory was established to evolve methods and techniques of developing and producing high-quality optical glass.

Nippon Kogaku used the name "NIKKO" for their scientific and photographic optics. In 1932 they produced a lens for general photographic use and coined the new trademark, "Nikkor." The first lens to bear the new name was a 10.5cm f/4.5 Tessar type. During the years 1938 to 1944, as a part of the Mitsubishi Trust, Nippon Kogaku established a chain of large plants to fulfill the optical needs of the government, but at the cessation of the war, all plants except the Ohi (Tokyo) and one satellite facility were closed.

On October 16, 1945, General Headquarters, Army of Occupation issued an order allowing Nippon Kogaku to resume production of peacetime products. But what could they produce which could be sold on the domestic market? The only people in Japan who had any money to spend were the individual military personnel of the occupation, mostly young men away from home for the first time. This group could hardly be expected to buy quantities of microscopes and telescopes much less transits. What other optical products would soldiers buy? Eye glasses maybe, but the Army supplied these free.

But how about cameras? Perhaps strangers in an exotic land would like to tour and take pictures as a remembrance of their adventures.

But the company had never made cameras! While they had never produced a complete instrument, the people at Japan Optical were familiar with 35mm cameras. During the thirties, they made a 50mm f/3.5 Nikkor lens and rangefinder assemblies used by Canon. Focusing mount mechanisms were also subcontracted from Nippon Kogaku by Canon.

So the few people left at Japan Optical, in order to save the company, set to work designing a 35mm camera. In November 1947, the first camera was ready for testing. They called it the NI(ppon)KO(gaku)N.

Co-author Paul Comon remembers his time as a GI.

"I was in the Army of Occupation from 1951 to 1952, and went to Japan with no photographic knowledge, or even a desire to own a camera. The beautiful country plus the many kind and generous people I met soon changed my mind. I had to record everything!

So I bought a camera which looked nice and was priced right. Photography buff GI's told me I had made a mistake. They said German cameras were the best.

But were they surprised by my pictures! I spent about one-third the price of an equivalent German camera and my images were sharper. Some told me my Japanese camera would soon break down. But reality turned out to be quite different. My camera saw some rough times in Korea.

Even though I don't use it any longer, I still have that camera. It still functions perfectly and has never needed a repair.

My experiences in the orient were such that after I got out of the service and returned to college, I changed my major to photography. In school, my Japanese camera suffered the same old "bamboo shutter" jokes, but my grades never suffered from poor resolution or shutter bounce.

Soon articles began to be published by famous photojournalists about the fabulous Nikon cameras and lenses. And there were some ex-GI's like me who reinforced these views. Now I'm proud I played a small part in helping America discover the Nikon."

The years immediately after the war saw a worldwide demand for cameras. Except for military models, virtually no new cameras had been available since 1941. It took some time for companies like Leitz, Frank & Heideke, Graflex and Bell & Howell to convert back to civilian production.

The Nikon story in the United States is more modern but equally interesting. Nikon cameras were first imported and sold in the United States by the Overseas Finance & Trading Company. Reprinted on the inside front cover of this book is one of their advertisements. It appeared in American photography magazines during 1951.

Shortly afterwards, Nikon distribution in the US was secured by Joseph Ehrenreich. The line of equipment was sold by Ehrenreich Photo Optical in the East, and Gary Lehmann Inc. in the West. These two companies merged and became Ehrenreich Photo-Optical Industries Inc., better known in the trade as EPOI.

Shortly after the introduction of the Nikon F, EPOI placed a Nikon in the hands of every influential news photographer. Coincidence was in Nikon's favor, because TV was changing everyone's lives at that time. People started watching history as it occurred. And surrounding each news event were the pros . . . all using Nikons! This promotion, a stroke of genius, could not have been successful, of course, unless it involved a quality product.

The Nikon F typifies the Nikon market position. When it was introduced in 1959, the rangefinder market was stagnant and the many flashy new SLR's seemed more featurefull, but the Nikon F had mystique; it was the camera of choice of top photojournalists. New meter prisms kept it somewhat abreast of the times. While the cameras of other manufacturers came and went, Nikon added new lenses and accessories to the line until it became the comprehensive system it is today.

Nikon has repeatedly dipped into the modestly priced camera market. Sometimes they were highly successful (Nikkormat), while other ventures might best be forgotten (Nikkorex). Over the years, other products in the line-up have included 8mm and Super 8 movie cameras, a slide projector (manufactured in the US by Sawyers), "point and shoot" cameras and video camcorders (some made by Matsushita and others by Sony). But through changing times, the top end cameras have secured Nikon's reputation.

Other milestones in the Nikon story include the acquisition of the Nikonos and its evolution and domination of that market, the popularity of the FM and FE in all their variations, the break-through that was called FA (regardless of poor sales figures when new, the camera is a classic already) and back-to-back smash hits in the N8008 and the F4 . . . a benchmark of historic proportions is the only way to sum up the sales figures (so far) of a camera in that price bracket.

While all this was going on, Nikon of Japan was expanding and opening new plants and offices. In 1981, Nippon Kogaku purchased the Ehrenreich organization and changed its name to Nikon Inc.

The story includes the manufacture of specialized products like equipment used in space. Nikon cameras made for use by NASA have flown on every manned flight since Apollo 15.

Many thanks go to Robert J. Rotoloni of the Nikon Historical Society of America who has done a complete history on the early Nikon years. Most of the early facts and dates used in this story were gleaned from Bob.

Even though Nikon cameras have been manufactured only since World War II, many of the earlier models have become collectors' items, particularly the rangefinders. Those interested in joining the society should contact Mr. Robert Rotoloni, Post Office Box 3213, Munster, Indiana 46321.

Nikon: A History of Innovation

The world of Nikon continues to expand on the strengths of many great events in our history and a pool of expertise accumulated over the years. Nikon is pressing forward in the industrial equipment, imaging/information and health/medical fields. Nikon is also exploring many new areas to maintain its creative challenge in the years ahead.

1917 Three of Japan's leading optical manufacturers merge to form a comprehensive, fully integrated optical company known as Nippon Kogaku K.K.

1918 Optical glass production and research begun.

1922 MICRON 4X, 6X ultra-small prism binoculars marketed.

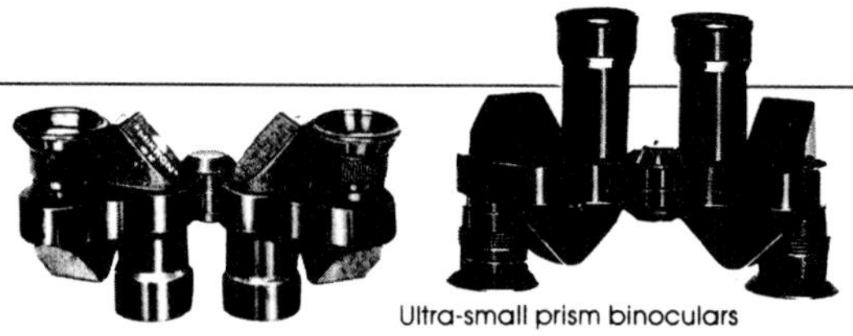

Ultra-small prism binoculars

1932 Nikkor adopted as brand name for camera lenses.

1945 Production shifted to cameras, microscopes, binoculars, surveying instruments, measuring instruments and eyeglasses after World War II to improve people's lives.

1946 Nikon brand name adopted for small-size cameras.

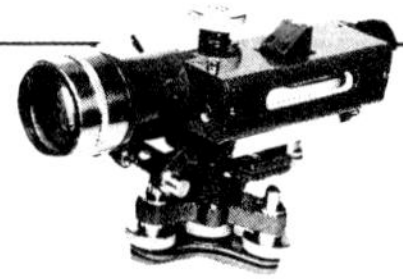

Level E

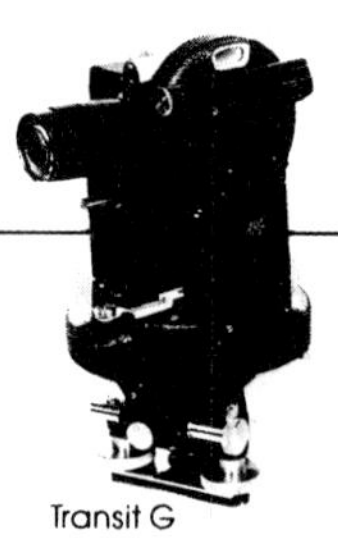

Transit G

1950 **The New York Times** *introduced the superior features of Nikon cameras and Nikkor lenses.*

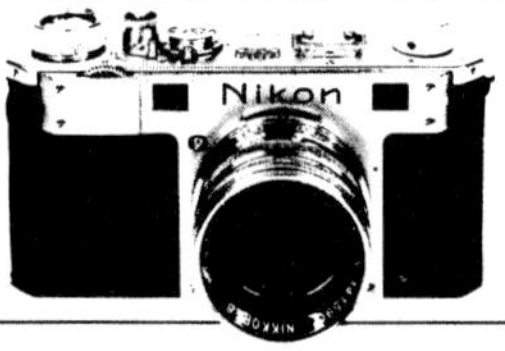

Nikon S

1951 Nikon S small-size camera marketed.

1963 NIKONOS all-weather camera marketed.

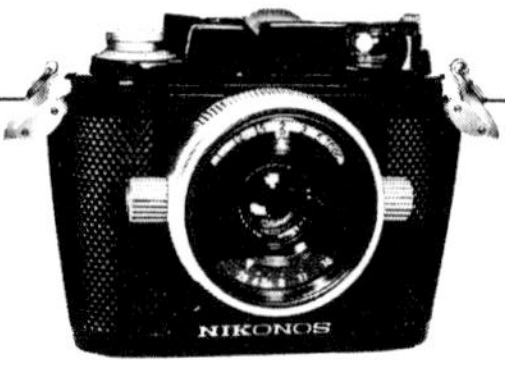

NIKONOS

1965 Nikkormat FT and FS SLR cameras marketed.

1971 Nikon F2 SLR camera marketed.

1972 Laser Interferometric X-Y Measuring System, a high-precision coordinate measuring instrument for IC use, marketed. Nikon sunglasses marketed. Nikkormat EL automatic exposure SLR camera marketed.

1974 105cm Schmidt-type telescope installed at Tokyo Astronomical Observatory.

1975 FB Line eyeglass frames marketed.

1980 NSR-1010G Step-and-Repeat Exposure System (Stepper) for VLSI manufacturing marketed. Nikon F3 and EM SLR cameras marketed. Planned development of dental root implant utilizing bioactive glass announced.

1981 TITEX eyeglass frames made of titanium marketed. Nikon's U.S. distributor, EPOI, became wholly owned subsidiary and renamed Nikon Inc. to begin direct sales. Nikon Fieldscope marketed. All solid-state electrochromic device (ECD) successfully developed.

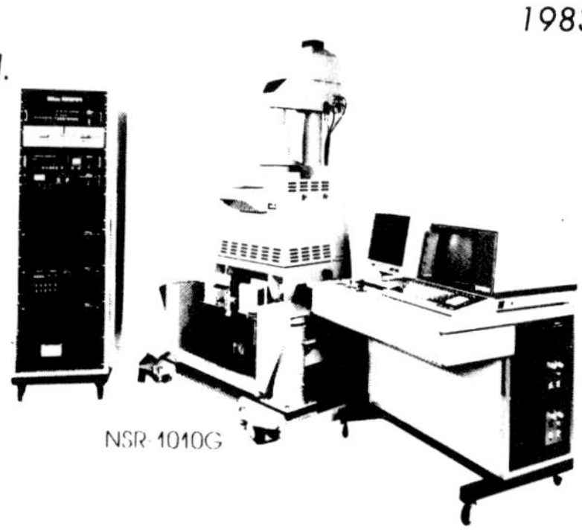

NSR-1010G

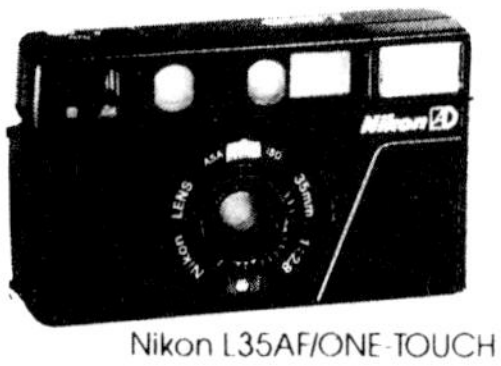

Nikon L35AF/ONE-TOUCH*

1983 Nikon markets its first autofocus compact camera, the Nikon L35AF/ONE-TOUCH. Nikon 6.5cm Refractive Equatorial Telescope for astronomy marketed. NFC-60 fundus camera marketed.*

1984 Nikon 35mm Film Direct Telephoto Transmitter NT-1000 marketed. Nikon FA received first Camera Grand Prix '84 in Japan. Optistation-2A IC wafer inspection device marketed.

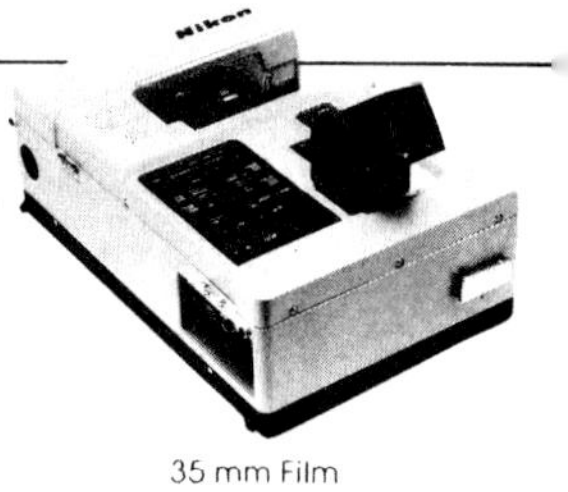

35 mm Film Direct Telephoto Transmitter NT-1000

1985 Total Station DTM-1 surveying instrument marketed. Compact binoculars 6x15CF marketed.

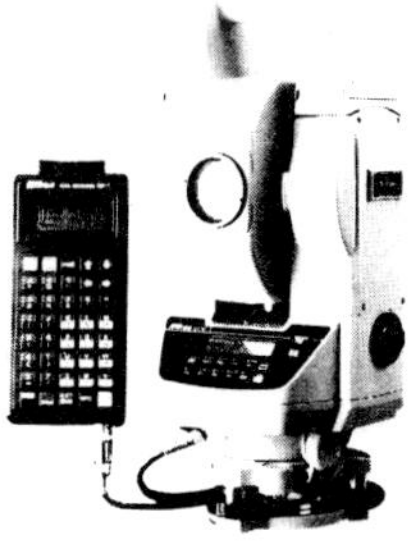

Total Station DTM-1

1910

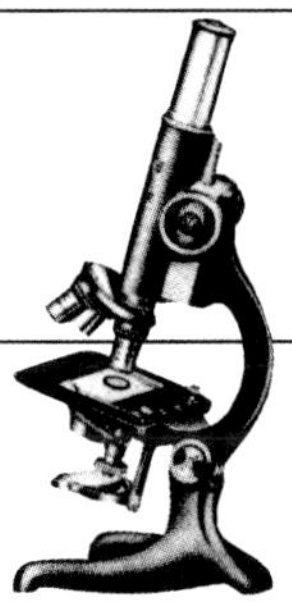

JOICO microscope

1920

1925 JOICO microscope marketed.

1930

1939 Listed on the Tokyo Stock Exchange.

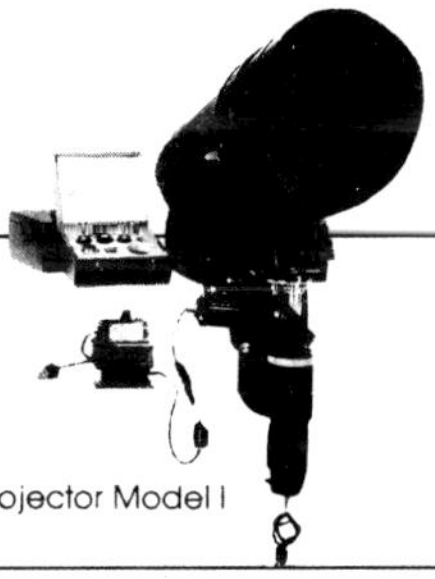

Profile Projector Model I

1940

1947 LEVEL E and TRANSIT G surveying instruments marketed. POINTAR eyeglass lenses marketed. Microscope model O marketed.

1948 Nikon I small-size camera marketed.

1949 Profile Projector Model I marketed.

1950

1952 Nikkor Club established to promote photography culture.

1957 Nikon SP small-size camera marketed.

1959 Nikon's first SLR camera, the Nikon F, marketed.

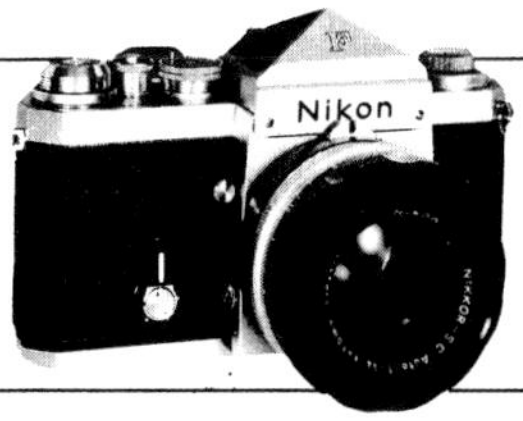

Nikon F

1960

1966 Nikon Super Zoom 8, an 8mm movie camera marketed.

1968 Rotary Encoder RIE digital measuring instrument marketed.

1970

1976 Nikon ORMA plastic lenses marketed.

1979 Auto Refractometer NR-1000, an automatic eye refractive index measuring machine, marketed. NASA chooses Nikon SLR cameras for space shuttle program. Nikon sunglasses styled by Hanae Mori and G. Giugiaro marketed.

1980

1986 TRISTATION three-dimensional coordinate measuring machine marketed. Nikon F-501/N2020** autofocus SLR camera marketed. Nikon F-501 received 1986 European Camera of the Year award.

1986 NSR-L7501G exposure system for large substrates marketed. Nikon LP-3000D high-precision laser imaging systems for printed circuits marketed.

1987 SX-5 X-ray stepper marketed. Nikon F-401/N4004** autofocus SLR camera marketed. Color Printer CP-1 for computer graphics use unveiled. NSR-1505EX excimer stepper unveiled.

1988 Nikon F-801/N8008** autofocus SLR camera marketed. Nikon F4 SLR camera marketed.

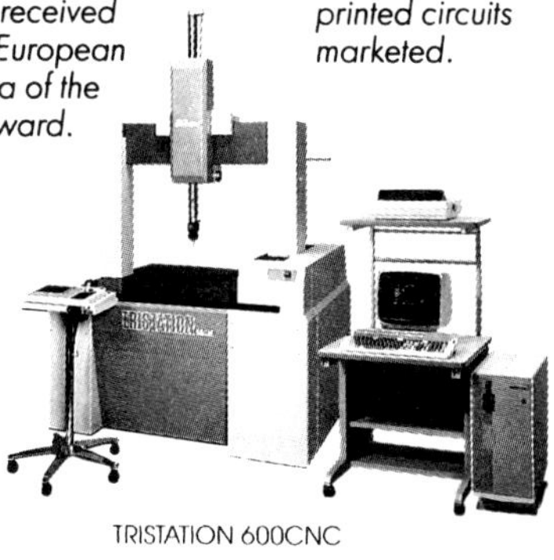

TRISTATION 600CNC

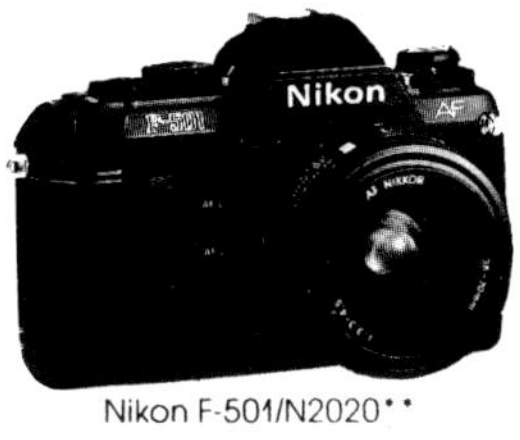

Nikon F-501/N2020**

*The name One-Touch is used only in the U.S.A. and Canada.

**The names N2020, N4004 and N8008 are used only in the U.S.A.

FEBRUARY 1960

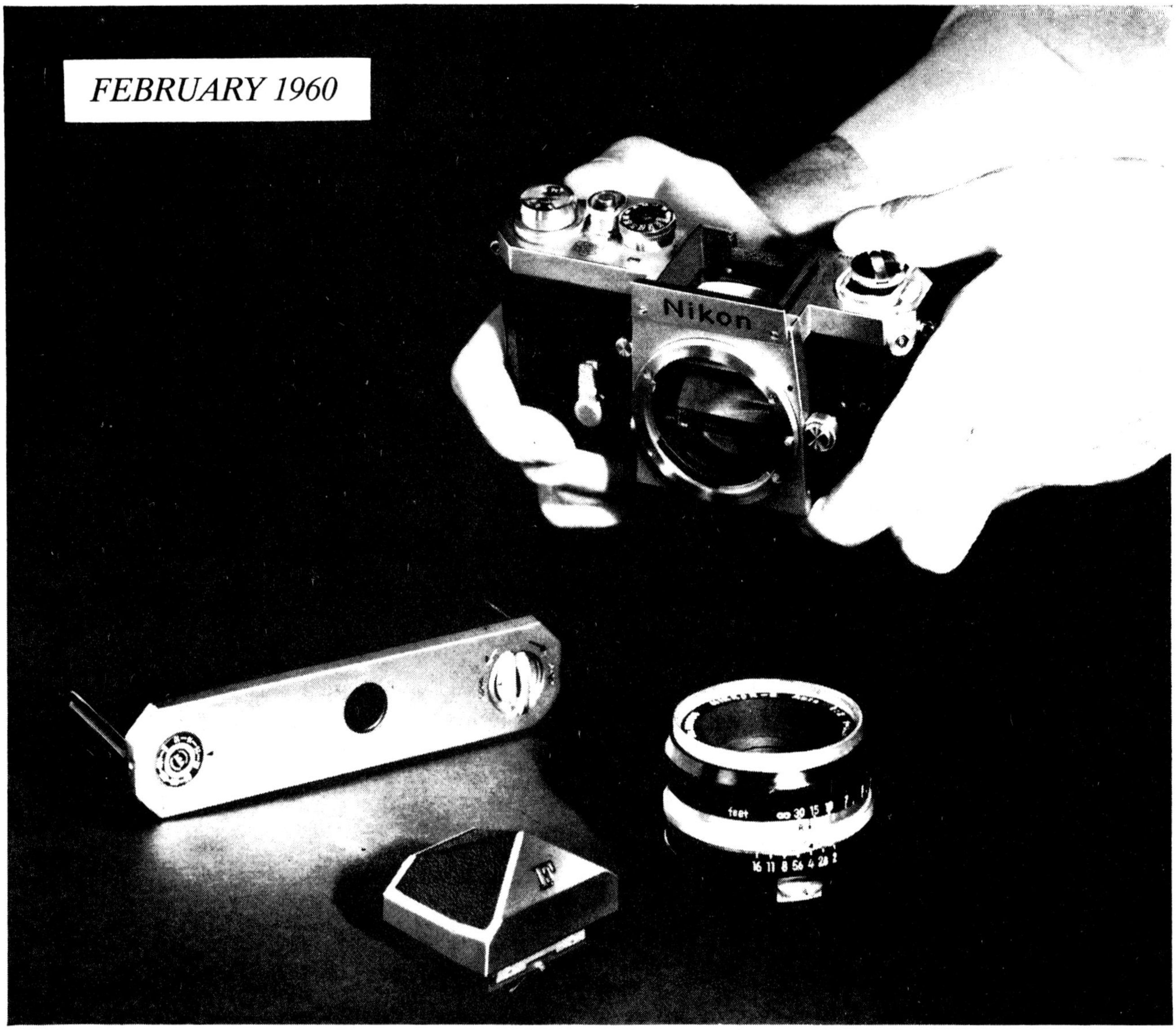

if you were designing the perfect 35mm reflex...
how many of these requirements would you include?

CONSTRUCTION A flawlessly built camera body, mechanically precise, meticulously finished—rugged and dependable under the severest conditions of climate and usage.

EYELEVEL FINDER Optically precise – screen area exactly matching usable film area – image bright and distinct, easy to view in its entirety even with glasses – interchangeable screens permitting use of other types, as preferred, or for special work and interchangeable finders for switching to waist-level viewing.

MIRROR Instant return – to eliminate image black-out – fully automatic—requiring no setting or adjustment of the camera—the action fast, smooth, virtually imperceptible—the mirror always returning to precise focus position even with camera held upside down.

LENSES Finest optical quality – in a wide variety of focal lengths – readily and quickly interchangeable – all providing flawless definition, high resolution even at full aperture.

LENS DIAPHRAGM Internally coupled – requiring no previous setting or adjustment of the camera – fully automatic – closing down for the exposure and reopening instantly to full aperture so that there is no dimming of the finder image.

FOCAL PLANE SHUTTER Accurate at all temperatures – covering a wide range of speeds, each synchronized for appropriate flash bulbs and speedlight – provision for delayed action.

ACCESSORIES Truly versatile accessories: a compact, battery-operated motor for shooting pictures in rapid succession, hand-held or remotely – an exposure meter that can be attached and coupled to both the shutter and the lens diaphragm – equipment for close-ups, copying, macro work and photomicrography – flash units, high quality filters, hoods and other essentials.

HANDLING EASE Above all, an instrument that is responsive, easy and fast to use – all controls conveniently located – requiring a minimum of effort and a minimum of manipulation.

The new Nikon F automatic reflex may or may not be the *perfect* camera. We are not even sure whether the perfect camera actually exists. But, of this we are certain – *the Nikon F is the closest approach to perfection ever achieved in a 35mm reflex.*

NIPPON KOGAKU TOKYO

Nikon F with 50mm Auto-Nikkor f2 lens, $329.50 – at your Nikon dealer. For further details write to Dept. MP2
NIKON INC., 111 Fifth Avenue, New York 3, New York
In Canada: Anglophoto Ltd., Montreal, P. O.

CHAPTER TWO

WARRANTY, SERVICE AND REPAIR

WARRANTY. All new Nikon products carry a warranty. The period of the warranty for photographic products is one year, both parts and labor. The term for video camcorders is one year for parts, 90 days for labor.

Each new product is packed with a warranty certificate. When making the purchase, the buyer is advised to check that the certificate is included. Items purchased from authorized Nikon dealers in the US include a warranty certificate issued by Nikon Inc., the Nikon Corporation's subsidiary in the US. He or she should also check to see that the nomenclature and serial number on the certificate match the product.

Since the warranty is for a limited period, purchasers are advised to thoroughly check each and every operation of the new equipment in order to determine if it is working properly. If a problem is encountered, the terms and conditions of the warranty should be enforced promptly.

The dealer is not a party to the warranty agreement, which is between the buyer and Nikon Inc. While this is a legality, it should be noted that many photographic equipment dealers (as opposed to other sorts of retail establishments) will often help customers with warranty problems.

CONDITIONS. The Nikon Inc. warranty is limited. It is valid in the continental US, Alaska, Hawaii, Puerto Rico and the Virgin Islands. The length of time is limited as described above. The warranty is extended only to the original purchaser. It is not assignable or transferable.

The warranty excludes "any product which has been subject to misuse, abuse, negligence or accident, any defects or damage directly or indirectly caused by the use of unauthorized replacement parts and/or service performed by unauthorized personnel (sic) and any batteries."

While cameras, lenses and other items are packed with the warranty certificate, a certificate is not always packed with each and every accessory. Nevertheless, the Nikon Inc. warranty is valid. In these instances, return the item for repair together with the sales receipt only.

IMPLIED WARRANTY. Some states in the US have laws which may supersede the terms and conditions of the Nikon warranty. In the case of a specific problem, you may wish to consult an attorney in to order to determine your rights. In some states this may mean that the time limitation of the Nikon warranty is invalid.

DOCUMENTATION. In order to perform warranty work, Nikon Inc. requires that the item be delivered to Nikon Inc., or one of its authorized repair stations, *together with a copy of the original sales receipt and part one of the 2-part warranty certificate.* It is very important, therefore, that when a new item is purchased, the sales receipt and warranty certificate be kept in a secure location. At the time of purchase, the buyer should make sure that the exact description of the item, together with its serial number, is listed on the receipt.

In order to safeguard the transaction, it is suggested that the buyer retain the original of both the receipt and the warranty certificate. Photocopies should be made to accompany the item delivered for repair.

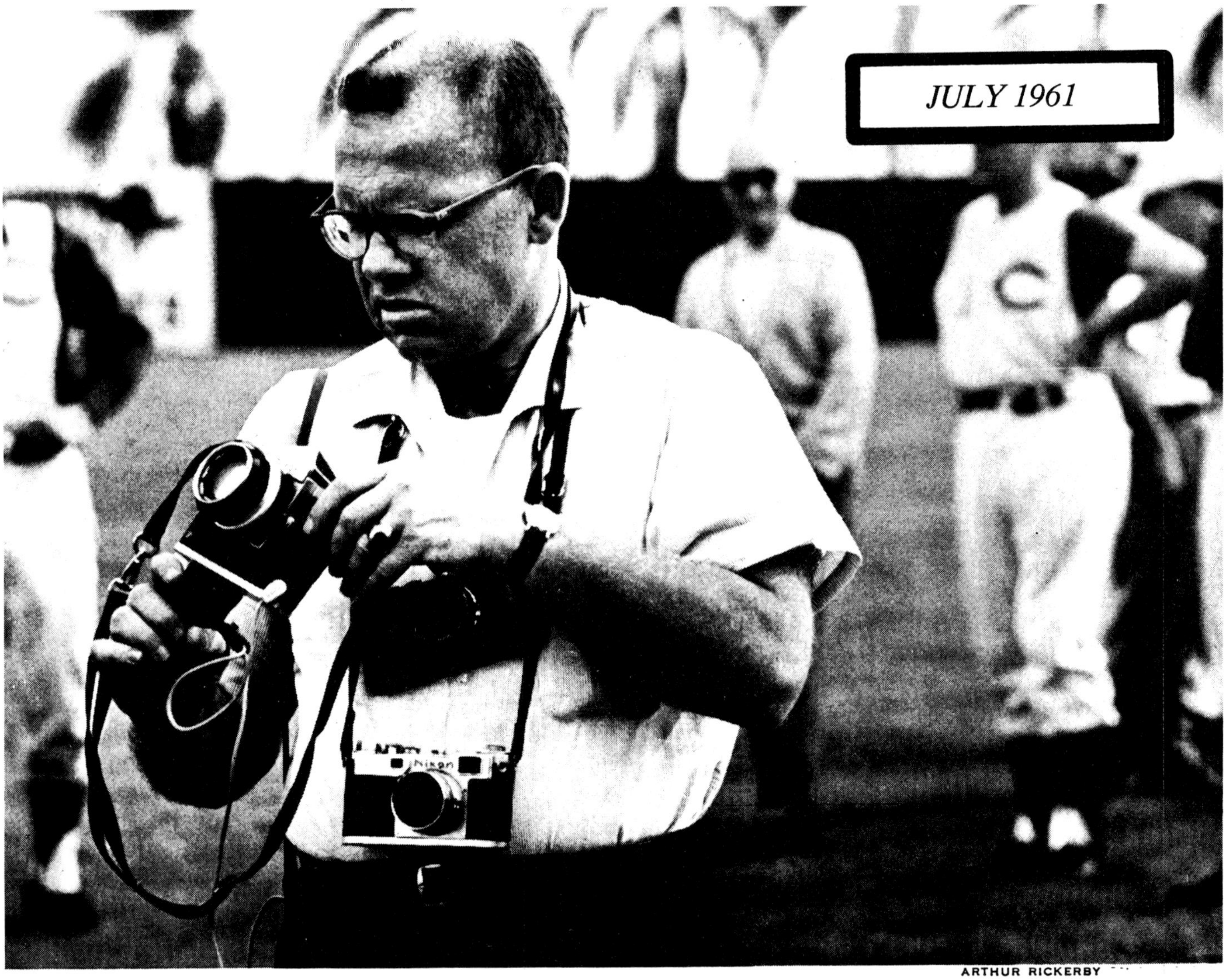

ARTHUR RICKERBY

Handling Speed and Ease

The Nikon F exemplifies the single-lens reflex in its most advanced state. Its automatic operation endows it with an almost incredible handling speed and ease. It responds smoothly, effortlessly. There is nothing to distract the user—nothing to divert him from the creative effort. And he feels a sense of greater command over every picture situation—a sense of power in the almost unbounded versatility of the instrument in his hands.

Lens Interchangeability

With the Nikon F, the user can interchange lenses with complete freedom. There are 19 Nikkor lenses to choose from. No finders are necessary. The image on the viewing screen is formed by the same lens that records the image on the film. There is no parallax, and not the slightest variance between the image seen in the screen area and the image recorded on the film.

Nikon F lens interchangeability assumes an even greater significance with the availability of three Auto-Nikkor zoom lenses. One zoom lens has a continually variable range of focal lengths from 35 through 85mm; the other, from 85 through 250mm; and the third, from 200 through 600mm. Thus equipped, there are no definable limits to the scope and versatility of the Nikon F.

Automatic Fire Power

One of the most dramatic examples of Nikon F versatility is the battery-operated Electric Motor Drive. This unique accessory fires the camera automatically. It automatically advances the film, winds and releases the shutter at varying rates—up to 3 exposures per second. So fast and smooth is the automatic mirror and diaphragm action of the Nikon F the finder image never seems to disappear from view, and it never dims.

The number of applications for the motor-equipped Nikon F is limited only by the imagination. It can be operated in-hand or remotely—manually, by radio impulse or other actuating device. It can be used for rapid sequences or time lapse studies. But, even more significant is the way the Electric Motor Drive frees the user from the mechanics of camera operation, and enables him to capture momentary action, split-second occurrences, fleeting expressions in pictures he could never have otherwise obtained.

Rangefinder or Automatic Reflex?

There is no doubt of the overwhelming trend to reflex. The reasons are self-evident. Yet if a rangefinder 35 is more compatible with the way you are accustomed to work, there is no reason for you to follow the trend. That is why Nikon makes both—the rangefinder-coupled SP and the F automatic reflex.

Examine both, for they differ only in the nature of their viewing systems. Each offers you the same meticulous quality, the same effortless handling ease, the same incomparable Nikkor optics, and the same rugged reliability. And for each there is a host of accessories to fit it for every conceivable application. Even the prices are the same: $329.50 with f2 lens, and $375 with f1.4.

For further details, write Dept. CT6

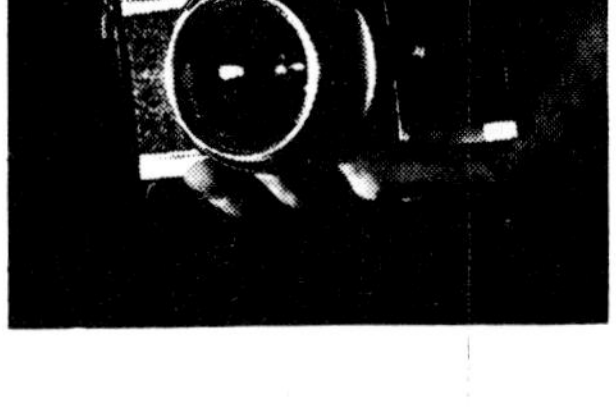

NIKON INCORPORATED
111 FIFTH AVENUE, NEW YORK 3,
Canada: Anglophoto Ltd., Montreal 8, P. Q.

The safest method of purchase is with a credit card. Then, if by chance the original receipt is lost, usually the credit card company can be prevailed upon to supply a copy of the credit card receipt. When a credit card is used to make a purchase, make sure the proper description and serial number(s) appear on the credit card receipt as well as on the dealer's invoice.

Remember, in order for Nikon Inc. to honor the warranty, the date of purchase must be established. If the purchase was not made by credit card, and if the original receipt has been lost, another avenue to explore is to request a duplicate receipt from the dealer. This is a good reason - among many others - for making purchases from reputable, authorized Nikon photographic dealers. (A photographic dealer is recommended as opposed to a department store or discount house since getting a duplicate receipt from such organizations is next to impossible.)

If the Warranty Certificate is lost, Nikon Inc. will still honor the warranty if the buyer presents the original receipt, and if the product was available new from Nikon Inc. at the time of purchase.

REGISTRATION. In the past, in order for the warranty to be valid, Nikon Inc. required the purchaser to fill out and mail to Nikon Inc. a "Nikon Owner Registration" form. In addition to name and address, the form asks a number of demographic and personal questions. These forms are still packed with most new Nikon products, *but they are no longer required* to validate the warranty.

Whether or not the form is filled out and mailed is entirely up to the purchaser. Nikon's purpose is " . . . for market research studies and reports - and will help us better serve you in the future." Sending in the form also may place the respondent on advertising mailing lists.

ORIGIN. If the item was purchased from an authorized Nikon dealer in the US, warranty repair will be performed either by Nikon Inc. or by a repair facility authorized by Nikon Inc. The names and locations of these facilities is listed in the first chapter of this book.

If the item was purchased in another country and brought to this country by the buyer, the warranty will be honored by Nikon Inc. In this case, the item, together with the documentation, must be delivered to the Nikon Inc. facility in Torrance, California or Garden City, New York. It may NOT be delivered to any other US Nikon facility, or to one of the authorized repair stations.

INTERNATIONAL WARRANTY REPAIR. When you are traveling outside the US, warranty repair is available in many other countries. The names and addresses of the authorized repair stations are listed in the first chapter of this book. When you embark on a trip with equipment still under warranty, you should take along copies of the purchase receipt and warranty certificate.

If you take an item out of the US and then return with it, you may be required by the US Customs Service to prove you purchased it in the US or pay duty. This is another reason it is a good idea to have a copy of the purchase receipt with you. An alternative strategy is to register the items with US Customs before leaving.

GRAY MARKET. Sometimes Nikon products are offered for sale on the so-called "gray market." This means that the item was not imported by Nikon Inc. Items imported by Nikon Inc. are distinctive in that they are accompanied by a Nikon Inc. warranty certificate.

Items sold in other countries have an international warranty certificate, not a Nikon Inc. certificate. In order for an international warranty certificate to be valid, the buyer must have a sales receipt issued by an authorized dealer in the country to which the item was originally exported from Japan (or from Japan itself if the item was purchased there).

Nikon Inc. does NOT honor non-Nikon Inc. warranties unless accompanied by a receipt proving the item was purchased in the country to which it was originally exported.

A Nikon product purchased in the US with a non-Nikon Inc. warranty will not be repaired under warranty either in the US or elsewhere!. Gray market products do NOT have a warranty.

This isn't to say that a gray market purchase is always a bad idea. Sometimes gray market items are priced at or only a little more than the used price for the same item. There are even occasions when some "used" items are priced higher than "new" gray market ones.

DELIVERY. Items for warranty repair must be delivered to Nikon Inc. or an authorized repair facility. The best course of action, if at all possible, is to personally deliver the item. Nikon customers are fortunate in that there are

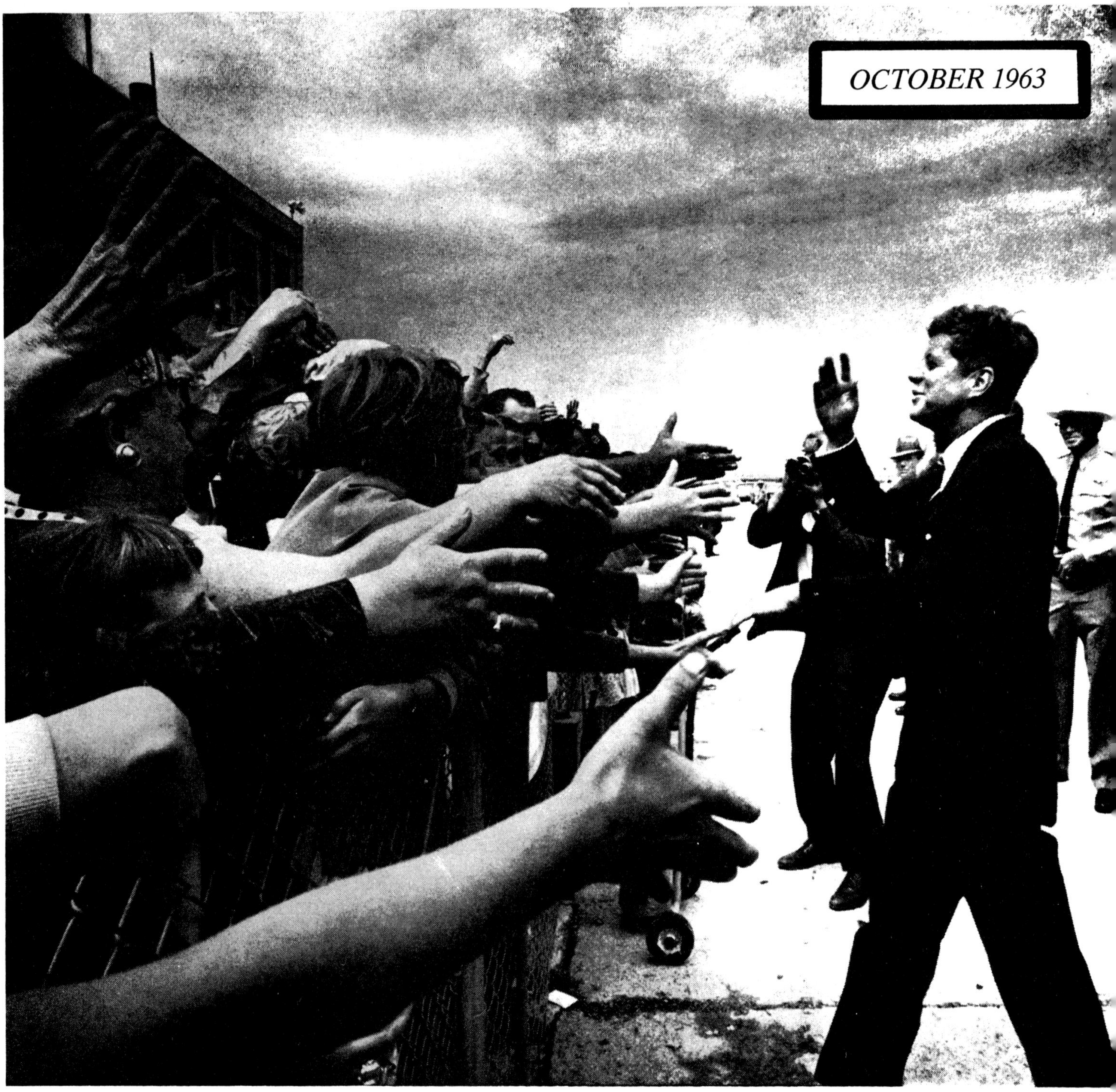

We salute George Tames of the New York Times Magazine, three-time winner of the White House News Photographers Association Grand Award: once in 1960, again in 1962, for his Nikon photo "Loneliest Job in the World", and now again in 1963, for his Nikon photo "The Personal Touch".

More of the outstanding work in photo-journalism is being done with Nikon because more of the top men in photo-journalism are Nikon users.

NIKON INCORPORATED, 111 FIFTH AVENUE, NEW YORK 3, N. Y. Subsidiary of Ehrenrich Photo-Optical Industries, Inc.

many repair stations. For most people, a facility is relatively nearby. If purchased there, most camera stores will ship warranty repairs to Nikon at no charge.

An alternative is to have the item delivered, by US mail, UPS or the like. In this instance, the item must be packed very carefully. For this reason, it is recommended that the original packing materials be retained after purchase. Even after the warranty period has expired, items may have to be sent for service or repair.

When an item is delivered for repair or service, just the product which is to be worked on should be included. Accessories should be removed. In the case of a camera body, the lens should be removed and a body cap installed.

When an item is delivered personally, be sure to get a receipt with the description and serial number accurately listed. If the item is to be sent by mail or UPS, it should be insured, and the receipt carefully preserved.

WARRANTY EXTENSION. A number of credit cards offer an extension of the manufacturer's warranty. American Express, as an example, doubles the original warranty. This would mean that a Nikon photographic product would have a two-year, rather than a one-year warranty. This provides another very good reason for buying with a credit card.

This warranty extension is provided by the credit card company, NOT Nikon Inc. The terms and conditions of the warranty provided by the credit card company should be carefully examined and preserved at the time of purchase. You must be very careful to retain the original sales receipt PLUS the credit card receipt. The credit card receipt should list the exact product description together with the serial number.

NIKON PROFESSIONAL SERVICES (NPS). Nikon has a staff, policy and equipment to support professional photographers. These services are available to qualified, full-time professionals. In order to receive these services, one must "join" the NPS.

To be considered for membership, write to Nikon Professional Services, 623 Stewart Ave., Garden City, NY 11530. The letter must be written on business stationery, either that of the photographer himself if he is self-employed, or on his employer's stationery. Membership is very restrictive and open exclusively to full-time working professional photographers.

There are a number of benefits:

1. Equipment is repaired on a priority basis. When an NPS member causes equipment to be delivered to Nikon Inc. for repair, the work is performed before repairs are done on other customers' equipment. This usually means three days maximum turn-around for repairs for which parts are on hand and two weeks when parts are not immediately available, or for major overhauls. Additionally, when an NPS member delivers equipment for repair or service, if there have been technical improvements since the original purchase, the equipment is updated.

2. On occasion, equipment is loaned to NPS members in cases of emergency (as in a critical assignment when the member's equipment is being repaired), for evaluation, or for the exploration of new ideas. These benefits are on an "as available" basis.

3. Membership includes a newsletter called, "NPS Advisory." The newsletter includes notices of new equipment which has been developed by Nikon, as well as articles of interest to professionals.

4. At some major news and sporting events, NPS provides on-site service to NPS members.

5. There are periodic lectures on photography and Nikon products for members only.

6. NPS has a staff of experts who will render advice on "unique photographic projects and assignments."

NIKON USA CLUB. When a new Nikon SLR camera is purchased in the US from an authorized dealer, an official application for warranty is included. Enrollment in the Nikon USA Club is accomplished by filling out the card (which accompanies the product) and mailing it to Nikon Inc.

There are no dues and members have no responsibilities. Basically, club membership means that you are on the Nikon Inc. mailing list. You will be informed about new products and any special offers the company may develop. There is also a periodic newsletter. In the past, the newsletter was sent two times a year. Starting in 1990, Nikon Inc. intends to publish quarterly.

Failure to send in the registration card does NOT invalidate the warranty. It only means you will not be on the mailing list.

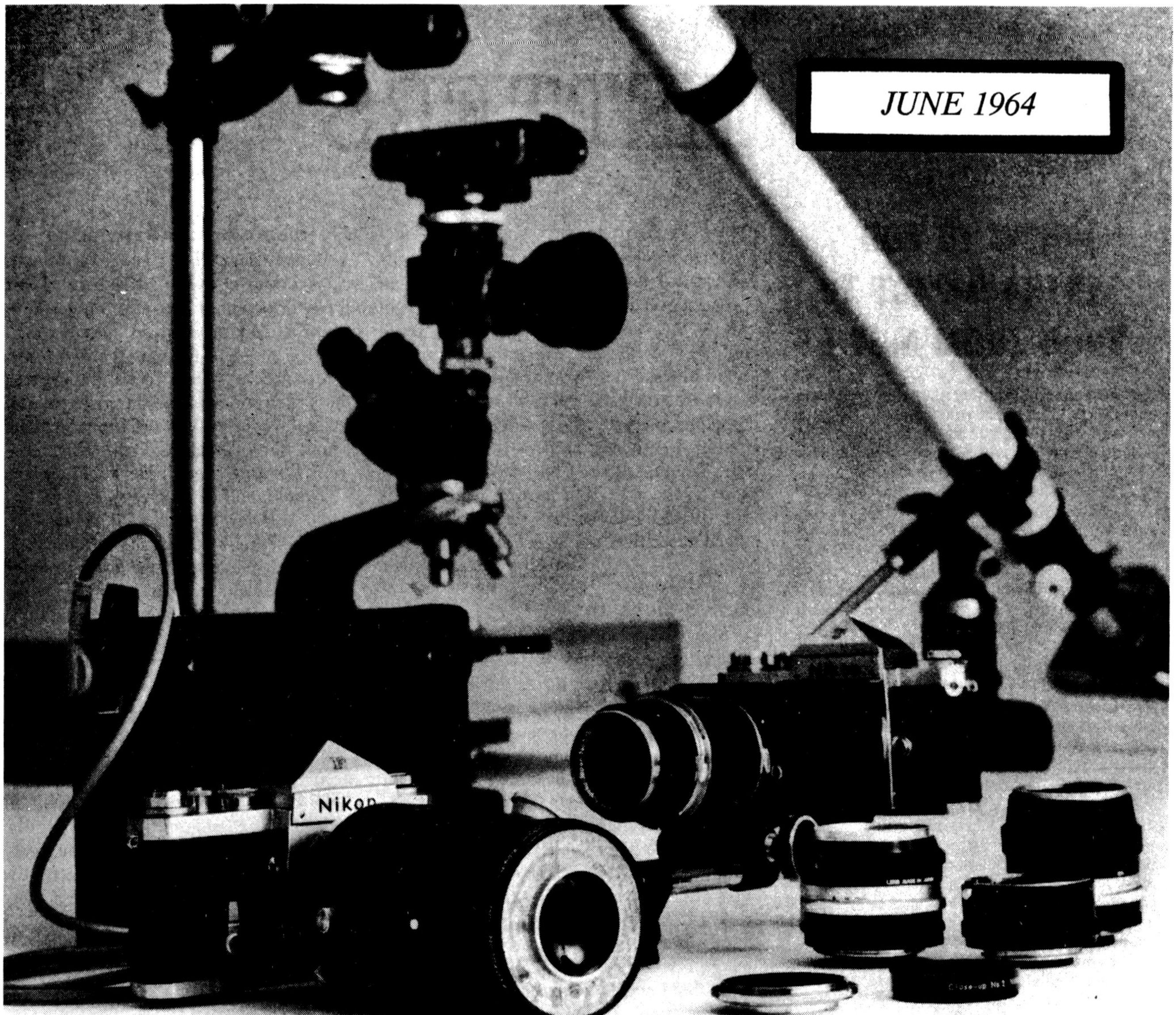

How special-purpose equipment helps make the Nikon F most versatile of all 35s

The picture capabilities of the Nikon F extend from microphotography to astro photography—from the infinitesimal to the infinite. There are special lenses, tubes, stands, bellows—an almost endless list of special purpose attachments and accessories—each contributing to the overall versatility of the Nikon F. Let us first consider the lenses.

The 55mm f3.5 Auto-Micro-Nikkor is a lens of almost incredible resolution. Moreover, it provides continuous focusing from infinity to ½ reproduction ratio. And a coupling tube further extends focus to 1:1 magnification. The automatic diaphragm is operative over the entire range, with automatic compensation for the close-up exposure factor.

The 200mm f5.6 Auto-Medical-Nikkor is no less unique and ingenious. There is no focusing scale in the conventional sense. The lens is preset for magnification within a range of 11 settings from 1/15th to 3 times actual size. The camera is used at that distance at which the image appears sharp.

This lens also incorporates its own light sources: four small incandescent bulbs to light the area for viewing, and a ring-light electronic flash for uniform, shadowless exposure illumination. Both are energized by a portable power-pack.

The diaphragm automatically stops down to correct taking aperture without presetting, and automatically compensates for the close-up exposure factor. The lens embodies facilities for identifying the film as to frame number or magnification.

The 135mm f4 Nikkor in Short Mount is another lens of special interest to the copyist. When used with the Nikon Bellows Attachment and B-F Adapter Tube, it covers a focusing range from infinity to 1:1 magnification.

Nikon F close-up accessories also include EXTENSION TUBES, FOCUSING BELLOWS and COPY-STAND OUTFITS, as well as AUXILIARY OPTICAL ATTACHMENTS for the lenses.

THE BELLOWS FOCUSING ATTACHMENT deserves special mention. Essentially, this accessory increases the focusing range of all lenses. In the case of the 135mm Nikkor in Short Mount, to 1:1 reproduction ratio and with the Micro-Nikkor, to 3.5:1. Also, when fitted with SLIDE-COPY ADAPTER, it is used for producing color-slide duplicates or negatives of either the entire slide (1:1), or a section enlarged.

The worker in photomicrography can choose between the MICROFLEX with its self-contained sighting system and shutter, and the simpler MICROSCOPE ADAPTER TUBE. The astronomer can use the TELESCOPE ADAPTER for astro photography.

See the Nikon F at your camera dealer or write Dept. PP-6.

EPOI NIKON INCORPORATED 111 Fifth Avenue New York 3, N. Y. Subsidiary of Ehrenreich Photo-Optical Industries, Inc.

PERIODIC SERVICE. Nikon recommends that each camera, lens and accessory be serviced at periodic intervals. The recommended intervals are:

1. Photojournalists and professionals in the field, each year.
2. Studio professionals, every two years.
3. Amateurs, every three years.

These recommendations, however, should probably be altered to meet individual needs and circumstances. Professionals who run many rolls through a camera might very well want to have service performed more frequently, as well as those who have subjected their equipment to severe environmental conditions.

Camera body servicing consists of checking the shutter speeds and, if necessary, adjusting for accuracy. Additionally, the body panels are taken off and any dust and dirt is removed. Finally, lubricant is applied as recommended by the factory.

REPAIRS. When repairs are necessary and the product is out of warranty, it is still best to return the equipment to Nikon or to one of the Authorized Repair Stations listed in Chapter 1. The reason for this is that Nikon supplies training to the technicians. And the training is ongoing. When new products are introduced, update training takes place. This is not true for technicians who work at non-authorized shops. Also, an authorized shop is more likely to have necessary parts on hand. If parts are needed and not in inventory, they must be ordered from Nikon, which takes additional time.

PARTS. A large supply of spare parts is maintained by Nikon Inc. in the US. The National Parts Center is located at the Torrance, California facility. Parts are sold directly to anyone who wishes to buy. It is not required that a purchaser be an authorized dealer, authorized repair shop or have any other qualification.

Parts can be purchased in person, by mail, telephone or FAX. Cash, checks or VISA/MasterCharge are accepted. To order by phone, call and give your credit card number and expiration date. Nikon will deliver any way you specify, including US Mail and Federal Express.

DAMAGE, LOSS AND THEFT. The acquisition of Nikon equipment can represent a considerable investment. It is inevitable that some photographers will encounter situations where equipment is damaged, lost or stolen. Before one of these unfortunate happenings occurs, it might be wise to anticipate such problems in order to minimize future losses.

The first thing to do upon the acquisition of additional equipment is to create an inventory, either on paper or computer memory. Then the inventory itself should be duplicated. The inventory should include a complete description of the equipment, date of acquisition, from whom the purchase was made, the amount paid and the serial numbers of each item.

Some police authorities recommend inscribing identification marks of some sort on the equipment. This may be helpful in terms of determining ownership in case of loss or theft, but such marks do decrease values when and if the equipment is offered for sale. In most instances, serial numbers are sufficient for identification. But you may want to consider making marks on items without numbers. Of course, a serial number is of no value unless you can demonstrate that you are the owner of the item with a particular number. Some authorities feel that individual marks will discourage a thief in the first place from taking such marked items, since they may be more difficult to fence. Be that as it may, each photographer must make his or her own decision in the matter.

It has already been mentioned that in order for the Nikon warranty to be valid, the purchaser must retain the original sales invoice. It is a good practice to retain invoices as long as you own the equipment. It should again be emphasized that the invoices should include serial numbers. Then, if there is ever any question as to ownership, there is documentary evidence.

INSURANCE. How about insurance? Many people have homeowners' or renters' insurance which covers the contents of their abode. Usually these policies cover camera equipment. All policies have limitations, and many have deductibles. At the point when you have acquired an amount of equipment which represents a significant investment for you, it is a prudent idea to examine your policy.

Many insurance companies will also write policies for photographic equipment alone. In order to obtain such coverage, most photographers seek out a company with whom they are already dealing with for their home or car. In addition to fire and theft, some companies also offer "drop" coverage to insure against damage.

NEW NIKON PROFESSIONAL CAMERA, THE F4

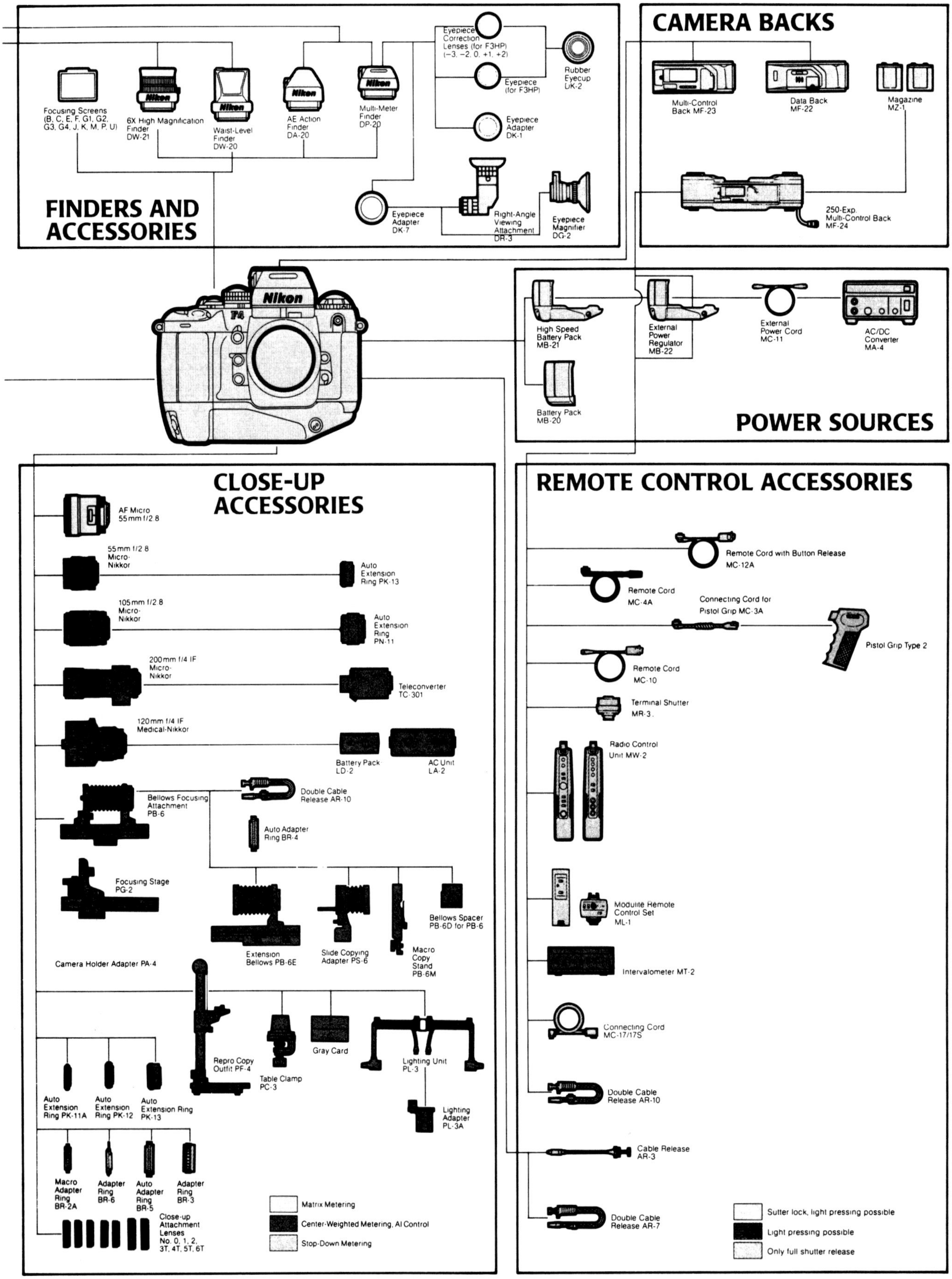

CHAPTER THREE

NEW PRODUCTS

This chapter has to do with products which Nikon Inc. has introduced to the US market during 1989. It also includes products introduced in 1990 until the date this book went to press. Some products introduced in the latter part of 1988 are also included. An example is the F4S. This camera was announced in 1988, but, for the most part, supplies did not appear on dealers' shelves until 1989.

The explanatory material in this chapter addresses itself to the rationale for the addition of the product as well as what is different about it. Product descriptions are found elsewhere in this book.

The current Nikon method of announcing a new product is via a press release from Nikon's public relations agency, Strear, David & Mitchell, Inc. Additionally, notices are mailed to authorized dealers from the sales staff and advertisements are placed in photography magazines. Just because an announcement has been made does not necessarily mean that an adequate supply will immediately be found on all dealers' shelves. New products are occasionally in short supply.

Sometimes a new product represents an improvement and replaces a previously offered item. In these instances, some dealers may have a supply of the replaced item on hand. Occasionally, items no longer current are offered for sale months or even years afterwards. Some dealers will then discount the product. If the new features have no significance to a potential purchaser, this may represent an opportunity to save. Discontinued items sold new by authorized dealers still carry the Nikon USA warranty.

NIKON F4S CAMERA BODY AND SYSTEM. This is a new professional autofocus SLR announced in late 1988, but not readily available until 1989. Nikon's previous professional autofocus SLR was the F3AF which as been discontinued. (The F3HP and F3P are still available.) The list price for the F4s body is a hefty $2428. As this book went to press, most dealers were selling bodies for less than $2000 and some for less than $1800.

The F4s is unlike any previous Nikon camera because it blends a vast array of electronic features into the professional workhorse that made Nikon famous. Another difference which caused industry analysts to watch its early progress was its price. At more than twice the price of any previous Japanese camera body, no one (including most Nikon personnel) believed it would meet with the resounding success it has enjoyed so far.

Its features, in addition to autofocus, include manual focus, automatic exposure in either shutter or aperture preferred mode, manual exposure control, matrix through-the-lens off-the-film flash exposure control, built-in motor drive, built-in viewfinder diopter adjustment and many others.

In the US, it is delivered in only the F4s configuration. Elsewhere, it can be purchased in the F4 configuration. The "s" signifies the large battery pack which will produce speeds up to 5.7 frames per second. The small battery pack can be purchased as an accessory, however.

MORE ACCESSORIES FOR THE F4S PROFESSIONAL SYSTEM

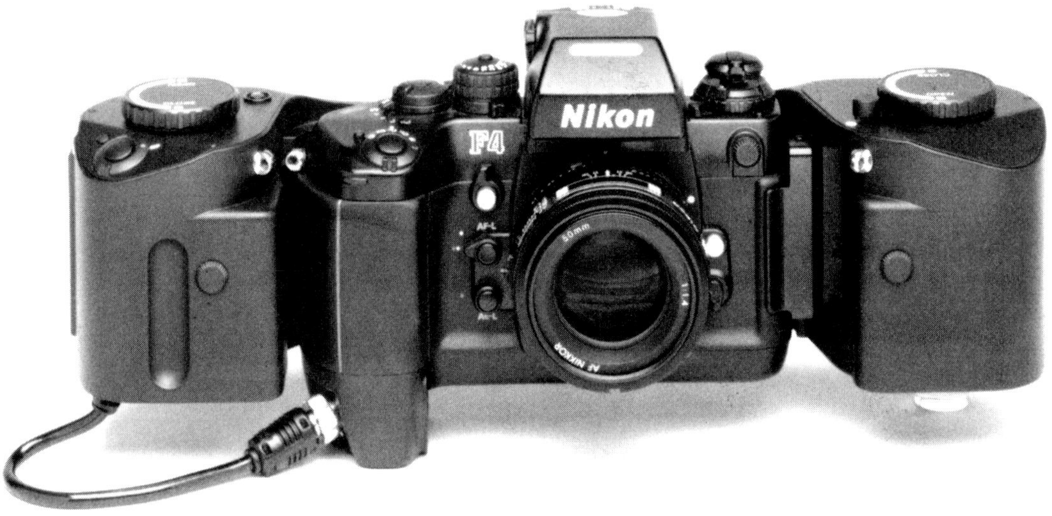

MF-24 BACK. (Announced February 22, 1990) This is a 250 exposure back for the F4. It must be used with an external power source, either from battery or through a power regulator from a 110v or 220v circuit.

The back not only handles long film rolls, but also imprints data and networks with the central processing unit (computer) in the camera body and AF lenses for automatic operation.

The operating features include focus priority, interval timing, automatic exposure bracketing, long exposure time and data imprinting, either between frames or in the picture area.

An intervalometer and a timer are built into the back to facilitate time-lapse photographs. The user keys in the starting time, interval time, number of pictures to be taken each time and the number of intervals. The camera and back do the rest. The long time-exposure function allows time exposures from 1 second to 999 hours, 59 minutes, 59 seconds.

The back can also control the camera to make up to 19 consecutive exposures with exposure values gradually shifted from the original metered value. The focus priority function will automatically trip the shutter when a subject comes to a preset distance from the camera.

ML-2 REMOTE CONTROL. (Introduced February 22, 1990) This is a three-channel, infrared remote control system that can trigger up to three cameras simultaneously or be used to synchronize remote flash units. The unit consists of an infrared light transmitter and a receiver to trigger the cameras or flashes. The system can turn on the camera body power, make a single shutter release, start and stop continuous motor operation, provide a three-second delay shutter release on single operation and send back a test signal for confirmation.

SD-8 BATTERY PACK. (Introduced February 22, 1990) This is a high performance pack intended for use with Nikon Speedlights SB-24, SB-22, SB-20 and SB-11. It reduces the recycling time by 60 to 75 percent and more than doubles the flash capacity. The pack accepts six AA alkaline or nickle-cadmium batteries. It is small and light enough (11.6 oz.) to carry in a shirt pocket or clipped to the user's belt.

MB-23 BATTERY PACK. This is an accessory battery pack which attaches to the bottom of the F4s camera body. It permits the use of nickel-cadmium batteries, but can also be used with alkaline batteries. The unit delivers increased performance and also improved operation at low temperatures when used with nicads. The pack increases the height of the camera slightly and adds 4.6 oz. F4 cameras are delivered in the US with the MB-21 battery pack making them F4s's. When the MB-23 is used the MB-21 is removed.

THE NIKON STILL VIDEO CAMERA SYSTEM

At the annual PMA conference held February 22, 1990 in Las Vegas, Nikon demonstrated its recently introduced black and white still video camera. A price was not announced and units are not yet available to dealers.

Named the QV-1000C, the camera records a high resolution image on a 2-inch floppy disc. The QV-1010T Monochrome Portable Transmitter allows instant playback and transmission. There are two dedicated zoom lenses: a 10-40mm f/1.4 and a 11-120mm f/2. There is an adapter which permits the use of any F mount Nikkor lens.

The camera and its controls are very similar to modern SLR 35mm film cameras. It features variable shutter speeds from 1 to 1/2000 seconds set by a dial, center-weighted TTL metering, choice of aperture priority, shutter priority, program or manual exposure control, a clear matte SLR viewing screen and an LCD information display in the finder.

The camera can shoot single frames or continuous sequences at 4 fps. The photographer can select one of three different film speed equivalents: 400, 800 or 1600 ISO. 25 high resolution or 50 lower-resolution images can be recorded on each 2-inch floppy disc.

The images can be viewed on a 4-inch screen built into the transmitter. The transmitter can be connected to any telephone line or to an acoustic telephone coupler for transmission anywhere. The digitized image can also be transmitted via radio or used in a personal computer for desk top publishing. The picture data can be received by standard wire service receivers or computers with appropriate software.

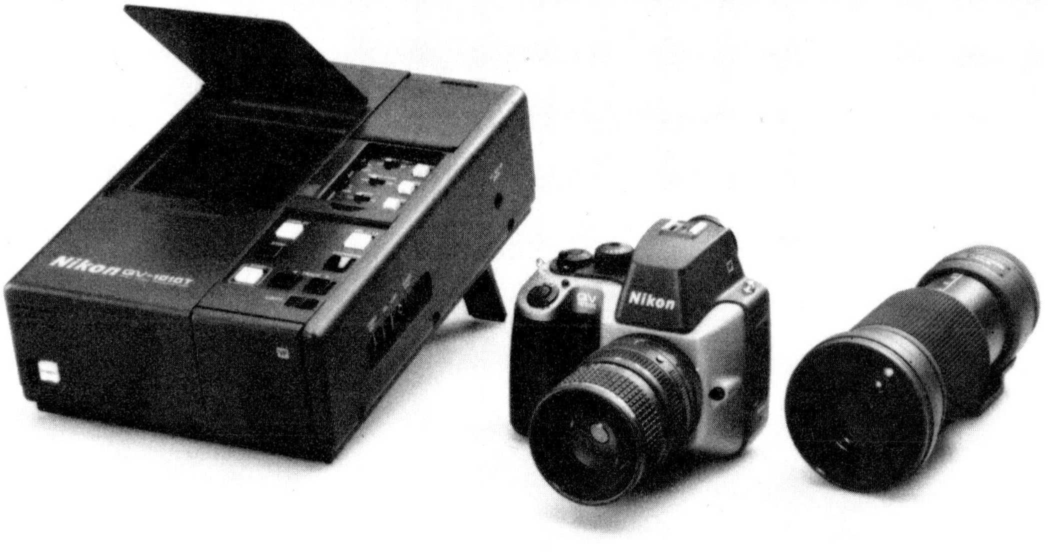

The new Nikon QV-1000C is in the center. On the left is the AV-1010T Monochrome Portable Transmitter for instant playback and transmission via telephone or radio. The dedicated 11-120mm f/2 zoom lens is on the right.

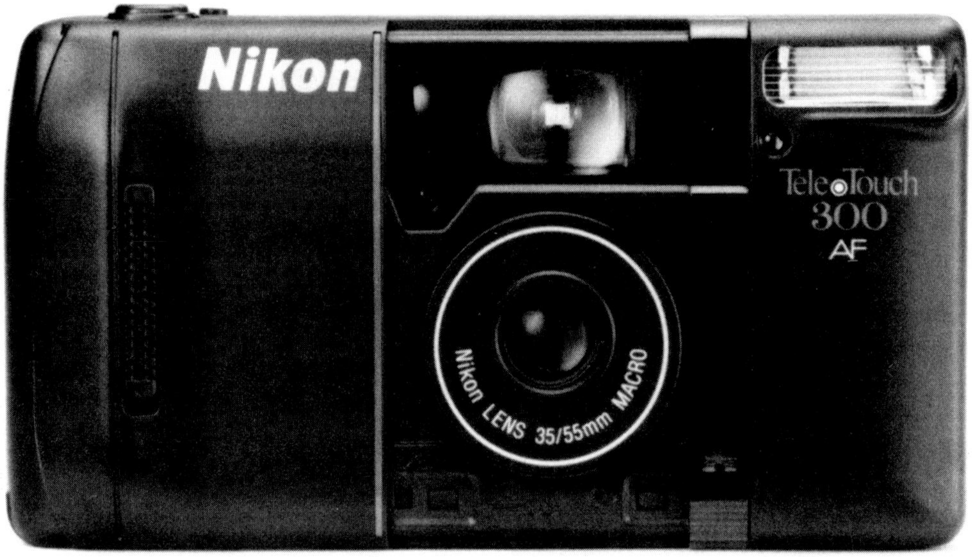

Nikon Tele•Touch 300

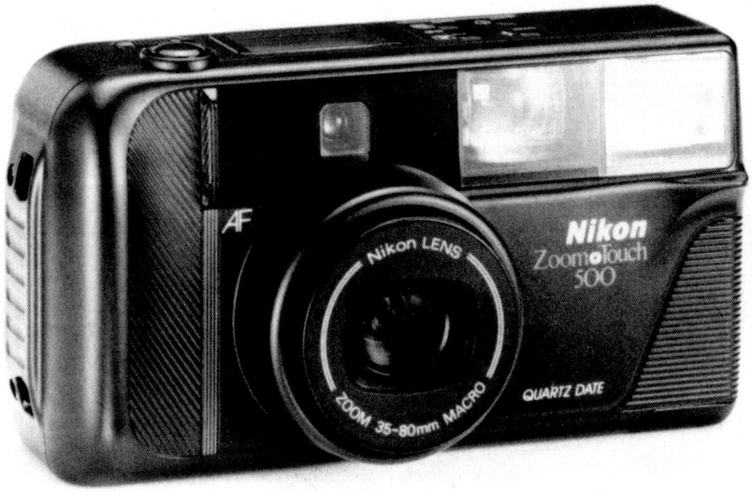

Nikon Zoom•Touch 500 Quartz Date

TELE-TOUCH 300 "POINT AND SHOOT" CAMERA. This autofocus compact was announced in April, 1989 with a list price of $275.

The camera features a dual focal length lens arrangement. The photographer can choose between a 35mm f/3.8 or a 55mm f/5.7. In addition to autofocus, some other features include focus-lock, automatic loading, built-in motor drive, automatic film rewind, self-timer and a "smart" flash which fires when the ambient light falls to a predetermined level.

TELE-TOUCH 300 QUARTZ DATE "POINT AND SHOOT" CAMERA. This camera, which was also announced in April of 1989, is the same as the Tele-Touch 300 with the addition of the quartz date feature. Its list price is $291.

The quartz date feature will imprint the month/day/year, the day/month/year, the year/month/day, the day/hour/minute or no imprint, as selected by the user. It also includes a 24-hour built-in clock with a timing accuracy within plus or minus 90 seconds per month at normal temperatures.

TELE-TOUCH DELUXE DATE "POINT AND SHOOT" CAMERA. This camera has the same characteristics as the Tele-Touch DeLuxe with a data back. The list price is $323.

ZOOM-TOUCH 500 "POINT AND SHOOT" CAMERA. This is the first Nikon "touch" camera with a zoom lens. The list price is $388. The f/7.8 lens zooms from 35mm to 80mm. The zoom operation offers single-frame or continuous automatic shooting at 3 fps either at a fixed focal length or during zooming at 5 selectable steps. The built-in flash recycles in 3 seconds and the 10-second self-timer features focus lock, interval control from 5 to 30 seconds, and a second exposure 5 seconds after the first exposure.

ZOOM-TOUCH 500 DATE "POINT AND SHOOT" CAMERA. The quartz date version has all the features of the Zoom-Touch 500 plus a data back that will imprint the month/day/year, hour/minute or no imprint. It includes a 24-hour clock accurate to 90 seconds a month. The list price is $404.

NIKON FM2n CAMERA. The FM was introduced in 1977, The FM2 in 1982, and the FM2n in 1989. It is a mechanical camera and presently the only one offered by Nikon. Since 1977, a number of improvements have been made, both in features and construction. The FM2n has not experienced an increase in price over the FM2.

While not apparent to users, the camera has undergone revolutionary internal changes. The most important feature improvement as far as photographers are concerned is an increase in the flash sync speed to 1/250.

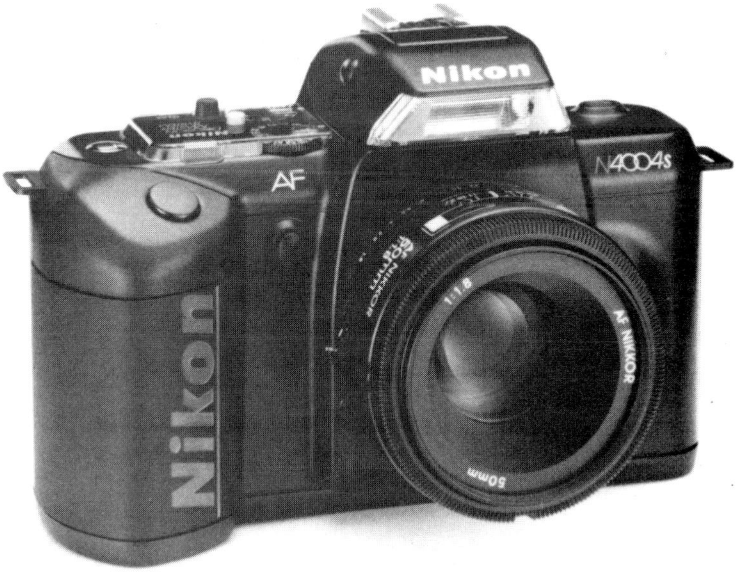

NIKON N4004s CAMERA BODY. This autofocus SLR body was announced in March, 1989. It replaced the N4004. The list price is $485.

The "s" version resembles its predecessor at first glance, but it is actually quite improved. The most significant change is a better autofocus mechanism. This results in faster and more positive autofocusing. The metering system was also improved. Both exposure control dials can now be locked in the automatic positions.

The N4004s, like its predecessor the N4004, is the only Nikon autofocus SLR which can only be used with autofocus lenses. The other Nikon autofocus cameras (N2020, N8008, F3AF, F4) all accept non-autofocus lenses, albeit in the manual mode.

NEW LENSES

20mm f/2.8 AF Nikkor. Lens available in April, 1989. List price: $647.50.

35mm f/2.0 AF Nikkor. Lens available in March, 1989. List price: $417.50.

60mm f/2.8 AF Micro Nikkor. List price: $494. (Replaces the 55mm f/2.8 AF Micro Nikkor.)

75-300mm f/4.5-5.6 AF Nikkor. Zoom lens available in March, 1989. List price: $657.50.

105mm f/2.8 AF Micro Nikkor. Introduced on February 22, 1990. To be available later in 1990. Price to be announced.

AF 35-70mm f/3.3-f/4.5 AUTOFOCUS LENS. This lens has been upgraded for the second time. This new (third) version has a depth of field scale and no window (the covering over the focusing scale). Additionally, the third version has a different optical formula which allows it to be physically shorter. The three versions can be differentiated from one another by serial number. Version number one started with 2,000,000; number two, 3,000,001; number three with 4,000,001.

MODIFIED AF LENSES.

One of the most recent changes involves making autofocus lenses more palatable to photographers who use them manually. The changes make the lenses easier to focus, whether they are mounted on an autofocus body or not.

The modifications to autofocus lenses include the addition of the following features: 1) A manual/auto switch which allows the lens to be used in the autofocus mode just like its predecessor. But when switched to manual, there is more drag on the focusing ring thus making focus less likely to creep. 2) There is an aperture locking switch which locks the aperture when the camera is used in either programmed or shutter priority mode so the f/stop cannot be accidentally moved. 3) There is a new focusing ring and grip. The tiny focusing ring on the earlier autofocus lenses made manual focusing difficult and the ring was hard to locate when not looking at it. The new ring and grip is considerably more "user friendly."

"N" LENSES. A process has been started recently to convert the present line of Nikkor lenses so that they are more "user friendly." The modifications include making the focusing ring wider, rubberizing the focusing grip and using more mar-proof construction materials. The "N" means new. These lenses are exactly the same as their predecessors optically. The lenses themselves are not marked, but the boxes and literature carry the "N" designation. Since the lenses are not inscribed, the only way to differentiate an N lens is by the serial number. Of course the physical differences are obvious if an "old" lens and an N lens of the same focal length and aperture are compared. The prices of the old and the N are, so far, the same. In each case, when an N lens is introduced, the previous lens of the same type, focal length and aperture is discontinued. Following is a list of N lenses introduced so far, together with the starting serial numbers:

LENS	*NON-N 1ST S/N*	*N 1ST S/N*
AF 35-135mm 3.5-4.5N	200,001	300,000
AF 50mm 1.8	2,000,000	3,000,001
AF 180mm 2.8N ED-IF	200,001	250,001
AF 300mm 2.8N ED-IF	200,001	300,001
AIS 200mm 2.0N ED-IF	information not available	information not available
AIS 600mm 5.6N ED-IF	information not available	information not available
AIS 600mm 4.0N ED-IF	information not available	information not available
PC 35mm 2.8N	information not available	information not available
Reflex 1000mm 11.0N	information not available	information not available
UW 15mm 2.8N UW	information not available	information not available

NEW NIKON 8MM VIDEO CAMCORDERS

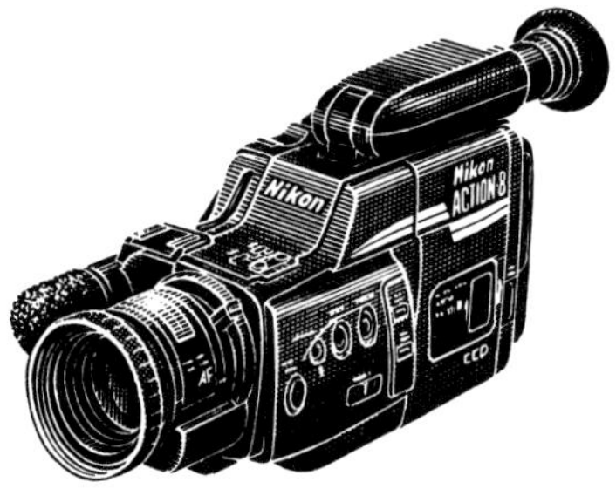

VN-830 8MM CAMCORDER. Video camera available in March, 1989. List price: $1300. This video 8mm format camera has a 6X power zoom lens (9mm to 54mm), macro capability and an illumination range of 4 lux to 100,000 lux. Its dimensions are 4 7/8" x 6 1/8" x 12 3/8" and it weighs 2 lb., 10 oz.

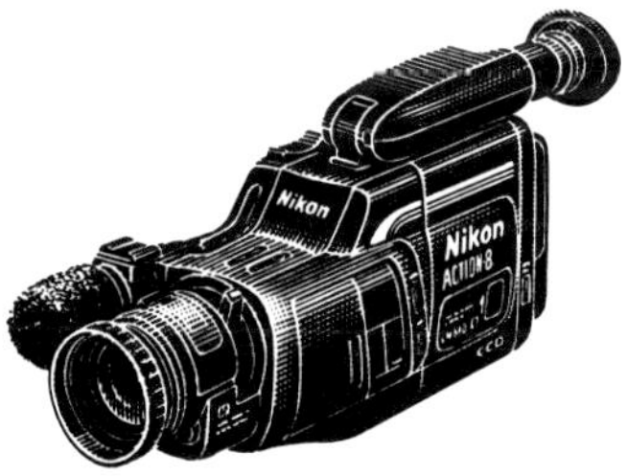

VN-840 8MM CAMCORDER. Video camera available in November, 1989. List price: $1400. This video 8mm format camera has an 8X power zoom lens (8.5mm to 68mm), macro capabilities and an illumination range of 3 lux to 100,000 lux. Its dimensions are 4 7/8" x 6 1/8" x 12 1/2" and it weighs 2 lb., 10 oz.

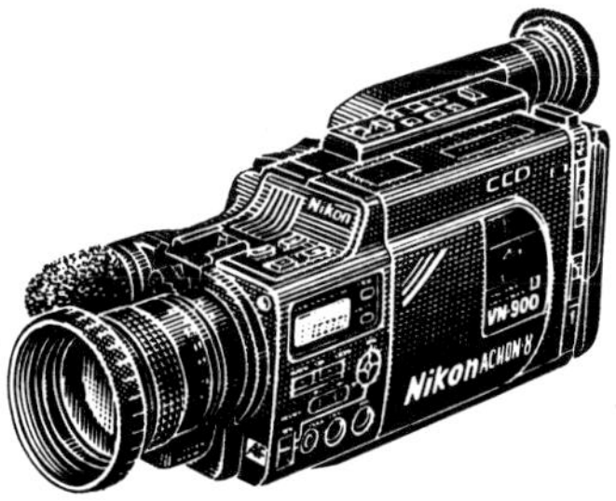

VN-900 8MM CAMCORDER. This video 8mm format camera has a 6X power zoom lens (12mm - 72mm) with macro capabilities, an illumination range of 5 lux to 100,000 lux, weighs 2 lbs., dimensions of 4 1/4" x 4 1/2" x ll 7/8."

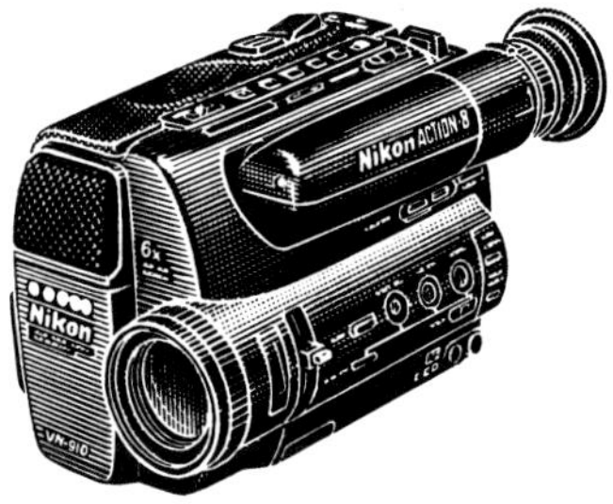

VN-910 8MM CAMCORDER. Video camera available in October, 1989. List price: $1500. This video 8mm format camera is noteworthy because it incorporates many features in a very small size. Its dimensions are 4 1/4" x 4 1/4" x 7" and it weighs only 1 lb., 12 oz. It has a 6X power zoom lens (11mm to 66mm) and an illumination range of 4 lux to 100,000 lux. Other features include macro capabilities, date and time recording plus title superimposition.

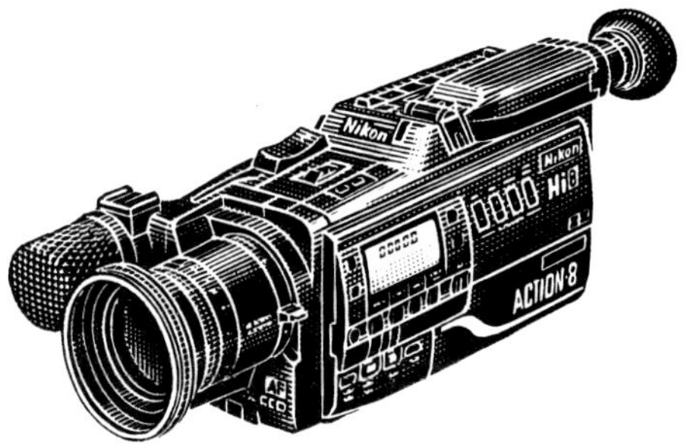

VN-950 8MM CAMCORDER. One of the "HI-8" series, the NV-950 offers 450 TV lines of horizontal resolution due to the new TSS (Tilted Sendust Sputtered) video head and separate Y/C input/output, which eliminates cross color and dot interference. The "HI-8" metal tape produces a higher density recording with horizontal magnetic particle orientation. The VN-950 has an 8X power zoom lens with macro capabilities, an illumination range of 4 lux to 100,000 lux, weighs 3 lbs., 5 oz. with dimensions of 5" x 5 3/8" x 13 7/8."

DECEMBER 1965

Meet the new Nikkormat Automatic Slide Projector with f3.5 Nikkor lens.

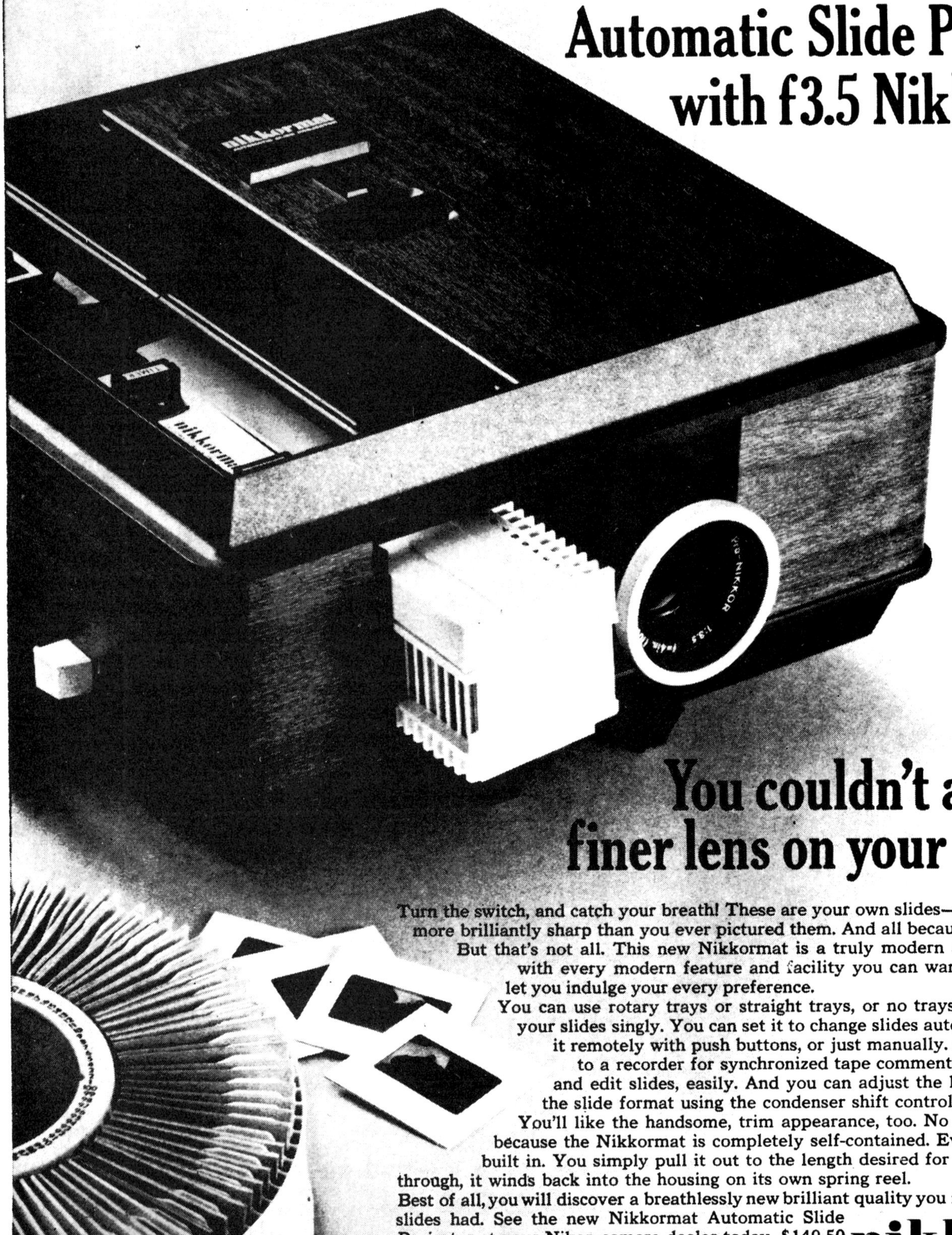

You couldn't ask for a finer lens on your camera.

Turn the switch, and catch your breath! These are your own slides—more colorfully alive, more brilliantly sharp than you ever pictured them. And all because of the Nikkor lens. But that's not all. This new Nikkormat is a truly modern automatic instrument with every modern feature and facility you can want. It was designed to let you indulge your every preference.

You can use rotary trays or straight trays, or no trays. You can even show your slides singly. You can set it to change slides automatically, or operate it remotely with push buttons, or just manually. Or you can connect it to a recorder for synchronized tape commentary. You can preview and edit slides, easily. And you can adjust the light system to match the slide format using the condenser shift control.

You'll like the handsome, trim appearance, too. No case to clutter things because the Nikkormat is completely self-contained. Even the power cord is built in. You simply pull it out to the length desired for use, and when you're through, it winds back into the housing on its own spring reel.

Best of all, you will discover a breathlessly new brilliant quality you never even knew your slides had. See the new Nikkormat Automatic Slide Projector at your Nikon camera dealer today. $149.50 complete. For complete, illustrated brochure, write:

nikkormat

Nikon Inc. Garden City, N.Y. 11533. Subsidiary of Ehrenreich Photo-Optical Industries, Inc.

CHAPTER FOUR

DISCONTINUED PRODUCTS AND PARTS

As time goes by, some new products are added to the Nikon line, while others are withdrawn or discontinued. This publication is updated periodically so that those who are active in selling or purchasing either new or used Nikon photographic products can continue to be knowledgeable.

When discontinued products are no longer available from the US supplier, these same items may still be available from retail outlets. Just because an item has been discontinued does not, of course, mean that it is no longer useful or desirable. But, at the same time, purchasers should keep in mind that many discontinued products are replaced with more advanced ones. It is entirely possible that the replacement products offer features which are important.

It is also significant to keep in mind that sometimes some dealers will offer discontinued items at significant savings. This could be because they have a large inventory and the replacement item sells better than the discontinued one. On occasion, when Nikon itself has a large unsold inventory of a soon to be discontinued item, it will sell to dealers at a price less than normal.

Discontinuations are not necessarily announced by Nikon Inc. One way to tell that an item has been withdrawn is to note that it no longer appears in the dealer price list. As of the publication date of this book, Nikon Inc. had not distributed a 1990 price list to dealers.

Following is a list of Nikon photographic products which were discontinued during 1989. Also included are items which Nikon Inc. has announced withdrawl in 1990. If known, the date of withdrawl is included in parenthesis.

Nikon is in a process of discontinuing AIS lenses. These are being replaced with AF lenses, which are also AIS.

SB-17 Speedlight (April 1990)

Cameras

Nikon N2020 camera body.
Nikon N4004 camera body.
(Replaced by the N4004s.)
Nikon FM2 camera body.
(Replaced by the FM2n.)
One Touch camera.
(Replaced by the New One Touch)
Fun Touch camera.
VN 830 Video Camcorder
VN 840 Video Camcorder
VN 900 Video Camcorder

Lenses

20mm f/2.8 AIS (April 1990)
24mm f/2.8 AIS (March 1990)
28mm f/2.8 AIS (March 1990)
28-85mm f/3.5-4.5 AIS (April 1990)
35mm f/2.0 AIS (April 1990)
35-105mm f/3.5-4.5 AIS (April 6, 1990)
50mm f/1.4 AIS (May 1990)
50mm f/1.8 AIS
85mm f/2.0 AIS (April 1990)
100-300mm f/5.6 AIS (April 1990)
180mm f/2.8 ED AIS
200mm f/4.0 (April 1990)
300mm f/2.0 ED-IF AIS
300mm f/2.8 ED-IF AIS
300mm f/4.5 ED-IF AIS (July 1990)
300mm f/4.5 AIS (April 1990)
35-135mm f/3.5-4.5 AIS
35-70mm f/3.3-4.5 AF
55mm f/2.8 Micro AF

Replaced by N lenses, Same Specifications

AF 35-135mm f/3.5-f/4.5
AF 50mm f/1.8
AF 180mm f/2.8 ED-IF
AF 300mm f/2.8 ED-IF
AIS 200mm f/2 ED-IF
AIS 600mm f/5.6 ED-IF
AIS 600mm f/4 ED-IF
PC 35mm f/2.8
Reflex 1000mm f/11
UW 15mm f/2.8

JUNE 1981

The only reason to buy a lesser camera is to take lesser pictures.

The F3.
Choice of the pros.

The FM. For full
manual control.

The FE. An automatic
you can grow with.

The EM. As easy to
afford as it is to use.

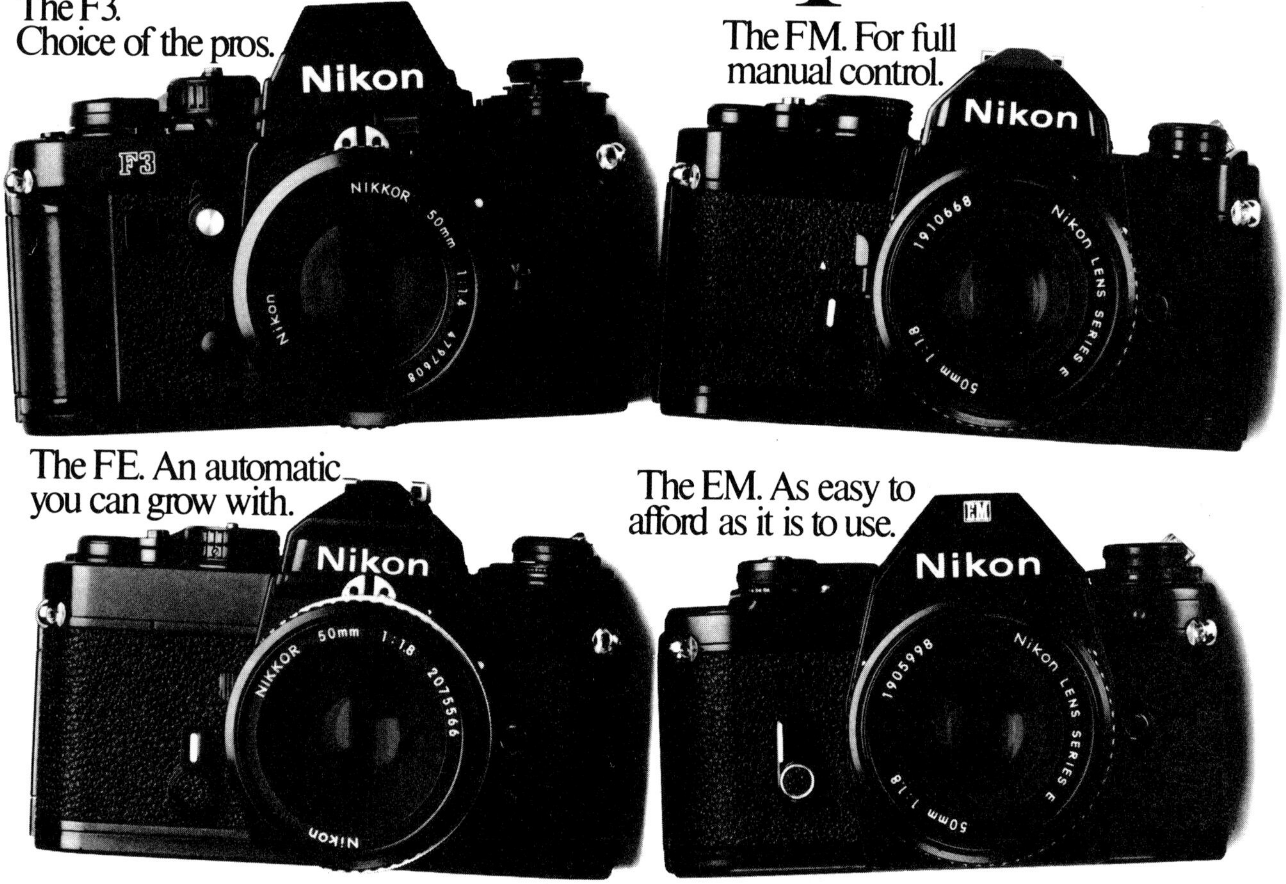

Nikon cameras have unquestionably been used by more professional photographers to take more award winning 35mm photographs than any other camera in the world.

For that reason, a lot of people think a Nikon is too much camera for them.

But it really isn't. Nikon makes a full line of cameras, with a full range of features, in a full range of prices. One of them is designed for you.

Whether you choose our professional automatic F3; our versatile, automatic FE; the fully manual metered FM; or the affordable, automatic EM, you'll be getting a Nikon. A camera subjected to an exacting system of design, manufacture and quality control.

If great pictures are what you're after, why buy a camera that gives you anything less?

Nikon

We take the world's greatest pictures.™

DISCONTINUED PARTS

For the most part, Nikon is very good about providing parts so that broken or defective products can be repaired. But there are items for which parts are no longer available. This means that such products cannot be repaired if they need parts, or it may cost more than it's worth to fabricate needed parts.

When contemplating the purchase of used products, it is significant to keep in mind items for which parts are not available. As time goes by, additional items will be added to the list. For this reason, this publication will be revised periodically and the discontinued parts list will be updated.

Following is a list of products for which parts are no longer available from Nikon:

All rangefinder camera bodies
Nikon EL2
All Nikkorex cameras
Nikonos I
All exposure meters
Photomic F finder
All non-AI (NAI) lenses
PC 28mm f/3.5
PC 35mm f/2.8
All rangefinder (RF) lenses
All short mount (SM) lenses
TC-1 Telextender
TC-2 Telextenders
S-36 motor drive
All Speed Magny backs
All flash guns (which use bulbs)
All strobes numbered before SB-11
1965 Underwater Flash Gun
Underwater Flash Gun for the Nikonos II
Underwater Flash Gun for the Nikonos III
Underwater Flash Gun SB-101
8mm movie cameras except R-10
(cine cameras, not video)

In addition, there are a number of products with parts in limited supply. Generally, this means no new parts are being produced and when the few on hand are sold, the product will join the category above in the next edition of this book. In some cases, it can be anticipated that the supply will not last out the current year.

All Nikkormat bodies
Nikonos II
Nikonos III
Photomic FTN Meter Prism
Photomic T Meter Prism
Photomic TN Meter Prism
All AI lenses
15mm f/2.8 UW
28mm f/3.5 UW
Auto Winder AW-1
F-250 motor drive
F-36 motor drive
MD-1 motor drive
MD-2 motor drive
MF-1 back
MF-2 back
MF-3 back
R-10 Super Zoom

Parts have been discontinued for the following products. Nikon USA, however, has a large supply of parts as of early 1990.

Nikon F
Nikon F2
MD-3 motor drive
Nikon F2 finders

SPECIAL NOTE REGARDING THE AIS 300MM F/2.0. ED-IF. This lens was introduced in 1984 with a retail price of $6000. Because of its speed, it became a favorite for professional motion picture use and many were converted to cinema camera mounts. In 1986, the price went to $6500, then jumped to $10,500 in 1987 and $11,525 in 1988. The 1989 dealer price catalog lists the lens but no price. There is a notation that the lens is a "special order item" and that the price will be furnished to a dealer upon request. In April 1990, co-author Paul Comon, a dealer, called to request the price and was informed that the lens is no longer available.

JANUARY 1960

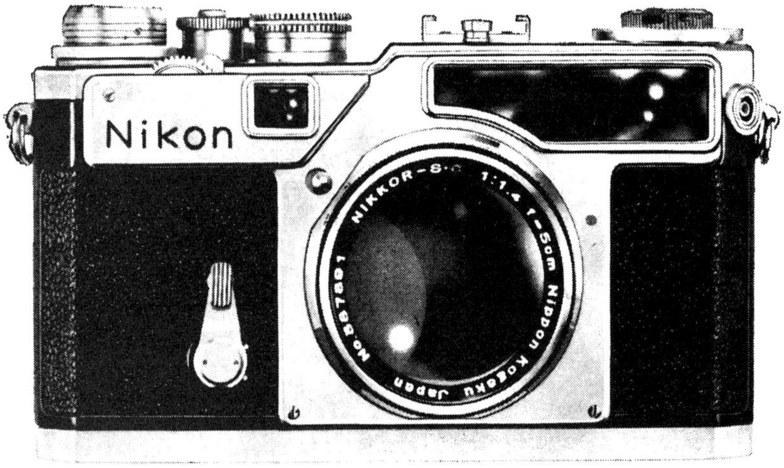

rangefinder-coupled or automatic reflex the finest '35' you can own is a **NIKON**

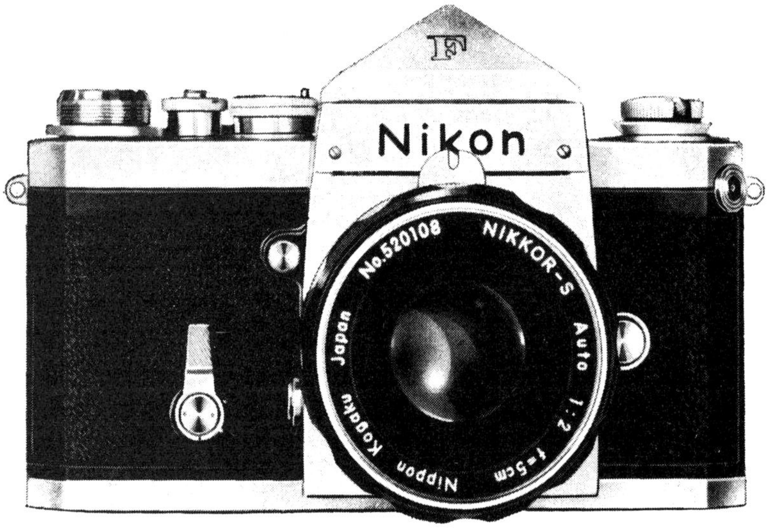

To say of one's camera — *"It's a Nikon"* — to say that it is equipped with a Nikkor lens, is to imply a measure of quality that has yet to be equalled — a quality that has achieved universal acknowledgement and recognition, especially among the knowledgeable, critical users of fine 35mm equipment.

Your choice between these two unusual instruments depends only upon your needs or preference — rangefinder or reflex. For they are both, in all other respects, the same — the same reputable, reliable make, the same meticulous quality, the same incomparable Nikkor optics and the same superb performance.

With a Nikon, you have every right to expect the finest results, for the instrument in your hands is the finest money can buy.

NIKON SP RANGEFINDER-COUPLED '35' with Universal Viewfinder System providing built-in finders for six different focal length lenses: 28, 35, 50, 85, 105 and 135mm, and 50mm Nikkor f/2 Lens, $329.50 (with f/1.4 lens, $375).

NIKON F AUTOMATIC REFLEX '35' with Fully Automatic Features: Instant-Reopen Diaphragm, Instant-Return Mirror and Instant-Action Preview Control, 50mm Auto-Nikkor f/2 Lens, $329.50.

See and examine both cameras at your Nikon Dealer. For further information write to Dept. MP-1

NIKON INCORPORATED, 111 Fifth Ave., New York 3, N. Y.
In Canada: Anglophoto Ltd., 880 Champagneur St., Montreal, P.Q.

CHAPTER FIVE

BUYING USED NIKON PHOTOGRAPHIC PRODUCTS

For many photographers, purchasing used equipment is a viable alternative to the acquisition of new products. Certainly the price will be less, and sometimes a photographer is able to get an item with specific characteristics which is no longer available new. But at the same time, wise used buying requires considerably more care than purchasing new products which come with a manufacturer's warranty.

Considerations. When purchasing a used camera, the three most important considerations are: condition, condition and condition. There are two parts to a consideration of condition: mechanical and cosmetic. Purchasers of used equipment seem to fall into two categories. One wants a fine camera in looks as well as operation, the other wants a serviceable one.

The first group consists of collectors, those who contemplate reselling the item, and users who appreciate cosmetically perfect equipment. The second group usually is more interested in the results produced by the camera than any other factor. If a camera is going to be subjected to rough use, it is not sensible to pay a premium for a cosmetically perfect specimen. A rough looking camera may wear out sooner than a nice looking one, but some cream puffs may be defective because inactivity has caused the lubricants to solidify.

Sometimes certain items are hard to find on the used market and decisions must be made on the spot. Judgments should always be made based on the appearance and operation of the item itself, not on the seller's conversation. The following discussion should help when making purchasing decisions.

Function. The first assessment should be, does everything function properly? Of course, mechanical problems can be rectified, but almost every repair technician has a minimum charge, usually between $30 and $50 (as times change, these prices may escalate). So if something doesn't work, ask yourself, "Would I pay at least $30 more?" Remember, only a repair technician can accurately estimate costs.

Many repairs require parts, and for some items, parts are simply no longer available from the manufacturer. This is the reason for the section in this book on discontinued parts. As an example, if you are considering a Nikonos I, you should be aware that parts cannot be obtained from Nikon Inc. Of course, given a sufficient amount of money, needed parts can be fabricated, but the cost will usually exceed the value of the repaired item.

Appearance. Cosmetic defects are usually permanent. Grading systems cannot always be accurate. As an example, black metal bodies often show wear more easily than chrome or polycarbonate ones. The black finish on Nikon metal cameras is baked enamel, and is easily worn, especially by poorly designed neck straps. Therefore, if you encounter a desirable black camera with some brassing, you may want to consider buying it. You can always upgrade later, but you can't retrieve the one that got away.

Chrome metal cameras can also show brass. If the brassing is smooth and evenly worn, the body has undoubtedly seen a lot of use. Some marks or bruises are indelible, but dirt and grime will come off and sometimes reveal a like-new finish underneath.

Problems with leather are serious from a cosmetic standpoint since leather is next to impossible to match. The texture, grain and finish are as unique as fingerprints. Even an expensive total re-leathering job may be unsuccessful because it just doesn't look right. The exception to this is leather blanks for the specific camera supplied by the manufacturer. Blanks may be difficult to obtain, especially for older models.

Always scrutinize the camera base plate. Many cameras which otherwise appear pristine show wear in this area.

Look at every lens surface from both sides and then look at a bright light through the lens. Look for surface scratches, irregular coating, element separation, fungus and foreign objects such as dust or lint. Of course, foreign objects can be removed by taking the lens apart, but the other problems cannot be so economically remedied.

Often a lens with any of these problems will perform well, but the price should be altered accordingly. Fungus is a unique problem since it is organic. Organisms may continue to grow and the problem could get worse unless rectified.

Mechanical Shutters. Generally speaking, earlier Nikons have mechanical shutters, and later ones, electronically timed ones. The exceptions to this are the FM, FM2 and FM2n which are later but mechanical. To check whether a camera is mechanical or electronic, remove the battery and trip the shutter at different speeds. Electronically timed shutters without electricity will work only at one speed, usually 1/90.

Mechanical shutters are timed by springs and gears. Although they are very accurate, problems can develop, particularly if the previous owner was not knowledgeable. Slow speeds, medium speeds and high speeds are on different trains. If the slow speeds are rarely used, the lubricant will gum up and the speeds will slow down. In extreme cases, the shutter will stick open. Inaccurate slow speeds can be detected by listening carefully. This problem is solved by total disassembly of the shutter, degreasing the parts, reassembling, lubricating and re-timing; obviously not a minor repair.

Mechanical Self-Timers. Timers are subject to the same problems that affect mechanical shutters. Inactivity is the culprit. Detection and the solution are the same. Owners of mechanical cameras are advised to work the slow shutter speed train and self-timer as often as possible, at least each time a new roll of film is loaded and advanced to the first frame.

Cloth and Titanium Foil Focal Plane Shutters. Early Nikon had cloth shutters. In 1959, Nikon started using coated Titanium foil. Everyone knows the sun's rays will burn a hole in paper when focused through a magnifying glass. If a camera with a cloth shutter is pointed at the sun and the lens focused on infinity, a hole in the shutter will result. Titanium shutters cannot be easily penetrated in this way, but the coating will melt. This may be more expensive to repair than a hole. This problem is usually confined to rangefinder models, since the mirror normally protects an SLR shutter. Holes in shutters can be detected by viewing a light through the shutter with the lens and back removed.

Iris Blades. Most Nikkor camera lenses have automatic diaphragms. If oil gets on the blades, they will not work rapidly enough. When this happens, the blades do not yield the proper aperture and severe overexposure results. This can be caused by storing lenses on their sides.

To check for oil, stop the lens down to its minimum opening and look carefully at the blades from both sides. Rotate the lens and look for oil.

Sometimes an iris blade will jump off its keeper. Look carefully while opening and closing the diaphragm. Look for irregularities in the blade pattern. Loose blades will not respond the same way as pinned ones.

Rangefinders. To test a rangefinder on any camera, be it a rangefinder-type or a single lens reflex, focus on the most distant object you can easily see. This object should be at least two times as far away as the farthest marking on the lens (other than infinity). Now look at the scale markings on the lens barrel. Is the mark at infinity? (This test is invalid for some telephotos, particularly mirror and ED lenses. Some will focus beyond the infinity mark and the point of infinity focus will vary with the temperature.)

Now measure carefully to find an object exactly six feet from the camera. Focus on the object and check the scale on the lens to see if it is at six feet. If a focusing system works at both infinity and six feet, you can be sure all is ok. If it does not check out, repeat the process with a different lens, since occasionally the lens can be at fault.

If a rangefinder camera is out of adjustment (the rangefinder may be out of adjustment either vertically or horizontally), the repair is usually relatively inexpensive.

If focusing is inaccurate on an SLR, this could signal expensive repairs. Some causes of SLR/rangefinder disagreement are: a damaged or misaligned lens mount, a mirror out of position or alignment problems in the prism. Use caution when you encounter this sort of a problem with an SLR.

Rangefinder lenses couple to the camera focusing mechanism via cams. Some older lenses may have worn cams that can be easily adjusted; but be sure the lens was made for the camera. Zeiss Contax rangefinder lenses will fit both Contax and Nikon since they have the same mount, but the cam systems are different.

If a lens for either an SLR or a rangefinder camera is out of adjustment to the extent that the finder and the lens scale do not agree, it is possible that the ring on the lens containing the focusing scale has slipped (inexpensive), or there are internal problems (probably expensive). So if you encounter a lens with focusing problems, look carefully for slipped rings, tampering or signs of trauma. Usually slipped rings are found on poorly manufactured after-market lenses.

Light Meters. Most Nikon cameras have a built-in light meter of one sort or another. Meters are easy to test. Simply compare one with another. The comparison should be made with both devices pointed at a large, evenly lit object such as a blank wall. Naturally, the reference meter (or camera with built-in meter) must be of known accuracy.

Flash Synchronization and Electronic Flash. These two subjects go hand in hand. The flash synchronization test for focal plane shutters is easy to perform if you have a camera and flash set-up allowing the flash to fire off the camera via a connecting cord. Remove or open the camera back, place a piece of white paper over the opening where the film would be (be careful not to touch the shutter). Some newer cameras will only work after the film counter passes zero. Normally, the counter only counts after the back door is closed. A lever in the body can be depressed to trick the counter. Remove the lens and point the flash at the lens mount. If you cannot remove the strobe from the camera and use a sync cord, aim the camera at a white wall about three feet away. Make sure the sync levers (if any) are set to "X" and the shutter is set to an appropriate speed. If the flash has a manual setting, position it there for this test. While looking at the paper, trip the shutter. If synchronization is perfect, there will be even illumination on the entire film plane represented by the paper. In order to observe the effect of improper synchronization, re-set the shutter to a speed faster than the maximum sync speed. To be sure, try several different speeds, both over and under the maximum sync speed. You will then observe the difference between in and out-of-sync.

To test synchronization with a between-the-lens shutter, with the lens mounted on the camera, open the aperture to its maximum. Use the same set-up as for a focal plane, but don't use the paper. While looking directly through the camera, when the strobe goes off, you will see a blinding flash of light. Close your eyes. With your eyes closed, because of retina fatigue, you will see the results of the flash. If you see a perfect circle of light, the synchronization is correct. An ellipse indicates almost perfect sync, while a star (in the shape of the shutter blades) indicates improper sync. Obviously, if you didn't see any light, there was no synchronization at all. It is advisable to try various shutter speeds in order to learn what perfect sync and slightly out-of-sync look like.

The tests described above will determine proper sync, but without elaborate test equipment, it is not possible to be sure automatic flash systems are functioning exactly as they should. There is, however, an easily performed test which will indicate correct operation with a reasonable degree of assurance. First, mount the flash on the camera. Then set the flash to the automatic mode you wish to test. While aiming at a blank wall, repeatedly fire the strobe at different distances between three and twenty feet. Don't look through the viewfinder; look at the wall. You should see a noticeable difference in flash intensities at different distances. Try all the different automatic modes.

When a sync cord is involved in a test and there is a failure, the first thing to mistrust is the cord. If you have two strobes and two cameras, it's easy to locate the problem through a process of elimination.

Batteries are the next most likely problem area. Even new ones can cause trouble. When there is a failure, first clean the contact points on both the batteries and the unit. Modern batteries seldom leak, but they often exude a film which eventually resembles white chalk dust.

That's the miracle of the Nikon F. It knows no obsolescence. Its designers seem to have anticipated every new idea development in slr design, and to have given it a timelessness no other camera has ever achieved.

The new Photomic T meter system is a unique example. First, it is interchangeable with every other Nikon F finder. Second, it determines exposure from the brightness of the lens-formed image on the viewing screen.

No extraneous light is permitted to upset its accuracy. The two CdS cells used to measure brightness are mounted behind double lens systems which "see" only the framed-in picture area on the screen. A special "black" coating is used to eliminate internal, glass surface reflections.

The Photomic T does not interfere with automatic diaphragm action. Cross-coupled, it responds to aperture as well as shutter speed changes, but the diaphragm remains wide open at all times. It stops down for the exposure when the shutter is released, and then automatically reopens.

We say of the Photomic T that it offers "thru-the-Nikkor" exposure control. Its use with the Nikon F implies its use with Nikkor lenses. This assurance of picture quality as well as exposure accuracy distinguishes it from all other thru-the-lens meter systems.

See the Nikon F with the new Photomic T meter system, priced at $371 with 50mm Auto-Nikkor f2 lens, and $433 with f1.4. Present Nikon F camera bodies require slight modification to accept the Photomic T, interchangeably. Write for complete details.

The old Nikon F has a new meter system.

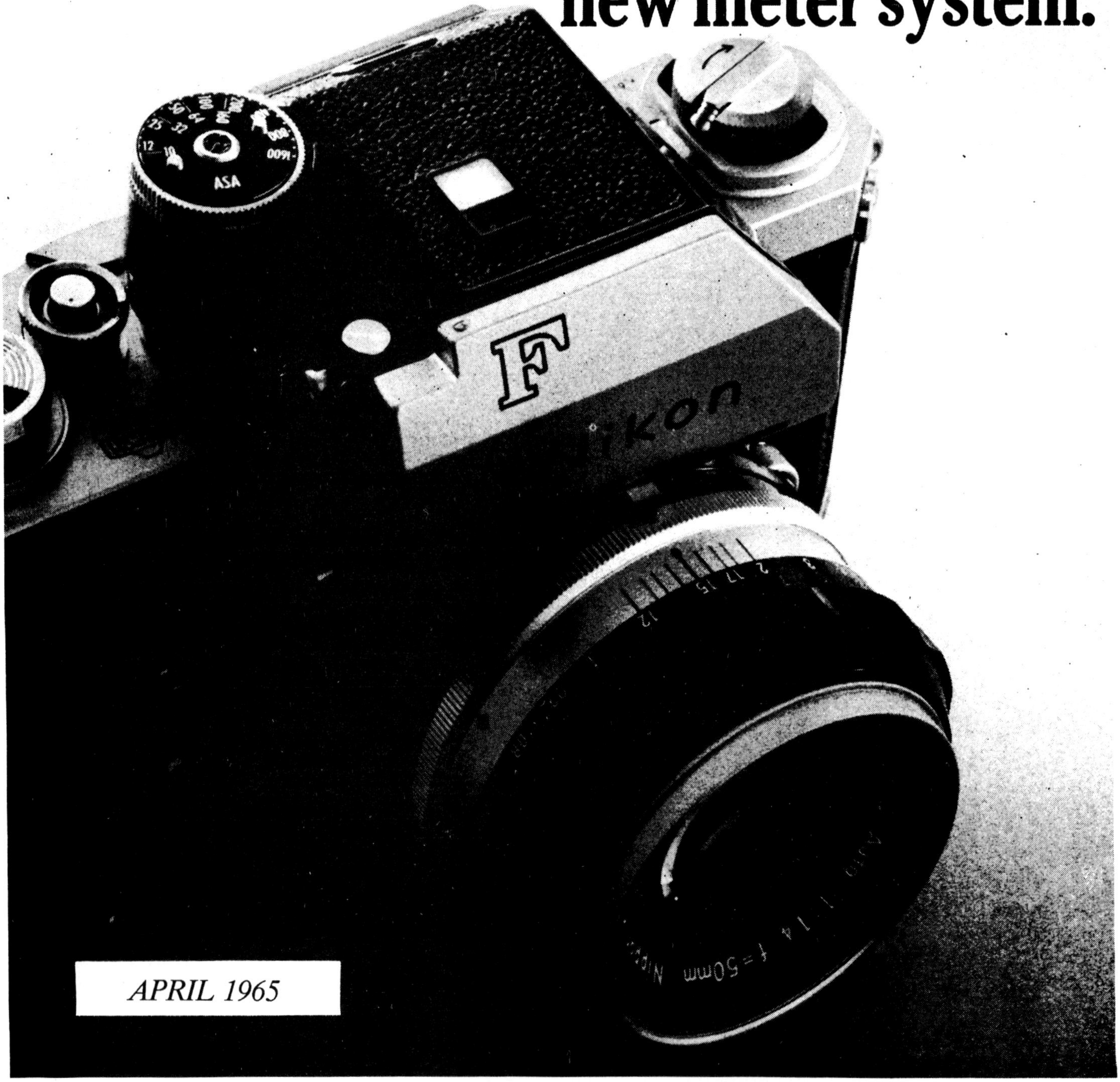

APRIL 1965

When this first occurs, it is invisible, but it can prevent proper electrical contact. Use an eraser (preferably an abrasive ink eraser) on both battery and unit contact points.

SLR Mirrors. The mirrors on Nikon SLRs are front surfaced. The mirror should never be touched. They should be cleaned only by a repair technician. The mirrors should be dusted only with canned air since the slightest touch of even the softest cleaning material can scratch them.

Inspect the mirror of a prospective purchase carefully. A mirror replacement is expensive. But keep in mind that the quality of the mirror affects only the viewing, not the photograph since the mirror is out of the way at the moment of exposure. The exception to this is the F2H which has a pellicle mirror (which does not move so marks on it WILL affect the image).

Electronic Cameras. All newer Nikon cameras are electronic except the FM series. Since they are more recently developed, there is less data upon which to rely. Electronic cameras contain fewer moving parts so there is less to wear. Many of the shells will not dent, and they certainly will not brass, so the amount of use they may have experienced can be more difficult to judge.

All of the functions should be carefully checked. Does the shutter appear to be accurate at all speeds? Does the strobe sync? Does the self-timer work? Does the light meter read accurately? The replacement of electronic components can be very costly.

Motor Drives and Winders. These are easily checked. Attach the drive to the camera. Load a roll of film and draw a line with a marker at the start of the first frame. Close the back and advance the film one frame with the motor or winder. Open the back and see if the mark advanced one full frame.

If the drive fails to function, first check the battery condition and the contacts. Next, look for a gap between the unit and the camera. Some motors don't seat easily.

If the unit still fails to function, it's probably better to pass.

Data Backs. Some data backs include batteries and others are powered by the battery in the camera body. To check, look at the back to see if there is a battery door or cover.

If the back functions, the data is visible in the display on the rear of the back. Test to see if the data can be changed by depressing the appropriate buttons. With the back mounted on the camera body with lens removed and no film loaded, release the shutter while looking through the lens mounting orifice. There should be a tiny flash of light at the location where the data is imprinted. This is easier to perform in a relatively dark location.

Bellows. Usually nothing goes wrong with bellows, but prudence requires a check before a used purchase. Move the rack through all of its movements to be sure it travels smoothly. Check all locks to see if they are secure in the locked position and that they unlock properly. Finally, insert a small flashlight inside the bellows to check for light leaks. The darker the room, the easier it is to see pin holes.

Motion Picture Cameras. Nikon does not presently produce motion picture cameras, but they have in the past. All of the tests applicable to a still camera should be applied to a motion picture camera plus checking the motor. First, listen to it run. Does it sound smooth and regular? Next, load some film and watch it run with the door open. Are top and bottom loops evenly maintained? Inspect the film which has gone through. Is it scratched? Are any of the perforations damaged?

Video Camcorders. Nikon presently distributes very fine quality video camcorders which are manufactured for Nikon by other concerns, presently Sony. The only sure way to test a used video camera is to tape a variety of subjects with different lighting conditions, and then play back under optimum conditions. If this is not possible, it would probably be wise to pass up the purchase.

JANUARY 1958

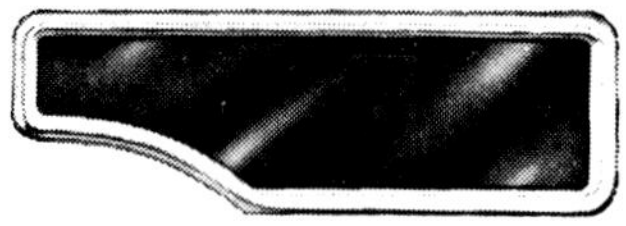

This one feature *alone*

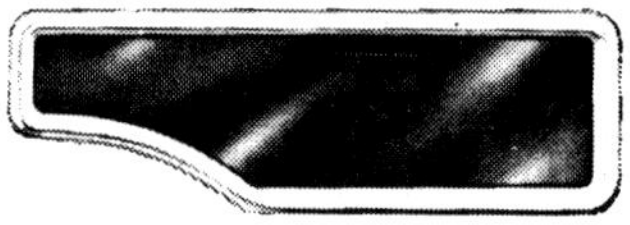

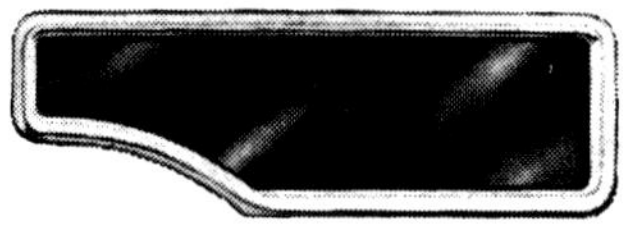

puts the new NIKON SP years ahead of any other '35' in the field

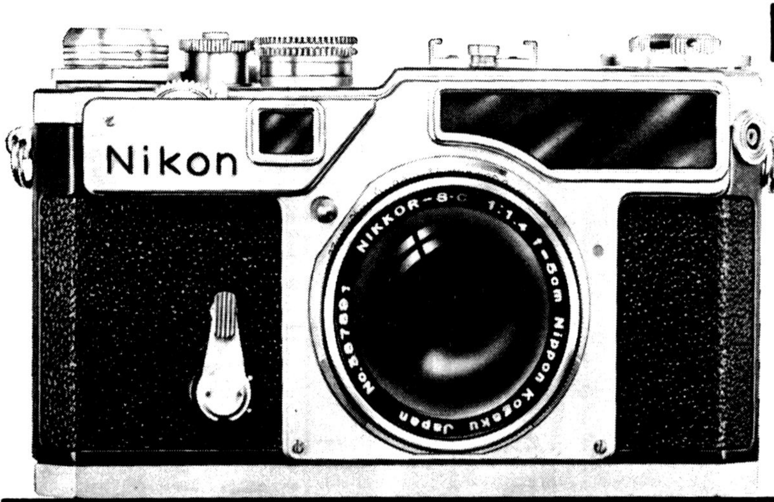

the Nikon SP Universal Viewfinder System

BUILT-IN VIEWING FIELDS FOR 6 FOCAL LENGTH LENSES
28, 35, 50, 85, 105 and 135mm — without any accessories

AUTOMATIC PARALLAX COMPENSATION
for "normal" and telephoto lenses: 50, 85, 105 and 135mm

LIFE-SIZE, ONE-TO-ONE VIEWING IMAGE
for "normal" and telephoto lenses: 50, 85, 105 and 135mm

WIDE ANGLE OPTICAL FINDER
for 28mm and 35mm wide angle lenses

6-LENS "PREVIEWER"
pre-selects the lens to use

Without the need for a single accessory finder, the built-in Universal Viewfinder System gives you the viewing fields for the six most-often-used focal lengths in 35mm photography. And it serves not only as a finder, but also as an efficient "previewer" to help you select the right lens to use. You can pick the lens faster; bring it into play faster; and put it to use with greater ease and speed than with any other '35.'

This one feature alone puts the Nikon SP years ahead of any other 35.' But, it is *not* alone, for the SP has many new features which easily make it the most complete, most advanced '35' in the fine camera field — like the new compensating flash-synch control, color-coded for bulb types and shutter speeds — the calibrated self-timer — the improved non-rotating speed dial — the automatic 'O' reset exposure counter and load indicator — and many others.

But above and beyond all features is the handling ease and speed of the SP. The single stroke film transport, the focusing wheel and body release in Nikon's traditional "advance-focus-shoot" grouping gives the Nikon owner an extra edge in every picture situation.

NIPPON KOGAKU TOKYO

Nikon SP with 50mm Nikkor f/2 $369.50; with 50mm Nikkor f/1.4 $415.
Nikon S2 with 50mm Nikkor f/2 $299.50; with 50mm Nikkor f/1.4 $345.

For complete description, write to Dept. MP-1 Nikon Incorporated, 251 Fourth Avenue, New York 10, N. Y. In Canada: Anglophoto, Ltd., 880 Champagneur Avenue, Montreal, P.Q.

CHAPTER SIX

NOMENCLATURE, CODES AND SERIAL NUMBERS

OVERSEAS NAMES. Nikon occasionally attaches different names to products intended for export to the United States.

US Designation	Non-USA Designation
Nikkormat	Nikomat
Nikkorex	Nikorex
N2000	F301
N2020	F501
N4004	F401
N4004s	F401s
N8008	F801

CAMERA CODES. Nikon point and shoot cameras have codes as well as names. Sometimes the name is on the camera; sometimes the code. Some of these point-and-shoot cameras have names on the cameras exported to the US. But the same model, sold elsewhere, may bear only the code.

One Touch	L35AF
One Touch Quartz Date	L35AD
Nice Touch	L135AF
One Touch (new)	L35AF2
One Touch Quartz Date (new)	L35AD2
Tele Touch	L35TWAF
Tele Touch Quartz Date	L35TWAD
Action Touch	L35AWAF
Action Touch Quartz Date	L35AWAD
New One Touch	AF3
New One Touch Quartz Date	AD3
Fun Touch	RF
Fun Touch Quartz Date	RD
Tele Touch Deluxe	TW2
One Touch 100	RF2
One Touch 100 Quartz Date	RD2
Zoom Touch 500	TW200M
Zoom Touch 500 Quartz Date	TW200MQD
Tele Touch 300	TW20
Tele Touch 300 Date	TW20D
Tele Touch Deluxe Data	TW2D

LENS CODES. In the past, Nikkor lenses were designated with a letter code. The code is inscribed on the lens ring. An example of how they are inscribed is "NIKKOR-Q." The code is always a single letter. This system was used until 1974 on both rangefinder and SLR lenses.

The letter indicates the number of elements in the lens. Within the production of a particular lens, the letter will not usually change. There is only one instance of changing the number of elements during the production of lenses with the same focal length and maximum aperture: the NAI 50mm f/2 went from S to H.

The following shows the significance of the letter code:

U	one element	H	six elements
B	two elements	S	seven elements
T	three elements	O	eight elements
Q	four elements	N	nine elements
P	five elements	D	ten elements

CAMERA SERIAL NUMBERS. Serial numbers are often of interest to collectors. Sometimes numbers are very significant. If, for instance, the first and last numbers of a specific product are known, this may indicate the number produced. This is not always true, however, since sometimes a manufacturer will assign a block of numbers in advance and then not produce a sufficient quantity to use all of the assigned numbers.

Serial numbers can also be significant by indicating when a product was manufactured. And they are obviously important in case of loss or theft. Some police authorities recommend making identification marks on camera gear. If you do make marks which are impossible to remove, you should be aware that the resale value of the equipment is lowered. If you have recorded the serial numbers of your equipment, this should be sufficient to identify you as the owner.

Some people believe that Nikon F and F2 camera's years of manufacture can be identified by the first two digits of the serial number, i.e. 66 meaning made in 1966. This is NOT the case. The Nikon F was first manufactured in 1958 and introduced in the US in 1959. There are no Nikon F's with serial numbers lower than 64. It is thought that in 1967, the year and serial number started to coincide and from then on Nikon continued using the first two digits of the serial numbers to indicate the year of manufacture. This seems, after a great deal of study, to be true. But no one the authors have interviewed can prove or disprove this hypothesis. Most people say that the first two digits in the F2 serial numbers also indicate the date of manufacture and less controversy rages around that issue. Exceptions to this are the F2/T and the F2H. The numbers for these cameras have no significance insofar as the date of manufacture is concerned.

When any Nikon camera has to be repaired and a top cover (the part with the serial number on it) is replaced, the new cover will NOT have the same serial number. Currently all new top covers have serial numbers. In the past, there were times when new replacement top covers were produced at the factory without a number inscribed.

When an F or F2 top cover is replaced by Nikon, an attempt is made to use a new cover with the first two digits the same as the damaged cover.

It should be kept in mind that many repair organizations keep a supply of used, usually damaged beyond economical repair, equipment on hand in order to cannibalize parts. This is particularly true of older bodies. So in this instance also, a repaired camera would receive a different number.

Except for the aforementioned instance of the F and F2 bodies, numbers assigned by Nikon to cameras and bodies have no significance. And there are duplications. There are some different cameras or bodies with the same number. For example, an FM2 and an FG-20 could have the same number. But the same number will NOT be found on two FE bodies.

LENS SERIAL NUMBERS. Unlike other photographic products, Nikon has kept track of the first number in the series of serial numbers assigned to a lens. This data has a number of uses. For instance, it can be determined by the serial number which lenses have been converted from NAI to AI. These lens serial numbers were provided to the authors by Nikon USA. Lenses exist bearing serial numbers that seem inconsistant with this chart. Data is presently being collected and future editions of this book may solve the puzzle.

FIXED FOCAL LENGTH LENSES

Lens	First #	Lens	First #
AI 6mm 2.8	628001	NAI 6mm 2.8	628001
AIS 6mm 2.8	629000	NAI 6mm 5.6	656001
NAI 7.5mm 5.6	880101	AI 8mm 2.8	242001
NAI 8mm 2.8	230011	AIS 8mm 2.8	243000
NAI 8mm 8.0	880101	NAI 10mm 5.6	180011
NAI 16mm 2.8	178051	AIS 16mm 2.8	185000
AI 16mm 3.5	280001	NAI 16mm 3.5	272281
AI 13mm 5.6	175021	NAI 13mm 5.6	175021
AIS 13mm 5.6	175901	AI 15mm 3.5	177051
AIS 15mm 3.5	180001	AI 15mm 5.6	340001
NAI 15mm 5.6	321001	AI 18mm 4.0	190001
NAI 18mm 4.0	173111	NAI 18mm 3.5	180051
AI 20mm 3.5	176121	NAI 20mm 3.5	421241
AIS 20mm 3.5	210001	AI 20mm 4.0	130001
NAI 20mm 4.0	103001	NAI 21mm 4.0	220111
AI 24mm 2.0	176021	AIS 24mm 2.0	200000
AI 24mm 2.8	525001	NAI 24mm 2.8	242821
AIS 24mm 2.8	700001	AI 28mm 2.0	450001
NAI 28mm 2.0	280001	AIS 28mm 2.0	575000
AI 28mm 2.8	430001	NAI 28mm 2.8	382011
AIS 28mm 2.8	635001	AI 28mm 3.5	1760201
NAI 28mm 3.5	195531	AIS 28mm 3.5	2100001
E 28mm 2.8	197900	PC 28mm 4.0	174041
PC 28mm 3.5	179000	AI 35mm 1.4	385001
NAI 35mm 1.4	350001	AIS 35mm 1.4	430000
AI 35mm 2.0	920001	NAI 35mm 2.0	690101
AIS 35mm 2.0	210001	E 35mm 2.5	1780801
AI 35mm 2.8	773111	NAI 35mm 2.8	255311
AIS 35mm 2.8	521001	PC 35mm 2.8	179000
NAI 45mm 2.8 GN	710101	AI 50mm 1.2	177051
AIS 50mm 1.2	250001	AI 50mm 1.4	3940001
NAI 50mm 1.4	532011	AIS 50mm 1.4	5100001
AI 50mm 1.8	1760801	AIS 50mm 1.8	2050001
AI 50mm 2.0	3500001	NAI 50mm 2.0	742111
AI 55mm 1.2	400001	NAI 55mm 1.2	184711
AI 55mm 2.8	179041	AI 55mm 3.5	940001
NAI 55mm 3.5	211001	AI 58mm 1.2	172011
AIS 58mm 1.2	185000	E 50mm 1.8	1055001
AF 80mm 2.8	182501	AI 85mm 1.8	410001
NAI 85mm 1.8	188011	AI 85mm 2.0	175111

Lens	First #	Lens	First #
AIS 85mm 2.0	270001	AIS 85mm 1.4	179091
E 100mm 2.8	1780701	AI 105mm 2.5	740001
NAI 105mm 2.5	194011	AIS 105mm 2.5	890001
AI 105mm 4.0	186956	NAI 105mm 4.0	174011
AIS 105mm 4.0	232001	AIS 105mm 2.8	182061
AIS 105mm 1.8	179091	NAI 105mm 4.0	910001
AI 135mm 2.0	190001	NAI 135mm 2.0	175011
AIS 135mm 2.0	201000	AI 135mm 2.8	770001
NAI 135mm 2.8	163011	AIS 135mm 2.8	900001
E 135mm 2.8	180001	AI 135mm 3.5	193501
NAI 135mm 3.5	111111	AIS 135mm 3.5	290001
AI 180mm 2.8	360001	AIS 180mm 2.8 ED	380000
NAI 200mm 2.0 ED-IF	176111	AIS 200mm 2.0 ED-IF	178000
AF 200mm 3.5	182501	AI 200mm 4.0	178021
AIS 200mm 4.0 IF	20000	NAI 300mm 2.8	603011
AI 300mm 2.8 ED-IF	605101	AIS 300mm 2.8 ED-IF	609000
AIS 300mm 2.0 ED	182121	AI 300mm 4.5	510001
NAI 300mm 4.5	173101	AI 300mm 4.5 ED	190001
AIS 300mm 4.5	550000	AI 300mm 4.5 ED-IF	200001
AIS 300mm 4.5 ED-IF	210000	AI 400mm 3.5 ED-IF	176091
NAI 400mm 3.5 ED-IF	175121	AIS 400mm 3.5 ED-IF	181500
NAI 400mm 4.5	400111	NAI 400mm 5.6	256031
AI 400mm 5.6 ED	261178	NAI 400mm 5.6 ED	260001
AI 400mm 5.6 ED-IF	280001	AIS 400mm 5.6 ED-IF	287601
NAI 600mm 5.6	600111	NAI 600mm 5.6 ED	650001
AI 600mm 5.6 ED	176091	NAI 600mm 5.6 ED-IF	176011
AIS 600mm 5.6 ED-IF	178500	AI 600mm 4.0 ED-IF	176121
AIS 600mm 4.0 ED-IF	178000	NAI 800mm 8.0	800111
NAI 800mm 8.0 ED	850001	AI 800mm 8.0 ED-IF	178041
AIS 800mm 8.0 ED-IF	179000	NAI 1200mm 11.0	120011
NAI 1200mm 11.0	150001	AI 1200mm 11.0 ED-IF	178051
AIS 1200mm 11.0 ED-IF	179000	Reflex 500mm 5.0	171011
Reflex 500mm 8.0	183201	Reflex 1000mm 11.0	111001
Reflex 2000mm 11.0	200111		

ZOOM LENSES

Lens	First #	Lens	First #
AI 25-50mm 4.0	178041	AIS 25-50mm 4.0	201000
AI 28-45mm 4.5	210001	NAI 28-45mm 4.5	174011
AI 35-70mm 3.5	760701	AIS 35-70mm 3.5	821000
AI 43-86mm 3.5	810001	NAI 43-86mm 3.5	438611
AI 80-200mm 4.5	270001	NAI 80-200mm 4.5	101911
AIS 80-200mm 4.0	180000	AIS 80-200mm 2.8 ED	181000
NAI 85-250mm 4.0-4.5	184711	NAI 85-250mm 4.0	157911
AI 50-300mm 4.5	980001	NAI 50-300mm 4.5	740101
AI 50-300mm 4.5 ED	175111	AIS 50-300mm 4.5 ED	183000
NAI 180-600mm 8.0 ED	174041	AIS 180-600mm 8.0 ED	174701
AIS 200-400mm 4.0 ED	182121	NAI 200-600mm 9.5	170111
AIS 200-600mm 9.5 ED	305001	NAI 360-1200mm 11.0 ED	170431
AIS 360-1200mm 11.0 ED	174000	E 75-150mm 3.5	1790801
E 36-72mm 3.5	1800701	E 70-210mm 4.0	2000001
AIS 50-135mm 3.5	811000	AI 35-105mm 3.5-4.5	1820869

LENS IMPROVEMENTS

Sometimes, during the production of a particular lens, Nikon made improvements. When this was done, a new initial first serial number was assigned. So the only way to ascertain if a lens is the latest (or an earlier) formula is to read the serial number. Following is a list of lenses which have been improved during their production. The years listed are the first years of production. These years are not necessarily the same as the years in which the lenses were first offered by Nikon Inc. in the US. Remember, this listing is NOT complete.

Lens	Year	First Serial Number
NAI 16mm 3.5	1973	272281
NAI 16mm 3.5	1975	280001
NAI 15mm 5.6	1973	321001
NAI 15mm 5.6	unknown	340001
NAI 24mm 2.8	1967	242821
NAI 24mm 2.8	1972	370001
NAI 24mm 2.8	1975	450001
NAI 28mm 2.0	1970	280001
NAI 28mm 2.0	1975	335001
NAI 28mm 3.5	1965	625611
NAI 28mm 3.5	1973	850001
NAI 28mm 3.5	1975	195531
NAI 35mm 1.4	1970	350001
NAI 35mm 1.4	1975	385001
NAI 35mm 2.0	1967	690101
NAI 35mm 2.0	1973	835001
NAI 35mm 2.0	1975	880001
NAI 35mm 2.8	unknown	350001
NAI 35mm 2.8	unknown	255311
NAI 35mm 2.8	1974	773191
PC 35mm 2.8	1968	851001
PC 35mm 2.8	unknown	900001
PC 35mm 2.8	1980	179000
NAI 45mm 2.8 GN	1968	710101
NAI 45mm 2.8 GN	1973	760001
NAI 50mm 1.4	1967	532011
NAI 50mm 1.4	1970	1280001
NAI 50mm 1.4	1974	2797021
NAI 50mm 1.4	1976	3750401

Lens	Year	First Serial Number
NAI 50mm 2.0	1967	742111
NAI 50mm 2.0	1972	2140201
NAI 50mm 2.0	1974	3100001
NAI 55mm 1.2	1968	184711
NAI 55mm 1.2	1972	250001
NAI 55mm 1.2	1974	350011
NAI 55mm 3.5	1968	211001
NAI 55mm 3.5	1970	600001
NAI 55mm 3.5	1973	730001
NAI 85mm 1.8	1964	188011
NAI 85mm 1.8	1973	390001
NAI 85mm 1.8	1975	410001
NAI 105mm 2.5	1964	194011
NAI 105mm 2.5	1970	407301
NAI 105mm 2.5	1972	500001
NAI 105mm 2.5	1974	673101
NAI 135mm 2.8	1967	163011
NAI 135mm 2.8	1973	380001
NAI 135mm 2.8	1975	430001
NAI 135mm 2.8	1976	730001
NAI 135mm 3.5	1966	720101
NAI 135mm 3.5	1969	865101
NAI 135mm 3.5	1973	111111
NAI 135mm 3.5	1975	158101
NAI 180mm 2.8	1970	312011
NAI 180mm 2.8	1975	350001
AI 200mm 4.0	1977	710001
AI 200mm 4.0	1979	178021
NAI 200mm 4.0	1966	270011
NAI 200mm 4.0	1969	420001
NAI 200mm 4.0	1973	570001
NAI 200mm 4.0	1975	670001
NAI 300mm 2.8	1971	603011
NAI 300mm 2.8	1975	604011
NAI 300mm 4.5	1964	304501
NAI 300mm 4.5	1975	480001
NAI 300mm 4.5	1975	173101
NAI 300mm 4.5	1964	400111
NAI 300mm 4.5	1974	410801

Lens	Year	First Serial Number
NAI 600mm 5.6	1964	600111
NAI 600mm 5.6	1973	611001
NAI 800mm 8.0	1964	800111
NAI 800mm 8.0	1973	810601
NAI 1200mm 11.0	unknown	120011
NAI 1200mm 11.0	unknown	131401
Reflex 500mm 8.0	1968	501001
Reflex 500mm 8.0	1974	530001
Reflex 500mm 8.0	1984	183201
Reflex 1000mm 11.0	1965	111001
Reflex 1000mm 11.0	1974	140001
Reflex 1000mm 11.0	unknown	142361
NAI 43-86mm 3.5	1963	438611
NAI 43-86mm 3.5	1973	570001
NAI 43-86mm 3.5	1975	774071
AI 80-200mm 4.5	1977	270001
AI 80-200mm 4.5	1977+	760801
NAI 80-200mm 4.5	1969	101911
NAI 80-200mm 4.5	1973	140001
NAI 80-200mm 4.5	1975	210001
NAI 50-300mm 4.5	1968	740101
NAI 50-300mm 4.5	1975	770401
NAI 200-600mm 9.5	1961	170111
NAI 200-600mm 9.5	1971	280001
NAI 200-600mm 9.5	1975	300001

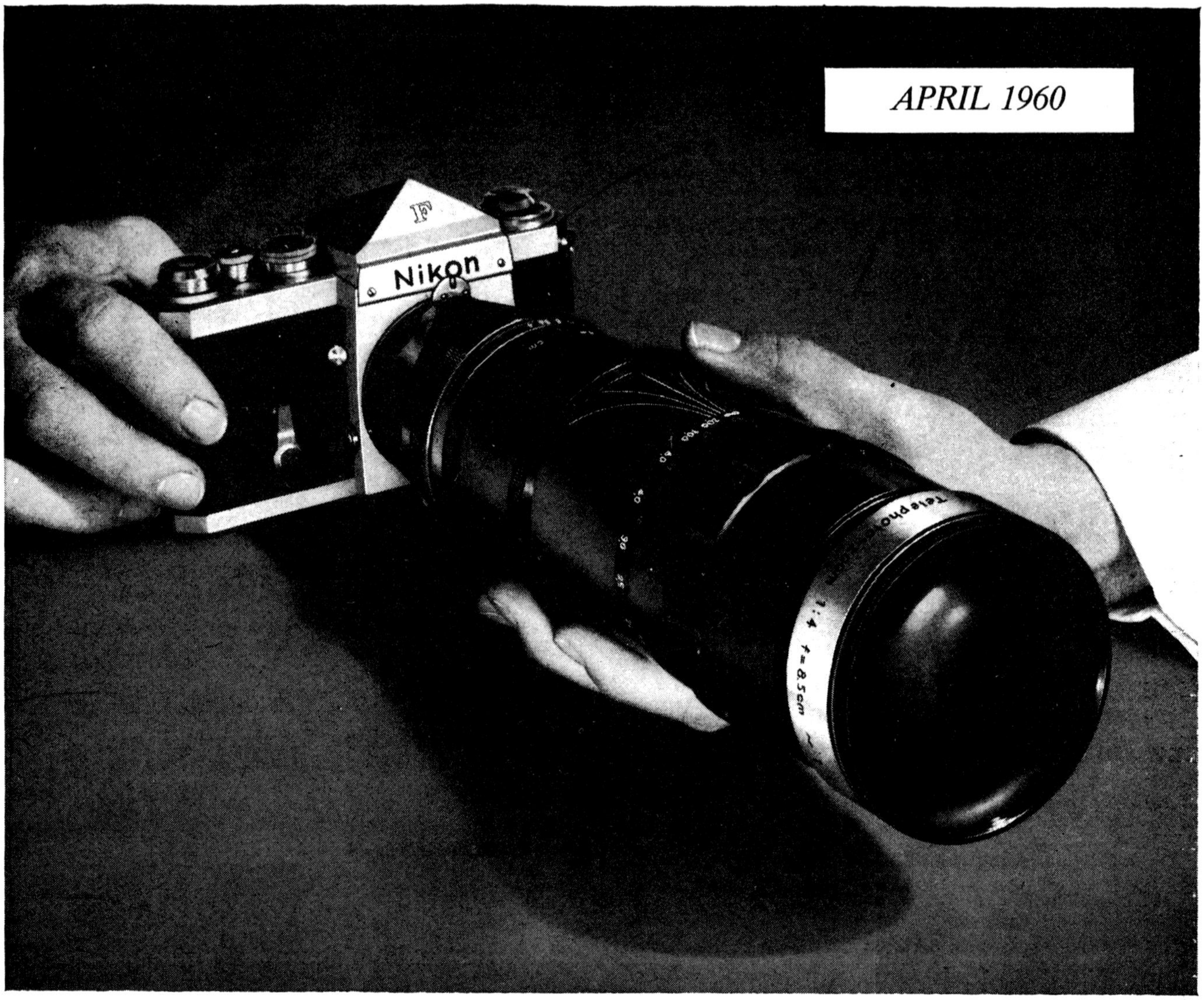

fabulous new f/4 auto-nikkor telephoto zoom can be used at any focal length from 85mm to 250mm

AUTOMATIC DIAPHRAGM COUPLES TO NIKON F AUTOMATIC REFLEX

The new Auto-Nikkor Telephoto Zoom is truly a phenomenal lens. In one instant it's an 85mm medium telephoto; in another, it's a long range 250mm objective; or any one of more than 165 intermediate focal lengths.

The change is simple, fast and smooth. You shift the selector ring and see the effect on image size through the reflex finder. When you have the magnification desired, you shoot. That's all there is to it. You focus the Auto-Nikkor Telephoto Zoom like any other lens—for any distance, from 7 feet to infinity. And once it is in sharp focus for the subject distance, it remains in sharp focus at every focal-length position. There is no re-adjustment or re-setting required. Even the effective 'taking' aperture remains constant at all focal lengths.

The new Auto-Nikkor Telephoto Zoom is internally coupled to the automatic diaphragm system of the Nikon F. Always at full aperture for focusing, viewing and focal-length selection, the lens automatically stops down to the 'taking' aperture —and then, instantly, reopens to f/4. There is no black-out; no dimming of the finder image.

The Auto-Nikkor Telephoto Zoom is an outstanding technical achievement—an achievement that speaks eloquently of the caliber of skill and creative ingenuity that is being devoted to all Nikon products.

Above all, the Auto-Nikkor Telephoto Zoom is a lens of flawless quality, exhibiting the same high resolution and color correction for which Nikkor lenses have become justly famous the world over. It is truly as fine a lens as it is unusual—a lens worthy of the most critical, discriminating user of 35mm equipment. Priced at $595, it fulfills the function of many lenses, the total cost of which would be many times that sum.

See the new Auto-Nikkor Telephoto Zoom at your Franchised Nikon Dealer. For further details write to Dept. PP-4.

NIKON INCORPORATED 111 Fifth Avenue, New York 3, N. Y. *In Canada:* Anglophoto Ltd., Montreal, P. Q.

CHAPTER SEVEN

AI LENS CONVERSIONS

In 1977, Nikon announced Automatic Maximum Aperture Indexing (AI) lenses and discontinued the previously offered semiautomatic indexing lenses. In late 1974, Nikon replaced the NAI 50mm f/2 with an AI version. But no one was told why the change was made, not even the sales force. Speculation and rumors circulated in the industry. As supplies of other NAI lenses were exhausted, they were replaced with the new AI versions. There were no changes in prices and the catalog designations remained the same. By 1977 when the first AI cameras were introduced, only AI lenses were being shipped to dealers.

Starting in 1977, Nikon Service Centers offered the capability of converting some of the older lenses to AI. Additionally, Nikon made the necessary conversion parts available so conversions could be performed by some independent repair technicians. Some technicians also offer a modified type of conversion. This allows an AI conversion of lenses that otherwise cannot be modified. This type of conversion may not look wonderful, but allows the modified lens to function in a satisfactory manner.

AIS conversions are not offered by Nikon. Additionally, it is not possible to convert any of the non-autofocus lenses to AF (autofocus).

A large number of used lenses are available which have been converted, both by Nikon and by independent repair technicians. The price for a conversion varies, but it is usually in the neighborhood of $40 to $60. At present, authorized conversions (authorized meaning a conversion performed by Nikon Inc. or a Nikon Authorized Repair Station) are being performed only in the US. Generally, the necessary parts are not available overseas.

A factory-type conversion or modification consists of the following: 1) A meter coupling ridge to enable automatic indexing of the lens' maximum aperture with the meter of any AI type camera for full-aperture exposure measurement. 2) A meter coupling shoe or prong with little holes in it to enable full-aperture exposure measurement with earlier non-AI type camera bodies. 3) An Aperture Direct Readout (ADR) scale so the photographer can read the aperture in the viewfinder of camera bodies with ADR capability. 4) An EE servo coupling post to enable EE servo-controlled metering. Converted lenses DO NOT include the aperture indexing post found on AI lenses.

Lenses which have been converted are usually referred to as AIed, AI'D or AID (used in this book). Their performance is the same as AI lenses. Obviously AID lenses are older than AI lenses. Most Nikkors produced after 1976 are AI.

Some independent repair facilities offer an AI conversion without using Nikon AI conversion parts. This type of conversion usually consists of re-machining existing lens parts. Naturally, this conversion is less desirable, but it does offer a chance for the conversion of a lens for which Nikon does not make parts. Some repair facilities can install a shoe (rabbit ears) on an E or AF lens so it will work with an older body as well as newer ones. This modification is simple and the cost is usually moderate.

Among major manufacturers of 35mm single lens reflexes, Nikon is unique. The same bayonet mount incorporated in the original Nikon F is still in use. Additionally, it has been and is used on all Nikon SLR bodies capable of lens interchangeability. Therefore, a lens purchased new today will work on all Nikon (as well as Nikkorex and Nikkormat) bodies. Granted, some of the newer functions may not operate, but the lens can be used.

An additional advantage that Nikon offers its customers is the very moderate cost of AI conversion. But no manufacturer can be expected to continue to make parts available for an indefinite period. Demand for AI conversions is diminishing and Nikon is currently only converting those lenses for which they still have parts on hand. Those who have non-AI lenses are advised to obtain the conversion before time runs out. Soon, non-AI lenses may decrease even further in value. Even if the AI features are not presently needed, the conversion is recommended.

In order to save money, some photographers purchase used non-AI lenses and then have them converted. Before indulging in this practice, it is important to know that not all non-AI lenses are capable of a factory authorized conversion. Following is a list of lenses Nikon accepts for conversion:

LENSES NIKON ACCEPTS FOR CONVERSION

LENS	SERIAL NUMBERS
13mm f/5.6	175021 and higher
15mm f/5.6	321001 and higher
18mm f/4.0	173111 and higher
20mm f/3.5	421241 and higher
20mm f/4.0	103001 and higher
24mm f/2.8	242821 and higher
28mm f/2.0	280001 and higher
28mm f/2.8	382011 and higher
28mm f/3.5	195531 - 301010, 625611 and higher
35mm f/1.4	350001 and higher
35mm f/2.0	717011 and higher
35mm f/2.8	255311 - 920110
50mm f/1.4	532011 and higher
50mm f/2.0	741111 and higher
55mm f/1.2	184711 - 970110
85mm f/1.8	219910 and higher
105mm f/2.5	234011 and higher
135mm f/2.0	175011 and higher
135mm f/2.8	189311 and higher
135mm f/3.5	111111 - 720100, 831211 - 904080
180mm f/2.8	312011 and higher
200mm f/4.0	304411 and higher
300mm f/4.5	326511 and higher
300mm f/4.5 ED	173101 and higher
400mm f/5.6	256031 - 260000
400mm f/5.6 ED	260001 and higher
6mm f/2.8	628001 and higher
8mm f/2.8	320011 and higher
16mm f/3.5	272281 and higher
45mm f/2.8 GN	710101 and higher
55mm f/3.5 Micro	238011 and higher
105mm f/4.0 Micro	174011 and higher
28-45mm f/4.5	174011 and higher
43-86mm f/3.5	438611 and higher
50-300mm f/4.5	740101 and higher
80-200mm f/4.5	101900 and higher
85-200mm f/4.0	184711 and higher

PARTS NO LONGER AVAILABLE FOR CONVERSION

As of 1990, parts are not available from Nikon Inc. in the US for the conversion of the following lenses:

LENS	SERIAL NUMBERS
13mm f/5.6	175021 and later
28mm f/2	all serial numbers
35mm f/2	all serial numbers
50mm f/1.4	635511 - 2797020
50mm f/1.4	532011 - 635510
50mm f/2	742111 - 785010
85mm f/1.8	410001 and higher
135mm f/2	175011 and higher
135mm f/2.8	730001 and higher
135mm f/2.8	189311 - 430000
135mm f/3.5	831211 - 865100
6mm f/2.8	all serial numbers
8mm f/2.8	all serial numbers
16mm f/3.5	all serial numbers
55mm f/3.5	238011 - 850000
43-86mm f/3.5	438611 - 774070
50-300mm f/4.5	all serial numbers
80-200mm f/4.5	all serial numbers

SPECIAL NOTE: All NAI 35mm f/1.4 lenses have the capability of stopping down to f/22. When these lenses are converted to AI, however, they lose f/22 and the aperture can be closed no smaller than f/16. The aperture of all 35mm f/1.4 lenses originally delivered as AI can be closed no smaller than f/16.

HAVING CONVERSION WORK PERFORMED

The most desirable conversion is one performed by Nikon Inc. or one of its authorized repair stations. Other types of conversion are available, but almost invariably, the resale value of a lens so modified is less.

A list of Nikon Service Centers as well as independent service organizations authorized by Nikon plus their locations and telephone numbers can be found in the first chapter of this book. A lens to be converted should be delivered to an authorized Nikon dealer or one of the listed repair facilities.

The problem with a Nikon Inc. authorized conversion is that this service is not available for all lenses. Other lenses can, however, be converted. There are a number of repair facilities in the US who perform this service. The easiest way to find such an organization is to look for their advertisements in *Shutterbug.*

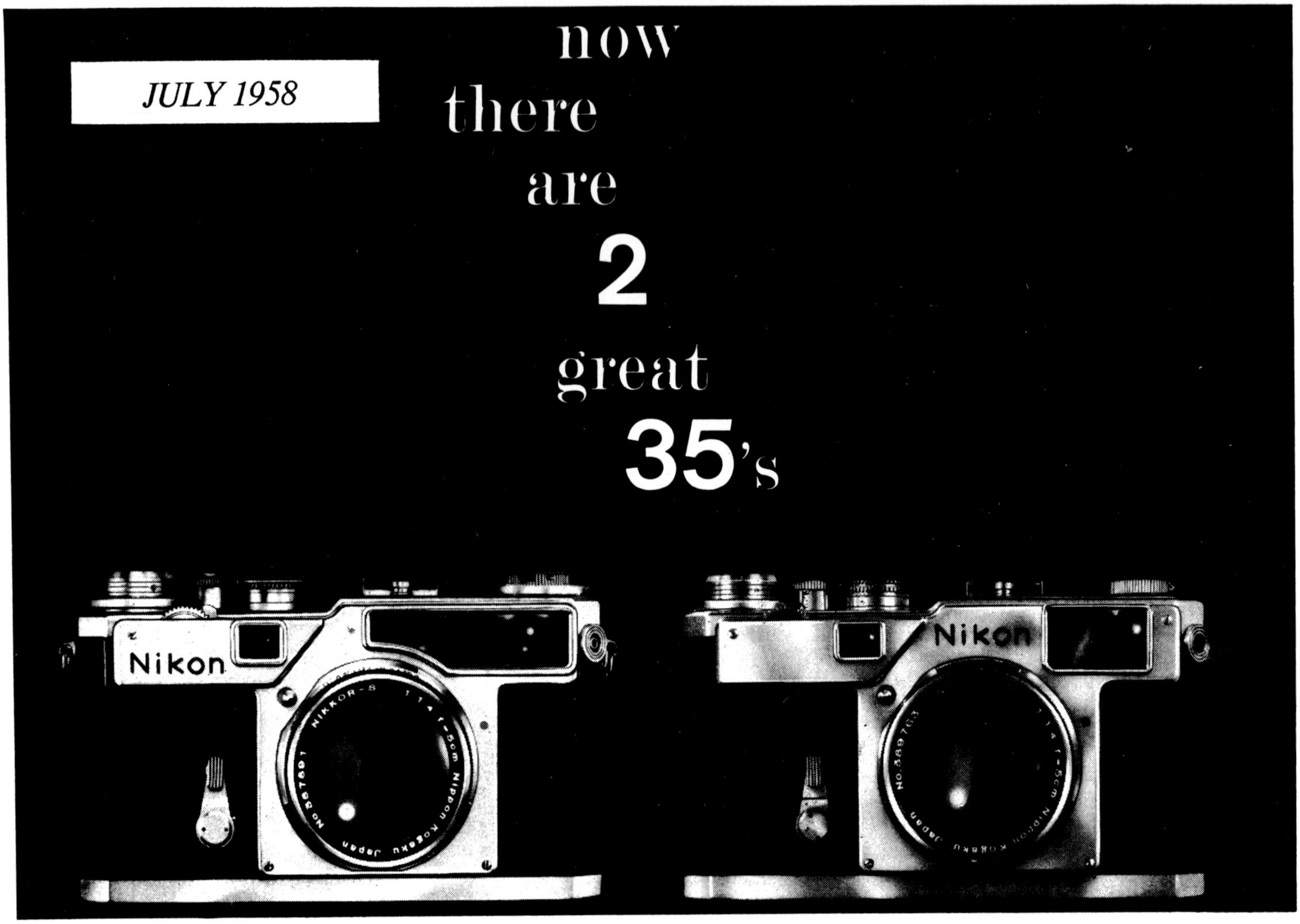

NIKON SP
and NIKON S-3

to give you complete command of the 35mm art

So responsive and smooth-working are these two new instruments, so easy and fast to handle, it is as if the photographer were suddenly liberated from all the distractions of camera mechanics—and free to perform his creative work. Never before has camera design been more perfectly suited to its task.

The new Nikon S-3 and Nikon SP are identical in body design and features, in rugged quality and precision. Only their viewfinders differ. The Nikon SP features the sensational built-in Universal Viewfinder System with viewing fields for six different lenses: 28mm wide angle through 135mm telephoto. The new Nikon S-3 introduces the built-in Trifocal Viewfinder for 35, 50 and 105mm lenses.

Accessories are fully interchangeable between models. Whether you select the SP or S-3 for your work, you can call upon the automatic fire-power offered by the Nikon Electric Motor Drive; the convenience of the shutter-coupled Exposure Meter; the unmistakable quality of Nikkor lenses; and the added versatility of a host of Nikon Accessories.

For complete details, write to: Nikon Incorporated, Dept. MP-7, 251 Fourth Avenue, New York 10, New York. In Canada: Anglophoto, Ltd., 880 Champagneur, Montreal, P. Q.

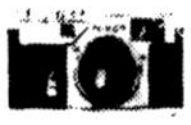

S-3 or SP, Nikon gives you an extra edge, in every picture situation

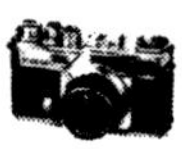

Nikon S-3 with 50mm Nikkor f/2 $309.50; with 50mm f/1.4 $355 • Nikon SP with 50mm Nikkor f/2 $369.50; with 50mm f/1.4 $415

CHAPTER EIGHT

CAMERA BODIES AND LENS COMPATIBILITY

In 1959, Nikon introduced the Nikon F. This was the first of a series of professional single lens reflex cameras known as the F series. The original was followed by the F2, the F3 and the F4.

One of the important features of the F bodies is that the viewfinders are interchangeable. The body can be fitted with a waist level finder or an eye level prism finder. In almost every instance, the camera was purchased new with a prism finder rather than a waist level finder. With the exception of the F3 and F4, if the camera includes a built-in light meter, it is a part of the prism finder.

When the prism contains a light meter, there is also a method of coupling the meter with the shutter speeds on the camera body and with the aperture of the lens. The system originally devised by Nikon to accomplish this may seem crude by today's standards, but it evolved while other manufacturers kept re-inventing the wheel. The Nikon evolution enables the latest lens to function on the earliest SLR body. In order to accommodate technological advances, other manufacturers have changed mounting systems entirely, thus precluding lens and body compatibility if they are from two different eras.

All meter prisms for F and F2 bodies couple to the shutter speeds via a pin and slot sitting piggyback over the shutter speed dial. When the dial is turned, it simultaneously sets the shutter speeds on both the camera body and the meter in the prism. In the F3 and F4, these functions take place inside the camera body. This evolution took place without damaging the integrity of the F system.

Cameras and lenses produced prior to 1977 coupled to one another with a prong which Nikon calls a shoe and most photographers call "rabbit ears." When a lens is fitted to a body, a pin fits in the slot between the ears to provide communication. After 1977, coupling is accomplished via a meter coupling ridge on the lens and a lever on the body. When a lens is coupled with the shoe and pin, indexing can be either manual or semiautomatic (NAI). When coupled with the ridge and lever, indexing is automatic (AI).

It is important to be able to identify both lenses and cameras in order to determine whether they are manual, semiautomatic or automatic. Manual and semiautomatic (NAI) camera bodies or prism finders have a round pin which fits into the shoe. Look for a round pin which would nestle between the rabbit ears. On some prisms, the pin can hide inside the housing. In order to see it, turn the camera upside down. Automatic indexing prisms and bodies have a flat lever instead of the round pin. The lever hugs the lens mounting flange and rides against the coupling ridge on AI lenses.

In manual indexing, the ASA (ISO) of the film as well as the maximum aperture of the lens must be set on the meter. When, for example, a 50mm f/1.4 is removed and replaced with a 135mm f/3.5, the dial must be readjusted for the aperture change.

In semiautomatic indexing, the extra step of re-setting the dial after a lens change is eliminated. But to make the system work, when a lens is mounted, its iris must be repeatedly fully opened and then fully closed until an audible click indicates the system is engaged. In automatic indexing, this opening and closing of the iris is not necessary; engagement is accomplished as soon as the lens is locked correctly in the mount.

The lenses used in either manual or semi-automatic indexing are the same. The difference is in the meter. In order to tell the difference, look at the ASA (ISO) dial. If there are a series of aperture numbers (1.4, 2, 2.8, etc.) on a ring next to the ASA numbers, then the meter provides manual indexing. If the ASA is set opposite an arrowhead or a point, indexing is not manual.

Therefore, to identify a body or prism finder, first look to see if there is a round pin or a flat lever. If there is a pin, it's non-automatic (NAI), if a lever, it is automatic (AI). Second, in the case of an NAI body or prism, look at the ASA (ISO) dial. If there is a ring of f stop numbers opposite the ASA/ISO scale, it is manual; if there is an arrow or point, it is semi-automatic.

All Nikon F bodies are the same. The only difference is in the removable prism finders. Many users who purchased cameras between 1959 and 1961 wanted a built-in meter, but none was then available. Subsequently most of them purchased a meter finder of one type or another. Pressing a button on the camera back pops out the old finder. Installing a new one converts the F to a Photomic, Photomic TN or whatever. The transformation can only be detected by checking the serial numbers against the dates of manufacture.

All Nikon F2 bodies are the same with the exception of the F2T, the F2 Titan and the F2HS. The difference in the other models is solely in the removable prisms. If a user purchased a Photomic AS finder in 1977 and installed it on his 1971 F2 body, the camera would become an F2 Photomic AS. The only way of discovering the transformation would be to check the camera serial numbers.

Not all Nikon lenses are compatible with every Nikon body. Sometimes attempting to mount an incompatible lens will result in damage to the meter coupling lever or the camera body's mirror. In other instances, a lens will mount, but will not perform all functions. And some lenses simply are impossible to mount.

First of all, rangefinder lenses will not mount on SLR bodies. The bayonet mounting systems of the rangefinder cameras and the SLRs are completely different. The rangefinder cameras use a Contax-type bayonet system while the SLRs have a mounting system unique to Nikon.

As far as SLR's are concerned, the most important thing to learn is that some earlier lenses cannot be mounted on some later bodies without sustaining damage to the mirror in the camera body. Earlier PC lenses cannot be mounted in some later bodies. Read the camera instruction book carefully. The unsuitable lens serial numbers are listed.

Some AI cameras have meter coupling levers which cannot be flipped up out of the way allowing NAI lenses to mount. Attempting to mount an NAI lens on such a body will cause damage. Read the camera instruction book in order to determine if the body will mount an NAI lens (see the chart on page 63).

E lenses can be mounted on NAI bodies, but they will not meter couple and so must be used via the stop down method of metering. It is possible to have a shoe (rabbit ears) installed on an E lens at a moderate cost.

SPECIAL NOTE REGARDING **N4004** AND **N4004s** CAMERAS. These cameras were designed for use with AF lenses. Although several non-AF lenses can be used, the automatic exposure and automatic focusing functions will be lost. AI, AIS and NAI converted to AI may be mounted. NAI lenses should NOT be mounted since they may cause damage to the camera. Some Reflex (mirror) and some PC lenses should not be mounted since they also may cause damage. The following Reflex Nikkors may be mounted: 500mm f/8, 1000mm f/11 (s/n 142360 or smaller or s/n 143001 or larger), 2000mm f/ll (s/n 200311 or larger). The following PC Nikkors may be mounted: 28mm f/3.5, 28mm f/4 (s/n 180901 or larger), 35mm f/2.8 (s/n 851000 or smaller or s/n 906201 or larger). The 120mm f/4 Medical Nikkor may be mounted and all Teleconverters except TC-16 and TC-16A.

When the lenses listed above are mounted, the focus indicator LED lights will light up when the subject is in focus, but the exposure indicator LEDs will not appear. An external exposure meter must be used.

TTL auto flash is possible with the built-in flash or flash guns with TTL capability, but programmed TTL auto flash is not. The aperture must be set on the lens aperture ring, not on the camera body.

CAMERA BODIES CLASSIFIED AS TO TYPE

1. Professional Bodies

All F models	Non-AI
F2	Non-AI
F2 Photomic	Non-AI
F2 Photomic S	Non-AI
F2 Photomic SB	Non-AI
F2T	Non-AI
F2H	Non-AI
F2 Titan	Non-AI
F2 Photomic A	AI
F2 Photomic AS	AI
F3	AI
F3HP	AI
F3/T	AI
F3AF	AI AF
F3P	AI
F4, F4s	AIS AF

2. Nikkorex Series

Nikkorex F	Non-AI

3. Nikkormat bodies

Nikkormat FT	Non-AI
Nikkormat FS	Non-AI
Nikkormat FTN	Non-AI
Nikkormat EL	Non-AI
Nikkormat FT2	Non-AI
Nikkormat ELW	Non-AI
Nikkormat FT3	AI
Nikon EL2	AI

4. Compact SLR bodies

Nikon FM	AI
Nikon FE	AI
Nikon EM	AI
Nikon FM2	AI
Nikon FG	AI
Nikon FE2	AI
Nikon FA	AIS
Nikon FG-20	AI
Nikon FM2n	AI

5. N Series Bodies

Nikon N2000	AIS
Nikon N2020	AIS AF
Nikon N4004	AIS AF
Nikon N4004s	AIS AF
Nikon N8008	AIS AF

SYSTEM CLASSIFIED AS TO CAMERA BODY

1. NAI (Non-Automatic Indexing)

   All Nikon F models
   Nikon F2 models Photomic, Photomic S, Photomic SB, T, H, Titan
   Nikkorex F
   Nikkormat FT, FS, FTN, EL, FT2, ELW

2. AI (Automatic Indexing)

   Nikon F2 Photomic A, Photomic AS
   Nikkormat FT3
   Nikon EL2
   Nikon FM, FE, EM, FM2, FG, FE2, FG-20, FM2n

3. AIS (Automatic Indexing Shutter)

   Nikon F3 models HP, /T, P
   Nikon FA
   Nikon N2000

4. AF (+AIS) (Autofocus)

   Nikon F3AF, F4, F4s
   Nikon N2020, N4004, N4004s, N8008

COMPARISON OF AI AND AIS LENSES

AI LENS

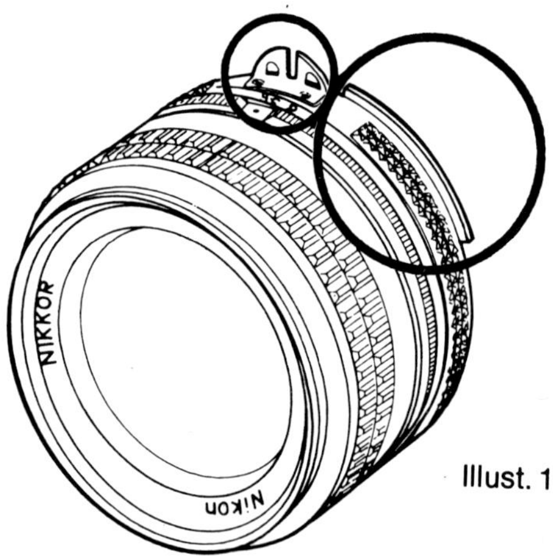

Illust. 1

AIS LENS

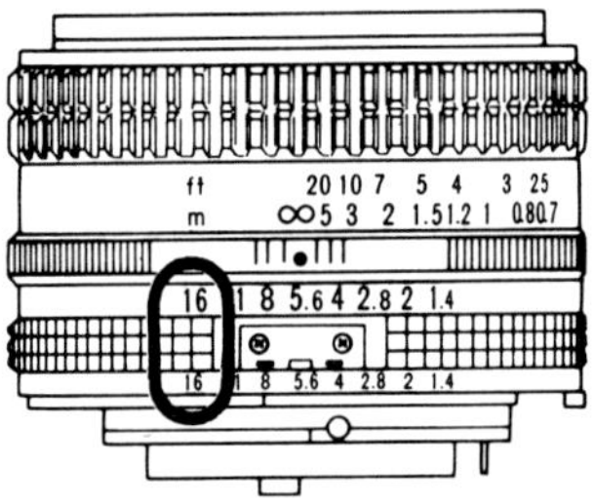

Illust. 2

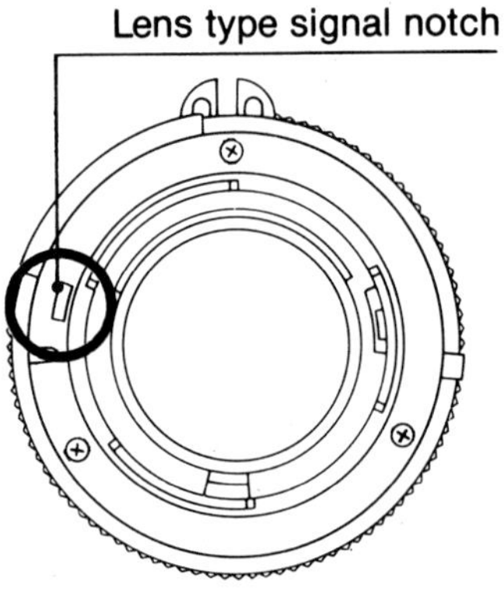

Illust. 3

The area encompassed by the small circle in illustration 1 shows the prong (rabbit ears) with the small holes. NAI lenses do not have holes. The area in the large circle shows the coupling ridge which connects with the flat lever on the camera body. E and AF lenses have no ears.

Illustrations 2 and 3 show the unique characteristics of AIS (and E) lenses. The smallest aperture is circled in illustration 2. The smallest aperture (largest number) is colored orange; others are not. The circle in illustration 3 shows the notch or signal groove in the mount.

CAMERA/LENS COMPATIBILITY CHART

This chart does NOT cover cameras introduced after 1983. Some lenses may damage some camera bodies. Consult the camera instruction book before mounting NAI lenses to any N series camera or any non-AF lens to a N4004 or N4004s.

CAMERA	NAI	AI	AID	NMC
Nikon F Series				
Nikon F (no meter prism)	+	+	+	+
Nikon F Photomic	+	+	+	+
Nikon F Photomic T	+	+	+	+
Nikon F Photomic TN	+	+	+	+
Nikon F Photomic FTN	+	+	+	+
Nikon F2 Series				
Nikon F2 (no meter prism)	+	+	+	+
Nikon F2 Photomic	+	+	+	+
Nikon F2A Photomic	o	+	+	+
Nikon F2S Photomic	+	+	+	+
Nikon F2SB Photomic	+	+	+	+
Nikon F2AS Photomic	o	+	+	+
Nikon F3	o	+	+	+
Nikon FM	o	+	+	+
Nikon FM2	x	+	~	+
Nikon FE	o	+	+	+
Nikon FE2	x	+	+	+
Nikon FG	x	+	~	x
Nikon FG-20	x	+	~	x
Nikon EM	x	+	~	x
Nikkormat EL	+	+	+	+
Nikkormat ELW	+	+	+	+
Nikon EL2	o	+	+	+
Nikkormat FS	+	+	+	+
Nikkormat FT	+	+	+	+
Nikkormat FTN	+	+	+	+
Nikkormat FT2	+	+	+	+
Nikkormat FT3	o	+	+	+
EE Servo DS-1	+	+	+	s
EE Servo DS-2	+	+	+	s
EE Servo DS-12	s	+	+	s

Code: + = Can be mounted without any loss in performance from original specifications. o = Requires stop down metering, but retains automatic diaphragm operation. s = Servo may be left on the camera, but metering must be done manually. ~ = No loss in metering performance. x = Cannot be mounted.

NAI = non-automatic indexing
AI = automatic indexing
AID = an NAI lens modified to AI
NMC = not meter coupled.

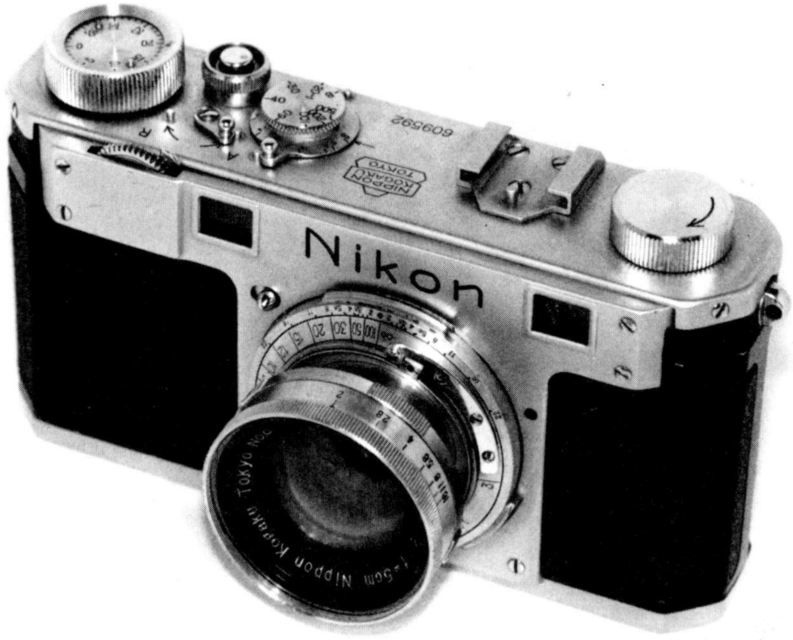

The Nikon I was the first camera manufactured by the Nikon Corporation. This is one of the two rarest Nikon cameras. A mint example will sell on the collector market for more than $5000.

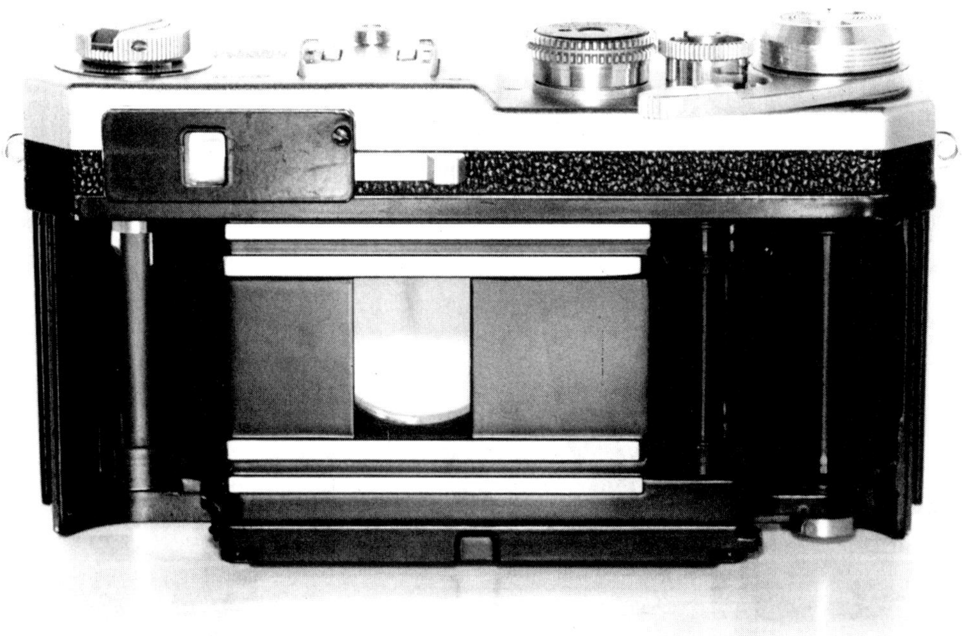

This back view of the Nikon S3M illustrates the half-frame format. This is the other of the two most rare models. (Both photographs are by Robert Rotoloni.)

CHAPTER NINE

STILL CAMERAS

Rangefinder Cameras

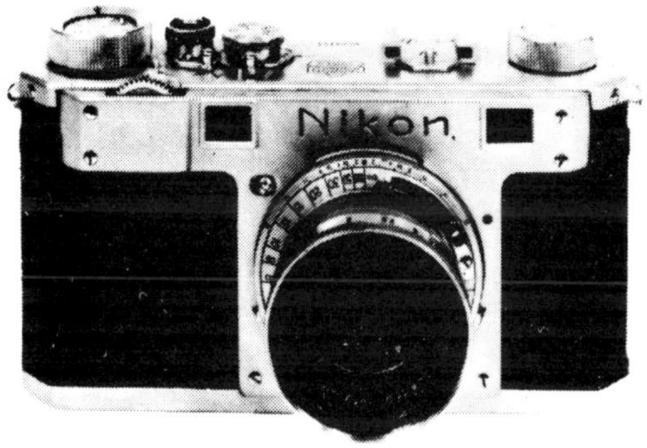

NIKON I (Introduced 1948, discontinued 1949) This first Nikon is similar in appearance to the Zeiss Contax II. It features a cloth focal plane shutter, rangefinder focusing and a Contax type bayonet lens mount (the mounts are the same, but the focusing cams are different). Its 24mm x 32mm format is unique. When this first model was current, it was called simply, the Nikon. When subsequent models were introduced, it was renamed the Nikon I. Identify by noting it has no flash sync terminal, and the frame counter is numbered past 40.

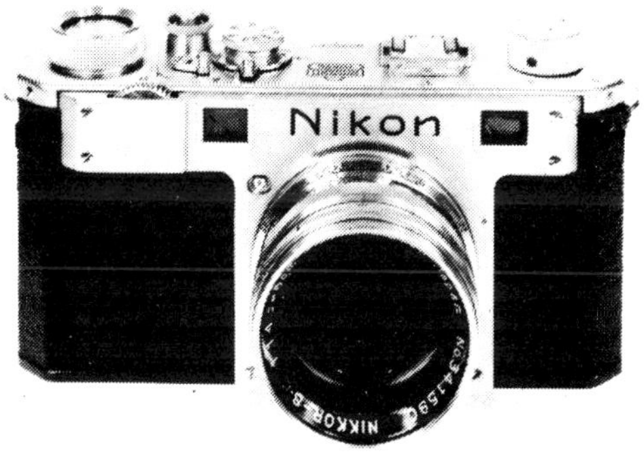

NIKON S (Introduced 1951, discontinued 1954) The standard 24mm x 36mm format is adopted by Nikon. Has flash synchronization. Identify by noting the top shutter speed of 1/500, the double prong flash sync outlet on the back of the body (marked electronic flash and flash bulbs) and the two locks on the bottom of the removable back.

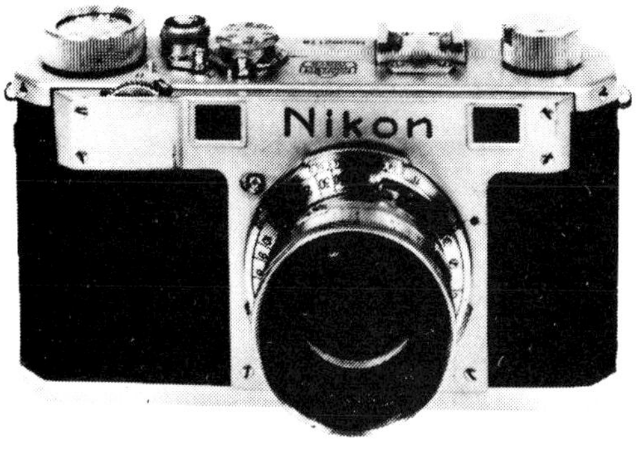

NIKON M (Introduced 1950, discontinued 1952) This model has the same features as the I with the format changed to 24mm x 34mm. Identify also by the lack of a flash sync terminal and frame counter numbers to 36.

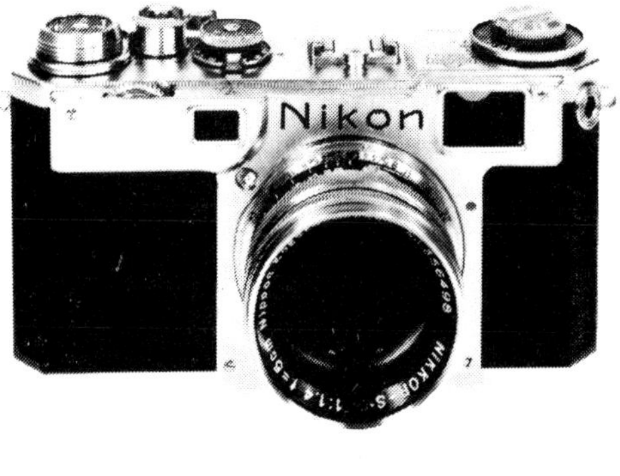

NIKON S2 (Introduced 1954, discontinued 1958) This is the first Nikon with a lever instead of a knob to advance the film. Identify by noting the single stroke film advance lever with a rewind crank which folds into its knob; also there is no self-timer.

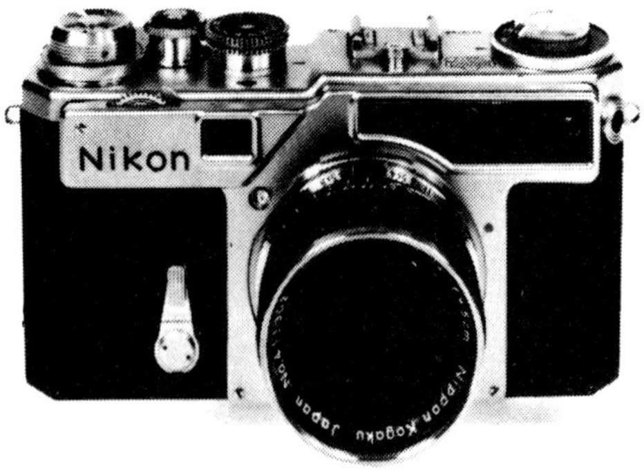

NIKON SP (Introduced 1957, discontinued 1965) The first Nikon with titanium shutter curtains as well as the first to accept an accessory battery powered motor drive. Identify by observing bright frame lines for six lenses from 28mm to 135mm.

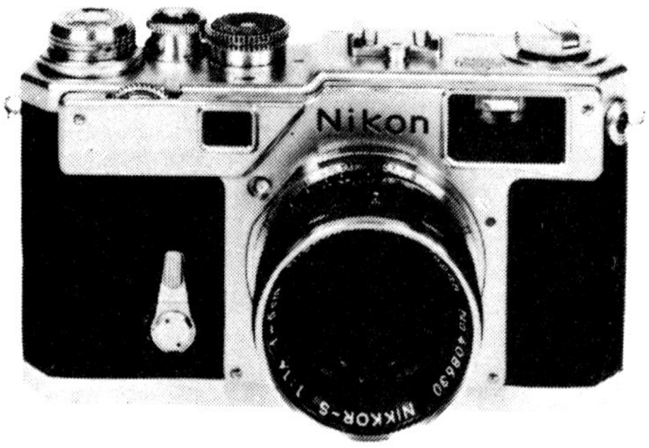

NIKON S3 (Introduced 1958, discontinued 1960) The S3 is a less expensive version of the SP. Identify by noting that there are frame lines for only three lenses: 35mm, 50mm and 105mm.

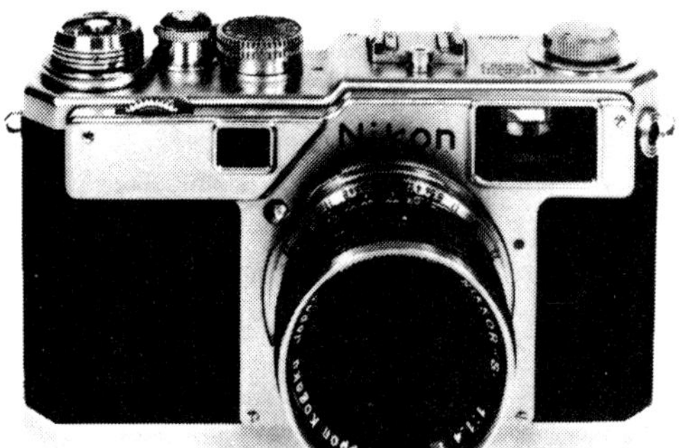

NIKON S4 (Introduced 1959, discontinued 1960) This was the lowest priced "S" type camera. The features are the same as the S3 except that there is no self-timer, no capability for mounting a motor drive and only bright frame lines in the viewfinder for 50mm and 105mm lenses. Identify by observing the frame lines in the viewfinder.

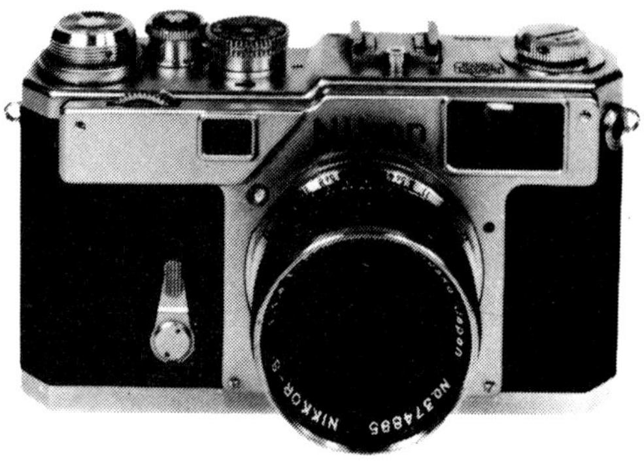

NIKON S3M (Introduced 1960, discontinued 1961) The unique aspect of the S3M is that it is a half-frame camera for 72 exposures with a format of 18mm x 24mm. It has all of the features of the S3 plus an improved viewfinder which provides views for different focal length lenses via a lever. To identify, note the frame counter goes to 72, there is a selector lever on the back, and it is the only half frame camera ever made by Nikon.

Professional Cameras

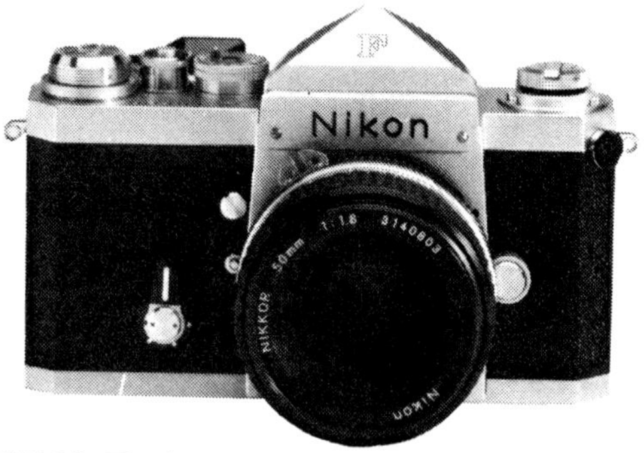

NIKON F (Introduced 1959, discontinued 1974) Nikon's first SLR featured interchangeable viewfinders and focusing screens. It also offered motor drive capability. It is easy to identify because the pentaprism has a large "F" on its face and has no light meter built into the prism.

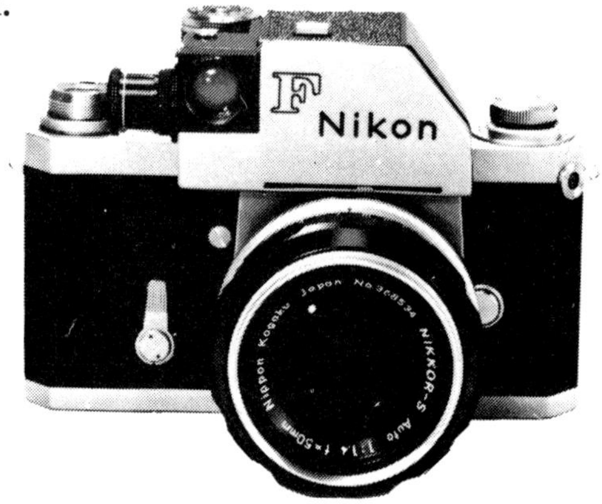

NIKON F Photomic (Introduced 1962, discontinued 1966) Viewfinder includes a built-in CdS cell exposure meter coupled to the lens aperture and shutter speed. The battery compartment is in the prism. This is the only Photomic finder without TTL metering.

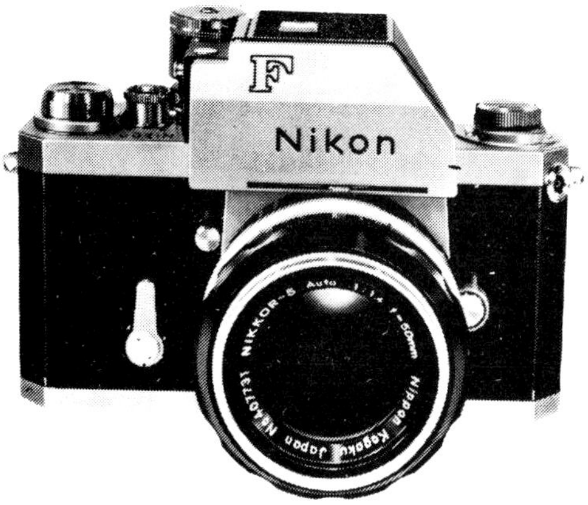

NIKON F Photomic T (Introduced 1965, discontinued 1966) The first Nikon camera with a built-in TTL exposure meter. To identify, note that while it is TTL, there is no "N" inscribed on the finder and no maximum aperture scale on its face.

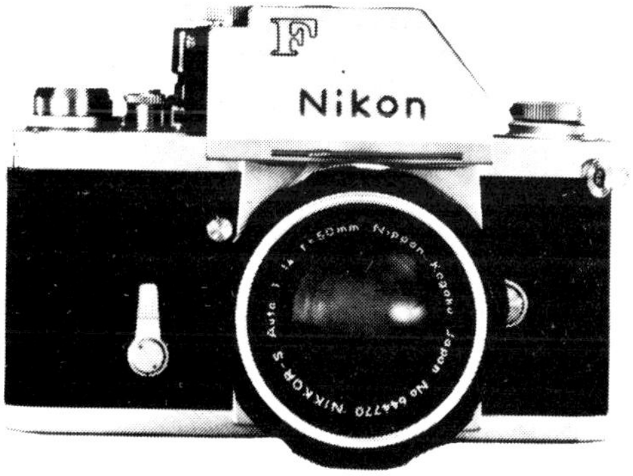

NIKON F Photomic TN (Introduced 1967, discontinued 1968) Center-weighted exposure measurement was added to the Photomic finder. Sixty percent of the exposure is read on a 12mm circle in the center of the viewfinder. It is identified by the letter "N" inscribed on the finder over the on/off switch.

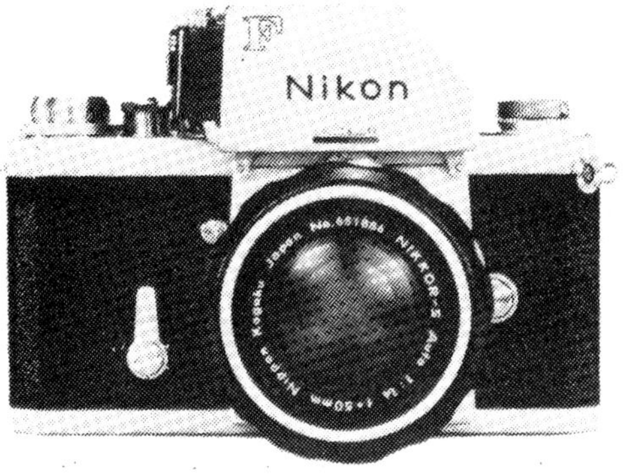

NIKON F Photomic FTN (Introduced 1968, discontinued 1974) This model introduced semiautomatic maximum aperture indexing and shutter speeds displayed in the viewfinder. To identify, note the maximum aperture scale visible on the face of the finder just above the lens. Also this is the only F Photomic finder with the shutter speed displayed in the viewfinder.

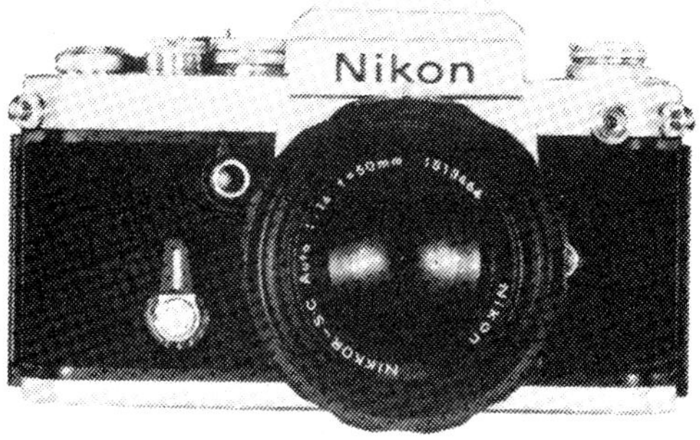

NIKON F2 (Introduced 1971, discontinued 1980) This camera was an improved version of the original F with shutter speeds from 10 seconds to 1/2000, built-in flash ready light and larger reflex mirror. The battery is in the camera body. Identify by "F2" inscribed on the top preceding the serial number. All other F2's have the inscription too, but this is the only one without a light meter in the prism housing.

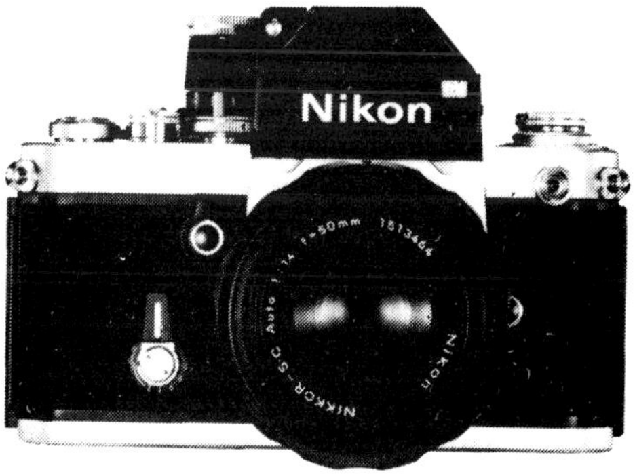

NIKON F2 Photomic (Introduced 1971, discontinued 1977) This improved meter/prism contains built-in TTL, full-aperture, center-weighted exposure meter; shutter speeds and a meter needle displayed in the viewfinder. To identify: 1) "F2" is inscribed preceding the serial number. 2) This is the only F2 with a needle movement for exposure evaluation. It is visible in the viewfinder.

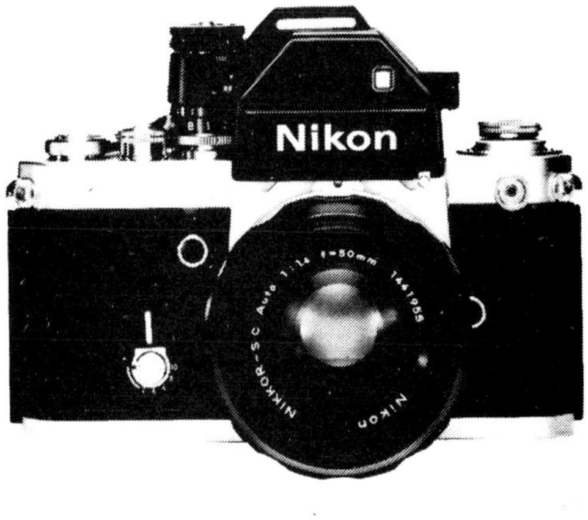

Nikon F2S Photomic (1973)

NIKON F2 Photomic S (Introduced 1973, discontinued 1976) Exposure information is observed via two sets of LEDs, one on top, the other in the viewfinder. Shutter-priority automation can be achieved with the EE Aperture Control Attachment DS-1. To identify, all of the following features must be present: 1) "F2" is inscribed preceding the serial number, 2) LED readouts, 3) no Automatic Indexing, 4) no eyepiece shutter.

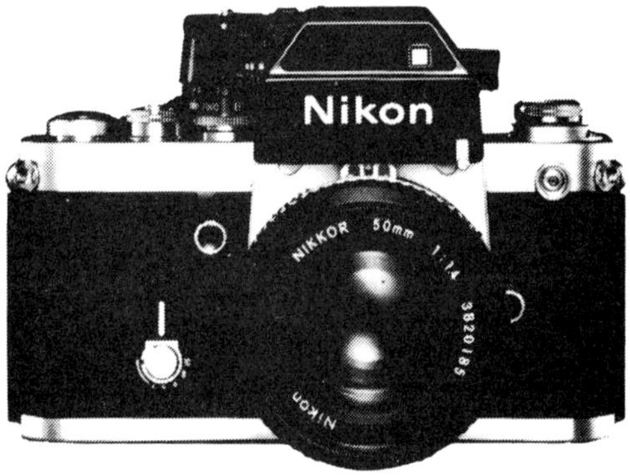

NIKON F2 Photomic SB (Introduced 1976, discontinued 1977) Silicon blue photodiode light metering cells and an eyepiece shutter made their debut on this model. To identify: 1) "F2" inscribed preceding the serial number, 2) The prism finder has an eyepiece shutter.

NIKON F2T (Introduced 1976, discontinued 1980) This camera has the same characteristics as the F2 except the body is made of titanium which is stronger and lighter than other metals (and more expensive). Identify by the serial number: the first two digits are 92.

NIKON F2H (Introduced 1976, discontinued 1980). This high-speed camera was made in black-finished titanium only. It yields up to 10 frames per second with the MD 100 motor drive. The mirror is pellicle (non-moving) rather than a conventional front surfaced mirror which swings out of the light path when the exposure is made. To identify, note the shutter speed dial has no T, B or 1/2000; has no self timer and has a non-removable Type B focusing screen.

NIKON F2 Titan (Produced in 1976) Special model for the US space program and some were purchased by NASA. Same as the F2T except for the inscription on its face. Identify by the word "Titan" inscribed on the face of the body.

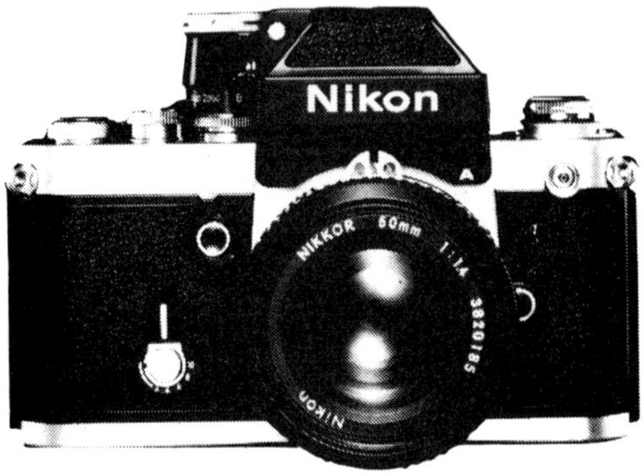

NIKON F2 Photomic A (Introduced 1977, discontinued 1980) This is the first Nikon to offer automatic indexing (AI) of the lens' maximum aperture. Identify by: 1) "F2" inscribed preceding the serial number. 2) A small white "A" inscribed on the face of the meter prism.

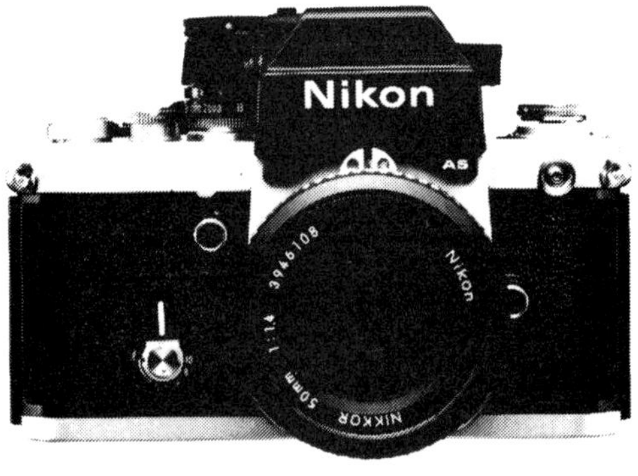

NIKON F2 Photomic AS (Introduced 1977, discontinued 1980) This is the AI version of the F2 Photomic SB. Shutter priority automation is possible via the EE Aperture Control Attachment DS-12. Idenfity by: 1) "F2" inscribed preceding the serial number. 2) A small white "AS" inscribed on the face of the meter prism.

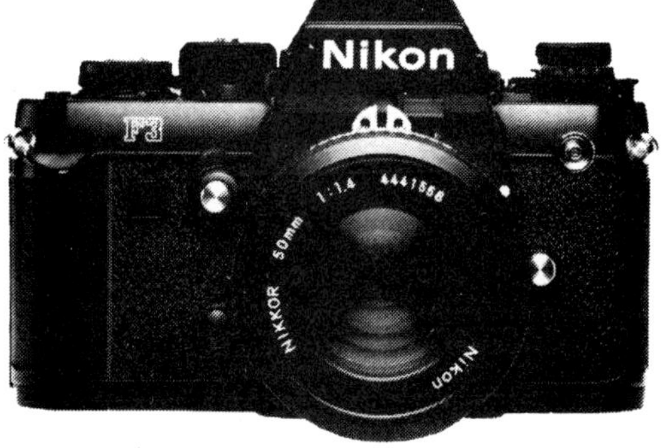

NIKON F3 (Introduced 1980, discontinued 1983) This fully electronic camera contains automatic exposure control with stepless shutter speeds from 8 seconds to 1/2000, quartz timing on manual and TTL flash exposure control. Identify by the "F3" inscribed on the camera's face and a prism housing that is not inscribed with any model designation.

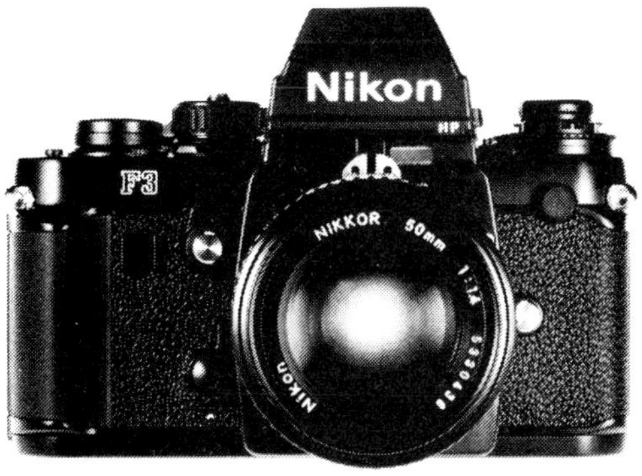

NIKON F3HP (high-eyepoint) (Introduced 1982, still available) An improved viewfinder on the F3 body allows eyelevel viewing up to 25mm away from the exit pupil. All the exposure information is visible in the viewfinder. Identify the body by the "F3" inscribed on its face and the prism finder by the small, white "HP" inscribed on its face.

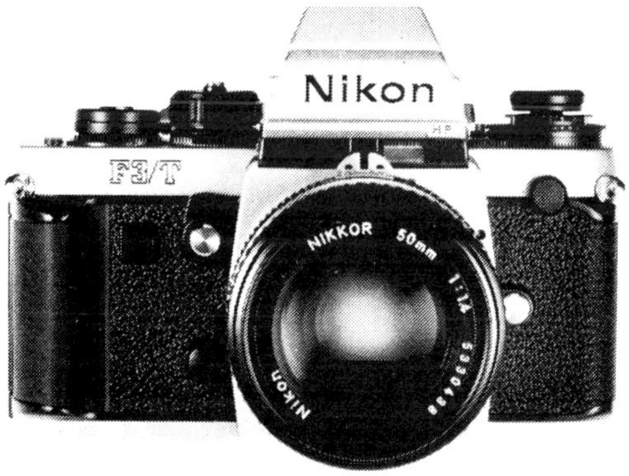

NIKON F3/T (Introduced 1982, still available) All of the features of the F3 in a titanium body. Identify by the "F3/T" inscribed on the face of the body.

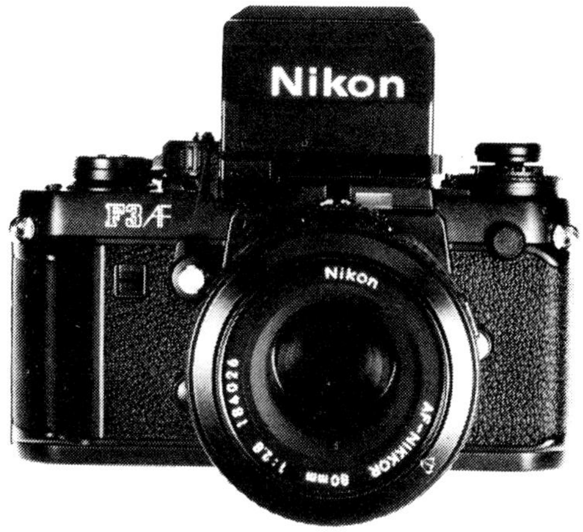

NIKON F3AF (Introduced 1983, discontinued 1988) Autofocus version of the F3. Identify the body by "F3AF" inscribed on its face.

NIKON F3P (Introduced 1983, still available) A ruggedized modification of the F3HP with the prism housing made from titanium. It is equipped with a MF-6B back and a built-in accessory shoe. Identify by: 1) "F3" inscribed on its face. 2) It is the only F3 without a built-in self-timer.

NIKON F4 (Introduced 1988, still available) Autofocus; manual, shutter or aperture priority; matrix TTL OTF flash exposure control, built-in motor drive. In the US, the F4 is available only as the F4s which indicates it is delivered with the large battery pack. Identify by "F4" inscribed on the face of the body.

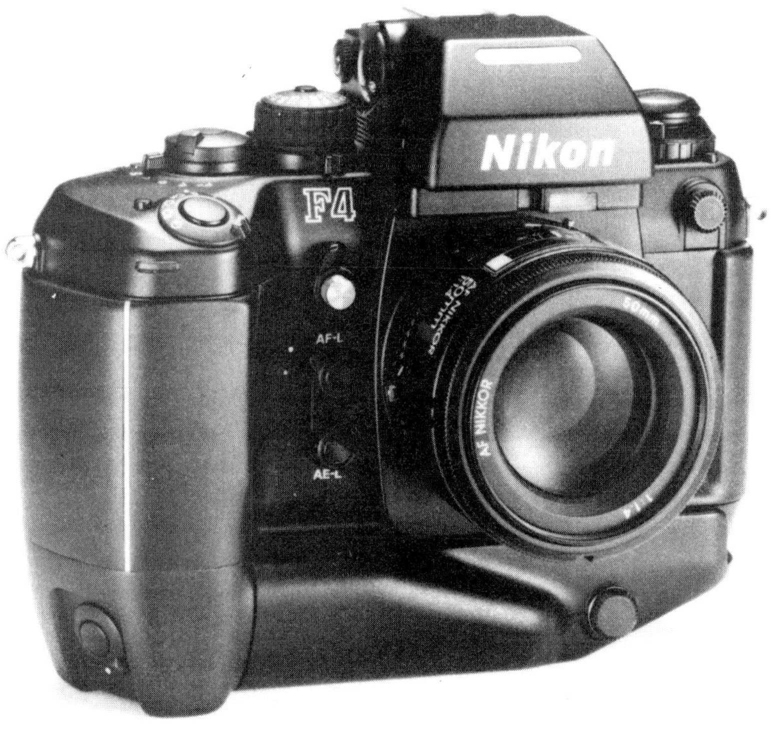

The Nikkorex Series

NIKKOREX 35 (Introduced 1960, discontinued 1961) This SLR has a fixed (non-interchangeable) 50mm f/2.5 lens. A built-in selenium light meter is coupled to the shutter and aperture controls. Identify by: 1) "Nikkorex" inscribed on the front of the prism housing. 2) It has a Citizen shutter ("Citizen" inscribed on the lens barrel).

NIKKOREX 35-2 (Introduced 1962, discontinued 1964) It has the same features as the 35, but with different shutter manufacturer. Identify by: 1) "Nikkorex" inscribed on the front of the prism housing. 2) It has a Seikosha-SLV shutter ("Seikosha-SLV" inscribed on the lens ring).

NIKKOREX F (Introduced 1962, discontinued 1965) It has provisions for interchangeable lenses via the Nikon "F" mount and a Copal Square focal plane shutter (which was the first metal vertical traveling focal plane shutter made). The bodies were made under contract for Nikon by Mamiya; the lenses were made by Nikon. Identify by: 1) "Nikkorex" inscribed on the front of the prism housing. 2) The only Nikkorex with provision for interchangeable lenses; all the other Nikkorex cameras have non-removable lenses.

NIKKOREX Zoom 35 (Introduced 1963, discontinued 1965) This camera has an f/3.5 43-86mm non-removable zoom lens and a built-in selenium cell meter. (It was the first still camera to be equipped with a non-interchangeable zoom lens.) The body was made by Mamiya; lens by Nikon. Indentify by: 1) "Nikkorex" inscribed on the front of the prism housing. 2) The only Nikkorex with a non-removable zoom lens.

NIKON Auto 35 (Introduced 1964, discontinued 1966) This is obviously a Nikkorex although the company calls it a Nikon. It has an f/2.0 48mm non-removable lens with the shutter coupled to a selenium cell light meter making it the only Nikkorex with fully automatic (shutter-preferred) exposure capability. The body was made by Mamiya; lens by Nikon. Identify by "Auto 35" inscribed on its face.

The Nikkormat Series

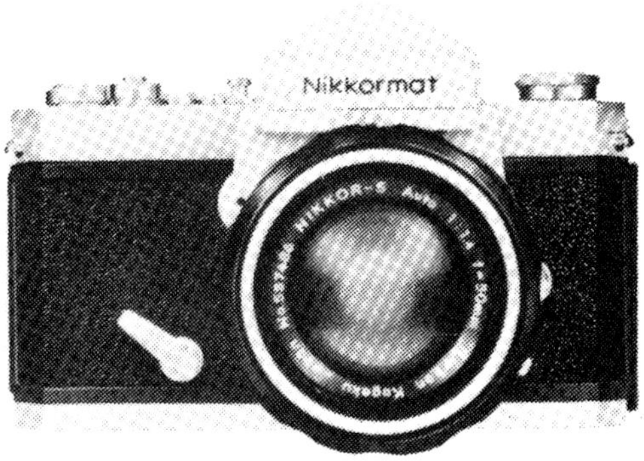

NIKKORMAT FT (Introduced 1965, discontinued 1967) This first of the Nikkormat series has a fixed pentaprism with through-the-lens (TTL) exposure metering. The meter needle is visible both in the viewfinder and on top of the camera. It features flash sync at 1/125 because of the Copal Square shutter. It was designed to accept many of the Nikon F accessories. Identify by: 1) "Nikkormat" inscribed on the front of the prism housing. 2) "FT" preceding the serial number on the top of the body.

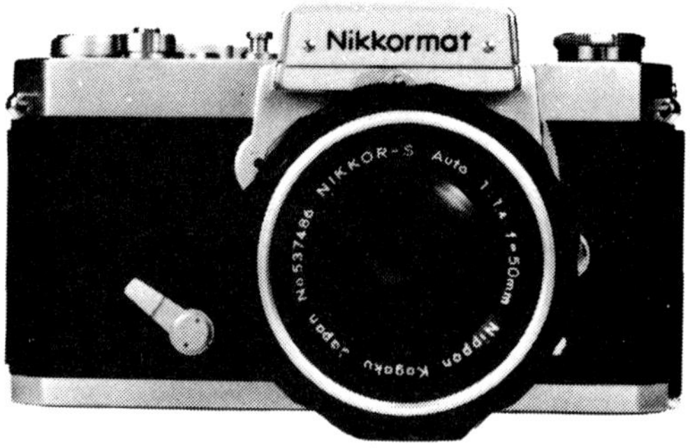

NIKKORMAT FS (Introduced 1965, discontinued 1971) This is a simplified and less expensive version of the FT without built-in meter or mirror lock-up capabilities. Identify by: 1) "Nikkormat" inscribed on the front of the prism housing. 2) "FS" preceding the serial number on the top of the body.

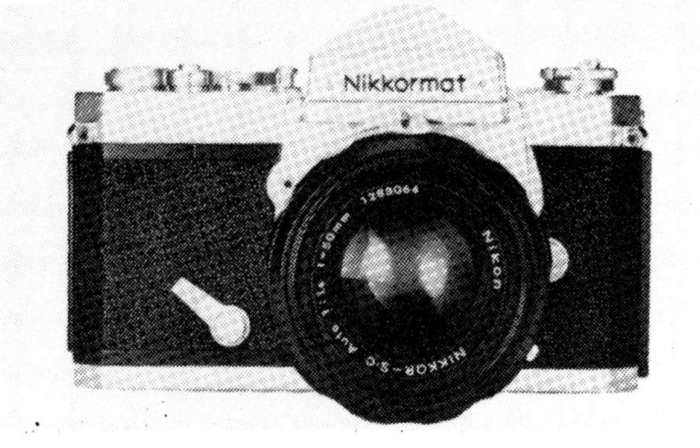

NIKKORMAT FTN (Introduced 1967, discontinued 1975) This model features center-weighted TTL metering and a vertical traveling focal plane shutter. There is a simplified method of setting the ASA/ISO and the shutter speed is visible in the viewfinder. Identify by: 1) "Nikkormat" inscribed on the front of the prism housing. 2) "FT" preceds the serial number and the letter "N" is inscribed on the top of the body beside the rewind knob above the external light meter window.

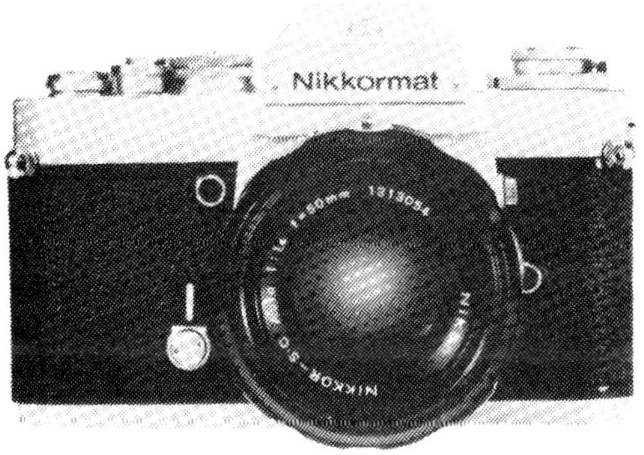

NIKKORMAT EL (Introduced 1972, discontinued 1977) The first fully automatic Nikkormat features aperture-priority automation with exposure memory lock as well as full manual exposure control. Identify by "EL" inscribed above the "Nikkormat" on the front of the prism housing.

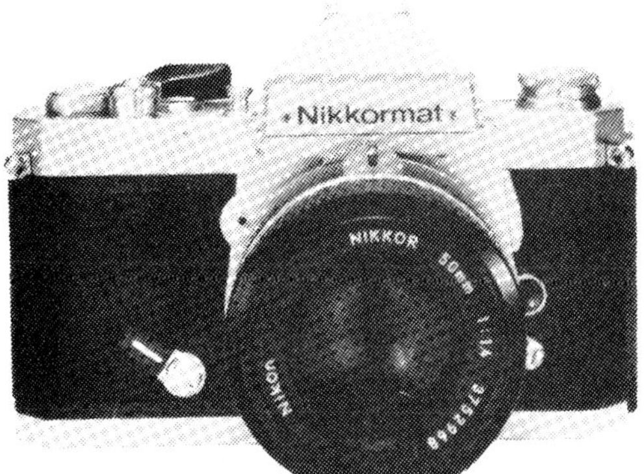

NIKKORMAT FT2 (Introduced 1975, discontinued 1978) This updated version of the Nikkormat FTN has a hot shoe contact built into the prism housing, a sync terminal with built-in automatic M-X switch and improved focusing via a microprism plus split-image screen. Identify by: 1) "Nikkormat" inscribed on the front of the prism housing. 2) "FT2" precedes the serial number on the top of the camera body.

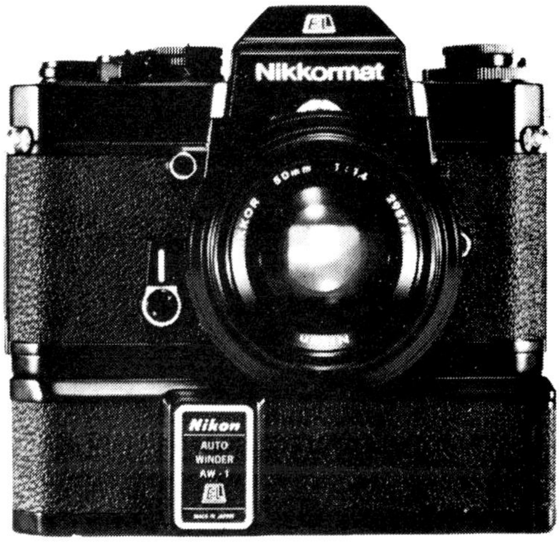

NIKKORMAT ELW (Introduced 1976, discontinued 1978) This model is the same as the EL with the added provision for an accessory automatic winder (AW-1). Identify by: 1) "EL Nikkormat" inscribed on the face of the prism housing. 2) "W" is the first character of the serial number.

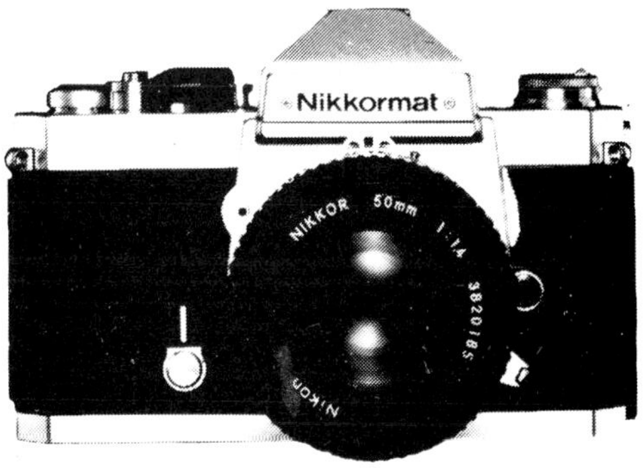

NIKKORMAT FT3 (Introduced 1977, discontinued 1979) This model has all of the features of the Nikkormat FT2 plus automatic indexing (AI). Identify by 1): "Nikkormat" inscribed on the front of the prism housing. 2) "FT3" preceds the serial number on the top of the camera body.

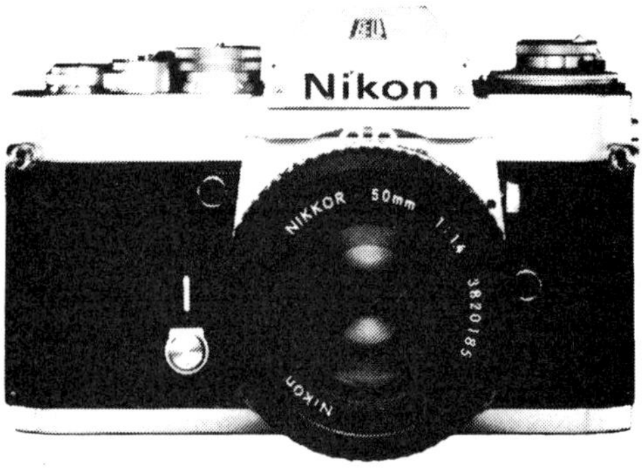

NIKON EL2 (Introduced 1977, discontinued 1979) This model has all of the features of the Nikkormat ELW plus automatic indexing (AI). It features SPD metering cells. This camera does not have "Nikkormat" inscribed on the face of the prism; it says, "Nikon." Identify by: 1) "EL" inscribed above "Nikon" on the face of the prism housing. 2) "EL2" precedes the serial number on the top of the camera body.

Compact SLR Cameras

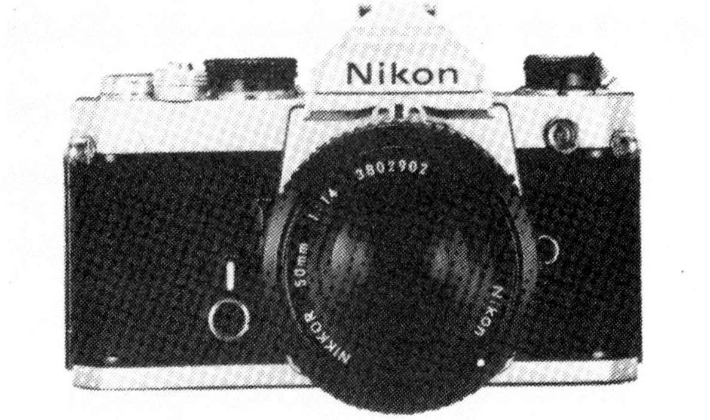

NIKON FM (Introduced 1977, discontinued 1984) This was the first compact SLR manufactured by Nikon. It features manual through-the-lens exposure metering with an LED display visible in the viewfinder. It also has double exposure capabilities. Identify by the "FM" preceding the serial number on the back of the camera body.

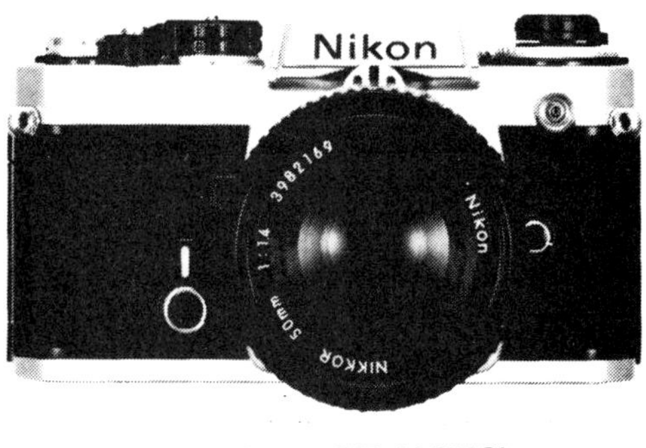

Nikon FE (1978)

NIKON FE (Introduced 1978, discontinued 1984) The FE has all of the features of the FM plus aperture preferred automatic exposure in addition to manual TTL metering. It is capable of accepting interchangeable focusing screens. Identify by the "FE" preceding the serial number on the back of the camera body.

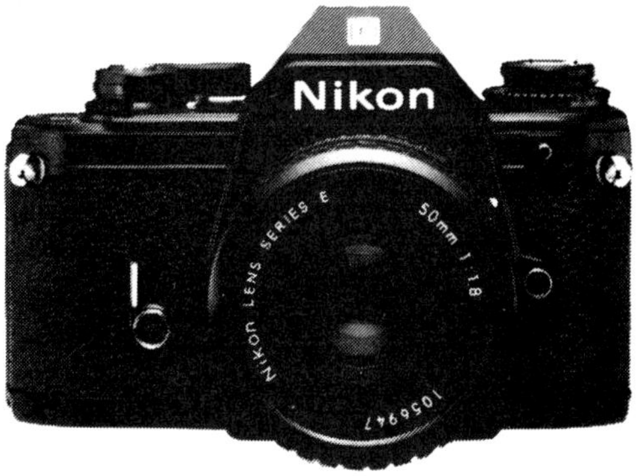

NIKON EM (Introduced 1979, discontinued 1985) This smallest of Nikon SLRs features aperture-priority automation only. The only manually selectible shutter speed is 1/90 for flash sync and emergency manual operation. Identify by the "EM" inscribed on the face of the prism housing.

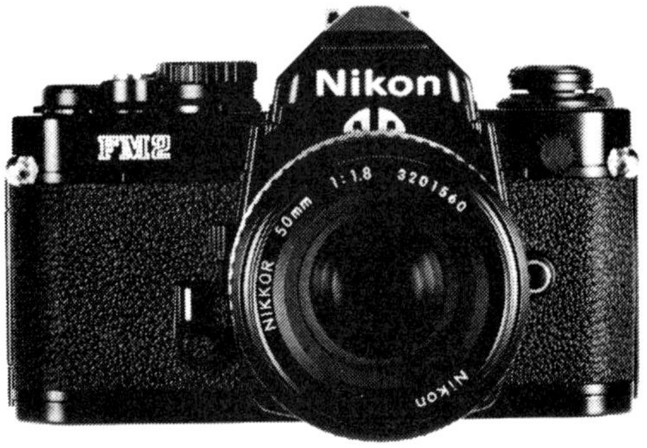

NIKON FM2 (Introduced 1982, discontinued 1988) This camera contains the same features as the FM plus a maximum shutter speed 1/4000, flash sync at 1/200. It features a mechanical shutter with vertically traveling titanium blades. The internal meter can be set from ASA/ISO 12 to 6400 and the focusing screens can be interchanged. Identify by the "FM2" on the face plate.

NIKON FG (Introduced 1982, discontinued 1987) This was the first Nikon camera to offer a programmed mode. It also offers aperture priority automation as well as manual exposure control. TTL flash metering is possible with the SB-15. The shutter is quartz timed and the shutter speeds are stepless. Identify by the "FG" inscribed on the face plate.

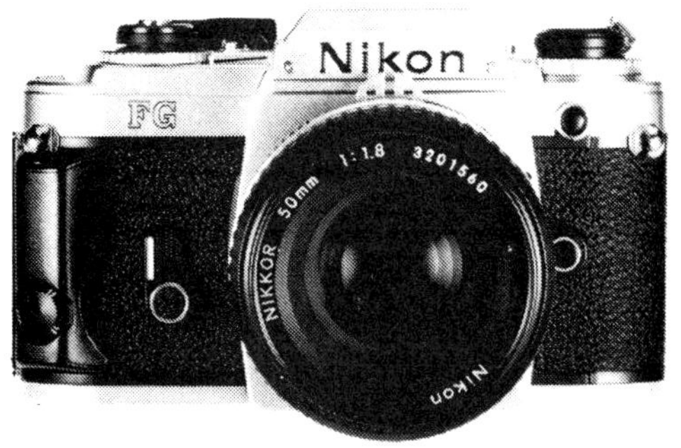

Nikon FG (1982)

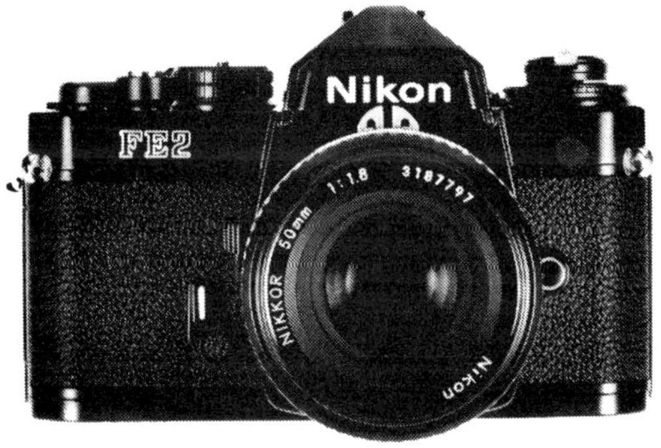

NIKON FE2 (Introduced 1983, discontinued 1989) This is an improved version of the FE with aperture-priority automation and manual exposure control, a top shutter speed of 1/4000, and flash synchronization at 1/250. Identify by the "FE2" inscribed on the face plate.

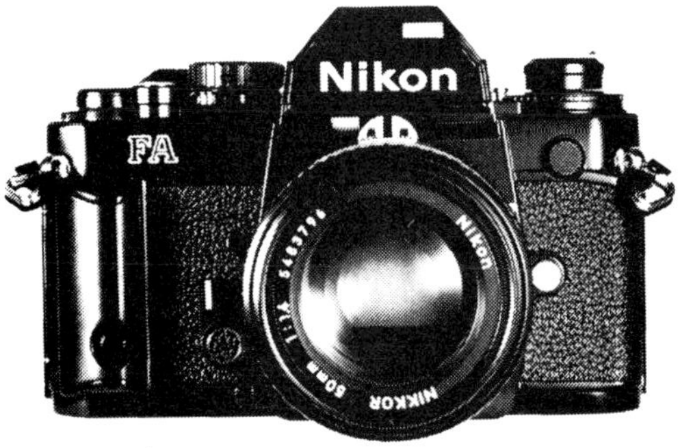

NIKON FA (Introduced 1983, discontinued 1989) Billed as "the technocamera," the FA introduced automatic multi-pattern matrix metering. It also features normal and high-speed programmed modes, shutter-priority, aperture priority and manual metering. There are shutter speeds to 1/4000, flash synchronization at 1/250 and TTL flash metering. Identify by the "FA" inscribed on the face plate.

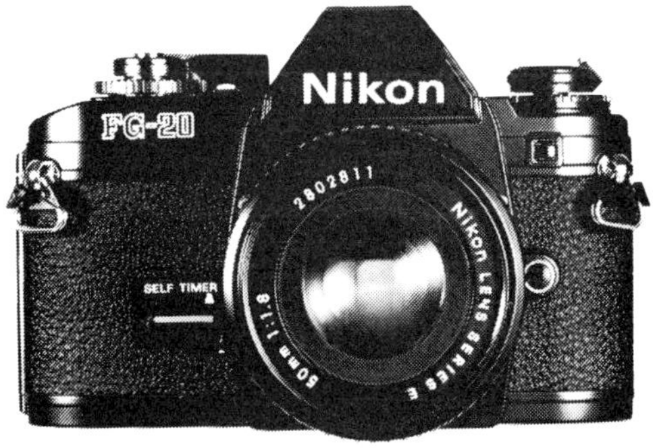

NIKON FG-20 (Introduced 1984, discontinued 1987) This scaled-down version of the FG features aperture priority with warning "beep," manual exposure controls and an exposure compensation button for backlit shots. FG features removed on the FG-20 are programmed automation and TTL flash metering. Identify by the "FG-20" inscribed on the face plate.

NIKON FM2n (Introduced 1989, still available) A further upgrade of the FM with 1/250 flash synchronization, a brighter focusing screen and a flash ready light in the viewfinder. FM2's are popular in some circles because they can be operated (except for TTL metering) without a battery. Identify by: 1) "FM2" inscribed on the camera face. 2) 1/250 flash synchronization and 3) An "N" preceding the serial number (later models only).

N Series Cameras

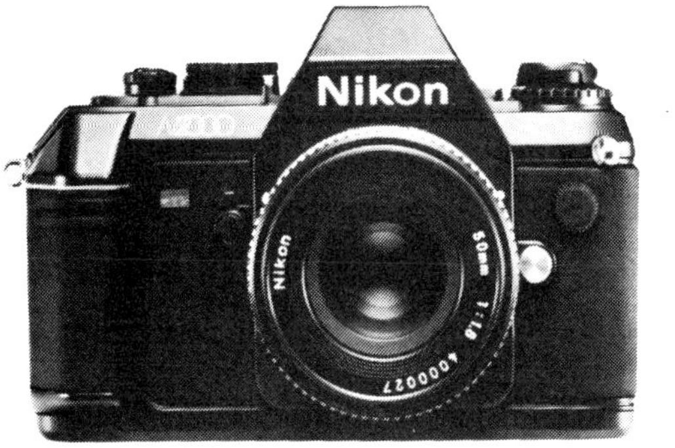

NIKON N2000 (Introduced 1985, still available) The first of the N series cameras features a built-in motor drive with up to 2.5 frames per second continuous shooting, manual focusing, programmed and aperture priority metering, manual metering and stepless shutter speeds to 1/2000. Identify by the "N2000" inscribed on the camera face.

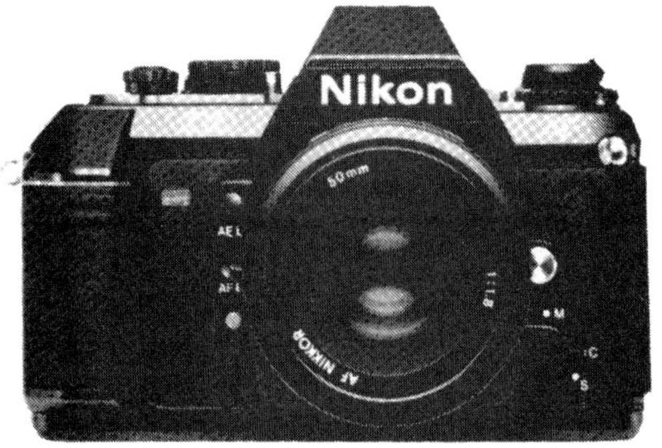

NIKON N2020 (Introduced 1986, discontinued 1989) This model has all of the features of the N2000 plus autofocus in either the single or continuous modes. Identify by the "N2020" inscribed on the camera face.

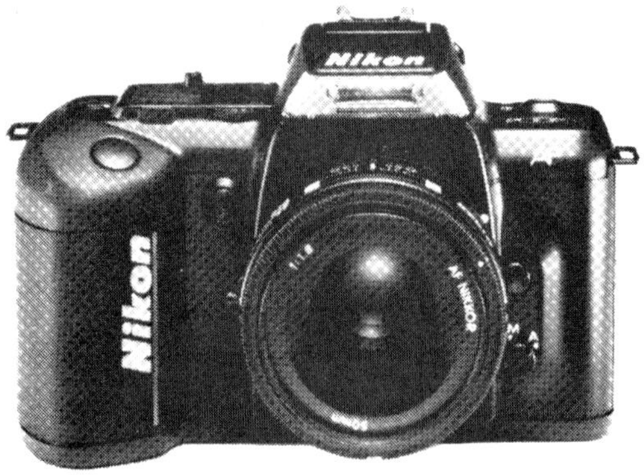

Nikon N4004 (1987)

NIKON N4004 (Introduced 1987, discontinued 1989) This camera has autofocus with built-in TTL flash, otherwise, the camera has the same features as previous N series cameras. It can only be used with AF lenses.Identify by "N4004" inscribed on the camera face.

SPECIAL NOTE: The N4004 and its successor, the N4004s, are unique among Nikon autofocus cameras. They can only be used with autofocus lenses. NAI lenses should not be mounted as camera damage may result. Other lenses may be used, but the internal metering functions will not work. See page 60.

NIKON N4004s (Introduced 1989, still available) This updated version of the N4004 features faster autofocusing, improved metering plus locking shutter speed and aperture control dials. Identify by the "N4004s" inscribed on the camera face under the self-timer button.

NIKON N8008 (Introduced 1988, still available) Autofocusing with matrix and center-weighted metering, six metering modes, stepless shutter speeds to 1/8000, flash synchronization to 1/250 and matrix TTL flash metering. Identify by "N8008" inscribed on the camera face directly below the mode button.

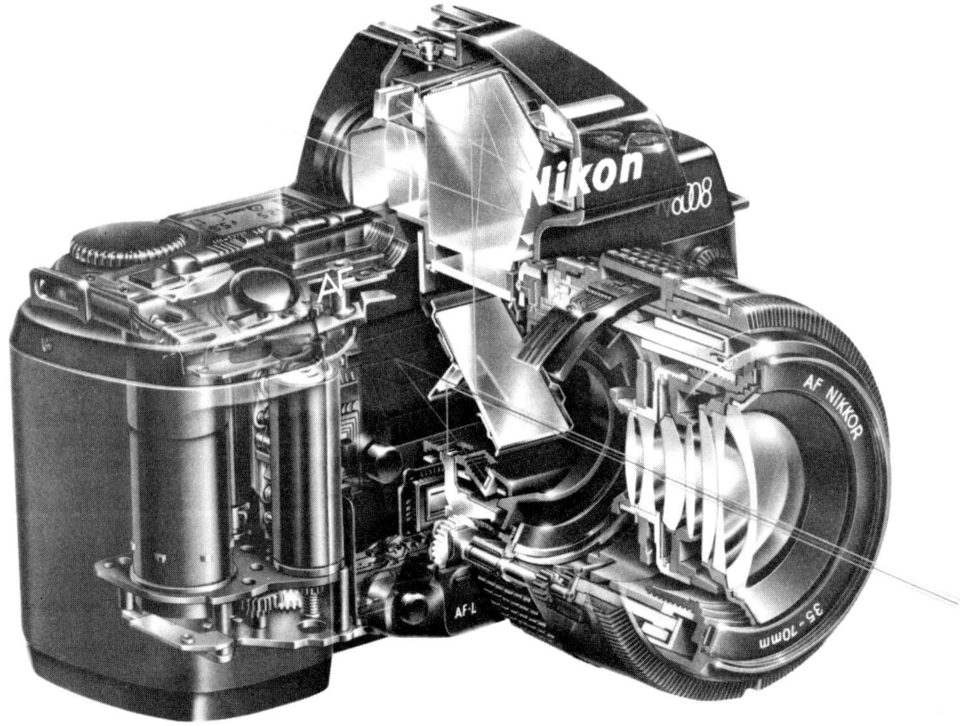

CUTAWAY OF **Nikon** *N8008*
W/35-70mm f/3.3 - 4.5 AF NIKKOR

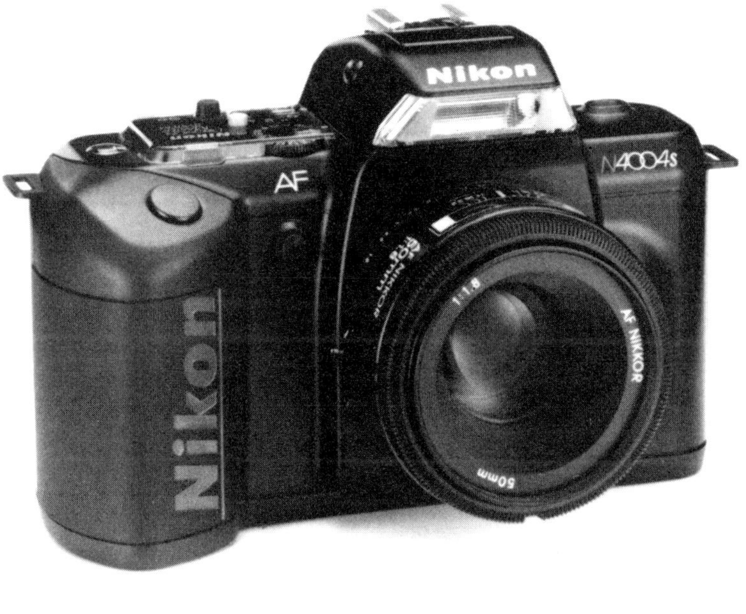

Nikon N4004S WITH 50mm f1.8 AF NIKKOR LENS

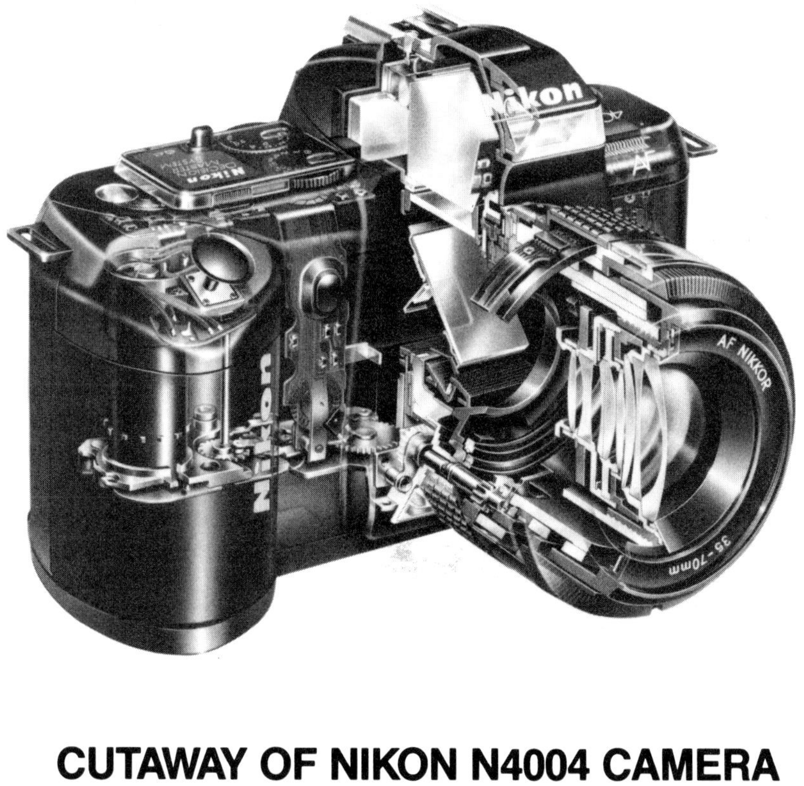

CUTAWAY OF NIKON N4004 CAMERA
WITH 35-70mm f3.3-4.5 AF NIKKOR

Point and Shoot Cameras

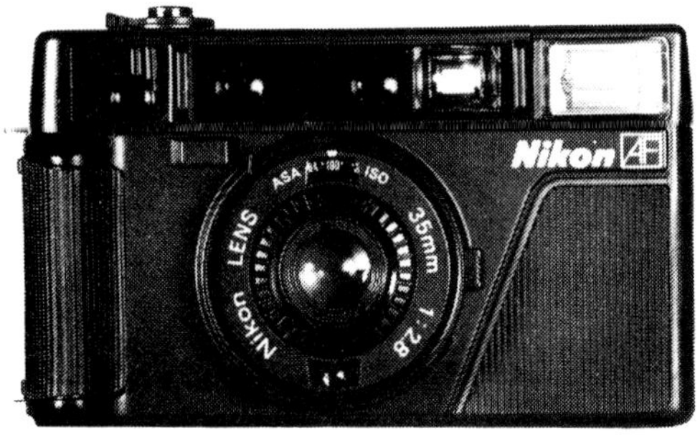

NIKON ONE TOUCH (L35AF) (Introduced 1983, discontinued 1984) Nikon's first autofocus, automatic exposure leaf-shutter camera with nine fully automatic features. Includes a built-in motor and fixed 35mm f/2.8 lens. Identify by the "L35AF" inscribed on the top plate.

NIKON ONE TOUCH QUARTZ DATE (L35AD) (Introduced 1983, discontinued 1984) This camera is the same as the One Touch plus a quartz timed date back. Identify by the "L35AD" inscribed on the top plate.

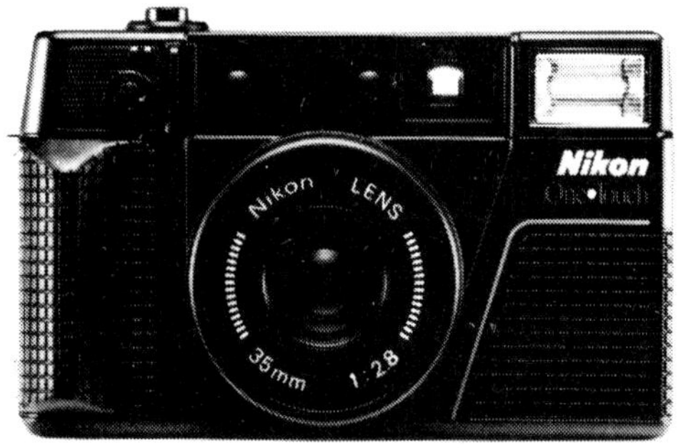

NIKON ONE TOUCH (L35AF2) (Introduced 1985, discontinued 1989) This is an upgraded L35AF with 11 automatic features, including a built-in lens cover (which is also the on-off switch) and DX coding. Identify by: 1) "One Touch" inscribed on the camera face under the flash. 2) The word "macro" does not appear on the lens ring.

NIKON ONE TOUCH QUARTZ DATE (L35AD2) (Introduced 1985, discontinued 1989) This camera is the same as the 1985 One Touch plus a quartz timed date back. Identify: same as a One Touch with a data back.

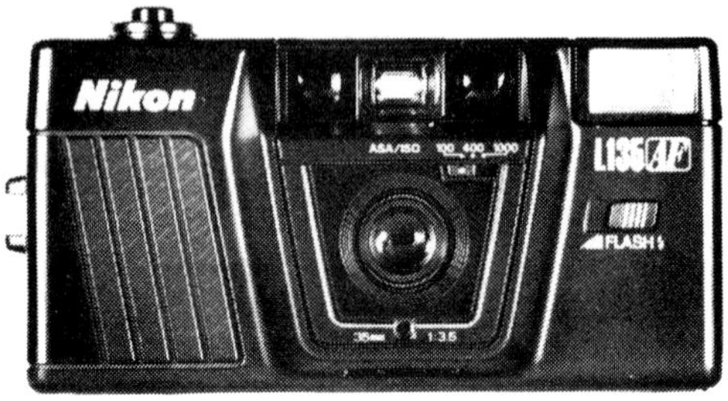

NIKON NICE TOUCH (L135AF) (Introduced 1984, discontinued 1989) This less expensive version of the One Touch has fewer automatic features, with a fixed 35mm f/3.5 lens and battery tester. Identify by the "135AF" inscribed on the camera face.

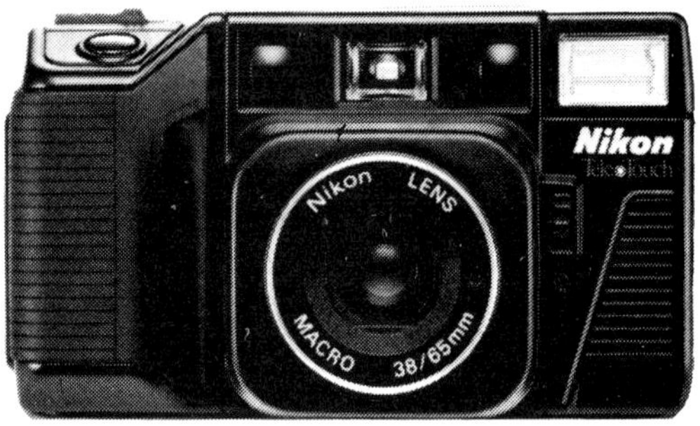

NIKON TELE TOUCH (L35TWAF) (Introduced 1986, discontinued 1989) All of the features of the 1985 One Touch plus three lens functions: 65mm telephoto, 38mm wide angle and macro. Stepless autofocus and automatic film rewind are added. Identify by: 1) "Tele Touch" inscribed on the camera face under the flash. 2) 38mm and 65mm lenses.

NIKON TELE TOUCH QUARTZ DATE (L35TWAD) Not sold in the US.

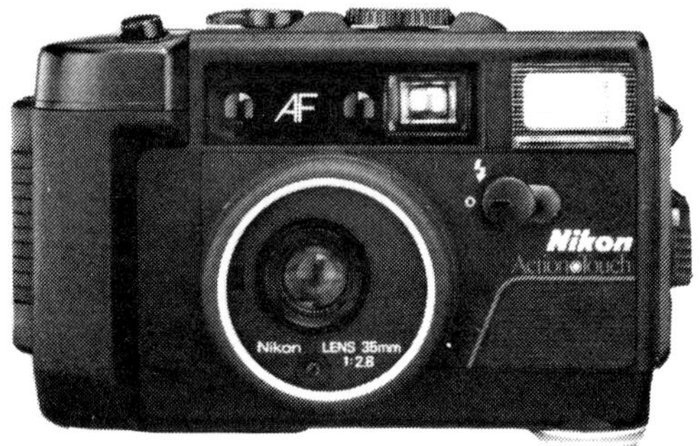

NIKON ACTION TOUCH (L35AWAF) (Introduced 1986, still available) All of the automatic features of the 1985 One Touch on land are combined in a waterproof body that will withstand depths of 3 meters/10 feet. The camera must be manually focused when used underwater. Identify by "Nikon Action Touch" inscribed on the camera body.

NIKON ACTION TOUCH QUARTZ DATE (L35AWAD) Not sold in the US.

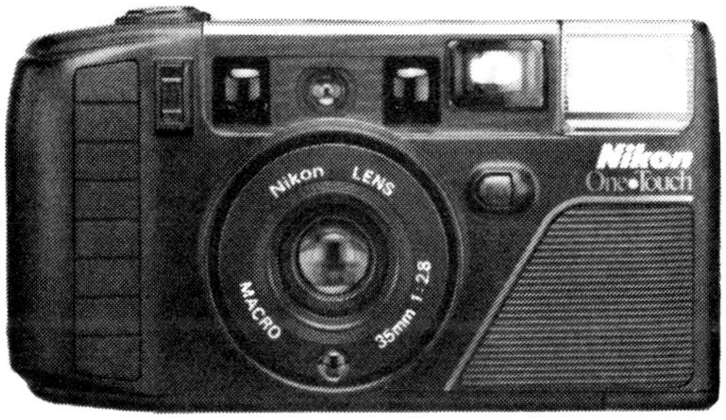

NIKON NEW ONE TOUCH (AF3) (Introduced 1987, discontinued 1989) Sixteen step autofocus with macro capabilities plus all the other 1985 One Touch features are incorporated in this model. Metering is via SPD instead of a CDS cell. The lens is threaded to accept filters. Identify by 1): "One Touch" inscribed on the camera face. 2) "Macro" inscribed on the lens ring.

NIKON NEW ONE TOUCH QUARTZ DATE (AD3) (Introduced 1987, discontinued 1989) This camera is the same as the New One Touch plus a quartz timed date back. Identify: same as a New One Touch with a data back.

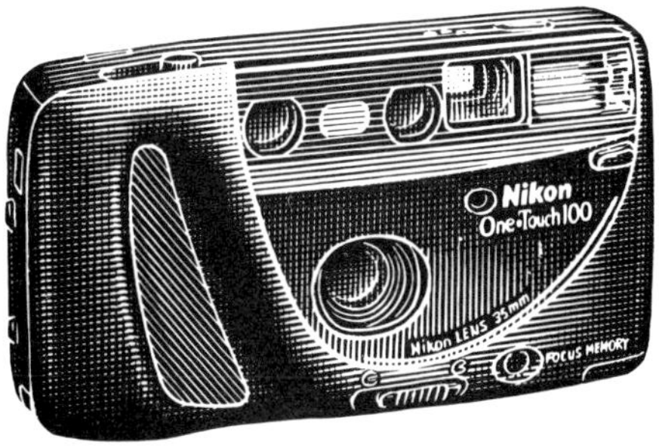

NIKON ONE TOUCH 100 (RF2) (Introduced 1988, still available) In this fourth version, focus memory and a double self-timer are added to the usual One Touch features on a re-styled body. Identify by the "Nikon One Touch 100" inscribed on the camera face.

NIKON ONE TOUCH 100 QUARTZ DATE (RD2) Not sold in the US.

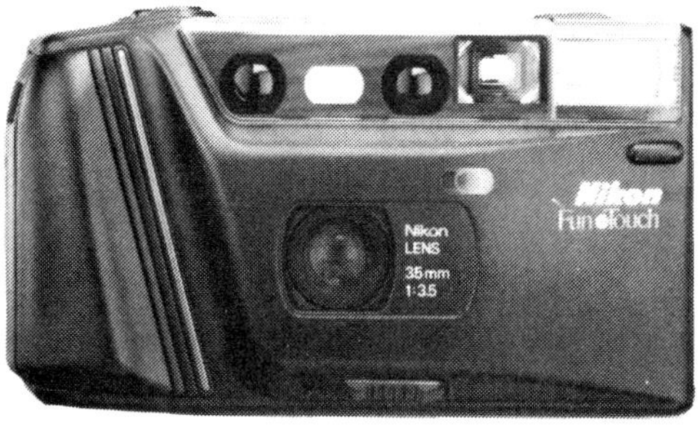

NIKON FUN TOUCH (RF) (Introduced 1987, discontinued 1989) This is a less expensive "Touch" camera with fewer automatic features. Includes a fixed 35mm f/3.5 lens, CDS meter, automatic exposure control, automatic flash, DX coding and a built-in lens cover. Identify by the "Nikon Fun Touch" inscribed on the camera face under the flash.

NIKON FUN TOUCH QUARTZ DATE (RD) Not sold in the US.

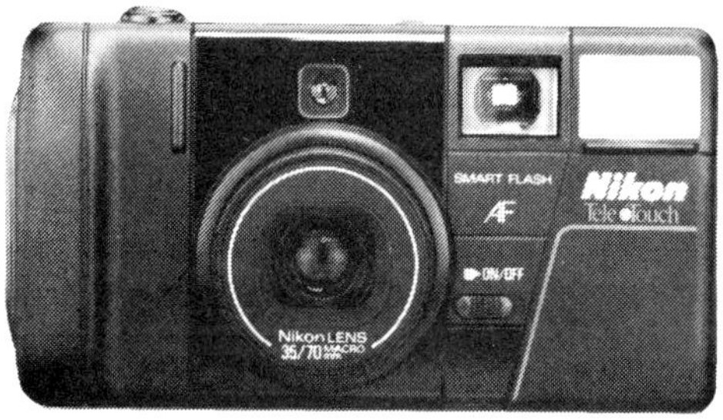

NIKON TELE TOUCH DELUXE (TW2) (Introduced 1987, still available) This model offers a choice of 35mm wide angle or 70mm telephoto and macro in an extremely small design. Identify by 1): "Nikon Tele Touch" inscribed on the camera face under the flash. 2) 35mm and 70mm lens positions.

NIKON TELE TOUCH DELUXE DATA (TW2D) (Introduced 1989, still available) Same as the Tele Touch Deluxe plus a quartz timed data back. Identify: same as a Tele Touch Deluxe with a data back.

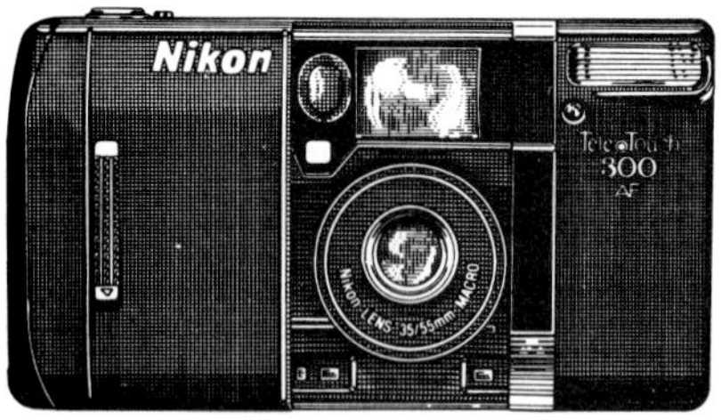

NIKON TELE TOUCH 300 (TW20) (Introduced 1989, still available) Offers a choice of 35mm wide angle or 55mm telephoto. Other features are focus lock, autoload, automatic film advance, automatic film rewind, self-timer and smart flash that fires only when needed. Identify by the "Nikon Tele Touch 300" inscribed on the camera face.

NIKON TELE TOUCH 300 DATE (TW20D) (Introduced 1989, still available) Same as the Tele Touch 300 plus a quartz timed date back. Identify: same as a Tele Touch 300 with a data back.

NIKON ZOOM TOUCH 500 (TW200M) (Introduced 1988, still available) All of the One Touch 100 features are combined with a 35mm to 80mm continuous zoom lens. Identify by the "Nikon Zoom Touch 500" inscribed on the camera face.

NIKON ZOOM TOUCH 500 DATE (TW200MQD) (Introduced 1989, still available) Same as the Zoom Touch 500 plus a quartz timed date back. Identify: same as a Zoom Touch 500 with a data back.

Underwater Cameras

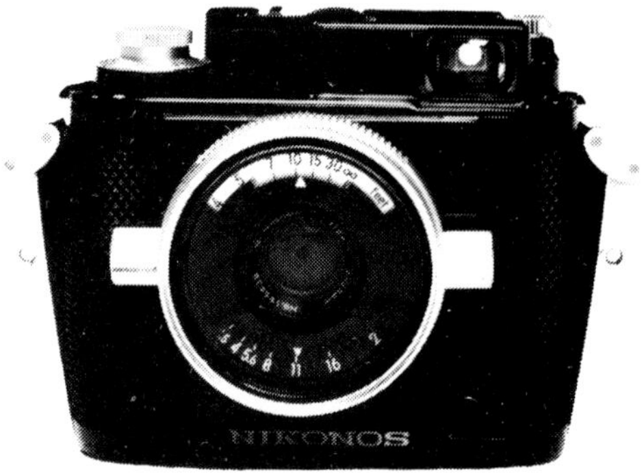

NIKONOS I (Introduced 1963, discontinued 1968) Nikon purchased the Calypso underwater 35mm still camera design from Jacques Cousteau. It was the first self-contained waterproof camera. It is an all manual, viewfinder type camera that contains no rangefinder but has interchangeable lens capabilities and accepts underwater flash units. It is easily identified since it is the only Nikonos with no model number inscribed on its face.

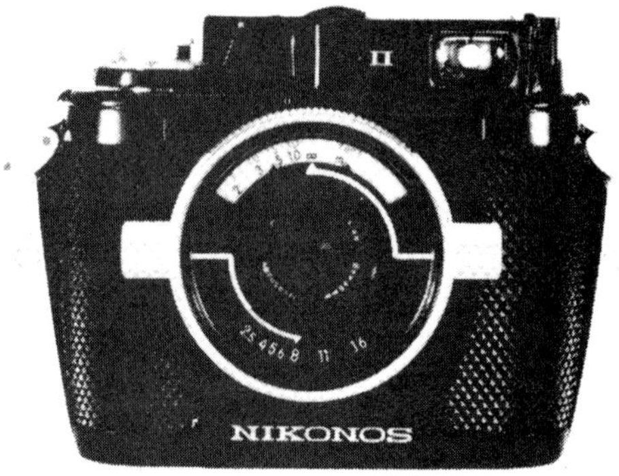

Nikonos II (1968)

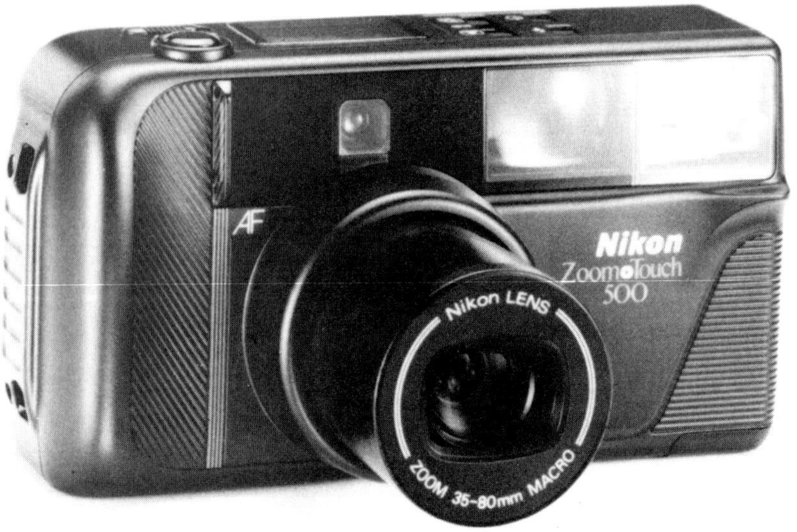

NIKONOS Nikonos II (Introduced 1968, discontinued 1975) This is an improved version of the Nikonos I with all of the features of the first model plus an improved rewind. The rewind selector is on the shutter speed dial. A rewind crank replaces a knob. Identify by: 1) "Nikonos" is inscribed on the bottom of the camera face. 2) "II" is inscribed next to the face of the viewfinder.

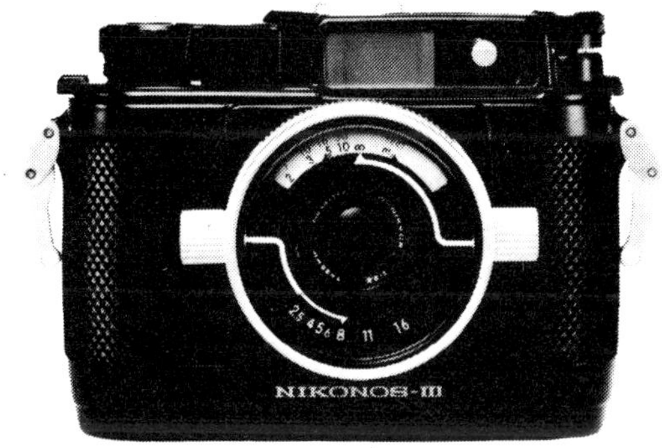

NIKONOS III (Introduced 1975, discontinued 1981) A further improvement features a single stroke film advance lever instead of the previous double stroke mechanism and a pressure plate which swings down for easier loading. Identify by the "Nikonos III" inscribed on the camera face under the lens mount.

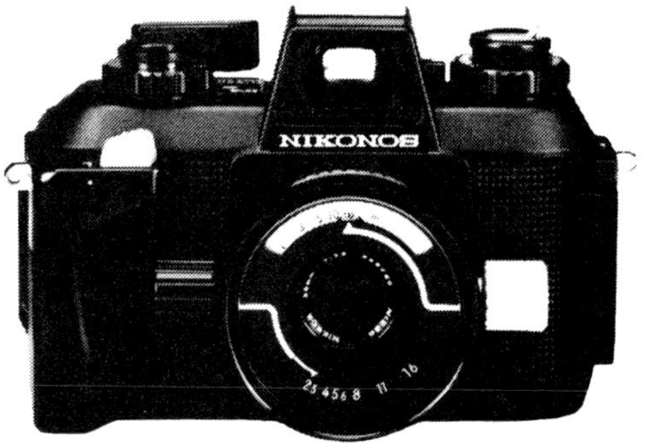

NIKONOS IV-A (Introduced 1980, discontinued 1985) Automatic TTL exposure control is added to the Nikonos line and a hinged back is incorporated for easier loading. Automatic flash exposure control is possible with the SB-101. All of the previously produced lenses function without sacrificing any of the new automatic features. Identify by: 1) "Nikonos" is inscribed on the face of the camera under the viewfinder. 2) "IV-A" is inscribed on the top next to the shutter speed dial.

NIKONOS V (Introduced 1984, still available) Manual exposure control and TTL flash exposure control are added to the IV-A features. Offered in either green or orange body covering (most imported into the US are orange). Identify by the "Nikonos V" inscribed on the face of the camera below the viewfinder.

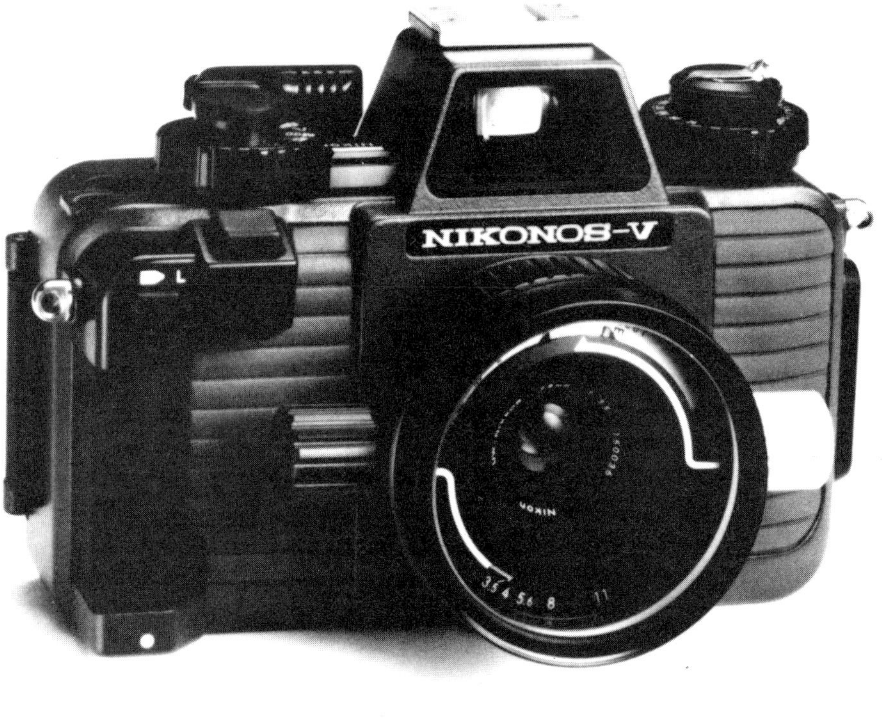

All-new Nikonos-V underwater camera with UW-Nikkor 28mm f/3.5 lens

now– thru-the-lens exposure control for the Nikon F PHOTOMIC T interchangeable thru-the-lens meter/finder system

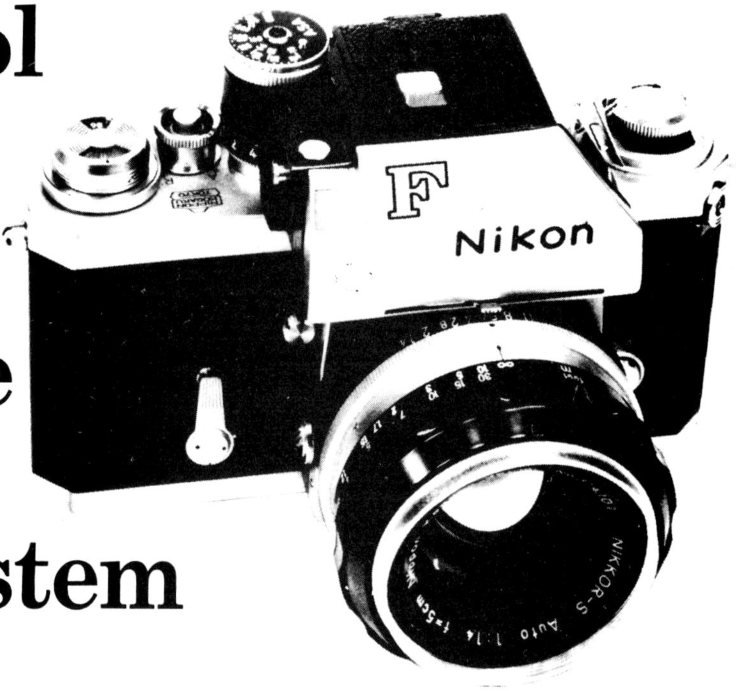

The makers of the Nikon F seem to have anticipated and allowed for every new development, every new advance in single-lens reflex design. They created an instrument whose capabilities are seemingly unlimited.

The owner of even the earliest Nikon F, for example, can enjoy the same modern advantages as if the camera had just come off the drawing boards. Likewise, the man selecting a Nikon F today can look to a lifetime of photographic activity with a camera that virtually defies obsolescence.

This year, as in previous years, the Nikon F offers proof again of its dynamic flexibility, this time with the new Photomic T meter system. Affixed to the Nikon F, it transforms this already remarkable camera into a totally new, totally integrated, ultra-modern instrument.

The Photomic T is a complete prism-finder-meter system designed for thru-the-lens exposure control. It interchanges with the standard prism finder or direct-reading Photomic, and is cross-coupled to the shutter speed dial and lens-aperture ring. Initially, the Photomic T will be supplied with Nikon F cameras only, but will soon be available as a separate accessory. Current camera bodies will require some modification.

Because it is a thru-the-lens system, the Photomic T automatically takes into account lens transmission, filter absorption, close-up exposure increase, etc. The need for calculating and allowing for these factors is therefore eliminated. The Photomic T reduces the problem of exposure determination to routine simplicity.

Nikon F/Photomic T with 50mm f2 Auto-Nikkor $371.00; with 50mm f1.4 Auto-Nikkor $433.00
Photomic T meter/finder system only, $109.50 (when available)

CHAPTER TEN

LIGHT METERS AND PRISMS

While Nikon no longer sells light meters as separate entities, all current and most Nikon cameras include a built-in light meter of one sort or another. These meter devices are a part of the interchangeable prism in the F and F2 cameras.

An important fact to remember is that while the prism finders are interchangeable on all of the professional bodies (F, F2, F3, F4), they are not interchangeable among the different series. A meter made for an F cannot be mounted on an F2, for example.

EXPOSURE METER MODEL A (Introduced 1957, discontinued 1965) This selenium cell unit fits into the accessory shoe on the SP, S3 and S4 rangefinder cameras. It couples directly with the shutter speed dial and gives direct f/ stop setting readouts. In low light conditions, the meter sensitivity can be increased via an amplifier cell or booster. An incident attachment was supplied with the meter.

EXPOSURE METER MODEL 3 (Introduced 1963, discontinued 1968) This selenium cell meter clips over the Nikon F's pentaprism and couples to both the f/ stop rabbit ears and the shutter speed dial. Meter needle alignment can be accomplished by turning either the lens f/ stop ring or the shutter speed knob. An incident light plate and a booster were included.

EXPOSURE METER MODEL D (Introduced 1963, discontinued 1970) This selenium cell meter clips over the Nikkorex F pentaprism and couples to the shutter speed dial and the rabbit ears on the lens. Moving either the aperture ring or the shutter speed dial moves the arrow on the meter to a needle which indicates the correct exposure. The meter takes reflected readings only.

PHOTOMIC F METER PRISM (Introduced 1962, discontinued 1967) This CdS cell exposure meter was Nikon's first unit which combined the metering function within the pentaprism housing. It is for the Nikon F body only. Although the meter couples to the lens aperture and shutter speed, it is of the external, non- TTL variety. The light gathering port is on the face of the meter and attachments can be screwed into it. An incident attachment and the angle of acceptance restrictor are stored, one on top of the other, on the side of the meter when not in use.

SPECIAL NOTES

Early Nikon F cameras (with serial numbers with the first two digits 68 and lower) needed a modification (by Nikon or an authorized repair facility) to accept any meter prism. Some cameras with 68 serial numbers have a red dot near the serial number. This indicates that they were modified at the factory before delivery.

Models with serial numbers with the first two digits less than 68 must be modifed to accept T, TN or FTN meter prisms.

APRIL 1978

A new meter system with extraordinary sensitivity is a vital part of this new high-performance professional Nikon.

The sun begins to disappear beneath the horizon. As it sinks, the light becomes dimmer, yet more and more fascinating–and photographically enticing. Subtle highlights of color twinkle on the water, changing constantly, demanding precise exposure. The failing light is far too dim for a meter reading with most cameras, or to illuminate the meter needle for that matter. But, with supreme assurance, this photographer adjusts lens and shutter and obtains a perfect exposure.

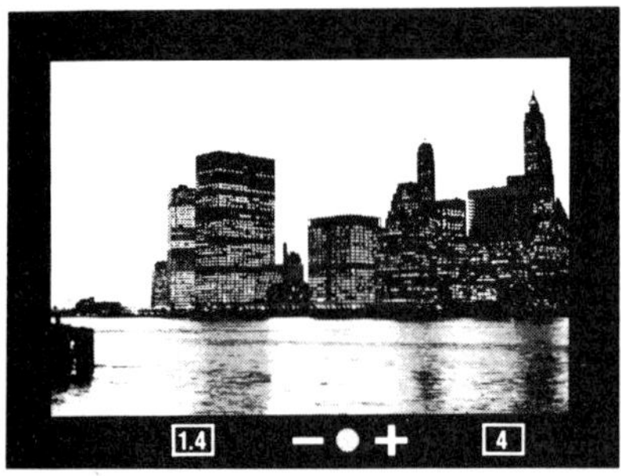

His camera is the remarkable new Nikon F2AS Photomic with meter sensitivity extending down to minus 2 EV. It can read accurately in light that would require an exposure of eight seconds at f1.4 with ASA 100 film. The exposure readout in the finder utilizes three light-emitting diodes that are as easy to see in the dark as in bright light. New silicon photo diode sensors combined with Nikon center-weighted metering provide accuracy to 1/5 f-stop, even in the most difficult lighting conditions. Add the new DS-12 EE Aperture Control, and aperture adjustment becomes fully automatic!

Nikon F2A: proven reliability with Auto Indexing

The standard F2A Photomic meter/finder provides unbeatable reliability, combining match-needle metering with the proven Nikon center-weighted system for truly exceptional accuracy. This is true center-weighting, with sensitivity over the entire viewing area, but more than half of it concentrated in the center of the screen. In all but the most difficult lighting, with any lens, no matter whether you're shooting a vertical or horizontal, you'll never need any special compensation.

Both F2A and F2AS Photomic finders are equipped for automatic maximum aperture indexing with the new AI Nikkor lenses. Simply put the lens in place, without regard for the aperture setting, and give it a quarter-turn twist. It will be locked firmly and precisely in place, the meter will be indexed and you'll be ready to meter at full-aperture! Previous Auto-Nikkor lenses can be used with stop-down metering or modified for AI capability at nominal cost. (If interested, write for Lit/Pak N-27.) Non-meter-coupled lenses work just as before. And, you have more than 55 lenses to choose from.

Whatever the finder, matchless accuracy

In addition to the two Photomics, the Nikon System includes a 6X Magnifying Finder, a Waist Level Finder, an Action Finder and, of course, the Standard Prism Finder. Plus 20 finder screens. Each finder has its own, special capabilities, but they share one unique quality: the most accurate viewing in 35mm photography. What you see in a Nikon finder is precisely what you get, to a degree unapproached by any other camera. When you're shooting any subject requiring precise framing, or working on special applications such as slide duping, there's simply no other camera that can do the job so perfectly.

High performance photography is a combination of unique Nikon qualities such as viewing accuracy. And especially the inimitable responsiveness of a Nikon with motor drive. For, in two decades of building motors, we have refined them into the most rugged, dependable and capable in photography.

Ruggedness approaching indestructibility

More than all other cameras combined, Nikon is the professional's choice. And the camera chosen by the most far-flung expeditions in and out of this world is inevitably Nikon. The paramount consideration is the Nikon level of proven reliability, which no other camera has even approached. Whether in outer space, on top of a mountain, or in the thick of the action – you've got to be able to depend on your camera, whatever the conditions. If you're serious about photography, you can't settle for anything less.

Nikon Information: *For details on the Nikon F2AS, check the Yellow Pages for the Nikon dealer nearest you, or write for Lit Pak N-38. Also, ask about the new two course travelling Nikon School of Photography. And in New York City, come to the new Nikon House at Rockefeller Center.*

Nikon Inc., Garden City, N.Y. 11530. *Subsidiary of Ehrenreich Photo-Optical Industries, Inc.*
(In Canada: Anglophoto Ltd. P.Q.)

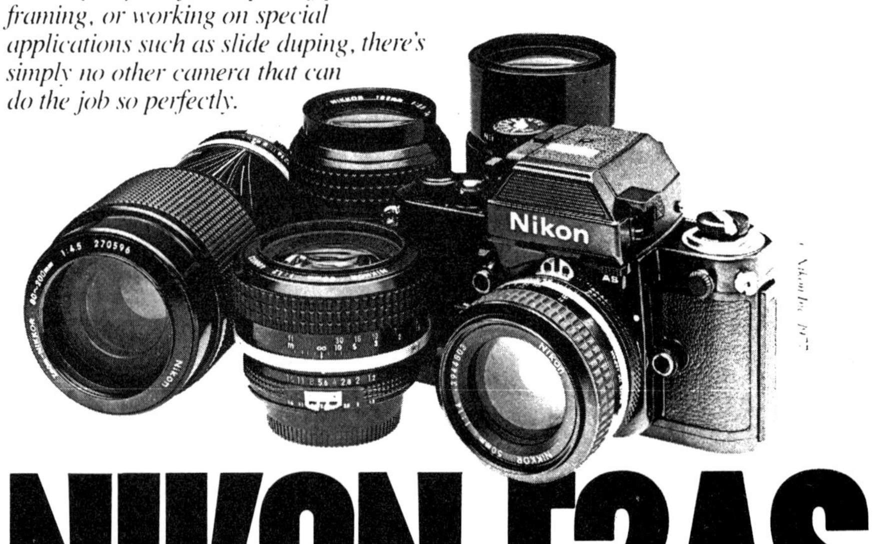

NIKON F2AS

PHOTOMIC T METER PRISM (Introduced 1965, discontinued 1968) This CdS cell exposure meter/prism was the first to provide TTL metering to the Nikon F system. Adjusting either the aperture or the shutter speed causes a needle to move. Centering the needle indicates the correct exposure. The film speed is set by aligning the ASA number opposite the maximum aperture of the lens in use. When a lens is changed, the setting must be adjusted.

PHOTOMIC TN METER PRISM (Introduced 1967, discontinued 1968) This unit is basically the same as the Photomic T, except that the metering function is center-weighted with approximately 60 percent of the reading concentrated within a 12mm central circular area. The remaining 40 percent is a reading from the balance of the area. This was a concept utilized by Nikon for many subsequent cameras and systems. The TN is for the Nikon F body only.

PHOTOMIC FTN METER PRISM (Introduced 1968, discontinued 1975) This unit introduced semiautomatic maximum aperture indexing. To accomplish this, the rabbit ear/meter pin connection must be made and registration assured by turning the aperture setting through its entire range until a click indicates locking. This is necessary for subsequent meter prisms until automatic indexing was introduced via the DP-12 on the F2 Photomic AS in 1977. Additional improvements over the TN include the display of shutter speeds in the viewfinder, a lever-type clamp to position and secure the unit snugly to the camera body and an engraved maximum aperture scale on the finder face. IMPORTANT: A modification by an authorized repair station is required for this unit to be installed on bodies with serial numbers below 6,900,001. The Photomic FTN is for the Nikon F body only.

PHOTOMIC F2 METER PRISM (Introduced 1971, discontinued 1978) This unit has built-in TTL, full aperture, center-weighted metering with shutter speeds and the meter needle displayed in the viewfinder. The galvanometer needle is displayed on top of the prism as well. The unit is for the Nikon F2 body only.

PHOTOMIC F2S METER PRISM (Introduced 1971, discontinued 1977) This unit is basically the same as the Photomic F2, except the needle is replaced with an LED readout displayed in the viewfinder as well as on top of the prism housing. It can also be used in conjunction with the EE Aperture Control Attachment DS-1. It is for the Nikon F2 body only.

PHOTOMIC F2SB METER PRISM (Introduced 1976, discontinued 1979) This unit features silicone photodiode (SPD) metering cells and incorporates a built-in eyepiece shutter. Otherwise it is the same as the Photomic F2S. It is for the Nikon F2 body only.

PHOTOMIC F2A METER PRISM (Introduced 1977, discontinued 1985) This meter prism introduced the Nikon Automatic Indexing (AI) system. It must be used in conjunction with AI lenses. It incorporates TTL and center-weighting and uses a galvanometer needle movement and CdS cells. It is for the Nikon F2 body only.

PHOTOMIC F2AS METER PRISM (Introduced 1977, discontinued 1985) This is the AI version of the F2SB prism employing silicone photodiode (SPD) cells and an LED readout. Shutter priority automation can be achieved when used in conjunction with the EE Aperture Control Attachment DS-12 on the Nikon F2 body.

UNDERWATER LIGHT METER FOR NIKONOS. Because the Nikonos I, II and III have no built-in metering system, Nikon offered this separate hand-held meter. It consists of two components: a clear lucite waterproof housing and a Sekonic Auto-Lumi Model L-86 meter. The meter is controlled by a large knob on the top of the housing and readings are made through the clear lucite.

AUGUST 1977

NIKON F2A

Professional photographers are the most demanding customers any camera maker can have. To a pro, a camera is the tool of the trade. It is significant that every year since 1959 a nation of professionals has chosen Nikon. It has been constantly refined, the best has been made still better. Today, as for these past 18 years, Nikon is the performance standard.

Nikon F2A Photomic with Auto Indexing

Now, the professional's Nikon, the famed F2, has evolved once again, into the new Nikon F2A Photomic. Its new, superbly reliable center-weighted meter system, with accurate match-needle control, allows you to change lenses instantly, with automatic aperture indexing, without concern for where the aperture ring is set. Add this new, time-saving feature to the rapid-fire capability of Nikon motor drive photography, and it's easy to see why we call this new F2A the high performance professional!

There is also a new F2AS Photomic. Employing an advanced form of metering cell, the Silicon Photo Diode, this extraordinary meter system offers a –2 to +17 EV range. Its LED finder readout indicates optimum exposure plus four levels of under- and over-exposure in 1/2-step increments in any light, or almost no light. Combined with a new Nikon EE Aperture Control, the F2AS provides full exposure automation.

The high-performance professional camera. Refined to a new level of perfection, with automatic lens indexing for the fastest, surest lens interchange ever!

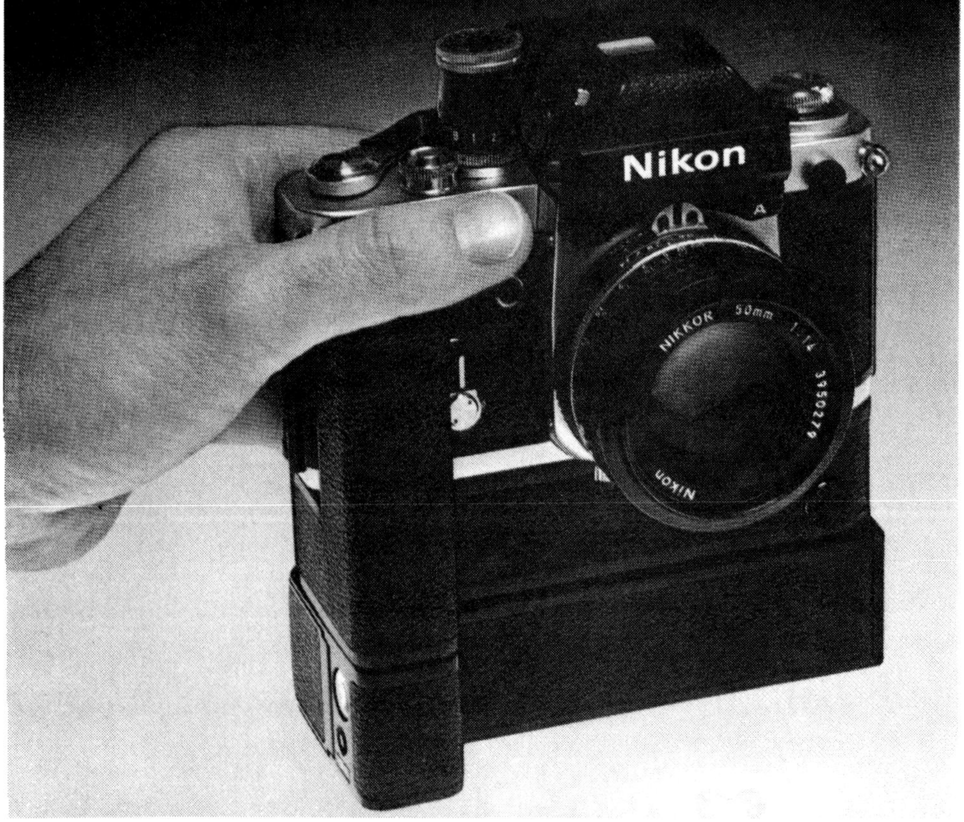

The ultimate in high performance: Nikon motor drive

Perhaps more than any other accessory, a Nikon motor drive transforms any Nikon F2/F2A/F2AS into the ultimate high performance image maker. The famous Nikon MD-2 is known as the world's finest. A new, low-priced model MD-3 will also be available. Both are products of more than two decades of Nikon motor drive experience and fully interchangeable.

New instant-interchange AI-Nikkor lenses

A full range of these lenses, 6mm through 600mm, permits instant interchanging on the Nikon F2A and F2AS Photomics. Any AI-Nikkor can be attached (or removed) with a quarter turn, regardless of its aperture setting, and is instantly ready for full-aperture metering. Non-meter-coupled Nikkors, through 2000mm, also fit the new cameras, as do non-AI Auto-Nikkors. These can be used with stop-down metering or, in most cases, modified at low cost for AI operation (write for Lit/Pak N-27, if interested).

The Nikon System: now more complete than ever

Long the most complete system in 35mm photography, the Nikon System has grown once again. Now, more than ever, it makes Nikon cameras the most capable, the most versatile in existence. Nikon F2A and F2AS cameras are, in fact, hundreds of cameras, ready to help you master any challenge you may ever encounter.

With this incomparable selection of accessories to choose from, your Nikon becomes an image-recording tool virtually without limitation. An instrument which you will never outgrow, whatever your ambitions and however they may change. If you wish to own the finest 35mm slr photography has to offer, your choice is clear: Nikon F2A/F2AS Photomic.

Visit your Nikon Dealer and see the complete line of Nikon cameras, Nikkor lenses and accessories. For the dates and locations of the famous Nikon School of Photography, write:

Anglophoto Ltd.,
160 Graveline St., Montreal, Quebec H4T 1R8.

CHAPTER ELEVEN

MOTOR DRIVES

S-36. (Introduced 1957, discontinued 1967) This motor was designed for use with the Nikon SP and S3 rangefinder cameras. This is the first motor drive designed to fit on a production model camera. It provides single framing or up to 3 fps continuous operation. The unit is powered by six 1.5 volt batteries which will expose up to 30 rolls. Nikon film cassettes are recommended because their construction results in less friction.

F-250. (Introduced 1959, discontinued 1984) This device is a 250-exposure magazine and motor for use with any F series camera. F bodies require modification in order to accept the unit. In addition to being a motor drive, the unit is an alternate camera back which allows loading bulk film up to 33 feet long producing 250 exposures. It can be operated by hand or remotely by cable, timer or radio. The standard battery pack has 8 C cells which will expose up to fifteen 250-exposure cassettes on single frame or up to 4 fps continuous operation. The full speed of 4 fps can be achieved only if the mirror is locked up.

F-36. (Introduced 1959, discontinued 1982) This motor is for use with any F series camera. F bodies require modification in order to accept the unit. It provides single framing or up to 4 fps continuous operation. There is a choice of battery packs, one powered by 8 C cell batteries (separate); the other by 8 AAs (attached). The full speed of 4 fps can be achieved only if the mirror is locked up.

SPECIAL NOTE. Each F-36 and F-250 must be adjusted to a specific camera body. They will not necessarily work with other F bodies.

KS-80a. (Produced in 1964) Made for the US Navy (Federal Stock Number VH 6720-689-9779). For use with a Nikon F, it includes a motorized shutter release and film advance, pistol-grip with 2-position shutter release trigger, internal nickle-cadmium battery and built-in charger. Provides motorized single frame exposure or sequential operation at 4 frames per second.

AUTO WINDER AW-1. (Introduced 1980, discontinued 1985) For use with the Nikon EL2 and Nikkormat ELW, this unit advances one frame per button depression. There is no continuous capability but a film winding speed of approximately 2 FPS is possible. It is powered by 6 AA batteries which drive up to 150 36-exposure rolls of film.

MD-E. (Introduced 1980, discontinued 1987) This motor is for the EM, FG and FG-20. Single exposure or 2 fps continuous operation are the choices. It is powered by 6 AA batteries which will drive more than 50 rolls of film.

MD-1. (Introduced 1971, discontinued 1975) This motor drive fits all camera bodies in the F2 series. It is capable of single frame and continuous exposure up to 5 fps. It will rewind a 36-exposure roll in about 7 seconds. The MD-1 requires an external power supply, either from the MB-1 cordless battery pack or the MA-2 AC/DC converter. The MB-1 uses 10 AA or 2 nicad NM-1 batteries, which yield up to 80 rolls with alkalines or 50 rolls with the nicads.

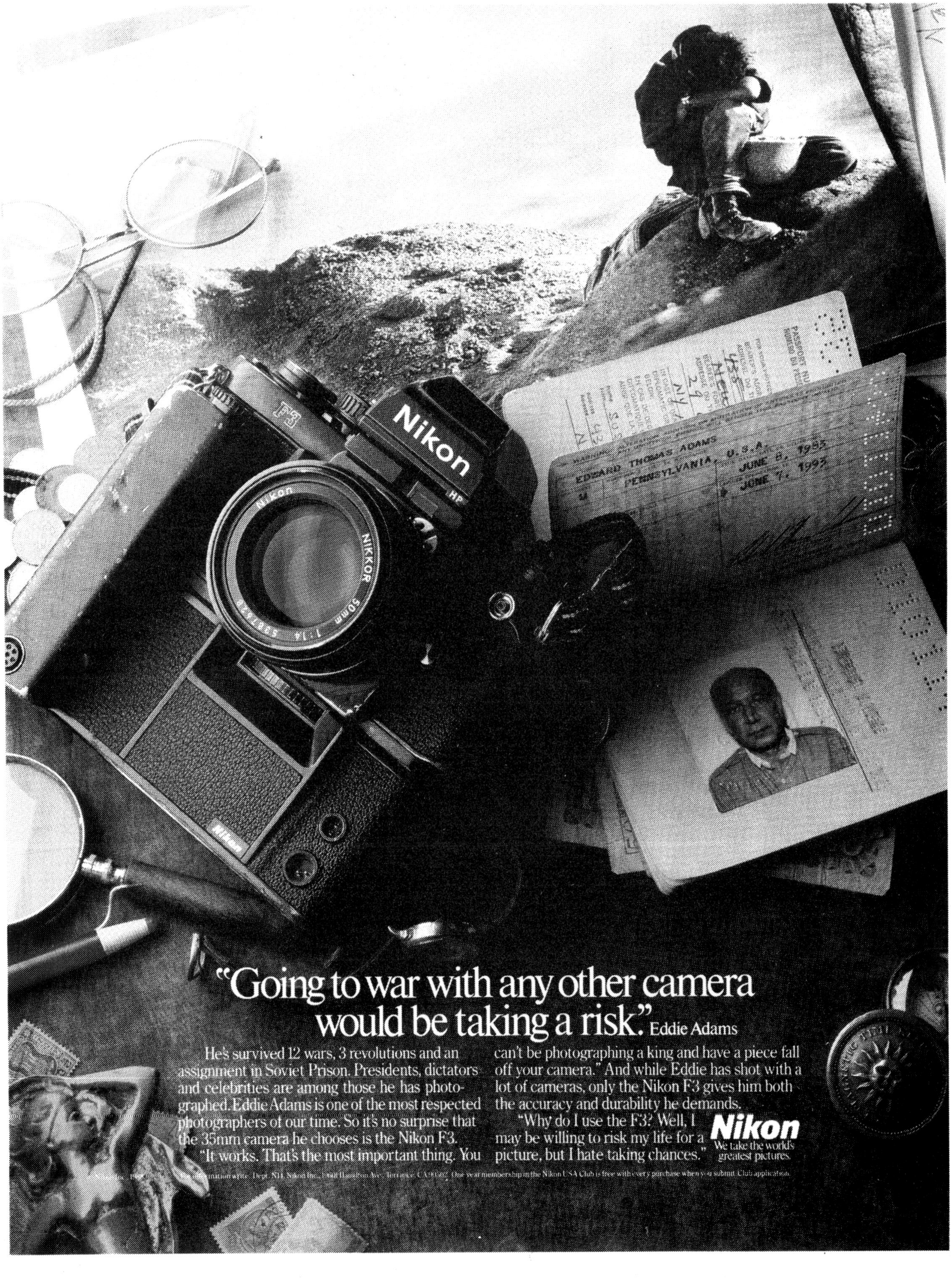
Nikon
F3
NIKKOR 50mm 1:1.4
EDWARD THOMAS ADAMS
PENNSYLVANIA, U.S.A.
"Going to war with any other camera would be taking a risk." Eddie Adams
He's survived 12 wars, 3 revolutions and an assignment in Soviet Prison. Presidents, dictators and celebrities are among those he has photographed. Eddie Adams is one of the most respected photographers of our time. So it's no surprise that the 35mm camera he chooses is the Nikon F3.
"It works. That's the most important thing. You can't be photographing a king and have a piece fall off your camera." And while Eddie has shot with a lot of cameras, only the Nikon F3 gives him both the accuracy and durability he demands.
"Why do I use the F3? Well, I may be willing to risk my life for a picture, but I hate taking chances."
Nikon
We take the world's greatest pictures.
One year membership in the Nikon USA Club is free with every purchase when you submit Club application.

MD-2. (Introduced 1974, discontinued 1985) This motor will function on the F2 series only. The drive selections vary from single exposure up to 5 fps. The MD-2 is a drive only and requires the MB-1, MB-2 or the AC/DC converter MA-4 to power it. It will automatically rewind a 36-exposure roll in 7 seconds; it also features a built-in relay for remote control by wire or radio, auto stops at the end of each roll and an impressive array of accessories. The MB-1 uses 10 AA or 2 nicad MN-1 batteries, which yield 80 rolls with the alkalines or 50 rolls with the nicads. The MB-2 uses 8 AA batteries which yield up to 30 rolls.

MD-3. (Introduced 1978, discontinued 1985) For the F2 series only, this motor provides for single exposures or up to 4 fps. The MD-3 is a drive only and requires power from the MB-1, MB-2 or the AC/DC converter MA-4. The MB-1 uses 10 AA batteries which can expose up to 160 rolls; the MB-2 uses 8 AA batteries which can expose up to 80 rolls.

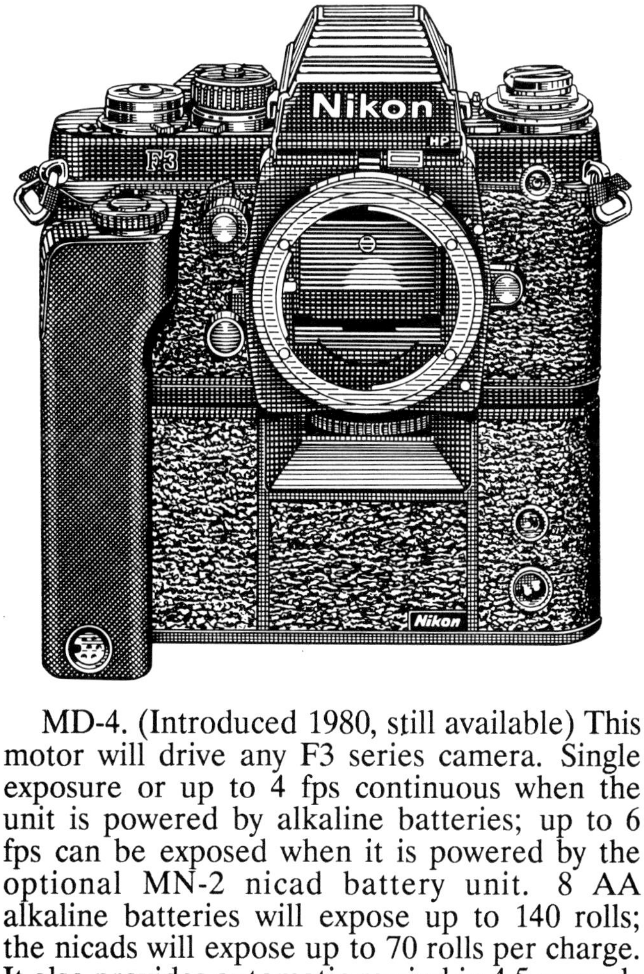

MD-4. (Introduced 1980, still available) This motor will drive any F3 series camera. Single exposure or up to 4 fps continuous when the unit is powered by alkaline batteries; up to 6 fps can be exposed when it is powered by the optional MN-2 nicad battery unit. 8 AA alkaline batteries will expose up to 140 rolls; the nicads will expose up to 70 rolls per charge. It also provides automatic rewind in 4.5 seconds with the alkalines or 8 seconds with the nicads.

MD-11. (Introduced 1977, discontinued 1980) This unit was designed for the FM or the FE. It will also fit on the FM2, FE2 or FA although Nikon does NOT recommend this utilization because there is no internal switching. This results in improper meter functioning and greatly shortened camera battery life. The unit provides single and up to 3.5 fps continuous operation. It is powered by 8 AA batteries which will expose up to 100 rolls.

MD-12. (Introduced 1980, still available) This motor replaced the MD-11. It fits the FM, FM2, FM2N, FE, FE2, FA and offers single exposure or up to 3.5 fps continuous operation. It is powered by 8 AA batteries which will expose up to 100 rolls. The difference between the MD-12 and the MD-11 is that the MD-12 provides internal switching for the FM2, FM2N, FE2 and the FA. It will function just as well as the MD-11 when used on the FM or FE.

MD-14. (Introduced 1982, discontinued 1987) This motor is for the EM, FG and FG-20. It will expose single frames or up to 3.2 fps continuously. It provides a choice of single, 2 fps or 3.5 fps. It is powered by 8 AA batteries which will expose up to 50 rolls.

MF-4. This 250 exposure back and motor drive is for the F3 series bodies. The unit is classified as a back by Nikon, but it includes a motor drive. It is described in Chapter 12.

MD-15. (Introduced 1984, discontinued 1989) Produced for the FA only, it provides single exposure or up to 3.2 fps continuous. Power for the FA body is supplied by the MD-15's batteries, so the FA will function even if the batteries in the FA are exhausted. It is powered by 8 AA batteries which will expose up to 70 rolls.

MD-100. This motor was made to be used only on the F2 High Speed motor driven camera. It provides either continuous or single operation. In the continuous mode, it will drive film at 10, 7.5, 6, 3.5 or 3 fps. It can be fired at the camera or via remote control. The unit is powered by the MB-100 Battery Pack which uses 4 MN-1 nickel cadmium batteries. The pack is charged via the MH-100 Quick Charger. The motor, battery pack and charger were not sold separately. When the camera was purchased, the motor, battery pack and charger were included.

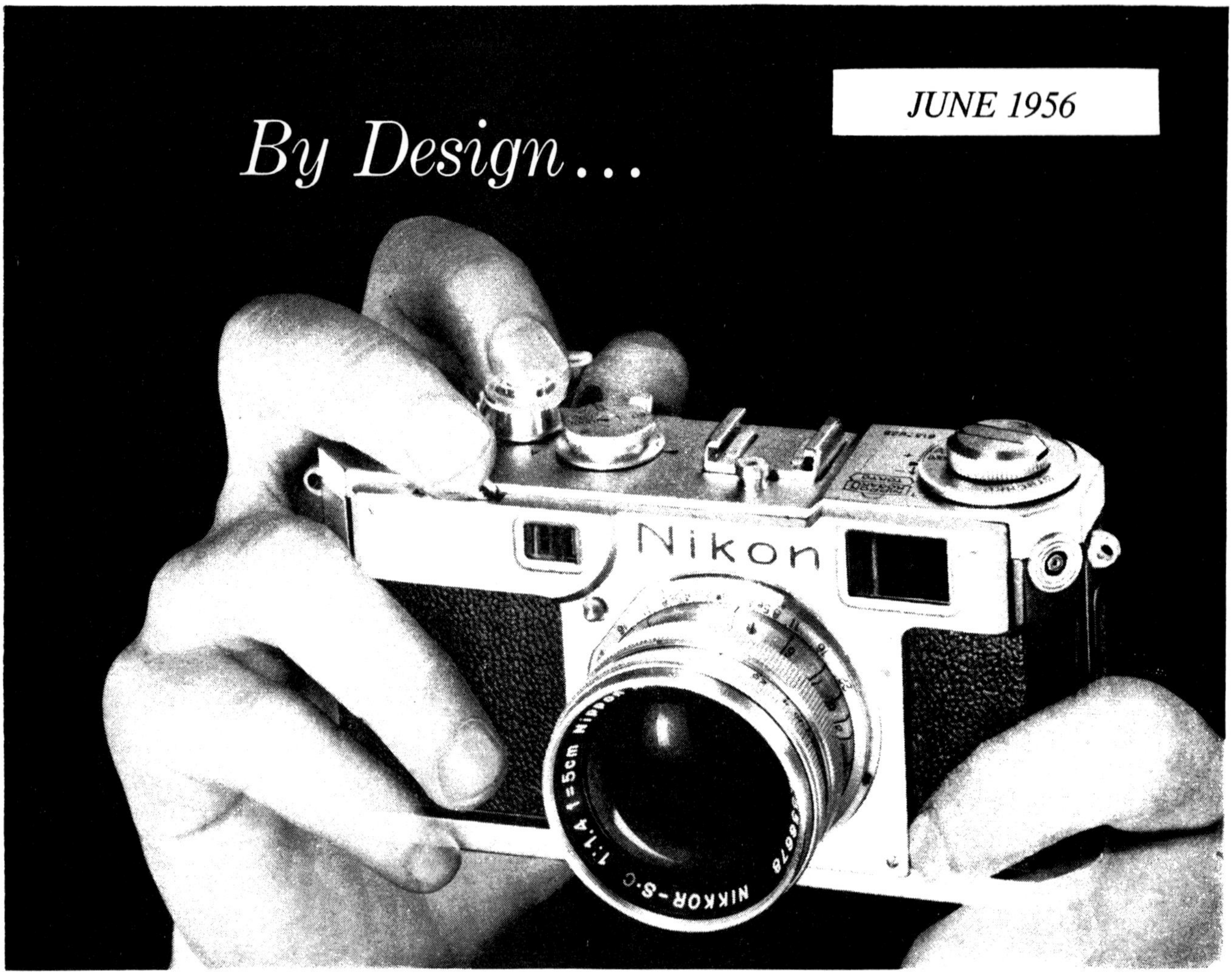

NIKON S-2

The Fastest Handling '35' in the Field

The vital question is – how **fast** can a fine camera deliver its precision and quality.

There is no waste motion when you use a Nikon S-2. You advance the film–focus the lens–and release the shutter using only three fingers. Here's how.

You hold the Nikon in your right hand so that the middle finger is on the focusing wheel–your forefinger rests on the body release–and your thumb is held ready at the transport lever. Now, start ... a short, single stroke of the lever advances the film and 'cocks' the shutter. Immediately, you adjust focus with your middle finger–your forefinger ready for the exposure.

Now, make this 1-2-3 test with any other 35. Advance the film–focus the lens–and shoot. Notice how many more movements are involved ... how much more time it takes ... and you will see how the **Nikon S-2**–by design–is *the fastest handling '35' in the field.*

Nikon S-2 with 50mm Nikkor f2 **$299.50**
Nikon S-2 with 50mm Nikkor f1.4 **345.00**

See Your Nikon Dealer or write to Dept. NF-2

NIPPON KOGAKU TOKYO

NIKON INCORPORATED • 251 Fourth Avenue • New York 10, N.Y.

Research microscopes, contour projectors, surveyors' transits, prism binoculars, and fine optical and ophthalmic instruments

CHAPTER TWELVE

BACKS

INTRODUCTION TO THE SPEED MAGNY ATTACHMENTS. Speed Magnys are backs for the F, F2 and F3 series which primarily produce large Polaroid photographs. These unique backs were designed and manufactured by the Speed Magny Company for use with Nikon F cameras at the 1964 Tokyo Olympic Games. The Model 100 back allowed pros who used Nikons to produce instant prints which could then be wire photoed seconds after each event directly from the stadiums to newspapers anywhere in the world.

After the Games, the US sales force assured the Nikon Corporation that at least 250 Speed Magnys could be sold each year. So Nikon bought out the Speed Magny Co and the first units appeared in the 1966 Nikon catalogue..

Polaroid roll film, Polaroid sheet film, Polaroid film packs or normal sheet film can be used depending on the model Speed Magny selected. Attaching a Speed Magny transforms a body into a large format SLR that retains such facilities as prism eyelevel viewing and focusing, automatic return mirror, automatic diaphragm and through-the-lens metering. While these attachments were originally designed for use with 200mm and longer lenses in order to avoid vignetting, excellent results have been obtained with shorter focal length lenses including fisheyes. The Speed Magny attachments incorporate an optical system which increases the effective focal length of the camera lens. The film holders are built into the backs designed to hold either rolls or packs of Polaroid film, but the user must purchase a holder (not made by Nikon) for the 4 X 5 system.

SPEED MAGNY 100. (Introduced 1966, discontinued 1975) Polaroid back for the Nikon F series only. Has a built-in holder to accept Polaroid 3 1/4 X 4 1/4 film packs such as 107, 108, 664, 665 and 669.

SPEED MAGNY 45. (Introduced 1967, discontinued 1975) 4 X 5 back for the Nikon F. Accepts any standard 4 X 5 holder including Polaroid. It also accepts the Polaroid Pack 550 Back.

SPEED MAGNY RF. (Introduced 1969, discontinued 1979) Polaroid back for the Nikon F. "RF" stands for roll film. It accepts Polaroid 3 1/4 X 4 1/4 roll film. In 1990, only the Type 42 and 47 Polaroid roll films are marketed. Both are black and white.

SPEED MAGNY 100-2 (Introduced 1972, discontinued 1976) Polaroid back for the Nikon F2 series only. Uses Polaroid 3 1/4 X 4 1/4 film packs.

SPEED MAGNY 45-2. (Introduced 1972, discontinued 1979) 4 X 5 back for the Nikon F2 series.

SPEED MAGNY 100-3. (Introduced 1982, discontinued 1987) Polaroid back for the F3. This performs the same function as the 100 and 100-2, but it is improved. It incorporates a 50mm f/2.8 El Nikkor (enlarging lens) to enlarge the image so that complete coverage of the 3 1/4 X 4 1/4 image is achieved. Vignetting is virtually eliminated on this model.

Unique attachments for Nikon F produce large photos with Polaroid and regular film

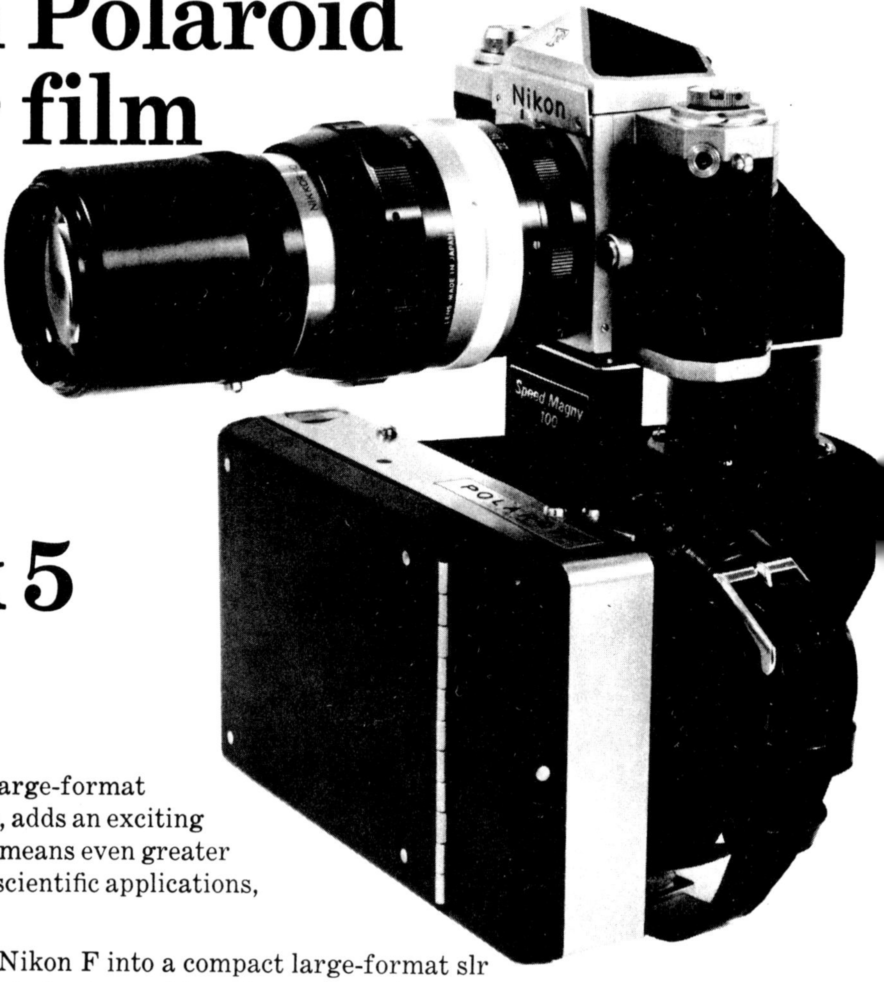

SPEED MAGNY

$3^1/_4$ x $4^1/_4$ • 4 x 5

The ability to use a Nikon F for "instant" large-format photography, in color and black-and-white, adds an exciting dimension to the entire Nikon F system. It means even greater versatility for commercial, industrial and scientific applications, as well as for news and sports coverage.

Attaching a Speed Magny transforms the Nikon F into a compact large-format slr that retains such facilities as prism eyelevel viewing and focusing, automatic-return mirror, automatic-reopen diaphragm, thru-the-lens metering, and the use of Nikkor optics.

There are 3 Speed Magny attachments. Model 100 accepts Polaroid® 3¼ x 4¼ film packs. Model 45 accepts standard 4 x 5 holders for Polaroid as well as regular sheet film. Model 'RF' uses Polaroid 3¼ x 4¼ roll film.

Speed Magny attachments were originally intended for use with 200mm and longer lenses to avoid vignetting. However, excellent results have been obtained with shorter lenses, too, including the Fisheye Nikkor.

The Speed Magny embodies an optical system which increases the effective focal length of the camera lens 3.2 times with the Models 100 and 'RF', and 4.1 times with the Model 45. Even when used for long-range telephotography, the Magny-equipped Nikon F is far smaller and lighter than many conventional large-format cameras.

Optical System

The Speed Magny optical system comprises a magnifying relay lens in combination with a coated field lens and 2 optically flat, surface-coated mirrors. With Models 100 and 'RF', the system increases the size of the picture 3.2 times to fill the 3¼ x 4¼ Polaroid format. Image size and picture angle are the same as if taken with a lens 3.2 times longer than the one used. With Model 45, the increase is 4.1 times.

Because of the difference in proportions between the 35mm and 3¼ x 4¼ /4 x 5 formats, slightly less picture length is recorded on the film than is shown in the Nikon F finder.

Use of Speed Magny units requires increases in exposure over those normally indicated by the emulsion speed: an 18-time increase with Models 100 and 'RF', and 20-time increase with Model 45. Photomic T TN and FTN systems can be programmed accordingly.

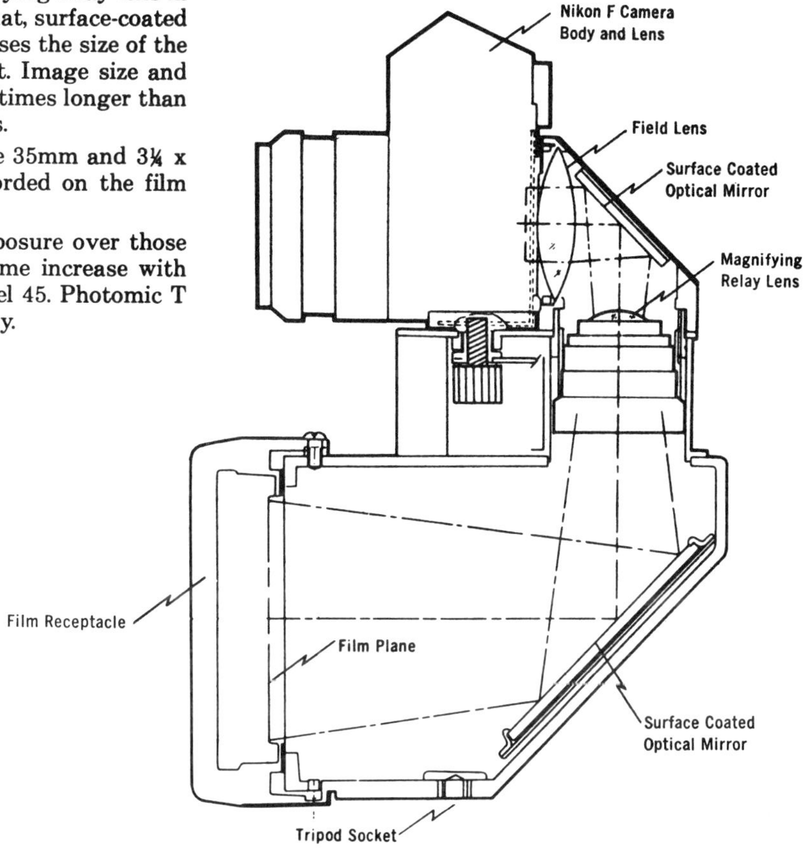

Film Holders

Speed Magny 100 has a built-in holder for Polaroid 3¼ x 4¼ film packs. Speed Magny 45 accepts standard holders for 4 x 5 Polaroid and regular sheet film. Speed Magny 'RF' accepts Polaroid 3¼ x 4¼ roll film.

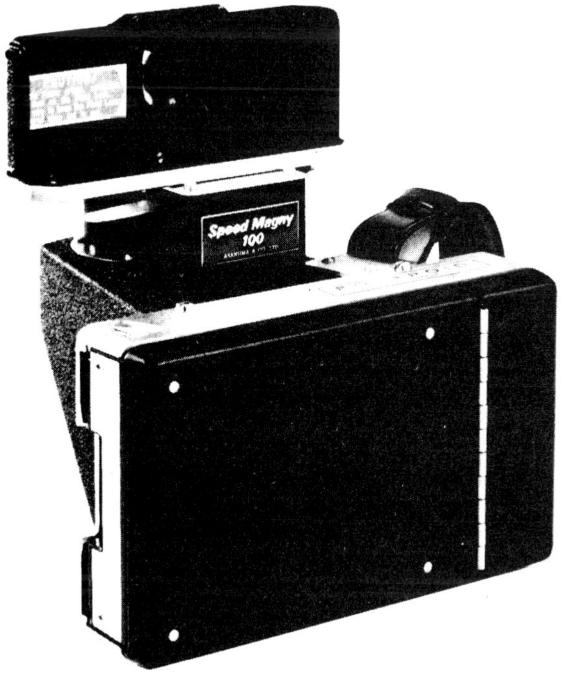

Technical Data

	Speed Magny 100	Speed Magny 'RF'	Speed Magny 45
Film format	3¼ x 4¼	3¼ x 4¼	4 x 5
Magnification	3.2x	3.2x	4.1x
Exposure increase factor	18	18	20
Effective rating of A SA 3000 film	ASA 170	ASA 170	ASA 150
Film holder	built in	built-in	extra
Dimensions:			
Depth	6.69″	7″	7.48″
Width	7.48″	12½″	8.66″
Height (to top of Standard Prism Finder)	9.65″	10″	9.84″
Weight (less camera)	4 lbs. 3 oz.	4 lbs. 12oz.	4 lbs. 3 oz.

Lens Chart

Lens on Nikon F	Effective focal length	
	Model 45	Model 100 and 'RF'
105mm f4	431mm	336mm
105mm f2.5	431mm	336mm
135mm f3.5	554mm	432mm
200mm f4	820mm	640mm
300mm f4.5	1230mm	960mm
400mm f4.5	1640mm	1280mm
600mm f5.6	2460mm	1920mm
800mm f8	3280mm	2560mm
1200mm f11	4920mm	3840mm
Zoom 85mm—250mm f4	349mm—1025mm	272mm—800mm
Zoom 50mm—300mm f4.5	205mm—1230mm	160mm—960mm
Zoom 200mm—600mm f9.5	820mm—2460mm	640mm—1920mm
Medical Nikkor 200mm f5.6	0.27X—12.3X	0.21X—9.6X

Note: Lenses other than those listed may be used. In each case the effective focal length is increased proportionately. With so lenses shorter than 200mm, there is the possibility of slight vignetting and image degradation around the edges of the print.

ON INC., Garden City, New York 11530. Subsidiary of Ehrenreich Photo-Optical Industries, Inc. Other offices in Chicago, Dallas, San Francisco, and Silver Spring, Md.

F-250. (Introduced 1959, discontinued 1984) This unit is both a back and a motor drive. It provides for the use of 33 feet, 250-exposure rolls. It is described in the previous chapter on motor drives.

MF-1. (Introduced 1974, discontinued 1985) This is a 250-exposure magazine designed to be used with the MD-1 or MD-2 on any F2 model camera. It has a separate shutter release button and two frame counters. One counter shows the number of frames exposed while the other shows the number remaining.

MF-2. (Introduced 1974, discontinued 1985) For the F2 series only. Used in conjunction with optional bulk film cassettes accepts 100-foot loads of film which yield up to 750 exposures per roll. The spools supplied with the film from most manufacturers can be loaded directly into the cassettes which makes the operation simple. The back has its own built-in motor which will drive the film at speeds up to 4 fps. Other controls and functions are the same as the MF-1.

MF-3. (Introduced 1974, discontinued 1985) For the F2 series only. This back can only be used in conjunction with the motor drive, MD-2. The back provides for automatic film rewind stop. The LED indicator lights up when rewinding is complete, which takes approximately 7 seconds for a 36-exposure roll.

MF-4. (Introduced 1982, still available) This unit is a 250-exposure magazine for the F3 series cameras. It has a built-in micromotor to drive the take-up magazine, a separate shutter release and both an additive and a subtractive frame counter. When the subtractive counter reaches zero, the drive automatically stops. It operates in the single mode or continuously up to 6 fps. It is powered by 8 AA batteries, an optional nicad unit (MN-2) or AC/DC converter (MA-4). It can expose twenty 33-foot rolls on one set of AA batteries.

MF-6. (Introduced 1980, discontinued 1985) This camera back was designed to be used exclusively with the MD-4 motor drive. It enables automatic film rewind and stops with the film leader outside the cartridge providing greater convenience in motor drive photography. As soon as rewinding is complete, the right hand LED indicator lights up.

MF-6B. (Introduced 1984, still available) Designed to be used with the MD-4 motor drive on the F3, this back enables automatic film rewind and stops with the film leader outside the cartridge.

MF-12. (Introduced 1982, discontinued 1984) This unit is for the FM, FM2, FM2N, FE and the FE2; it records the date (year/month/day or the time (date/hour/minute) on the film as it is exposed. It is supplied with a connecting cord which must be connected to the PC terminal on the camera body, without which the back will not imprint data on the film.

MF-14. (Introduced 1982, still available) This back fits F3 cameras. It imprints either the year/month/day, the day/hour/minute or it will number the frames at the moment of exposure. The frames can be numbered with any sequence from -2 to +2000. It has a built-in clock which can be set to ring every day at a set time.

MF-15. (Introduced 1982, discontinued 1987) Made for the FG, this motor imprints either the year/month/day, the day/hour/minute or it will number the frames at the moment of exposure. The frames can be numbered with any sequence from -2 to +2000. It has a built-in clock which can be set to beep at a previously set time.

MF-16. (Introduced 1983, still available) This back is for the FM2, FM2N, FE2 or FA. It will not work on the FM or FE since these cameras do not have data back contacts. It imprints either the year/month/day, the day/hour/minute or it will number the frames at the moment of exposure. It has a built-in clock which can be set to beep at a previously set time.

MF-17. (Introduced 1983, still available) This is a data back which can be used only with the 250 exposure back magazine MF-4. It is for the F3 series and imprints either the year/month/day, the hour/minute/second or a handwritten memo. The imprint is via a short duration electronic strobe which operates even during continuous operation of the motor drive. It is also usable in conjunction with Nikon speedlights.

MF-18. (Introduced 1985, still available) This back is for the F3 series in conjunction with the motor drive MD-4. It imprints either the year/month/day, the hour/minute/second or the frame number in the space between the frames, thus providing information without affecting the image.

MF-19. (Introduced 1985, still available) This unit is for the N2000 and the N2020. It imprints the year/month/day, the month/day/year, the day/hour/minute or it will count and number frames from 1 to 999999. It is automatically programmed and adjusted for leap years. It can be programmed to function as a timer or a time-lapse device. In the timer mode, up to 99 shots can be taken at a desired time each day for up to 99 days, or a selected day of each month for up to 99 months. The intervalometer function allows setting intervals between successive shootings and varying the number of shots per shooting. Timing intervals can be set for a maximum of 99 hours, 59 minutes, 59 seconds. Up to 99 shots can be taken between intervals up to 99 times. When used with the N2020, it will perform in the autofocus function, i.e. the shutter is automatically released when the picture is in focus.

MF-20. (Introduced 1988, still available) This data back, for the N8008 only, imprints either the year/month/day, day/hour/minute (24 hour clock), day/month/year or no imprint.

MF-21. (Introduced 1988, still available) This data back is for the N8008 only. It imprints a choice of 8 different data: year/month/day, month/day/year, day/month/year, day/hour/minute, frame count, sequence number, desired fixed number or shutter speed and aperture setting. It allows shooting up to 19 continuous frames, each with a different exposure. It allows taking a specified number of shots at specified intervals. The MF-21 facilitates long time exposures and the freeze focus function.

MF-22. (Introduced 1988, still available) A data back for the F4 only, It imprints either year/month/day, day/hour/minute (24 hour clock), month/day/year, day/month/year or no imprint.

MF-23. (Introduced 1988, still available) For the F4 only. This multi-control back will imprint data either between the frames or on the frame itself. It will print not only the year, month, day, hour, minute and second in assorted combinations, but also a fixed number, frame count, shutter speed, aperture or exposure combination. It can also be used as an intervalometer extending time exposure duration up to 999 hours, tripping the shutter when the subject enters a predetermined position; performs automatic bracketing functions, delays exposure for a preset time up to 99 hours, sounds an alarm at any given second or sounds an alarm when the film reaches a preset number of frames. It can also be programmed to lock the shutter and sound the alarm when the film reaches a preset number of frames.

MF-24. (Introduced 1989, still available) This is a 250-exposure back for F4 only. It is used with two 250-exposure MZ-1 magazines for loading up to 10 meters (33 feet) of bulk film. It must be powered by an external source, either the Nikon High Speed Battery Pack MB-21 or the External Power Regulator MB-22.

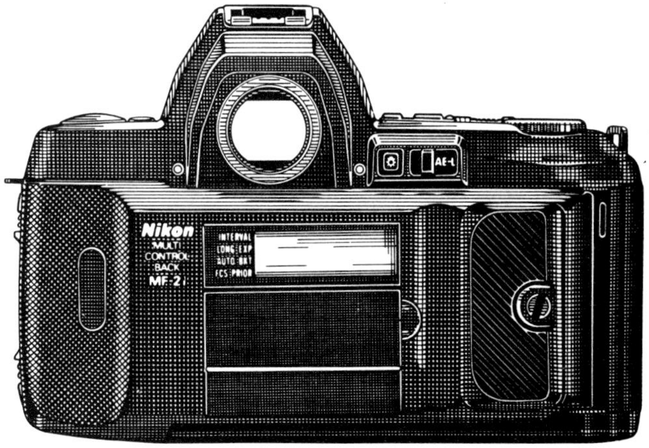

Nikkor Lens Table

Description	Optical Construction	Picture Angle	Minimum f-stop	Closest Focusing Distance	Filter Size	Lens Hood	Lens Case	Weight	Dimensions	TC 201	TC 301	TC 14A	TC 14B
Wide-angle													
13 mm f/5.6 Nikkor	16-12	118	f/22	0.3 m (1 ft)	4 Filters Supplied	built-in	CL-14	1200	115 × 99 (88.5)	○	x	○	x
15 mm f/3.5 Nikkor	14-11	110	f/22	0.3 m (1 ft)	4 Filters Supplied	built-in	CL-17	630	90 × 94 (83.5)	○	x	○	x
18 mm f/3.5 Nikkor	11-10	100	f/22	0.25 m (0.9 ft)	72 mm	HK-9	CL-37	350	75 × 72.5 (61.5)	○	x	△	x
20 mm f/2.8 Nikkor	12-9	94	f/22	0.25 m (0.85 ft)	62 mm	HK-14	CL-30S, No. 61	260	65 × 54 (42.5)	○	x	○	x
24 mm f/2 Nikkor	11-10	84	f/22	0.3 m (1 ft)	52 mm	HK-2	CL-31S, No. 61	300	63 × 63 (51.5)	○	x	○	x
24 mm f/2.8 Nikkor	9-9	84	f/22	0.3 m (1 ft)	52 mm	HN-1	CL-30S, No. 61	250	63 × 57 (46)	○	x	○	x
28 mm f/2 Nikkor	9-8	74	f/22	0.25 m (0.9 ft)	52 mm	HN-1	CP-31S, No. 61	360	63 × 68.5 (58.5)	○	x	○	x
28 mm f/2.8 Nikkor	8-8	74	f/22	0.2 m (0.7 ft)	52 mm	HN-2	CL-30S, No. 61	250	63 × 53 (44.5)	○	x	○	x
35 mm f/1.4 Nikkor	9-7	62	f/16	0.3 m (1 ft)	52 mm	HN-3	CL-31S, No. 61	400	67.5 × 74 (62)	○*	x	○	x
35 mm f/2 Nikkor	8-6	62	f/22	0.3 m (1 ft)	52 mm	HN-3	CL-30S, No. 61	280	63 × 59.5 (51.5)	○	x	○	x
Normal													
50 mm f/1.2 Nikkor	7-6	46	f/16	0.5 m (1.7 ft)	52 mm	HS-12, HR-2	CL-34A, No. 61	380	68.5 × 59 (47.5)	○	x	△	x
50 mm f/1.4 Nikkor	7-6	46	f/16	0.45 m (1.5 ft)	52 mm	HS-9, HR-1	CL-34A, No. 61	250	63 × 50.5 (40)	○	x	○	x
50 mm f/1.8 Nikkor	6-5	46	f/22	0.45 m (1.5 ft)	52 mm	HS-11, HR-1	CL-30S, No. 61	220	63.5 × 48 (37)	○	x	○	x
Telephoto													
85 mm f/1.4 Nikkor	7-5	28 30	f/16	0.85 m (3 ft)	72 mm	HN-20	CL-17, No. 62	620	80.5 × 72.5 (64.5)	○*	x	○	x
85 mm f/2 Nikkor	5-5	28 30	f/22	0.85 m (3 ft)	52 mm	HS-10	CL-31S, No. 61	310	63 × 60.5 (52.5)	○	x	○	x
105 mm f/1.8 Nikkor	5-5	23 20	f/22	1 m (3.5 ft)	62 mm	built-in	CL-15S, No. 62	580	78.5 × 88.5 (80.5)	○*	x	○	x
105 mm f/2.5 Nikkor	5-4	23 20	f/22	1 m (3.5 ft)	52 mm	built-in	CL-32S, No. 62	435	64 × 77.5 (69.5)	○	x	△	x
135 mm f/2 Nikkor	6-4	18	f/22	1.3 m (4.5 ft)	72 mm	built-in	CL-15S, No. 62	860	80.5 × 103 (93.5)	○*	x	○	x
135 mm f/2.8 Nikkor	5-4	18	f/32	1.3 m (4.5 ft)	52 mm	built-in	CL-32S, No. 62	435	64 × 91.5 (83.5)	△	x	○	○
180 mm f/2.8 Nikkor ED	5-5	13 40	f/32	1.8 m (6 ft)	72 mm	built-in	CL-35A	800	78.5 × 138 (130)	○*	x	○	x
200 mm f/2 Nikkor IF-ED	10-8	12 20	f/22	2.5 m (10 ft)	122 mm	built-in	CL-63	2400	138 × 222 (214)	○	x	△	○
200 mm f/4 Nikkor	5-5	12 20	f/32	2 m (7 ft)	52 mm	built-in	CL-13, No. 63	510	65 × 124 (116)	△	x	○	x
300 mm f/2 Nikkor IF-ED	11-8	8 10	f/16	4 m (13 ft)	52 mm	built-in	CT-300	7100	195 × 346.5 (338.5)	△	○	△	○
300 mm f/2.8 Nikkor IF-ED	8-6	8 10	f/22	4 m (13 ft)	122 39	built-in	CL-63	2500	138 × 249 (241)	x	○	△	○
300 mm f/4.5 Nikkor	6-5	8 10	f/32	3.5 m (11.5 ft)	72 mm	built-in	CL-20A	1200	78.5 × 202 (194)	x	○	△	○
300 mm f/4.5 Nikkor IF-ED	7-6	8 10	f/32	2.5 m (10 ft)	72 mm	built-in	CL-36	990	80 × 200 (192)	x	○	x	○
400 mm f/2.8 Nikkor IF-ED	11-9	6 10	f/22	4 m (13 ft)	52 mm	built-in	CT-400	6050	172 × 342 (333.5)	△	○	△	○
400 mm f/3.5 Nikkor IF-ED	8-6	6 10	f/22	4.5 m (15 ft)	122 39	built-in	CL-61A, No. 57	2800	134 × 304 (296)	x	○	△	○
400 mm f/5.6 Nikkor IF-ED	7-6	6 10	f/32	4 m (13 ft)	72 mm	built-in	CL-27A	1200	85 × 262 (254)	x	○	x	○
600 mm f/4 Nikkor IF-ED	8-6	4 10	f/22	6.5 m (24 ft)	160 39	built-in	CT-601	6300	177 × 460 (452)	x	○	x	○
600 mm f/5.6 Nikkor IF-ED	7-6	4 10	f/32	5.5 m (20 ft)	122 39	built-in	CL-62A, No. 57	2700	134 × 382 (374)	x	○	x	○
800 mm f/8 Nikkor IF-ED	9-7	3	f/32	10 m (35 ft)	122 39	built-in	CT-1203	3300	134 × 460 (452)	x	○	x	○
1200 mm f/11 Nikkor IF-ED	9-8	2	f/32	14 m (45 ft)	122 39	built-in	CT-1203	3900	134 × 577 (569)	x	○	x	○
Reflex													
500 mm f/8 Reflex-Nikkor	6-6	5	–	1.5 m (5.25 ft)	39 mm	HN-27 Supplied	CL-39	840	89 × 116 (104.5)	○	x	○	x
1000 mm f/11 Reflex-Nikkor	5-5	2 30	–	8 m (25 ft)	39 mm	built-in	CL-29	1900	119 × 241 (233.5)	△	□	△	□
2000 mm f/11 Reflex-Nikkor	5-5	1 10	–	18 m (60 ft)	built-in	–	Hard Case	17500	262 × 598 (593.5)	△	○	x	○
Zoom													
35-70 mm f/3.3-3.5 Zoom-Nikkor	8-7	62 -34 20	f/22	0.35 m (1 ft)	52 mm	HN-2	CL-31S, No. 61	255	63 × 69 (61)	○	x	○	x
35-105 mm f/3.5-4.5 Zoom-Nikkor	16-12	62 -23 20	f/22	0.27 m	52 mm	HK-11	CL-33S, No. 63	510	64 × 95 (86.5)	○	x	○	x
35-135 mm f/3.5-4.5 Zoom-Nikkor	15-14	62 -18	f/22	0.4 m (1.3 ft)	62 mm	HN-22	CL-33S, No. 62	600	68 × 112 (104)	○	x	○	x
80-200 mm f/4 Zoom-Nikkor	13-9	30 10 -12 20	f/32	1.2 m (4 ft)	62 mm	HN-23	CL-35A, No. 63	810	73 × 162 (154)	○	x	△	x
50-300 mm f/4.5 Zoom-Nikkor ED	15-11	46 -8 10	f/32	2.5 m (8.5 ft)	95 mm	HK-5	CL-64, CE-2	1950	98 × 247 (239)	○	x	○	x
100-300 mm f/5.6 Zoom-Nikkor	14-10	24 20 -8 10	f/32	0.7 m	62 mm	HK-24	CL-40	930	74 × 207 (199)	○	x	○	x
180-600 mm f/8 Zoom-Nikkor ED	18-11	13 40 -4 10	f/32	2.5 m (8.5 ft)	95 mm	HN-16	CZ-1860	3600	105 × 402 (395)	x	○	x	○
Fisheye													
6 mm f/2.8 Fisheye-Nikkor	12-9	220	f/22	0.25 m (0.9 ft)	built-in	–	Hard Case	5200	236 × 171 (160)	○	x	○	x
8 mm f/2.8 Fisheye-Nikkor	10-8	180	f/22	0.3 m (1 ft)	built-in	–	CL-11	1100	123 × 139 (128)	○	x	○	x
16 mm f/2.8 Fisheye-Nikkor	8-5	180	f/22	0.3 m (1 ft)	4 Filters Supplied	–	CL-30S, Nr 61	330	63 × 66 (55.5)	○	x	○	x

CHAPTER THIRTEEN

CAMERA LENSES

I. EVOLUTION OF THE NIKON SYSTEM

BAYONET LENSES FOR RANGEFINDER CAMERAS. The first Nikon camera was styled after the German Contax of the thirties and so was its lens mount. Contax lenses seem to function on Nikon rangefinder cameras and vise versa, but the rangefinders of the two cameras are cammed differently which produces focusing problems. This is not as pronounced with lenses of 55mm or less focal lengths because the depth of focus overcomes the slight differences, but images from longer lenses will be noticeably out of focus. Nikon manufactured some lenses cammed for Contax cameras. These can be identified by a "C" engraved on the lens barrel. This "C" should not be confused with the "C" (located on the ring between the front element and the filter retaining ring) which signifies that the lens is coated.

THE NIKON F MOUNT. In 1959, Nikon introduced the Nikon F, the company's first single lens reflex camera. At the same time, a bayonet lens mount was introduced which is called the Nikon F mount. All Nikon SLR and Nikkormat (as well as the one lens-interchangeable Nikkorex) cameras use this mount. Nikon rangefinder and underwater (Nikonos) cameras do NOT use the F mount.

NON-METER COUPLED (NMC) LENSES. Most Nikkor lenses utilize some method of communicating the aperture setting to the camera body, but a few do not. These lenses may have preset diaphragms and require stop-down metering or, as in the case of mirror lenses, they may have no iris at all so there is nothing to couple. Some current examples of non-meter coupled lenses are the PC and Reflex (mirror) lenses.

AUTO NIKKORS. At the same time Nikon introduced the Nikon F, Auto Nikkors were made available in the F mount. The mount allows the lens and camera body to communicate with one another through levers on both. This permits automatic diaphragm operation and full aperture metering. Automatic diaphragm operation means that the photographer sees the scene in the viewfinder at the maximum aperture of the lens. When the shutter is released, the lens stops down to the selected aperture and re-opens after the exposure. Full aperture metering means that the metering system built into the camera body or prism can be utilized with the lens at maximum aperture.

NON-AUTOMATIC INDEXING (NON-AI) LENSES. Indexing means that the lens aperture settings are communicated to the camera body. Before 1977, Nikon systems did not automatically index. The photographer had to set both the film speed (ASA) and the maximum lens aperture on the light meter dials. Later, a semiautomatic system was devised that reduced, but did not eliminate extra steps when changing lenses.

Both of these old systems are referred to by most photographers as Non-AI, abbreviated in this book to NAI. NAI lenses are identifiable by their solid meter coupling shoes, the famous rabbit ears. (AI and AIS have little holes in each ear or, in the case of E and AF lenses, they have no ears at all.)

When a NAI lens is mounted to a camera, a pin on the body or the prism housing fits between the ears, thus coupling the lens to the light meter. During the mounting process, the pin must be placed at a register point, the iris ring on the lens set to f/5.6 and the bayonet engaged and locked while keeping the pin between the ears.

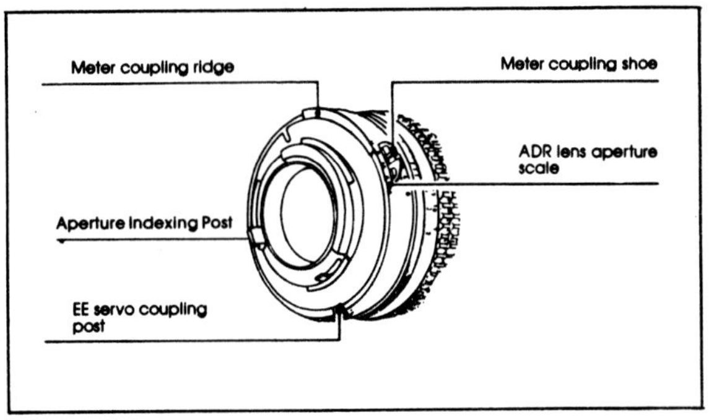

AUTOMATIC INDEXING (AI) LENSES. Automatic indexing was introduced by Nikon in 1977. Before then, Nikkor lenses employed semiautomatic indexing (see Non-AI lenses). Automatic means that when the lens is mounted, the indexing feature is automatically engaged. The engagement is accomplished by a projection on the back of the lens which Nikon calls a Meter-Coupling Ridge. AI lenses can be mounted on all Nikon bodies. They will automatically index with bodies designed for them and they will also semi-automatically index on earlier bodies with the registration pins. AI (and AIS) lenses are distinguished from Non-AI lenses in that the shoes have little holes in them (one in each ear to facilitate Aperture Direct Readout of the aperture in the viewfinder) or they have no ears at all (E and AF). As AI lenses were introduced, most non-AI lenses were phased out.

MODIFIED AI NIKKOR LENSES. A modified AI Nikkor is a non-AI Auto Nikkor which has been modified to AI specifications. (See the chapter in this book on AI conversions.

AUTOMATIC INDEXING-SHUTTER (AIS) LENSES. AIS lenses were introduced in 1984. AIS lenses accomplish everything AI lenses do plus operating in shutter preferred and programmed modes with camera bodies which include these features. AIS lenses can be identified by the signal groove in the mount. Additionally, the smallest aperture on the scale is colored orange. AIS lenses can be mounted on all Nikon SLR bodies. They have the same shoe with holes as do AI lenses which allow them to index with older bodies (except E and AF). When AIS was introduced, AI lenses were discontinued. AIS lenses are gradually being phased out and being replaced with AF lenses (which are also AIS).

E LENSES. E lenses were introduced in 1979. They are also AIS, but they do not have a meter coupling shoe as do non-AI, AI and AIS lenses. As a consequence, E lenses do not meter couple with earlier bodies. E lenses are less expensive than Nikkor lenses. The savings was accomplished by the substitution of some plastic parts in place of metal as well as the elimination of the shoe, plus the utilization of different optical formulas with fewer elements. It is possible to have the shoe added to an E lens.

AUTOFOCUS (AF) LENSES. Nikon AF lenses are made to focus automatically when used with a Nikon autofocus camera body (F3AF, N2020, N4004, N8008, F4). All Nikon AF lenses are on AIS mounts. AF lenses can be used on ANY Nikon SLR. AF lenses do not have shoes and consequently will not meter couple with pre-1977 bodies. They can, however, be used in the stop-down mode. It is possible to have the shoe added to AF lenses.

AF Nikkors are easy to identify because they say, "AF Nikkor" on them. They are earless (unless retrofitted) otherwise all factors regarding AI and AIS lenses also apply. They focus manually on all Nikon bodies and automatically on all Nikon autofocus bodies. They also focus manually on autofocus bodies by switching the focus mode selector (located below the lens release button on the camera body) to "M." No preparation is necessary in order to mount and focus an AF lens on a manual focus body.

Some AF lenses also have an A/M switch on the lens. When the lens is switched to M, drag is applied to the focusing ring which makes focusing more positive and less easy to inadvertently move. At the end of 1989, the AF lenses with an A/M switch were: 60mm F/2.8 Micro, 180mm f/2.8 ED-IF, 300mm f/2.8 ED-IF, 300mm f/4 ED-IF, 80-200mm f/2.8.

"N" LENSES. Recently Nikon has been adding an "N" designation to some lenses. The "N" stands for new. These "new" lenses have a textured metallic finish and a wider focusing ring. Otherwise they are the same. When a lens is offered with the N, the lens it displaces is no longer available from Nikon Inc. An example is the AF 35-135mm f/3.5-f/4.5. This lens was introduced in 1986. In 1989, an N version was announced and the original is no longer available. Some dealers, however, will have stocks of the old, or non-N lenses after an N version is introduced. So far, the list and dealer prices have remained the same. If contemplating a new lens purchase, it would be wise to examine the N improvements and then determine if an N version is available.

P. The 500mm 4.0 ED-IF is designated "P." The P stands for the P in CPU (Central Processing Unit or computer). This means the lens is equipped with electronic circuitry to enable its use in all exposure modes with the N series autofocus bodies.

EARLIER LENSES ON LATER CAMERAS. Can lenses without AI or AIS be used with AI or AIS camera bodies? Earlier Nikkor lenses, basically those produced before 1977 (non-AI and manual), can be used on most later Nikon bodies, but only in the stop-down metering mode. These lenses can only be used on those AI cameras having a movable meter coupling lever. The lever must be locked up before the lens can be mounted. A careful reading of the camera instruction book is recommended. Non-AI lenses CANNOT be mounted on the FM2, FE2, FG and EM camera bodies or any of the N series.

A camera with the AI or AIS feature contains a meter-coupling lever which must be locked up to permit exposure measurement via the stop-down method. Should a lens without AI, AIS or any non-meter coupled lens (of any brand) be forced onto the camera when the coupling lever is not locked up, damage can result. The instruction book for each camera body gives details of procedures for stop-down metering. The AI index coupler on the FM2, FE2, FG, EM and N bodies is not movable. Therefore, do not attempt to force lenses which do not easily mount.

AI, AIS AND AF LENSES ON EARLIER BODIES. The Nikon F bayonet mount is unchanged since its introduction. When an AI or AIS lens is used on an earlier camera body, it will mount and operate in the same way as do non-AI lenses. This is because of the inclusion of the shoe on AI and AIS lenses. This is NOT true of E and AF lenses which do not have the shoe. E and AF lenses can be used, but only in the stop-down metering mode. Rabbit ears can be installed on most Nikkors with automatic diaphragms. All E lenses can be fitted as well as most AF lenses. AF lenses with two dimples on the iris ring near the f/5.6 marking definitely can be retrofitted. If there are no dimples, only a qualified repair person can tell (see the authorized repair list).

II. SPECIAL APPLICATION LENSES

BELLOWS MOUNT LENSES. Some Nikkors are made for use solely with Nikon bellows attachments. The lenses include either an F mount or the Nikon rangefinder Contax-type mount. But they cannot be focused unless they are used in conjunction with either a bellows attachment or extension tubes. No data is transmitted between the lens and body, so if an internal camera metering system is used, it must be the stop-down mode.

CLOSE-UP ATTACHMENT LENSES. Some photographers call these lenses diopters. They increase magnification but have no effect on exposure. They come in various strengths and can be stacked together to provide even greater magnification. Unlike some after-market lenses of this type, Nikon diopters are of fine quality. They are described in detail in Chapter 16: Close-Up Equipment.

ED NIKKORS. These lenses are constructed with special glass called extra-low dispersion, hence "ED." These lenses allow better registration of colors and fewer aberrations thus producing a sharper image. They are always more expensive than non-ED lenses and usually in short supply.

IF NIKKORS. IF means internal focusing. Most photographic lenses use screw-thread helicoids to move lens elements back and forth or the entire lens is moved back and forth to effect focusing. IF lenses use a cam which does not change the length of the lens. The cam also allows the photographer to focus more rapidly with less barrel rotation. Some IF lenses have larger maximum apertures and/or allow closer minimum focusing.

ED-IF (EDIF) NIKKORS. Some Nikkors are both ED and IF in which case they include the designation ED-IF.

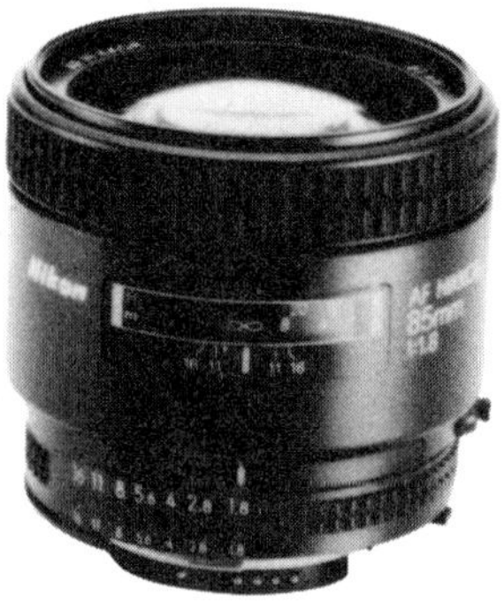

85mm f1.8 AF NIKKOR

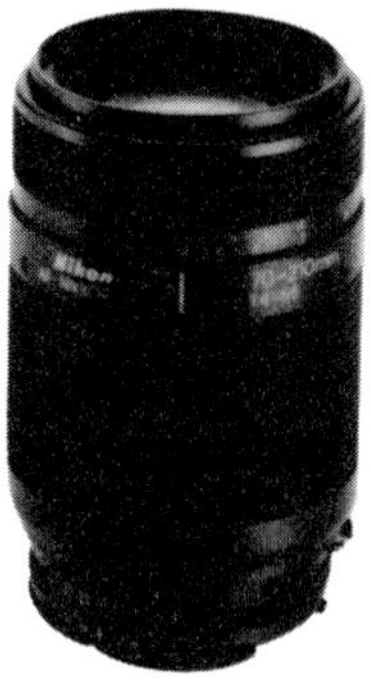

70-210mm f4.5-5.6 AF NIKKOR ZOOM

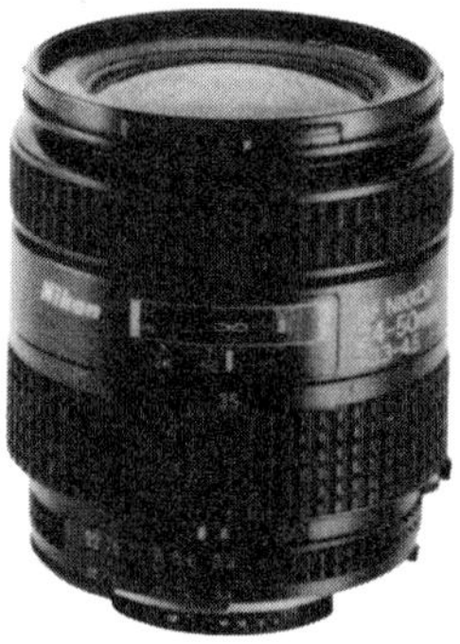

24-50mm f3.3-4.5 AF NIKKOR ZOOM

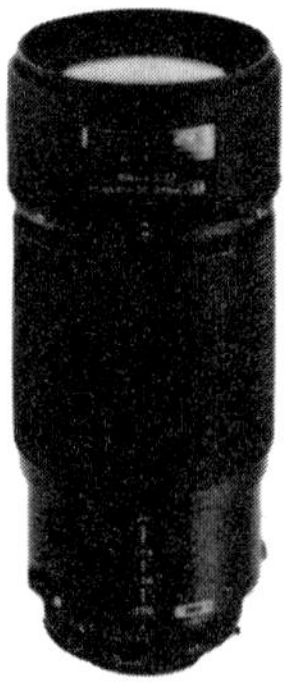

80-200mm f2.8 AF NIKKOR ZOOM

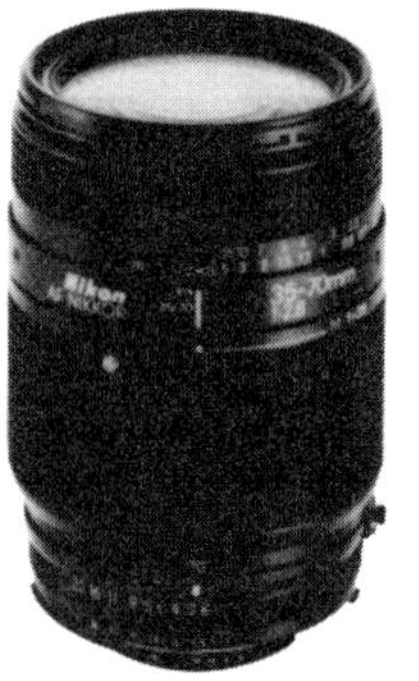

35-70mm f2.8 AF NIKKOR ZOOM

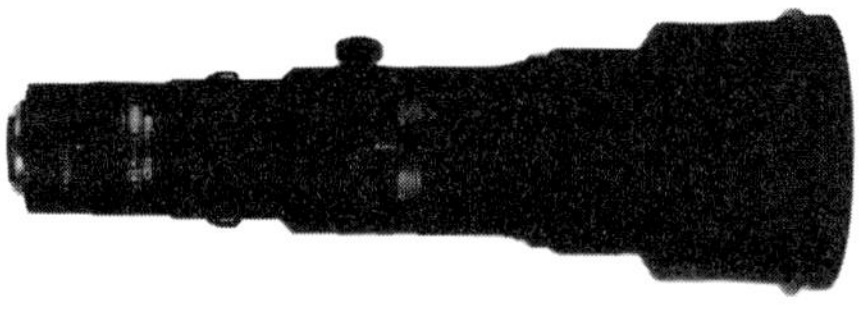

ED-1F 500mm f4 P

FISHEYE LENSES. These lenses see the world the way a fish might; 180 degrees or more at a time. Straight lines on the periphery are bowed in, creating the famous fisheye characteristic: extreme barrel distortion. Nikon makes two different kinds of fisheye lenses: circular, covering 23mm in diameter and full-frame, covering 24mm x 36mm. The only full-frame Nikkor is the 16mm (AI, AIS or NAI).

GN LENS. Before the era of flash automation, Nikon made a 45mm f/2.8 lens which is designated, "GN." The initials stand for "guide number." A linking system couples the focusing mechanism to the lens diaphragm. When coupled, the aperture of the lens automatically adjusts during focusing, assuring correct flash exposure at any distance. Thus the guide number/distance/aperture calculations are eliminated.

MEDICAL NIKKORS. These lenses offer a virtually automatic approach to close-up work. Instead of conventional focusing, a number of settings are provided based on reproduction ratios. The camera is then placed at the distance from the subject at which the image is sharp in the finder. The lenses incorporate their own light source which consists of a small bulb for focusing and a synchronized ring-light strobe which produces a uniform, shadowless light. The diaphragm automatically stops down to the correct aperture when the magnification is chosen. They are available with either an AC power source or a battery pack. The various lenses are described in detail in Chapter 17: Close-Up Equipment.

MICRO LENSES. Nikon calls a lens designed for extreme close-ups - magnifications of 1:2 to 1:1 - "micro." Most photographers call these lenses, "macro." This, naturally, can lead to some confusion. Nikkor Micro lenses are described in detail in this book in Chapter 17: Close-Up Equipment.

NOCTURNAL (NOCT) LENSES. Nocturnal lenses are made for taking pictures at night where there are large dark areas and very bright lights. When a normal lens is used for this purpose, a halo results around the light. The front element of nocturnal lenses is aspherical, which eliminates the halo effect.

OP FISHEYE. "OP" stands for "orthographic projection." This is a special formula which can be used to record an area's exact distribution of illumination brightness. The lens can also be used for normal fisheye operation.

PC NIKKOR LENSES. Two lenses, a 28mm 3.5 and a 35mm 2.8, are perspective control (PC) lenses. This means that the forward portion of the lens can move laterally. The purpose of this is to enable the photographer to correct or distort perspective in much the same way as the shifting front of a view camera does. These lenses are not AIS or AI because they do not have automatic diaphragms and so must be used in the stop-down mode if internal camera metering is utilized. Extreme caution must be employed in using earlier PC lenses on some later camera bodies as their use can cause damage. These earlier lenses can only be identified by their serial numbers. Read the camera instructions carefully before using a PC lens.

PRESET LENSES. A preset lens is a step up from a totally manual lens. With a manual lens, the photographer determines the aperture required, sets it on the lens and then makes the exposure. With a preset, the photographer can set the aperture in advance while the iris remains open. Just before making the exposure and without looking at the lens, the photographer turns the aperture ring to a stop at the preset opening.

Nikon produced a few preset lenses, most during earlier years. In the price listings in this book, there is a notation after the model designation if a lens is preset.

REFLEX NIKKOR LENSES. Most photographers call these mirror lenses. They use curved front-surfaced mirrors in combination with lenses to produce an image. They are shorter and lighter than conventional lenses and do not have adjustable apertures. Metering must be done in the stop-down mode. Proper exposure is obtained by adjusting the shutter speed or affixing neutral density filters or both. All Reflex Nikkors can be used with all Nikon and Nikkormat SLR bodies (and the Nikkorex F). A Reflex Nikkor is easily identifiable since the mirror is readily visible through the front of the lens. One Reflex lens was made with the Nikon rangefinder mount while the subsequent ones have the Nikon F mount.

Filter Selector Chart

LENS	FILTER
6mm f2.8	Built-in (Skylight, Y-48, Y-52, O-56, R-60)
8mm f2.8	Built-in (Skylight, Y-48, Y-42, O-56, R-60)
13mm f5.6	Supplied with Bayonet Type (Y-48, O-56, R-60, Neutral)
15mm f3.5	Supplied with Bayonet Type (L1BC, O-56, A-2, B-2)
16mm f2.8	Supplied with Bayonet Type (L1BC, O-56, A-2, B-2)
18mm f4	series 9 drop-in (Lenshood acts as retainer for series 9 drop-in)
18mm f3.5	72mm
20mm f2.8	62mm
20mm f3.5	52mm
24mm f2, 24mm f2.8	52mm
28mm f2, 28mm f2.8, 28mm f2.8E, 28mm f3.5	52mm
28mm f4 PC & 28mm f3.5 PC	72mm
35mm f1.4, 35mm f2, 35mm f2.5E, 35mm f2.8	52mm
35mm f2.8 PC	52mm
50mm f2, 50mm f1.8, 50mm f1.8E, 50mm f1.4, 50mm f1.2, 50mm f1.4 AF, 50mm f1.8 AF	52mm
55mm f2.8 Micro	52mm
58mm f1.2 Noct.	52mm
85mm f1.4	72mm
85mm f1.8	62mm
85mm f2	52mm
80mm f2.8 AF	52mm
100mm f2.8E	52mm
105mm f1.8	62mm
105mm f2.5	52mm
105mm f2.8 Micro & 105mm f4 Micro	52mm
135mm f2	72mm
135mm f2.8, 135mm f3.5	52mm
180mm f2.8, 180mm f2.8 ED, 180mm f2.8 ED-IF AF	72mm
200mm f2 ED-IF (new)	39mm
200mm f3.5 ED-IF AF	62mm
200mm f4/200mm f4 Micro	52mm
300mm f2 ED-IF	52mm (supplied w/L37C)
300mm f2.8 ED-IF	39mm
300mm f4 ED-IF AF	39mm, 82mm
300mm f4.5, 300mm f4.5 ED-IF	72mm
400mm f5.6 ED-IF	72mm
400mm f3.5 ED-IF, 600mm f5.6 ED-IF, 600mm f4 ED-IF, 800mm f8 ED-IF, 200mm f11 ED-IF	39mm (supplied with L-37C)
400mm f2.8	52mm (supplied w/L37C)
800mm f5.6	52mm (supplied w/L37C)

LENS	FILTER
500mm f8	39mm (supplied with R-60, Y-52, O-56, ND-4X, L-37C), 82mm
1000mm f11	39mm (supplied with ND-4X, L-37C, O-56, A-2, B-2)
2000mm f11	Built-in (L-39, Y-48, O-56, R-60)
24-50mm f3.3-4.5 AF Zoom	62mm
25 50mm f4 Zoom	72mm
28-50mm f3.5 Zoom	52mm
28-45mm f4.5 Zoom	62mm
28-85mm f3.5-4.5 Zoom AF	72mm
35-70mm f2.8 AF Zoom	62mm
35-70mm f3.3-4.5 Zoom AF	52mm
35-70mm f3.5 M Zoom	62mm
35-70mm f3.5 Zoom	72mm
36-72mm f3.5 E Zoom	52mm
35-105mm f3.5-4.5 Zoom	52mm
35-105mm f3.5-4.5 Zoom AF	52mm
35-135mm f3.5-4.5 Zoom	62mm
35-135mm f3.5-4.5 Zoom AF	62mm
35-200mm f3.5-4.5 Zoom	62mm
50-135mm f3.5 Zoom	62mm
50-300mm f4.5, 50-300mm f4.5 ED	95mm
70-210mm f4 E Zoom	62mm
70-210mm f4 AF Zoom	62mm
70-210mm f4-5.6 AF Zoom	62mm
75-150mm f3.5 E Zoom	52mm
80-200mm f4.5 Zoom	52mm
80-200mm f4 Zoom	62mm
80-200mm f2.8 ED AF Zoom	77mm
80-200mm f2.8 ED Zoom	95mm
100-300mm f5.6 Zoom	62mm
180-600mm f8 Zoom	95mm
200-400mm f4 Zoom	122mm
200-600mm f9.5 Zoom	82mm screw-in or series 9 drop-in (Lenshood acts as retainer for series 9 drop-in)
360-1200mm f11 Zoom	122mm
200mm f5.6 Medical	38mm
50mm f4 EL Nikkor	34.5mm
50mm f2.8 EL Nikkor	40.5mm
63mm f2.8 EL Nikkor	40.5mm
63mm f3.5 EL Nikkor	40.5mm
75mm f4, 80mm f5.6, 105mm f5.6 EL Nikkor	34.5mm
135mm f5.6 EL Nikkor	43mm
150mm f5.6 EL Nikkor	47mm
180mm f5.6 EL Nikkor	58mm
210mm f5.6 EL Nikkor	68mm
240mm f5.6 EL Nikkor	77mm
300mm f5.6 EL Nikkor	95mm
360mm f5.6 EL Nikkor	120mm
R-8 Movie	52mm
R-10 Movie	67mm (72mm with rubber hood HR-3)
Super 8X, 5X	52mm

The following filters are available from Nikon: 39mm, 52mm, 62mm, 72mm, 82mm, Series 9, 95mm, 122mm, 160mm. Refer to Page 12 for Prices.

SHORT MOUNT LENSES. Short mount lenses were made in longer than normal focal lengths. The lens includes two bayonet mounts, one inside the other. One mount is the Nikon rangefinder Contax-type mount. Short mount lenses can be used on any Nikon rangefinder camera in conjunction with a reflex housing. The other bayonet is for use with an adapter (N-f Adapter Tube) which permits their use with Nikon cameras which use the Nikon F mount.

UNDERWATER LENSES. These lenses are designed for use with Nikonos bodies and cannot be used with other bodies. All Nikonos mount lenses can be used with any model Nikonos camera body. Those designated "UW" can be used underwater only. Those designated "LW" can be used above water only. Those without designation can be used both above and underwater.

UV LENSES. UV means that the lens was specially designed for ultraviolet photography. Other lenses focus visible rays and ultraviolet rays at different focal distances. With the UV lens, there is virtually no variation in the focus position between visible and ultraviolet rays, thus eliminating clumsy focus adjustments. Special coating is applied to the air-to-glass surfaces of the lens element to reduce reflections under ultraviolet light. At all focused distances in every wavelength range, aberration is minimal and distortion is eliminated. Fluorspar is applied to some elements to insure adequate transmission of ultraviolet rays. The lens can also be used for ordinary photography with visible light. Currently there is one UV lens available, the 105mm f/4.5.

III. NIKON OPTICAL TERMS

APERTURE-DIRECT-READOUT. Aperture-direct-readout or ADR means that when an AI or AIS Nikkor lens is used with a Nikon camera body which includes the ADR facility, the aperture in use is shown in the viewfinder via a direct readout from the secondary aperture scale at the rear of the lens. The small holes in the rabbit ears help make this possible.

COATING. When Nippon Kogaku returned to civilian production after World War II, the company started to coat lenses. Because of this, all lenses made for Nikon cameras, whether rangefinder or SLR, are coated on each air to glass surface. In order to advertise this innovation, until the late fifties, the identification ring on Nikkors was inscribed with a red letter "C." There is no difference between lenses with the "C" and those without. The first coating was a single, thin layer of magnesium flouride.

INTEGRATED COATING (IC) Some Nikkors have a designation, "IC." This first appeared in 1974. Integrated coating is what Nikon called multicoating. This means that not only are all air to glass surfaces coated, but also they are coated in varying layers of different thicknesses. Multicoated lenses transmit more light, reduce flare and ghosts as well as providing better contrast. The "IC" designation was used when the feature was first introduced and later the use of the initials was discontinued.

NIKON INTEGRATED COATING (NIC). In 1979, Nikon started using the term Nikon Integrated Coating and the initials, "NIC." The designation only appears in print, not on the lenses themselves. The new name only indicates a change in terminology. Nikon lenses have been multicoated since 1974.

CLOSE RANGE CORRECTION (CRC). Some Nikon lenses are designated CRC (such as the AF Nikkor 20mm f/2.8, AIS 55mm f/2.8 Micro and the AIS 85mm f/1.4). Most lenses perform best from medium distances to infinity. When they are focused at extremely close distances, the image they produce is less satisfactory. This problem is addressed by constructing lenses with "floating elements." This means some elements shift position in relationship to the others when the focus is changed. Nikon has designated floating element Nikkors, "CRC."

LETTER CODES. Some earlier Nikkors have a letter inscribed on the identification ring. The letter is a code which indicates the number of elements. (See Chapter Six.) This practice was discontinued in the early seventies. But, lo and behold, all of a sudden the AI 50mm 2.0 HC introduced in 1977 is designated "HC." The H indicates six elements and the C means coated!

THE NIKON PHOTOGRAPHER'S SYSTEM

"Visual variety is so important," says Paul Fusco. "The great array of Nikon lenses is such an advantage because it gives you variety in approach and feel and look. It's amazing how much variety you can carry around in one camera bag! Competition is so keen that you're always looking for a way of seeing a subject that's just a little different."

Fusco includes 20, 24, 28, 50, 55, 180, 200, 300 and 500mm Nikkor Lenses in his system. "I especially like the dimensional quality of the shorter lenses," he says. "Like the 20mm—extreme wide angle with a lot of depth, minimum distortion. It's a sculptural feeling. But I also use the 180 a lot. It's light, easy to carry around, but can stand up to the kind of abuse professional photographers put equipment to."

Ken Biggs has 24, 35PC, 50, 55 Micro, 105, 105 Bellows, 400, 43-86 and 80-200mm zoom lenses, of which he identifies 24, 35PC and 80-200 as favorites. "The 24 can add a stylish look to your picture," he explains, "I use it a lot for annual report work. It will focus down to 12-inches, and it takes all my regular Nikon filters. Using the 35mm Perspective Control Lens is almost like having a 4x5 view camera. This lens has saved me many, many times when I had to shoot tall objects that had to be free of distortion. And the 80-200 Zoom! I got that for the zoom effects, but after making some lens tests, I could hardly believe the sharpness! Now it's one of my all-time favorite lenses."

Because Doug Kirkland's work is so extremely varied, his favorite lens on any given day may be his 15, 20, 24, 28, 50, 55, 85, 105, 135, 180, 300, 500 or 1000mm Nikkors. Yes, he has one of the incredible new 15mm f5.6 wide angles. "I like it a lot!" he says. "It's the last word in wide angles. It's the widest, has the most depth of field, reflex viewing... I don't know what more they can give us after this!"

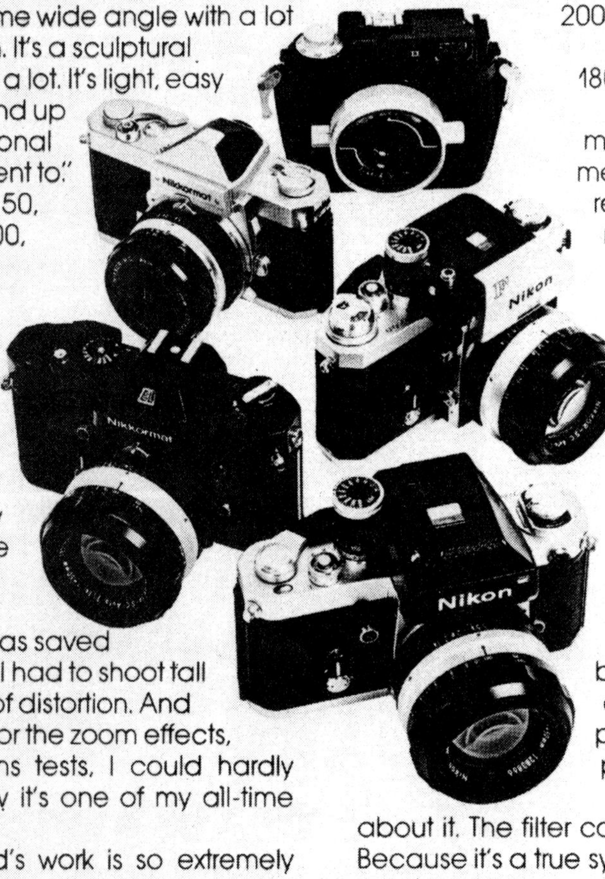

Filters: one size fits almost all

Ken Biggs listed nine Nikkor lenses in his arsenal. One of the more interesting things about them is that eight of them (all except the 400) take the same 52mm Nikon filters. For a guy who makes the extensive and creative use of filters that Biggs does, that's vital. "I usually carry about 50 glass filters around with me. Can you imagine the problems I'd have trying to carry 50 different filters in two or three different sizes?" Actually, every Nikkor between 24 and 200mm takes the same 52mm filters, with the lone exception of the 180mm f2.8. That even includes the 80-200mm zoom. "This feature makes the Nikon System a must for me," adds Biggs. It's one of the best reasons why any pro worthy of the name refuses to have any lenses other than Nikkor in his Nikon System. Another is the durability under professional abuse that Fusco talked about.

What's in a system?

Everybody talks about systems, but not everybody has them. Not by our standards.

Because a system is more than just a wide array of accessories. It does happen that the Nikon System is the most complete in 35mm photography, but that's not the whole point. The difference is in the way the components work together. Ken Biggs puts it this way: "The Nikon System is a total system. That's what I like about it. The filter compatibility is just one example. Because it's a true system, I can carry a lot of equipment and accessories in an average size case. You might find another camera that's a few ounces lighter, but the system will be bigger and heavier because you have to carry a lot of incompatible lenses and accessories." Professional or aspiring amateur, can you afford less than a truly complete system? In 35, there's only one. The name is Nikon.

CHAPTER FOURTEEN

TELECONVERTERS

NIKON TELECONVERTERS, sometimes called extenders, are accessory lenses mounted between the camera body and a prime or zoom lens. Their purpose is to increase the focal length of the lens. In doing so, the amount of light transmitted is decreased. They are also sometimes called "tele-extenders" or "doublers," although this last is somewhat of a misnomer since the focal length is not always doubled; sometimes it is more than doubled, sometimes less.

A teleconverter is a lens made up of glass elements. Each time light passes through an element, the amount transmitted is diminished. Therefore, when a teleconverter is utilized, the effective aperture of the prime lens is decreased. The amount of the decrease is a multiple of the extension. A 2X teleconverter decreases the light by two f/ stops. For example, when using an f/4 lens and a 2X teleconverter, the effective aperture becomes f/8.

Obviously, since the teleconverter involves the introduction of additional optical elements, a certain amount of decrease in the image quality will be experienced. In order to obtain the best possible quality, a prime lens of the needed focal length should be used. A teleconverter is a compromise between quality on the one hand and size plus cost on the other.

There are many "after-market" converters on the market, some good, some so-so and many quite awful. Nikon teleconverters, on the other hand, are fine optical instruments. If the use of a teleconverter is a good solution, in order to obtain the best possible quality under the circumstances, Nikon teleconverters should be the choice.

Each Nikon teleconverter is designed to be used with certain Nikon lenses. When a Nikon teleconverter is used with a Nikon lens for which it was not designed, there may be image problems such as vignetting or uneven exposure.

Any Nikon teleconverter can be mounted on any Nikon SLR body; there is no possibility of damage. Of course, those later teleconverters which incorporate AI, AIS or AF functions will not provide these functions on camera bodies which do not have the function(s).

‡ TELECONVERTER SELECTOR CHART

TC-201, TC-14A

Wideangle
13mm f/5.6
15mm f/3.5
18mm f/3.5°
20mm f/3.5
24mm f/2
24mm f/2.8
28mm f/2
28mm f/2.8
28mm f/3.5
35mm f/1.4
35mm f/2
35mm f/2.8

Normal
50mm f/1.2°
50mm f/1.4
50mm f/1.8

Telephoto
85mm f/1.4•
85mm f/2
105mm f/1.8•
105mm f/2.5°
135mm f/2•
135mm f/2.8△
(TC-14B also usable)
135mm f/3.5
(TC-14B also usable)
180mm f/2.8 ED•
200mm f/2 IF-ED°
(TC-14B also usable)•
200m f/4

Reflex
500m f/8
(TC-14B usable)•
1000mm f/11°
(TC-301 and TC-14B also usable)•

Fisheye
6mm f/2.8
8mm f/2.8
16mm f/2.8

Zoom
25-50mm f/4
35-70mm f/3.5
35-105mm.f/3.5-4.5
50-135mm f/3.5
50-300mm f/4.5 ED
80-200mm f/2.8 ED°
80-200mm f/4°

Special Purpose
Noct 58mm f/1.2•
Micro 55mm f/2.8
AF80mm f/2.8
AF200mm f/3.5 ED
(TC-301 and TC-14B also usable)

Series E
28mm f/2.8
35mm f/2.5
50mm f/1.8
100mm f/2.8
135mm f/2.8•
Zoom 36-72mm f/3.5
Zoom 75-150mm f/3.5
Zoom 70-210mm f/4

TC-301, TC-14B

Telephoto
300mm f/2.8 IF-ED
(TC-14A also usable°)
300mm f4 IF ED AF
300mm f/4.5 IF-ED
300mm f/4.5
(TC-14A also usable°)
400mm f/3.5 IF-ED
(TC-14A also usable°)
400mm f/5.6 IF-ED
600mm f/4 IF-ED
600mm f/5.6 IF-ED
800mm f/5.6 IF-ED
800mm f/8 IF-ED
1200mm f/11 IF-ED

Zoom
180-600mm f/8 ED
200-600mm f/9.5
360-1200mm f/11 ED•

Reflex
1000mm f/11
(TC-201 and TC-14A also usable°)•
2000mm f/11
(TC-201 also usable)

Special Purpose
Micro 105mm f/4
(TC-201 also usable)
Micro 200mm f/4 IF
(TC-14A also usable)
AF200mm f/3.5 ED
(TC-201 and TC-14A also usable)

TC-1 (Introduced 1978, discontinued 1982) 2X: doubles the focal length. For non-AI lenses of 200mm or less plus the 500mm f/8 reflex and the 50-300mm 4.5 zoom. (Some vignetting may result with the zoom lens at some focal lengths.) It should not be used with lenses which require mirror lock-up or the 105mm f/4 micro.

TC-2 (Introduced 1978, discontinued 1984) 2X: doubles the focal length. For non-AI lenses of 300mm or more except the 500mm f/8 reflex.

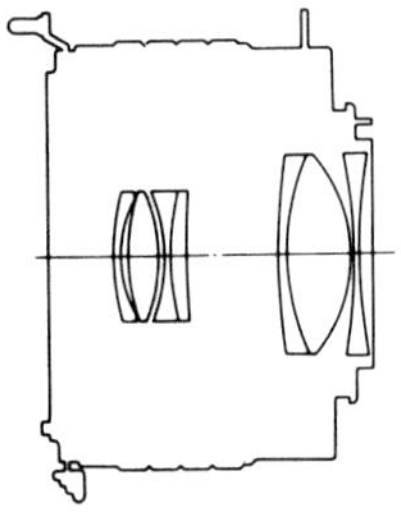

TC-1

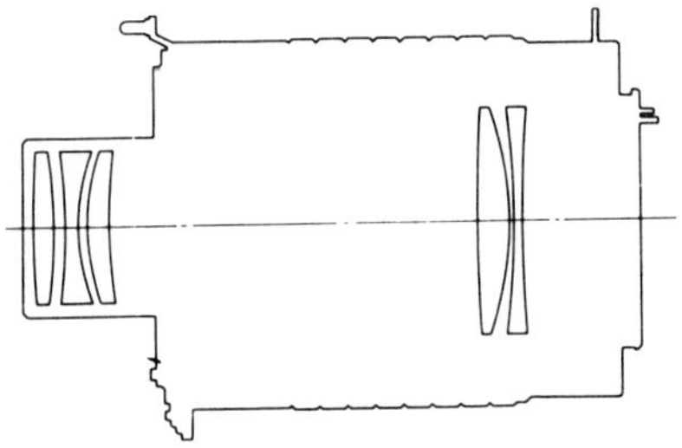

TC-2

TC-200 (Introduced 1978, discontinued 1984) 2X: doubles the focal length and creates a two-stop loss in exposure. For AI lenses of 200mm or less. For lenses without deeply recessed rear elements.

TC-300 (Introduced 1978, discontinued 1984) 2X: doubles the focal length and creates a two-stop loss in exposure. For AI lenses of 300mm or more. For lenses with recessed rear elements.

Lens			TC-200	TC-300
Fisheye	AI	6mm f/2.8	O	X
	AI	8mm f/2.8	O	X
	AI	16mm f/2.8	O	X
Wideangle	AI	13mm f/5.6	O	X
	AI	15mm f/3.5	O	X
	AI	18mm f/4	O	X
	AI	20mm f/3.5	O	X
	AI	24mm f/2	O	X
	AI	24mm f/2.8	O	X
	AI	28mm f/2	O	X
	AI	28mm f/2.8	O	X
	AI	28mm f/3.5	O	X
	AI	35mm f/1.4★	O	X
	AI	35mm f/2	O	X
	AI	35mm f/2.8	O	X
Normal	AI	50mm f/1.2	O	X
	AI	50mm f/1.4	O	X
	AI	50mm f/1.8	O	X
	AI	50mm f/2	O	X
	AI	55mm f/1.2★	O	X
Telephoto	AI	85mm f/2	O	X
	AI	105mm f/2.5	O	X
	AI	135mm f/2★	O	X
	AI	135mm f/2.8★	O	X
	AI	135mm f/3.5	O	X
	AI	180mm f/2.8★	O	X
	AI	200 f/4	O	X
	AI	ED300mm f/2.8 (IF)	△	O

Lens			TC-200	TC-300
Telephoto	AI	300mm f/4.5★	△	O
	AI	ED300mm f/4.5 (IF)	△	O
	AI	ED400mm f/3.5 (IF)	△	O
	AI	ED400mm f/5.6	△	O
	AI	ED400mm f/5.6 (IF)	△	O
	AI	ED600mm f/5.6 (IF)	△	O
	AI	ED800mm f/8 (IF)	△	O
	AI	ED1200mm f/11 (IF)	△	O
Zoom	AI	25 ~ 50mm f/4	O	X
	AI	35 ~ 70mm f/3.5	O	X
	AI	43 ~ 86mm f/3.5	O	X
	AI	ED50 ~ 300mm f/4.5	O	X
	AI	80 ~ 200mm f/4.5	O	X
PC		28mm f/3.5	△	X
		35mm f/2.8	△	X
Noct	AI	58mm f/1.2★	O	X
Micro	AI	55mm f/2.8	O	X
	AI	105mm f/4	△	O
	AI	200mm f/4 (IF)	△	O
Reflex		500mm f/8	O	X
Series E		28mm f/2.8	O	X
		35mm f/2.5	O	X
		50mm f/1.8	O	X
		100mm f/2.8	O	X
		135mm f/2.8	O	X
		36 ~ 72mm f/3.5	O	X
		75 ~ 150mm f/3.5	O	X

Notes

O = Perfectly matched.
△ = Usable but vignetting or other performance deterioration may be noticeable in the image recorded on the film.
X = Not usable.
★ = When these lenses are used at apertures smaller than f/11 with high shutter speeds there is occasional unevenness of illumination on the film.

TC-14 (Introduced 1979, discontinued 1984) 1.4X: multiplies the focal length by 1.4. For AI lenses.

TC-14C (Introduced 1986, discontinued 1987) 1.4X: multiplies the focal length by 1.4. This teleconverter is matched specifically to the AIS 300mm f/2.0 EDIF, is supplied with the lens at the time of purchase and is to be used with that lens only.

Lens			TC-14
AI		135/3.5	O
AI		180/2.8	O
AI	IF-ED	200/2	O
AI	IF-ED	300/2.8	O
AI		300/4.5	O
AI	IF-ED	300/4.5	O
AI	ED	400/5.6	O
AI	IF-ED	400/5.6	O

Lens			TC-14
AI	IF-ED	400/3.5	O
AI	IF-ED	600/5.6	O
AI	IF-ED	600/4	O
AI	IF-ED	800/8	O
AI	IF-ED	1200/11	O
	Reflex	500/8	△
	Reflex	1000/11	△
AI	Zoom	50-300/4.5	O

O : Perfectly matched.
△ : Use without the filter.

TC-14A (Introduced 1984, still available) Multiplies the focal length by 1.4 and creates a one-stop loss in exposure. For AI and AIS lenses under 200mm. Use with the GN 45mm lens can damage the teleconverter.

TC-14B (Introduced 1984, still available) Multiplies the focal length by 1.4 and creates a one-stop loss in exposure. For AI and AIS lenses over 300mm.

Lens		TC-14A	TC-14B
Fisheye	AI 6mm f/2.8S	O	×
	AI 8mm f/2.8S	O	×
	AI 16mm f/2.8S	O	×
Wideangle	AI 13mm f/5.6S	O	×
	AI 15mm f/3.5S	O	×
	AI 18mm f/3.5S	△	×
	AI 20mm f/3.5S	O	×
	AI 24mm f/2S	O	×
	AI 24mm f/2.8S	O	×
	AI 28mm f/2S	O	×
	AI 28mm f/2.8S	O	×
	AI 28mm f/3.5S	O	×
	AI 35mm f/1.4S	O	×
	AI 35mm f/2S	O	×
	AI 35mm f/2.8S	O	×
Normal	AI 50mm f/1.2S	△	×
	AI 50mm f/1.4S	O	×
	AI 50mm f/1.8S	O	×
	AI 50mm f/1.8	O	×
Telephoto	AI 85mm f/1.4S*	O	×
	AI 85mm f/2S	O	×
	AI 105mm f/1.8S*	O	×
	AI 105mm f/2.5S	△	×
	AI 135mm f/2S*	O	×
	AI 135mm f/2.8S	O	O
	AI 135mm f/3.5S	O	O
	AI 180 mm f/2.8 ED*	O	×
	AI 200mm f/2S IF-ED*	△	O
	AI 200mm f/4S	O	×
	AI 300mm f/2S IF-ED*	△	O
	AI 300mm f/2.8S IF-ED	△	O
	AI 300mm f/4.5S IF-ED	×	O
	AI 300mm f/4.5S	△	O
	AI 400mm f/3.5S IF-ED	△	O
	AI 400mm f/5.6S IF-ED	×	O

Lens		TC-14A	TC-14B
Telephoto	AI 600mm f/4S IF-ED	×	O
	AI 600mm f/5.6S IF-ED	×	O
	AI 800mm f/8S IF-ED	×	O
	AI 1200mm f/11S IF-ED	×	O
Zoom	AI 25~50mm f/4S	O	×
	AI 28~50mm f/3.5S	O	×
	AI 35~70mm f/3.5S	O	×
	AI 35~105mm f/3.5~4.5S	O	×
	AI 50~135mm f/3.5S	O	×
	AI 50~300mm f/4.5S ED	O	×
	AI 80~200mm f/2.8S ED*	△	×
	AI 80~200mm f/4S	△	×
	AI 180~600mm f/8S ED	×	O
	AI 200~400mm f/4S ED*	×	O
	AI 360~1200mm f/11S ED*	×	O
AF	AI 80mm f/2.8	O	×
	AI 200mm f/3.5 IF-ED	O	O
Noct	AI 58mm f/1.2S*	O	×
Micro	AI 55mm f/2.8S	O	×
	AI 105mm f/2.8S	O	×
	AI 105mm f/4S	×	O
	AI 200mm f/4S IF	△	O
Reflex	500mm f/8	△	□
	1000mm f/11	△	□
	2000mm f/11	×	O
Series E	28mm f/2.8	O	×
	35mm f/2.5	O	×
	50mm f/1.8	O	×
	100mm f/2.8	O	×
	135mm f/2.8*	O	×
	36~72mm f/3.5 Zoom	O	×
	70~210mm f/4 Zoom	O	×
	75~150mm f/3.5 Zoom	O	×
PC	28mm f/3.5	×	×
	35mm f/2.8	×	×

• Never attach the TC-14A to the GN-Nikkor 45mm f/2.8, or the lens or TC-14A could be damaged.

Notes:

O = Perfectly matched
□ = Usable, but without filter
△ = Usable, but vignetting or other image deterioration may occur.
× = Not usable, because it cannot be mounted or vignetting or other image deterioration will ruin the photo.
* = When these lenses are used at apertures smaller than f/11 with high shutter speeds, there is occasional unevenness of illumination on the film.

TC-201 (Introduced 1984, still available) Doubles the focal length and creates a two-stop loss in exposure. Designed for AIS lenses under 200mm, it also works with AI lenses.

TC-301 (Introduced 1984, still available) Doubles the focal length and creates a two-stop loss in exposure. Designed for AIS lenses over 300mm, it also works with AI lenses.

Lens/Teleconverter Compatibility

The following table lists various Nikkor and Nikon Series E lenses which can be used in conjunction with Nikon Teleconverters TC-201 and TC-301; compatibility is detailed in the right-hand columns.

	Lens	TC-201	TC-301
Fisheye	[A] 6mm f/2.8	◎	×
	[A] 8mm f/2.8	◎	×
	[A] 16mm f/2.8	◎	×
Wideangle	[A] 13mm f/5.6	◎	×
	[A] 15mm f/3.5	◎	×
	[A] 18mm f/3.5	◎	×
	[A] 20mm f/3.5	◎	×
	[A] 20mm f/2.8	◎	×
	[A] 24mm f/2	◎	×
	[A] 24mm f/2.8	◎	×
	[A] 28mm f/2	◎	×
	[A] 28mm f/2.8	◎	×
	[A] 28mm f/3.5	◎	×
	[A] 35mm f/1.4	◎	×
	[A] 35mm f/2	◎	×
	[A] 35mm f/2.8	◎	×
Normal	[A] 50mm f/1.2	◎	×
	[A] 50mm f/1.4	◎	×
	[A] 50mm f/1.8	◎	×
Telephoto	[A] 85mm f/1.4*	◎	×
	[A] 85mm f/2	◎	×
	[A] 105mm f/1.8*	◎	×
	[A] 105mm f/2.5	◎	×
	[A] 135mm f/2*	◎	×
	[A] 135mm f/2.8	○	×
	[A] 135mm f/3.5	◎	×
	[A] 180mm f/2.8 ED	◎	×
	[A] 200mm f/2 IF-ED*	◎	×
	[A] 200mm f/4*	○	×
	[A] 300mm f/2 IF-ED*	◎	◎
	[A] 300mm f/2.8 IF-ED	×	◎
	[A] 300mm f/4.5 IF-ED	×	◎
	[A] 300mm f/4.5	×	◎
	[A] 400mm f/3.5 IF-ED	×	◎
	[A] 400mm f/5.6 IF-ED	×	◎

	Lens	TC-201	TC-301
Telephoto	[A] 600mm f/4 IF-ED	×	◎
	[A] 600mm f/5.6 IF-ED	×	◎
	[A] 800mm f/8 IF-ED	×	◎
	[A] 1200mm f/11 IF-ED	×	◎
Zoom	[A] 25~50mm f/4	◎	×
	[A] 28~50mm f/3.5	◎	×
	[A] 35~70mm f/3.3~4.5	◎	×
	[A] 35~70mm f/3.5	◎	×
	[A] 35~105mm f/3.5~4.5	◎	×
	[A] 35~135mm f/3.5~4.5	◎	×
	[A] 50~135mm f/3.5	◎	×
	[A] 50~300mm f/4.5 ED	◎	×
	[A] 80~200mm f/2.8 ED*	◎	×
	[A] 80~200mm f/4	◎	×
	[A] 100~300mm f/5.6	△	×
	[A] 180~600mm f/8 ED	×	◎
	[A] 200~400mm f/4 ED*	△	□
	[A] 360~1200mm f/11 ED*	×	◎
AF	[A] 80mm f/2.8	◎	×
	[A] 200mm f/3.5 IF-ED	△	◎
Noct	[A] 58mm f/1.2*	◎	×
Micro	[A] 55mm f/2.8	◎	×
	[A] 105mm f/2.8	◎	×
	[A] 200mm f/4 IF	×	◎
Reflex	500mm f/8	△	×
	1000mm f/11	△	□
	2000mm f/11	△	◎
Series E	28mm f/2.8	◎	×
	35mm f/2.5	◎	×
	50mm f/1.8	◎	×
	100mm f/2.8	◎	×
	135mm f/2.8	◎	×
	36~72mm f/3.5 Zoom	◎	×
	70~210mm f/4 Zoom	◎	×
	75~150mm f/3.5 Zoom	◎	×
PC	28mm f/3.5	×	×
	35mm f/2.8	×	×

Notes:

◎ = Perfectly matched
□ = Usable, but without filter
○ = Usable, but at a close focused distance, vignetting or other image deterioration may occur.
△ = Usable, but vignetting or other image deterioration may occur.
× = Not usable, because it cannot be mounted or vignetting or other image deterioration will ruin the photo.

TC-16. (Introduced 1984, still available) For the F3AF body and the DX-1 AF finder only. It increases the focal length by 1.6X and causes a 1 1/3-stop decrease in exposure. It provides autofocus via a built-in micromotor which enables the teleconverter lens elements to move. It can be used with a variety of AI and E lenses between 24mm and 300mm. Non-AI lenses cannot be used with the TC-16. Lenses other than those listed on the table to the right, including non-AI lenses converted to AI and non-Nikon lenses, cannot be used with the TC-16. Damage to the lens and/or the teleconverter may result.

The following table lists a variety of AI-type Nikkor and Nikon Series E lenses which can be used with the Nikon AF Teleconverter TC-16.

Wideangle	[A] Nikkor 24mm f/2
	[A] Nikkor 24mm f/2S
	[A] Nikkor 28mm f/2 (Product number 540021 or higher)
	[A] Nikkor 28mm f/2S
	[A] Nikkor 35mm f/1.4S
	[A] Nikkor 35mm f/2 (Product number 931001 or higher)
	[A] Nikkor 35mm f/2S
Normal	[A] Nikkor 50mm f/1.2
	[A] Nikkor 50mm f/1.2S
	[A] Nikkor 50mm f/1.4 (Product number 3980001 or higher)
	[A] Nikkor 50mm f/1.4S
	[A] Nikkor 50mm f/1.8
	Nikkor 50mm f/1.8S
	Series E 50mm f/1.8
	[A] Nikkor 50mm f/2 (Product number 3640001 or higher)
	[A] Nikkor 55mm f/1.2
	[A] Noct Nikkor 58mm f/1.2
	[A] Noct Nikkor 58mm f/1.2S
Telephoto	[A] Nikkor 85mm f/1.4S
	[A] Nikkor 85mm f/2
	[A] Nikkor 85mm f/2S
	[A] Nikkor 105mm f/1.8S
	[A] Nikkor 135mm f/2
	[A] Nikkor 135mm f/2S
	[A] Nikkor 200mm f/2 IF-ED
	[A] Nikkor 200mm f/2S IF-ED
	[A] Nikkor 300mm f/2S IF-ED

TC-16A. (Introduced 1984, still available) Multiplies the focal length by 1.6, and used with Nikon autofocus cameras, it converts certain non-AF lenses to autofocus. Only AI (not AI converted) or AIS lenses can be used. Only the listed lenses can be used; mounting other lenses may damage the teleconverter.

NOMENCLATURE

1. Lens type signal pin
2. Lens release button
3. Lens mounting index
4. Camera mounting index
5. AF coupling
6. Aperture indexing post
7. Focal length indexing notch
8. AF contacts
9. Meter coupling ridge

Thank you for your kind patronage of Nikon.
Before using your Autofocus Converter TC-16A, read the following carefully so you get the most out of your TC-16A now and for years to come.

IMPORTANT!

The Autofocus Converter TC-16A **cannot** be used with any camera other than the Nikon F-501/N2020.*
*The Nikon N2020 and N2000 are sold exclusively in the U.S.A. and Canadian markets.

LENS/TC-16A COMPATIBILITY

Only the AI-type (excluding AI-modified) lenses listed below can be used with the TC-16A; use of other lenses may *damage* the TC-16A.
Also note that the TC-16A/lens assembly cannot be attached to another teleconverter.

AF	AF Nikkor 50mm f/1.8 AF-Nikkor 80mm f/2.8
Fisheye	Nikkor 6mm f/2.8 Nikkor 8mm f/2.8 Nikkor 16mm f/2.8
Wideangle	Nikkor 24mm f/2 Nikkor 24mm f/2.8 Nikkor 28mm f/2 (No. 540021 or larger) Nikkor 28mm f/2.8 (No. 500001 or larger) Nikkor 35mm f1.4 (Use AI-S type lens only)* Nikkor 35mm f/2 (No. 931001 or larger) Nikkor 35mm f/2.8 (No. 880001 or larger)
Normal	Nikkor 50mm f/1.2 Nikkor 50mm f/1.4 (No. 3980001 or larger) Nikkor 50mm f/1.8 Nikkor 50mm f/1.8(N) Nikkor 50mm f/2 (No. 3640001 or larger) Nikkor 55mm f/1.2
Telephoto	Nikkor 85mm f/1.4 Nikkor 85mm f/2 Nikkor 105mm f/1.8 Nikkor 105mm f/2.5 Nikkor 135mm f/2 Nikkor 135mm f/2.8 [Only infinity (∞) to 1.7m (5.58 ft)]** Nikkor 180mm f/2.8 ED [Only infinity (∞) to 2.5m (8.2 ft)]** Nikkor 180mm f/2.8 [Only infinity (∞) to 2.5m (8.2 ft)]** Nikkor 200mm f/2 IF-ED Nikkor 300mm f/2 IF-ED*** Nikkor 300mm f/2.8 IF-ED***
Zoom	Zoom-Nikkor 80-200mm f/2.8 ED
Special	Noct-Nikkor 58mm f/1.2 Micro-Nikkor 55mm f/2.8 Micro-Nikkor 105mm f/2.8 [Only infinity (∞) to 0.55m (1.8 ft)]**
Series E	28mm f/2.8 35mm f/2.5 50mm f/1.8 100mm f/2.8 135mm f/2.8 [Only infinity (∞) to 1.7m (5.58 ft)]**

*AI-S type lenses can be distinguished by the **orange** minimum aperture indication on the aperture-direct-readout scale.
**For an in-focus image, set the lens focus ring to a setting within the specified distance range.
***Use smallest possible aperture (largest f-number).

MOUNTING THE LENS ON THE TC-16A ——— A1•A2

Position the lens in the TC-16A's bayonet mount, lining up the aperture index on the lens with the lens mounting index on the TC-16A. Twist lens counterclockwise until it clicks into place.
To mount telephoto lenses having a tripod collar, twist the TC-16A clockwise until it click stops.
To remove: Press the lens release button on the TC-16A and turn the lens clockwise until it comes off. With telephoto lenses having a tripod collar, turn the TC-16A counterclockwise instead.

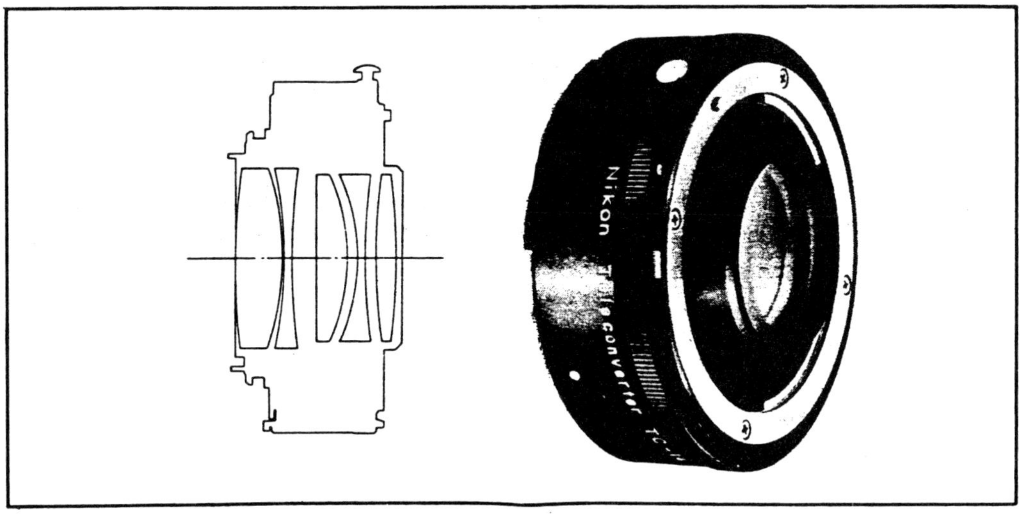

Teleconverter TC-14

CAMERA/FLASH COMBINATION

Flash Unit / Camera Type	Speedlight SB-11 SB-14 SB 140	Speedlight SB-17 SB-16A	Macro Speedlight SB-21A SB-21B	Speedlight SB-15 SB-16B SB-20 SB-22*, SB-23	Speedlight SB-E SB-19 SB-10	Repeating Flash Unit SB-6	Ringlight SR 2 Macro Ringlight SM 2	120 mm medical Nikkor lens
Nikon F3	TTL control w Sensor Cord SC-12 or w AS-7	direct TTL control also w TTL Sensor Cord SC-14	(SB-21A) ☆ direct	w/Flash Unit Coupler AS-4 or w AS-7	w Flash Unit Coupler AS-4 or w AS-7	w Flash Unit Coupler AS-3 SC-9	w built-in sync cord	SC-20 or SC-22 and AS-4 or w AS-7
Nikon FE2 FA	TTL Control w/SC-23	w Flash Unit Coupler AS-6 Manual Only	(SB-21B) ☆ direct	TTL Cont. Remote Cord SC-17	☆ direct	w Flash Unit Coupler AS-2 SC-9	w built-in sync cord	SC-20 or SC-22
Nikon FE FM/FM2	SC-11 or SC-13	w Flash Unit Coupler AS-6 Manual Only	(SB-21B) ☆ direct	☆ direct	☆ direct	w Flash Unit Coupler AS-2 SC-9	w built-in sync cord	SC-20 or SC-22
Nikon FG N2020* N2000 N4004*	TTL Control W SC-23	w Flash Unit Coupler AS-6 Manual Only	(SB-21B) ☆ direct	TTL Cont. Remote Cord SC-17	☆ direct	w Flash Unit Coupler AS-2 SC-9	no provision	SC-22

*NOTE: SB-20, SB-22, SB-23, AF Speedlight provides autofocus illumination at low light levels with the Nikon N4004 and N2020 camera only; with other cameras, flash operation without AF assist is provided as described in the table.

TTL MULTIFLASH SYSTEM CHART

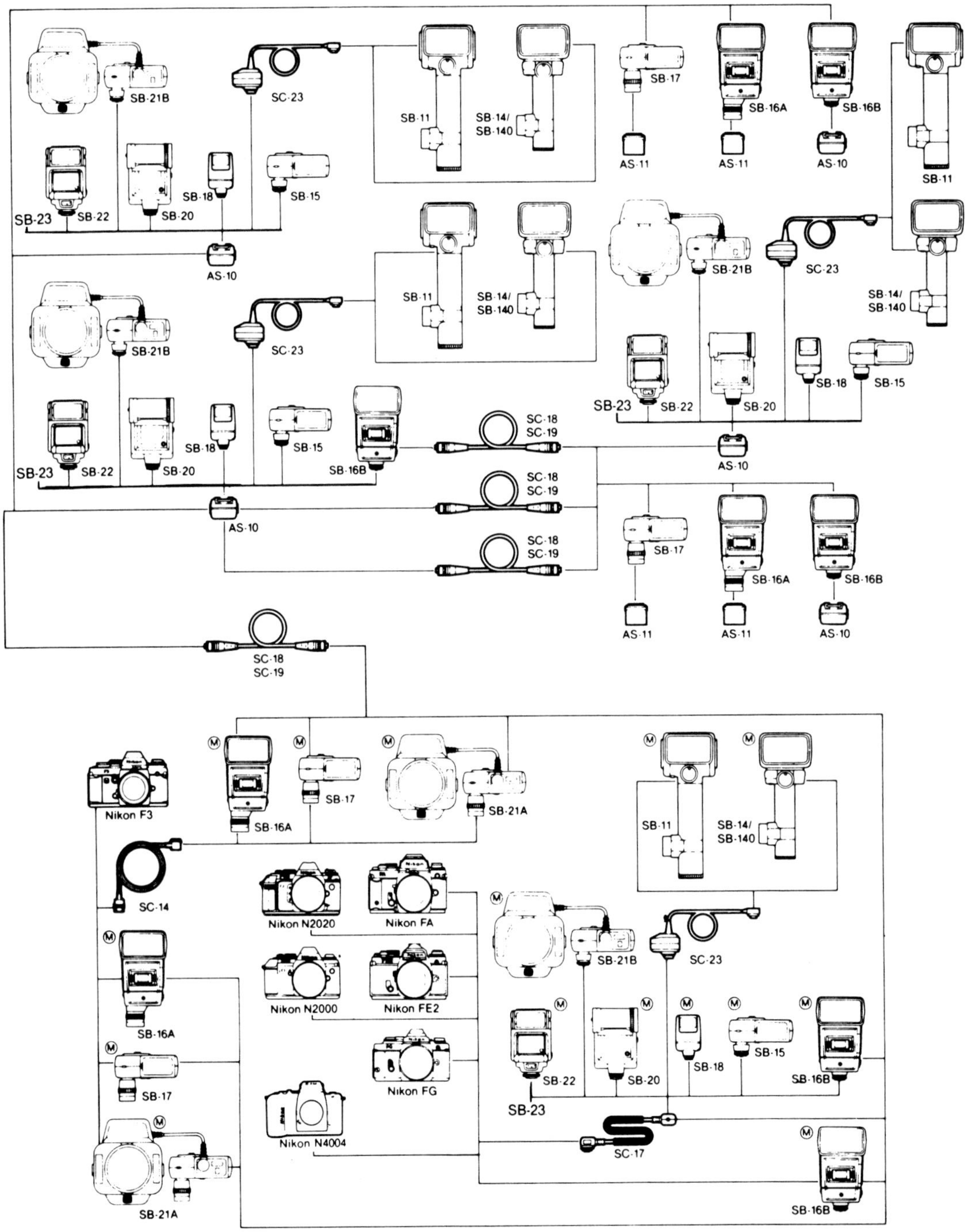

Ⓜ indicates the "master" flash unit.

CHAPTER FIFTEEN

FLASH UNITS

BC-1 No information.

BC-2 No information.

BC-3. (Introduced ?, discontinued 1961) This unit, which was designed for the S series cameras, uses a standard 22.5 volt battery and accepts regular midget bayonet base type bulbs such as the #6. There are two built-in test bulbs to check the camera circuit continuity and the battery-capacitor charge. Included were a connecting cord, extension outlet, bulb ejector, folding camera bracket and snap-off battery case.

BC-4. (Introduced 1956, discontinued 1959) This is a more compact and less expensive flash gun which uses #6 bulbs. It was designed for the S2 and SP rangefinder cameras.

BC-5. (Introduced ?, discontinued 1967) This compact unit fits the accessory shoe on the Nikon F by means of Coupler FLP 364. It makes electrical contact without requiring a connecting cord. The tilting head reflector permits bounce flash and is a collapsing, fan-fold type. It uses a standard 22.5 volt battery and has a built-in test light.

BC-6. (Introduced ?, discontinued 1967) This is a compact unit which fits into the accessory shoe of the camera. It takes the small AG-1 flash bulb and uses a standard flash cord connection and a 15 volt battery.

UNDERWATER FLASH GUN. (Introduced 1965, discontinued 1975) Designed to be used with the Nikonos I. It mounts via a camera holder and can be moved up, down, forward or aft with a long shaft at the base of the unit. Its integrity is maintained with O-rings and waterproof couplings. It is powered by a #412, 22.5v battery and uses either #6, #6B, 26 or 26B bulbs.

BC-7. (Introduced 1967, discontinued 1983) An inexpensive fan-type unit for #5, 6, 6B, 26 or 26B flash bulbs designed to fit on the F or F2 series. It takes a 22.5 volt battery.

REPEATING STROBE, AC POWER. (Introduced 1969, discontinued 1975) No information.

REPEATING STROBE, BATTERY. (Introduced 1969, discontinued 1975) No information.

SB-1. (Introduced 1969, discontinued 1973) This is a handle mount strobe which can be powered either by nicad batteries in the handle or dry cells in the SD-2 battery pack. It is a completely manual unit with an ASA 125 guide number of 149 (ft) which yields 80 flashes with fully charged nicads, 300 with D cells or 700 with a type 497 battery. The recycle time is 1.5 seconds with the 497, 4 seconds with D cells or 5 seconds with nicads. The nicad battery charger can also be used an AC power supply.

SM-1. (Introduced 1971, discontinued 1974) This is a macro ringlight which must be used with the SB-1 power supply. It is designed to attach to any Nikkor lens fitted to a bellows in the reverse position. The unit has a built-in illuminator to aid in focusing. It cannot be used with the 510v battery. Nikon recommends testing and has not established a guide number.

SR-1. (Introduced 1971, discontinued 1974) This is a macro ringlight which must be used in conjunction with the SB-1. It plugs into the side of the SB-1 power supply and is powered by whatever source has been chosen for the SB-1. The SR-1 screws into any lens with a 52mm filter thread. It has a two-position switch which will change the flash from full to 1/4 power. Otherwise its characteristics are the same as the SB-1.

SR-2. (Introduced 1975, discontinued 1989) This macro ringlight screws into any lens with a 52mm filter thread. It is powered by the LD-1 DC battery or the LA-1 AC power supply. (These power supply units are also used with the 200mm f/5.6 Medical Nikkor. Earlier power supply units cannot be used) The guide number at 100 ASA/ISO is 16 (m) 52 (ft) at full power or 8 meters/26 feet at 1/4 power. The recycling time is 12 seconds at full power, 5 seconds at 1/4 power. The battery pack delivers up to 600 flashes at full power and 1400 at 1/4 power.

SM-2. (Introduced 1975, discontinued 1989) This macro ringlight is for extreme close-ups and attaches to lenses mounted on bellows in the reverse position. It is powered by either the LD-1 or LA-1 with other characteristics the same as the SR-2. Nikon recommends testing and has not established a guide number.

UNDERWATER FLASH FOR THE NIKONOS II. (Introduced 1975, discontinued 1986) Same as the underwater flash gun designed for the Nikonos I, except for the Nikonos II flash connector socket.

UNDERWATER FLASH FOR THE NIKONOS III. (Introduced 1975, discontinued 1986) Functions with all M, MF and FP bulbs and can use AG1 bulbs with an AG1 bulb adapter. It is most versatile with the FP bulbs since they better match the camera's sync requirements. It is powered by two 15v batteries. The mounting hardware and sync cord have been improved over the previous underwater guns.

SB-2. (Available only during 1977) This flash was designed to fit F and F2 series cameras directly through the F mounting foot. It has 3 automatic ranges plus manual. The recycling time on manual is approximately 8 seconds and can be less than 2 seconds on automatic. Powered by 4 AA cells which yield approximately 140 manual flashes or up to 1400 on automatic. The range is up to 6 meters/20 feet; the guide number at ISO 100 is 25 (m) 82 (ft).

SB-3. (Available only during 1977) The SB-3 has the same specifications as the SB-2 but it was designed for the Nikkormat EL, FT2 and FTN as well as the Nikon R8 and R10 8mm movie cameras. It contains an ISO hot shoe.

SB-4. (Introduced 1977, discontinued 1979) Designed for any Nikon with an ISO hot shoe. It can be operated on manual or it has one automatic range. Two AA alkaline cells yield 140 manual flashes or up to 1000 automatic. Recycles on manual between 9 and 13 seconds or in less than one second on automatic. Range is to 13 feet with a guide number at ISO 100 of 16 (m) 52 (ft).

SB-5. (Introduced 1977, discontinued 1981) This is a high performance, handle-mount strobe which will function on any Nikon if the proper connection is made. It has three automatic modes and on manual will operate at full power, 1/4 power or continuous at up to 3.8 frames per second. The unit is powered by Nikon Nicad Battery Pack SN-2 or Nikon High Voltage Pack SD-4. The SN-2 yields 75 flashes on manual or 420 on automatic and recycles in 2.6 seconds on manual or 1/4 second on automatic. The SD-4 yields 250 manual flashes or up to 3000 on automatic and recycles in 1.5 seconds on manual or 1/4 second on automatic. The range is up to 8 meters/26 feet with a guide number at ISO 100 of 32 (m) 105 (ft).

SB-6. (Introduced 1978, still available) The Nikon Repeating Flash SB-6 is a sophisticated unit which offers a host of features. It incorporates full flash synchronization with motor driven cameras up to 3.8 fps or with motion picture cameras up to 24 fps in addition to complete stroboscopic operation up to 40 flashes per second. When used in conjunction with Sensor Unit SU-1 and Extension Cord SC-9, it then becomes an automatic, energy saving unit providing correct exposure at various flash-to-subject distances. It mounts directly to F2 series bodies and with a coupler to Nikkormat bodies. It must be used in conjunction with the AC Power Unit SA-3.

SB-7E. (Available only during 1978) Designed to fit F and F2 series cameras through the F foot. It has two automatic ranges plus manual. The unit is powered by 4 AA batteries which yield approximately 160 flashes on manual and recycles on manual in 8 seconds. The range extends to 6 meters/20 feet with a guide number at ISO 100 of 25 (m) 82 (ft).

SB-8E. (Available only during 1978) This unit has the same characteristics as the SB-7E except it fits on all cameras that contain an ISO hot shoe.

SB-9. (Introduced 1977, discontinued 1980) This is a small, light-weight strobe unit designed for the occasional user. Contact is made through an ISO hot shoe. It can be used on a camera without a hot shoe with a PC cord and the Nikon SC10 accessory shoe. It is powered by two AA batteries which yield up to 55 exposures. It has two automatic ranges, but no manual control. The range is 5 meters/17 feet and it has a guide number of 14 (m) 46 (ft) at ISO 100. The recycling time is 9 to 13 seconds.

SB-10. (Introduced 1978, discontinued 1985) Designed primarily for the FE. When used on the FE, it sets the camera (in auto) to X (the camera's sync shutter speed) and provides a ready light in the viewfinder. The unit has two automatic ranges as well as manual at full power. It is powered by 4 AA cells which yield 160 flashes on manual and recycles in 8 seconds. The range of light extends to 6 meters/20 feet with a guide number at ISO 100 of 25 (m) 82 (ft).

SB-11. (Introduced 1980, still available) This handle-mount strobe is dedicated to the F3. It provides TTL automatic when used with an F3 and automatic or manual with any other camera. In TTL automatic, the duration of the flash is controlled by the light measuring system in the camera body. It must be used with the Sensor Cord SC-12 between the strobe unit and the hot shoe on the camera body. A Wide-Angle Attachment SW-3 for the 28mm lens is available. Guide number at ISO 100: 36 (m) 118 (f). 170 flashes on manual per 8 AA alkaline batteries. Maximum distance: 25.5 meters/84 feet.

SB-12. (Introduced 1980, discontinued 1984) Designed exclusively for the F3, this "F Foot" mounted strobe provides TTL automatic control. It can be used off-camera with the F3 via a SC-14 cord (or any other camera with a PC terminal on manual only). It has seven automatic ranges as well as manual on full-power. The unit is powered by 4 AA cells, reaches to 6.2 meters/20.3 feet on manual and recycles in eight seconds. The guide number with ISO 100 is 25 (m) 82 (f).

SB-14. (Introduced 1982, still available) Dedicated to the F3. Provides TTL automatic when used with the F3 and automatic or manual with any other camera. In TTL automatic, the duration of the flash is controlled by the light measuring system in the camera body. The automatic sensing unit - SU-2 - is detachable (for non-TTL automatic). Guide number at ISO 100: 32 (m) 105 (ft). 270 flashes with Battery Pack SD-7 (6 C batteries). Maximum distance: 8 meters/26 feet.

SB-15. (Introduced 1982, discontinued 1988) Dedicated to the FA, FE2 and the FG. It provides TTL automatic when used with these cameras or manual with any other camera. Guide number at ISO 100: 25 (m) 83 (ft). 160 flashes per 4 AA alkaline or 60 with NiCad batteries. Maximum distance: 6.2 meters/20 feet.

SB-16. (Introduced 1983, still available) The SB-16 is a flash head only. It must be used with one of two detachable Flash Unit Couplers. Depending on the coupler attached, the unit becomes SB-16A or SB-16B. Actually the SB-16 has two flash heads. The main head can be tilted and rotated while a small auxiliary head always points straight ahead. This small head provides fill-in light. The angle of the main flash can be adjusted to match the focal length of the lens in use. An accessory - Wide-Flash Adapter SW-7 - allows the use of a 24mm lens. Provides four modes: 1) TTL automatic when used with a compatible camera, 2) self-regulated automatic at two different intensities, 3) manual and 4) a reduced power manual for sequential flashes when using a motor drive. Guide number at ISO 100: 32 (m) 105 (ft). 100 flashes per 4 AA alkaline or NiCad batteries. Maximum usable distance: 8 meters/26 feet.

SB-16A. Dedicated to the F3. The AS-8 Flash Unit Coupler attaches to the F3 and all its variations: F3T, F3HP and F3AF.

SB-16B. Dedicated to the FA, FE2, FG and N series bodies. The AS-9 Flash Unit Coupler fits on a standard shoe or ISO hot shoe.

SB-17. (Introduced 1983, discontinued 1990) Dedicated to any F3 including the F3AF. Unit includes a mounting foot to fit the F3. Can be used with any standard ISO shoe with Adapter AS-6. Has four modes: 1) TTL automatic with the F3, 2) self-regulated automatic at two different intensities, 3) manual and 4) reduced power manual (MD) for sequential flashes when using a motor drive. When used with the F3, FA, FE2, FG and FG-20, on automatic the flash will set the camera shutter speed to X sync. Has a Wide-Flash Adapter SW-6 for use with the 28mm lens. Guide number at ISO 100: 25 (m) 82 (ft). 160 flashes per 4 AA alkaline, NiCad or carbon-zinc batteries. Maximum usable distance: 6.2 meters/20 feet.

SB-18. (These units were sold by Nikon Inc. as a part of a package, never separately. It never appeared in the dealer price list; there was no suggested list price.) This is a shoe mounted unit designed for the FG, FE2 or FA. It can also be used with the Nikonos V (above water) via the V type sync cord. It operates on either TTL or manual. There are no automatic settings other than TTL. 250 manual flashes from 4 AA cells and a recycle time of 6 seconds. The maximum distance is 10 meters/32 feet with a guide number at ISO 100 of 20 (m) 66 (ft).

SB-19. (Introduced 1984, discontinued 1988) Intended for use with the FG-20 and EM, but can be used with any camera with an ISO hot shoe. Can be used with self-regulated automatic or manual. When used with the FG-20 or the EM and a lens with an Aperture Indexing Post (AIS, AI, E), offers a choice of six aperture settings on automatic. With other cameras, there is only one aperture choice. Guide number at ISO 100: 20 (m) 66 (ft). 250 flashes per 4 AA alkaline batteries. Maximum usable distance: 10 meters/33 feet.

SB-E. (Introduced 1979, discontinued 1987) Intended for use with the FG-20 and EM, but can be used with any camera with an ISO hot shoe. Has only one mode: self-regulating automatic. With an FG-20 or EM and a lens with an Aperture Indexing Post (AIS, AI, E), offers a choice of three aperture settings. With other cameras, there is only one aperture choice. Guide number at ISO 100: 17 (m) 56 (ft). 80 flashes per 4 AAA alkaline batteries. Maximum usable distance: 3 meters/10 feet.

SB-20. (Introduced 1986, still available) Intended for use with the N2020, but also dedicated to the N2000, FE2 and FA. Provides TTL automatic with the dedicated cameras. Additionally, provides an infrared light source to help the N2020 focus automatically in dim light. Can be used with the FG-20 and EM for manual flash. Must be used with lenses with an Aperture Indexing Post (AIS, AI, E). Guide number at ISO 100: 30 (m) 98 (ft). 150 flashes per 4 AA alkaline, nicad or carbon zinc batteries.

SB-21. (Introduced 1986, still available) This macro system is composed of two units: the controller and the ring flash. A complete unit is produced by combining the SB-21 with the AS-12 or the AS-14 to make the SB-21A or SB-21B respectively. The controller is usually mounted on the camera ISO shoe and the flash assembly around the lens via the filter threads. In addition to TTL, the unit operates on full, 1/4 and 1/16 manual. It is powered by 4 AA cells which provide 200 flashes on manual. The range is 1.3 meters/4.25 feet with a guide number at ISO 100 of 13 (m) 43 (ft).

SB-21A. For the F3. The AS-12 has a special foot for attaching to the F3 enabling the unit to be used for TTL.

SB-21B. For any ISO shoe. The AS-14 has an ISO mounting foot which enables the unit to be used for TTL operation with the FA, FE2, N2020, N2000 or FG.

SB-22. (Introduced 1987, still available) This ISO shoe-mounted unit is designed primarily for use with Nikon autofocus cameras. It provides programmed TTL with the N series and F4 plus the FA, FE2 and FG. It provides automatic and manual on any camera with an ISO hot shoe. There are two automatic ranges plus TTL and manual. It is powered by 4 AA cells which yield 200 flashes on manual and recycles in 4 seconds. The maximum range is 20 meters/66 feet with a guide number at ISO 100 of 25 (m) 82 (ft).

SB-23. (Introduced 1988, still available) This is an inexpensive ISO shoe mounted strobe designed primarily for Nikon autofocus cameras. It operates on TTL with the N series bodies plus the F4, FA, FE2 and FG. In addition to TTL, there is a manual mode, but no automatic modes. It is powered by 4 AA cells which provide 400 manual flashes and a recycling time of 2 seconds. The maximum range is 10 meters/32 feet with a guide number at ISO 100 of 20 (m) 66 (ft).

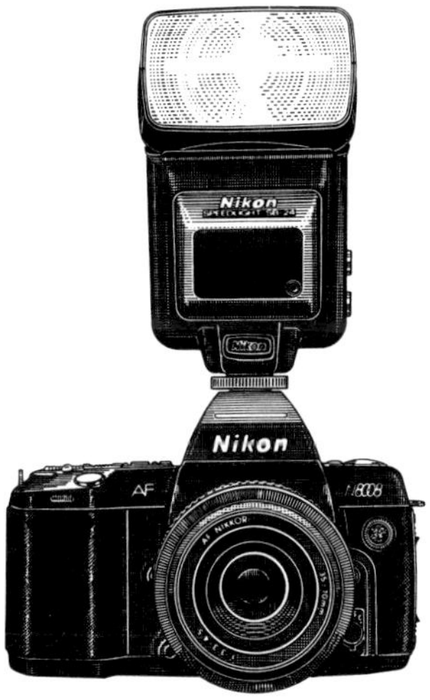

N8008 with 35-70mm Lens
SB-24 Speedlight

SB-24. (Introduced 1988, still available) This is a very sophisticated shoe mounted unit with cybernetic-sync flash, first and second curtain flash sync, matrix balanced fill-flash, matrix TTL flash, center-weighted flash fill and center-weighted TTL flash when used with the appropriate Nikon camera. TTL, automatic and manual can be used with the N series, FA, FE2, FG or F3. All of the modes operate with the N8008 and F4. It is powered by 4 AA cells which provide 100 flashes on manual and recycle in 5 seconds. The maximum range is 20 meters/66 feet with a guide number at ISO 100 of 42 (m) 138 (ft).

SB-101. (Introduced 1980, discontinued 1985) This is an underwater unit offering fully automatic operation when used with the Nikonos IV-A. It can be taken to depths of 50 meters/160 feet. It can also be used on earlier Nikonos bodies on manual. There are two automatic modes and either full or 1/4 power on manual. It is powered by 8 AA cells which yield 150 flashes on manual and recycles in 8 seconds. The underwater maximum range is 4 meters/13 feet (above water: 8 meters/26 feet) with an underwater guide number at ISO 100 of 16 (m) 52 (ft)f; above water: 32 (m) 104 (ft).

SB-102. (Introduced 1985, still available) This unit is an amphibious high performance strobe designed for use with the Nikonos V, IV-A and III. It can be submerged to a depth of 50 meters/160 feet. In combination with the Nikonos V, it offers TTL automatic and when coupled with the optional sensor unit SU-101, it can be used for non-TTL automatic with the Nikonos III, IV-A and V. In addition to the TTL and automatic modes, it operates on full, 1/4 and 1/16 on manual. It is powered by 6 C cells which provide 120 flashes on manual and recycles in 14 seconds. The underwater maximum range is 5.6 meters/18 feet (above water: 11 meters/36 feet) with an underwater guide number at ISO 100 of 16 (m) 52 (ft); above water: 32 (m) 104 (ft).

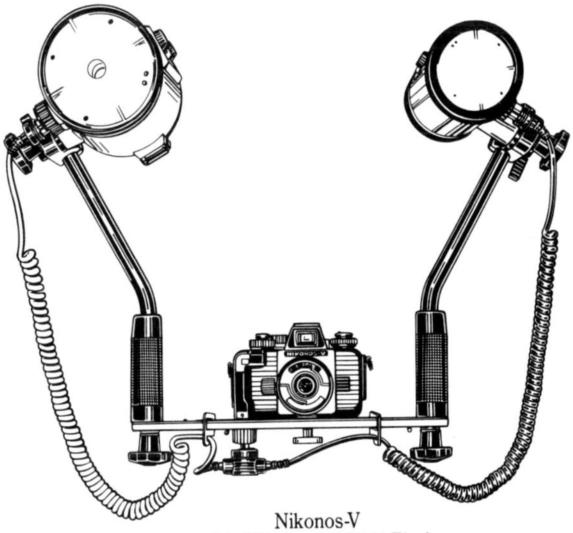

Nikonos-V
with SB102 and SB103 Flash

SB-103. (Introduced 1985, still available) This is a small, high performance amphibious unit designed by use with the Nikonos III, IV-A and V. It can be submerged to 50 meters/160 feet. With the Nikonos V, it offers TTL automatic flash exposure control. It can be used with the Nikonos III and IV-A on manual. Powered by 4 AA cells, the unit provides 130 flashes on automatic and recycles in 6 seconds. The maximum underwater range is 3.5 meters/11.5 feet (above water: 7 meters/23 feet) with an underwater guide number at ISO 100 of 10 (m) 33 (ft); above water: 20 (m) 66 (ft).

SB-140. (Introduced 1986, still available) This is a sophisticated, handle mounted strobe which offers great versatility when used with a wide variety of accessories. It will work with any camera and can be equipped with filters making it useful for infrared and ultaviolet photography. It has three automatic ranges, TTL plus full and 1/4 power on manual. It is powered by 6 C cells which provide 270 flashes on manual and recycles in 4 seconds. The maximum range is 8 meters/26 feet with a guide number at ISO 100 of 32 (m) 105 (ft).

Flash Compatability Chart

Flash \ Camera	F3 Series 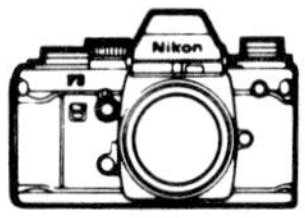	FA/FE2/N2000 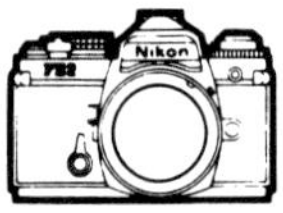	FM2 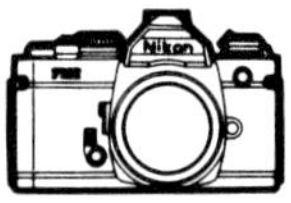	N2020 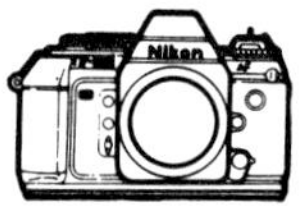
SB-11 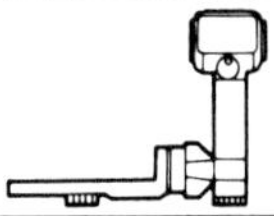	Via SC-12 ●	Via SC-23 ●		Via SC-23 ●
	▲	Via SC-13 ▲	Via SC-13 ▲	Via SC-13 ▲
SB-14 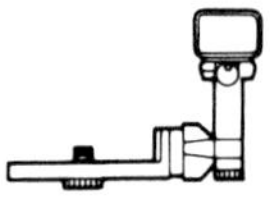	Via SC-12 ●	Via SC-23 ●		Via SC-23 ●
	▲	Via SC-13 ▲	Via SC-13 ▲	Via SC-13 ▲
SB-140 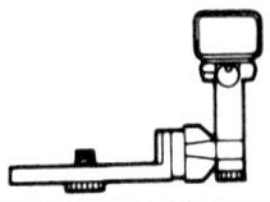	Via SC-12 ●	Via SC-23 ●		Via SC-23 ●
	▲	Via SC-13 ▲	Via SC-13 ▲	Via SC-13 ▲
SB-16A 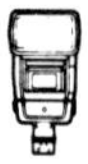	Direct or Via SC-14 ●			Via SC-13
	▲	Via Coupler AS-6 ▲	Via Coupler AS-6 ▲	▲
SB-16B 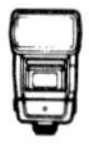		Direct or Via SC-17 ●		●
	Via Coupler AS 4/7 ▲	▲	Direct or Via SC-17 ▲	▲
SB-17 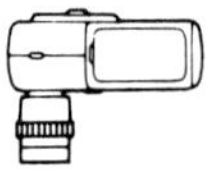	Direct or Via SC-14 ●			Direct or Via SC-17
	▲	Via Coupler AS-6 ▲	Via Coupler AS-6 ▲	Via Coupler AS-6 ▲
SB-20/22 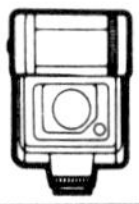		Direct or Via SC-17 ●		Direct or Via SC-17
	Via Coupler AS-4/7 ▲	▲	▲	▲
SB-21A 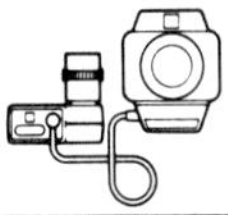	Direct ●			
		Via Coupler AS-6	Via Coupler AS-6	Via Coupler AS-6
SB-21B 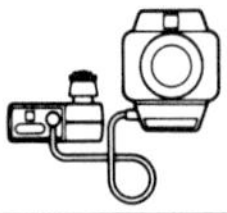		Direct ●		Direct ●
	Via Coupler AS-4/7		Direct	
SB-6 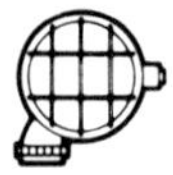				
	Via SC-9	Via SC-9	Via SC-9	Via SC-9

● TTL Automatic Control

▲ Sensored Automatic Control

Manual Control

AF-Illumination

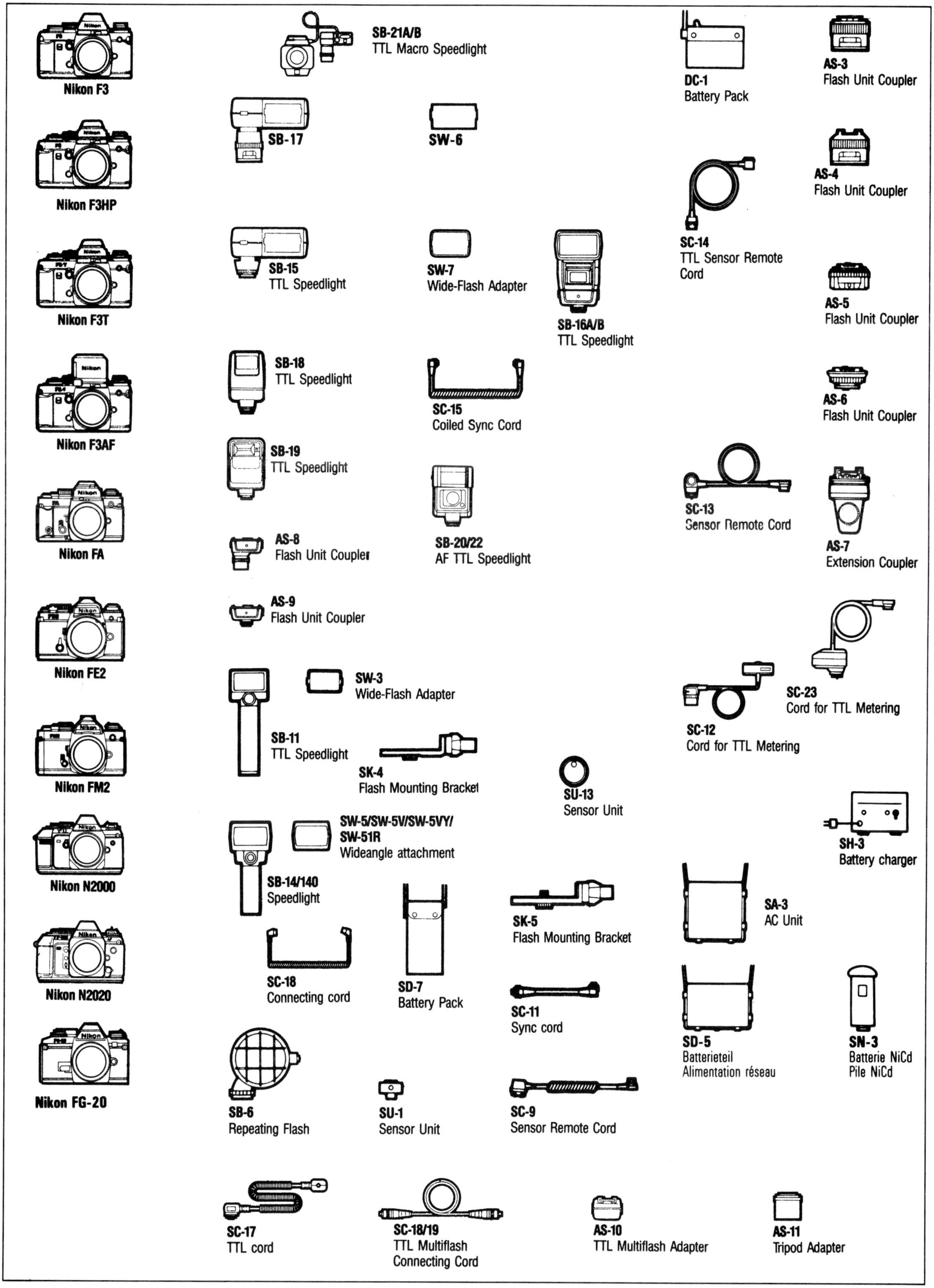

Nikon F3
Nikon F3HP
Nikon F3T
Nikon F3AF
Nikon FA
Nikon FE2
Nikon FM2
Nikon N2000
Nikon N2020
Nikon FG-20
SB-21A/B
TTL Macro Speedlight
SB-17
SW-6
SB-15
TTL Speedlight
SW-7
Wide-Flash Adapter
SB-16A/B
TTL Speedlight
SB-18
TTL Speedlight
SC-15
Coiled Sync Cord
SB-19
TTL Speedlight
SB-20/22
AF TTL Speedlight
AS-8
Flash Unit Coupler
AS-9
Flash Unit Coupler
SW-3
Wide-Flash Adapter
SB-11
TTL Speedlight
SK-4
Flash Mounting Bracket
SW-5/SW-5V/SW-5VY/
SW-51R
Wideangle attachment
SB-14/140
Speedlight
SC-18
Connecting cord
SD-7
Battery Pack
SK-5
Flash Mounting Bracket
SC-11
Sync cord
SB-6
Repeating Flash
SU-1
Sensor Unit
SC-9
Sensor Remote Cord
DC-1
Battery Pack
AS-3
Flash Unit Coupler
AS-4
Flash Unit Coupler
SC-14
TTL Sensor Remote
Cord
AS-5
Flash Unit Coupler
AS-6
Flash Unit Coupler
SC-13
Sensor Remote Cord
AS-7
Extension Coupler
SC-23
Cord for TTL Metering
SC-12
Cord for TTL Metering
SU-13
Sensor Unit
SH-3
Battery charger
SA-3
AC Unit
SD-5
Batterieteil
Alimentation réseau
SN-3
Batterie NiCd
Pile NiCd
SC-17
TTL cord
SC-18/19
TTL Multiflash
Connecting Cord
AS-10
TTL Multiflash Adapter
AS-11
Tripod Adapter

JANUARY 1959

why a
NIKON SP

Photography has come to mean a great deal to you. It's a world in which you are the prime mover. There is no one to restrain you; no one to goad you. There is only you and your will to create, your own burning desire to express yourself, to be heard—in pictures.

You want a camera, yet, more than a camera. You want an instrument that responds fluently; an instrument you can command, and it obeys; that works with you and helps you achieve the results you visualize and strive to create. *That is why you have a Nikon SP.*

From the moment you take it in your hands, it becomes alive, part of you. You bring it up to your eyes, and instantly you behold your picture—life-size—and you see it as it will compose with any one of six different lenses. One of them frames the very picture you want. In a moment, the appropriate lens is in position—advance, focus, shoot—and you have it. The picture is yours, all yours. *That is why you have a Nikon SP.*

Finally, the negatives are processed. You examine them—they're just as you expected. You have learned that you can count on Nikkor lenses to give you needle-sharp detail definition—at every aperture. And the exposures—day, night —bright light, dim light—it evidently makes no difference as long as there is light enough to see by! What a rare combination of speed and resolution! *That is why you have a Nikon SP.*

There is more—a long list of things you've discovered in the Nikon SP—each of which adds to the realization that the SP is truly the greatest 35mm camera of all time. But, not one of these is so important as the discovery that you are suddenly creating the kind of pictures you've often seen and admired—only this time they are yours. And so, the world of creative photography is yours—beyond even the horizons... *all because you have a Nikon SP.*

If *you* haven't as yet discovered the magic in Nikon photography, ask to see the Nikon SP at your photo dealer. For fully illustrated camera, lens and accessory brochures, write: Dept. P-1

NIPPON KOGAKU TOKYO

NIKON INCORPORATED

251 Fourth Avenue, New York 10, New York • In Canada: Anglophoto Ltd., 880 Champagneur Avenue, Montreal, P.Q.

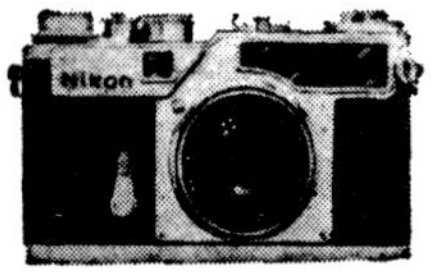

Nikon SP (left) with Universal 6-lens Viewfinder System and 50mm Nikkor f2, $369.50; with 50mm Nikkor f1.4, $415. Nikon S3 (right—identical to SP except for 35, 50 and 105mm Trifocal Finder) with f2, $309.50; and with f1.4, $355.

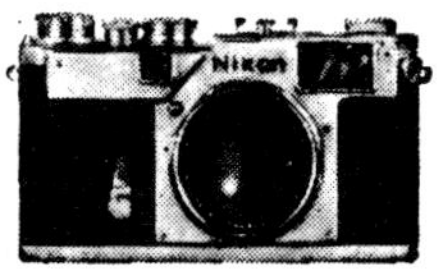

CHAPTER SIXTEEN

CLOSE-UP EQUIPMENT

BELLOWS

BELLOWS FOCUSING ATTACHMENT PB-4. This is a four-track, bellows focusing attachment with a range of 43mm to 185mm and a reproduction ratio from 1:1.2X to 1:3.6X with a 50mm 1.8 lens in the normal position. It offers horizontal swings through an arc of 25 degrees, shifts of 10mm to either side and a tripod head movement of 152mm.

BELLOWS FOCUSING ATTACHMENT PB-5. This two-track bellows focusing attachment has a reproduction ratio of 1:1.2X to 1:3.5X with a 50mm 1.8 lens in the normal position and a range of 43mm to 185mm.

BELLOWS FOCUSING ATTACHMENT PB-6. This mono-rail bellows focusing attachment has a tripod head traversing plate. Therefore the single rail unit performs like a 4-track unit. Automatic diaphragm control is possible when it is used with the double cable release AR-4. The reproduction ratio is 1:1.1X to 1:4X with a 50mm lens in the normal position. The lens can also be mounted in the reverse position without a need for accessories. The bellows has a range of 48mm to 205mm. The tripod head movement is 180mm.

EXTENSION BELLOWS PB-6E. Fits onto the PB-6. Increases the amount of extension to 438mm and extends the reproduction ratio from 1:1.6X to 1:8.5X. This enables much higher magnification ratios than with the bellows alone. Voids the PB-6 automatic diaphragm feature.

COPY STANDS

REPRO-COPY OUTFIT PF-1. The unit consists of a tubular column secured to a folding baseboard which doubles as a storage case. The uncounterbalanced saddle and camera cradle slide up or down the column making a sturdy set-up for copying or photographing small objects.

REPRO-COPY OUTFIT PF-2. Similar to the PF-1, except is has a two-piece column for greater versatility and easier storage. The knobs and controls are improved.

REPRO-COPY OUTFIT PF-3. This unit is taller and sturdier than the PF-1 and PF-2. The column is rectangular rather than tubular which insures that the film plane remains parallel to the subject. The reproduction ratio scale facilitates precise copying. Includes a gray card centering target on the baseboard; does not fold for storage.

REPRO-COPY OUTFIT PF-4. A refined version of the PF-3. Makes centering the camera plus accessories such as motors and bellows simple. Special provision to reduce vibrations included. With the PC-3 Table Clamp, attaches to a table or bench without giving up any bench space.

RINGS AND TUBES

MACRO ADAPTER RING BR-2. Allows lenses with a 52mm front thread to be mounted in the reverse position. When mounted directly to the camera body, the ring and reversed lens allow closer focusing than normally. Used with a bellows, a greater than life-size image is obtained.

AUTO RING BR-4. This ring, when used with the AR-4 double cable release, provides automatic exposure control with a PB-4 or PB-5 Bellows. The ring is mounted between the lens and bellows, adding an additional 9mm of extention.

EXTENSION RING SET K. The set consists of 5 different rings (K-1, K-2, K-3, K-4, K-5) which can be used singly or in combination to provide extensions from 5.8mm to 46.6mm. They may be used between the body and lens or between the body and bellows or other close-up devices to increase magnification.

EXTENSION RING E2. This ring can be used with or without bellows to increase the lens-to-film distance. It includes a semiautomatic diaphragm control.

EXTENSION RINGS PK-1, PK-2, PK-3. These automatic extension rings add 8mm, 14mm and 27.5mm respectively. They are for NAI lenses.

EXTENSION TUBE PK-11A. This AI tube adds 8mm to the lens-to-film distance and can be used in conjunction with any other close-up device.

EXTENSION TUBE PK-12. Adds 14mm to the lens-to-film distance and can be used in conjunction with any other close-up device.

EXTENSION TUBE PK-13. Adds 27.5mm to any close-up system. It was made as a companion to the AI 55mm Micro Nikkor. Without the tube, the lens is capable of reproduction ratios up to 1:2; with the tube, 1:1 is possible.

EXTENSION TUBE PN-1. Adds 52.5mm. Made to be a companion to the NAI 105mm Micro Nikkor. Without the tube, the lens is capable of reproduction ratios up to 1:2; with the tube, 1:1 is possible.

EXTENSION TUBE PN-11. Same as the PN-1 for the AI 105mm Micro Nikkor.

COMPATABILITY OF EXTENSION RINGS WITH AI & NON-AI PRODUCTS

EQUIPMENT	COMBINATION			
*CAMERA TYPE	**EXTENSION RING TYPE	LENS TYPE	MAX APERTURE INDEXING	METERING
1. AI	—	AI or AIS	Automatic	Full Aperture
2. AI	AI	AI or AIS	Automatic	Full Aperture
3. AI	Non-AI	None	Stopped-Down	
4. AI	—	Non-AI	None	Stopped Down
5. AI	AI	Non-AI	LENS CANNOT BE MOUNTED	
6. AI	Non-AI	Non-AI	None	Stopped-Down
7. Non-AI	—	AI or AIS	Semi-Automatic	Full Aperture
8. Non-AI	AI	AI or AIS	None Stopped-Down	None
9. Non-AI	Non-AI	AI or AIS	Semi-Automatic	Full Aperture
10. Non-AI	—	Non-AI	Semi-Automatic	Full Aperture
11. Non-AI	AI	Non-AI	LENS CANNOT BE MOUNTED	
12. Non-AI	Non-AI	Non-AI	Semi-Automatic	Full Aperture

*Camera Type: AI—Nikon F3, F2A Photomic, F2AS Photomic, FA, N2000, FE2, FM2, FE, FM, EM, EL-2 and Nikkormat FT-3
Non-AI—Nikon F2 Photomic, F2SB Photomic, Nikkormat EL/ELW & FT2

**Extension Ring Type: AI—PK-11, PK-12, PK-13 & PN-11
Non-AI—PK-1, PK-2, PK-3 & PN-1

SLIDE COPYING DEVICES

SLIDE COPYING ADAPTER PS-4. Fits PB-4 and PB-5 bellows. This unit allows copying negatives or transparencies, mounted or not, either full-size or cropped and magnified. The image copied can be moved up and 6mm vertically or 9mm horizontally to facilitate cropping. Lenses from 20mm to 85mm function properly. Reproduction ratios of 1:1.2X to 1:4.4X can be realized with a 50mm lens in the normal or reversed position.

SLIDE COPYING ADAPTER PS-5. Fits PB-4 and PB-5 bellows. This is a simplified version of the PS-4. It has a reproduction ratio range of 1:1.2X to 1:4.4X using a 50mm lens. It will accept both mounted transparencies and unmounted strips. It has no provision for the movement of the original image.

SLIDE COPYING ADAPTER PS-6. For use with the PB-6. Allows a 6mm rise and fall plus a 9mm lateral shift. Can be used with lenses from 20mm to 55mm. It has a reproduction range of 1:1.1X to 1:2.9X with a 50mm lens.

DIOPTERS

CLOSE-UP ATTACHMENT LENS NUMBER 0. This 52mm lens has a diopter rating of .7; with a 50mm lens, it is capable of reproduction ratios of up to 1:5.4.

CLOSE-UP ATTACHMENT LENS NUMBER 1. This 52mm lens has a diopter rating of 1.5; with a 50mm lens, it is capable of reproduction ratios of up to 1:4.4.

CLOSE-UP ATTACHMENT LENS NUMBER 2. This 52mm lens has a diopter rating of 3. With a 50mm lens, it is capable of reproduction ratios of up to 1:3.3.

CLOSE-UP ATTACHMENT LENS NUMBER 3T. This 52mm lens was designed to be used with telephoto lenses. It has a diopter rating of 1.5; with a 200mm lens, it is capable of reproduction ratios of up to 1:2.

CLOSE-UP ATTACHMENT LENS NUMBER 4T. This 52mm lens was designed to be used with telephoto lenses. It has a diopter rating of 2.9; with a 200mm lens, it is capable of reproduction ratios of up to 1:1.2.

CLOSE-UP ATTACHMENT LENS NUMBER 5T. This 62mm lens was designed to be used with telephoto lenses. It has a diopter rating of 1.5; with a 105mm lens, it is capable of reproduction ratios of up to 3.3.

CLOSE-UP ATTACHMENT LENS NUMBER 6T. This 62mm lens was designed to be used with telephoto lenses. It has a diopter rating of 2.9; with a 105mm lens, it is capable of reproduction ratios of up to 2.2.

MICRO NIKKOR LENSES

RF 50mm 3.5 (Introduced 1956, discontinued 1963) This lens is for Nikon rangefinder cameras. It is in a two-position mount that allows focusing from 3 feet to infinity or 1.5 feet to 3 feet in the macro position.

NAI 55mm f/3.5 (Introduced 1963, discontinued 1977) This lens uses the same Petzval optical formula as the rangefinder micro, but it was redesigned and placed in a barrel and mount for Nikon reflex cameras. It is capable of reproduction ratios up to 1:2. Together with the PK 3 Auto Extension tube, it will reproduce at ratios up to 1:1.

AI 55mm f/3.5. (Introduced 1977, discontinued 1979) This is the same as the NAI 55mm Micro Nikkor but in an AI mount.

AI 55mm f/2.8. (Introduced 1980, discontinued 1984) This flat field lens is truly multipurpose. It performs well as a normal lens and is superb for all close-up work where positioning the camera close to the subject is not a problem. It will focus from infinity to 0.25 meters/0.9 feet and is capable of ratios up to 1:2. Together with the PK-13 Auto Extension tube, it will reproduce at ratios up to 1:1.

SPECIAL NOTE. NAI tubes must be used in the stopped-down mode when mounted on AI, AIS or AF cameras. AI tubes on NAI cameras must be used in the stopped-down mode. NAI and AI tubes do not transfer S or AF functions to any camera. The N4004 and N4004s cameras, when used with ANY tube, require stopped-down metering.

CAUTION. The PK-1, PK-11, BR-4 and K-1 cannot be mounted directly on AF lenses.

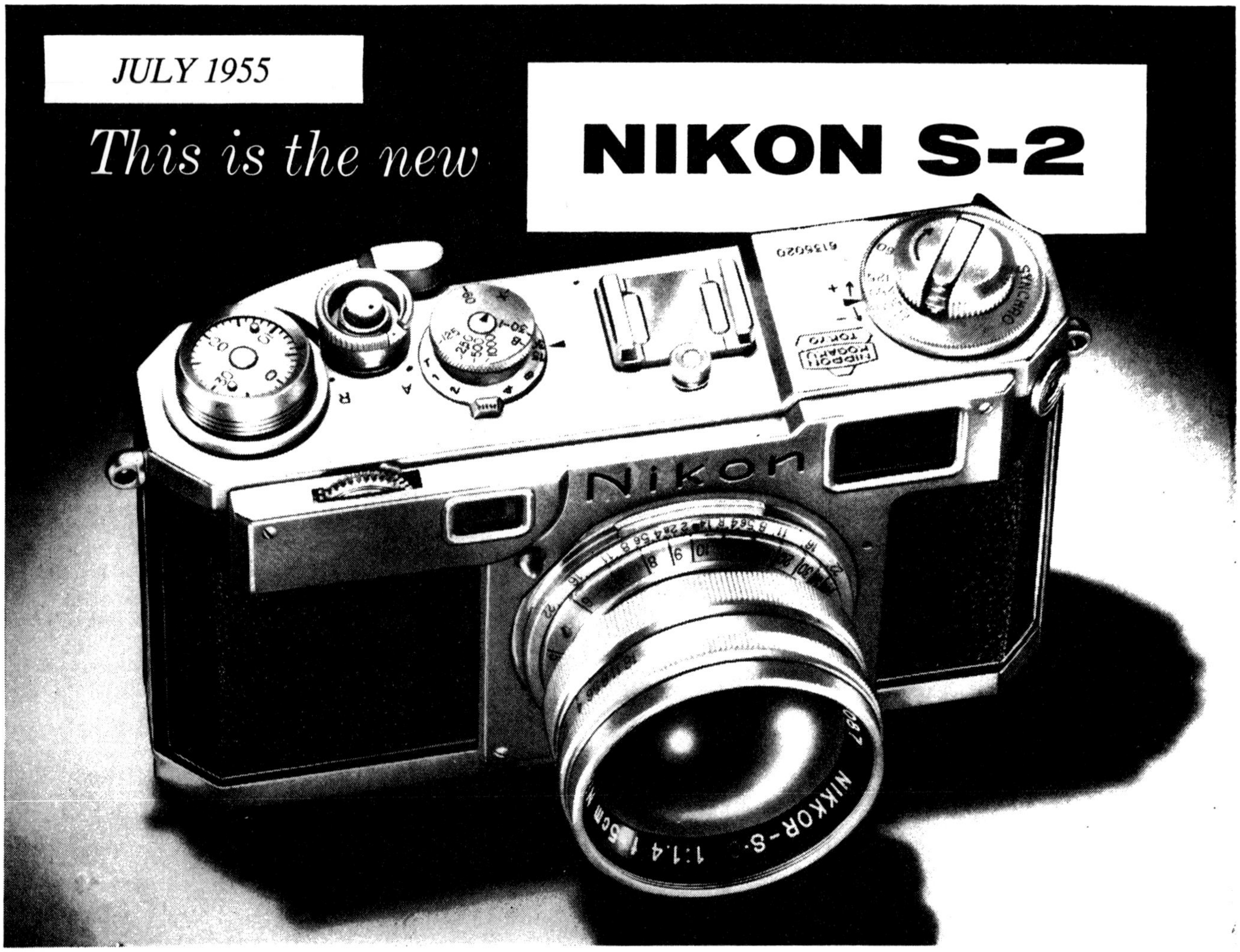

...and these are the **5** *Most Talked About Features*

LIFE-SIZE IMAGE RANGEFINDER/VIEWFINDER
Large 1 to 1 image simplifies focusing and viewing. Internal luminous rectangle frames subject and aids in composition. Can be used with both eyes open.

RAPID FILM TRANSPORT
Single-stroke lever advances film and simultaneously sets shutter for next exposure. Permits sequence pictures in rapid succession without danger of double or partial exposures.

HI-SPEED FILM REWIND
Convenient crank-lever permits a completed 36-exposure roll to be rewound in less than 20 seconds. When not used, lever folds and nests flush in rewind knob.

POSITIVE SYNCH SELECTOR
Dial settings permit perfect synchronization at all shutter speeds to 1/1000th second. For various types of flashbulbs. Speedlight units synched at 1/50th second.

NIKKOR LENSES
Exhibiting unusually high resolution at high speeds, the NIKKOR Lenses have contributed immeasurably to the technique of Available Light Photography. This is only one of the many reasons why NIKKOR Lenses are the most wanted in the field—sought for every make of 35mm camera.

And there are many more features you will like. In fact, the NIKON S-2 combines more features in one instrument than any other '35' on the market today.

NIKON S-2 with Nikkor 50mm f2 lens . . **$299.50**
NIKON S-2 with Nikkor 50mm f1.4 lens . **345.00**

At your Nikon dealer, or write for complete description to Dept. TG-2.
NIKON Incorporated, 277 Fifth Avenue, New York 16, N. Y.

NIPPON KOGAKU TOKYO

Research microscopes, contour projectors, surveyors' transits, prism binoculars, and fine optical and ophthalmic instruments.

AIS 55mm f/2.8 (Introduced 1984, still available) This lens is the same as the AI 55mm f/2.8 but in AIS mount.

AF 55mm f/2.8. (Introduced 1986, discontinued 1989) This is a flat field multipurpose lens. It performs well as a normal lens and is superb for close-up shots where a short camera-to-subject distance is not a problem. It will focus from infinity to .25 meters/0.9 feet and produces reproduction ratios up to 1:2.

AF 60mm f/2.8 (Introduced 1989, still available) This versatile new lens performs well on manual focusing bodies as well as autofocus ones. It produces ratios up to 1:1 without the need of tubes or rings. This lens should NOT be used with the following rings as they may damage the lens CPU contacts: PK-11, K-1, BR-4, BR-2 or K-2.

NMC 105mm f/4.0 Bellows-Nikkor. (Introduced 1969, discontinued 1977) This lens is for use with bellows focusing attachments and offers continuous focusing from infinity to 1.3X when used with either the PB-4 or the PB-5. Optically optimized at close distances, it still performs well at greater distances, but contains no meter coupling or auto-diaphragm (the iris must be set manually or can be preset).

NAI 105mm f/4.0 (Introduced 1974, discontinued 1977) This lens is primarily designed for close-up work, but it is also a valuable medium-length telephoto. It has high resolution and excellent contrast. It will achieve reproduction ratios up to 1:2 and up to 1:1 when used in conjunction with the PN-1 extension ring.

AI 105mm f/4.0 (Introduced 1977, discontinued 1984) This lens is the same as the NAI 105mm f/4.0 but in AI mount.

AIS 105mm f/4.0 (Introduced 1984, discontinued 1985) This lens is the same as the AI 105mm f/4.0 but in AIS mount.

AIS 105mm f/2.8. (Introduced 1984, still available) This lens is ideal when more lens to subject distance than a 55mm or 60mm lens will allow. It has a minimum focusing distance of 0.41 meters/1.34 feet and provides a reproduction ratio of 1:2 or 1:1 when used with the PN-11 Auto Extension Tube.

AF 105mm f/2.8 (Introduced 1990, still available) This lens features a focusing range from infinity to 1:1. It has a close-range correction floating element design for excellent quality over the entire focusing range. It is truly a multi-purpose lens.

AI 200mm f/4.0 IF (Introduced 1979, discontinued 1984) This telephoto lens allows close-up photography from a greater distance than any of the shorter focal length micro lenses. It will focus to a minimum distance of 0.71 meters/2.34 feet and provides a reproduction ratio of 1:2. Even greater magnification can be achieved when used in conjunction with the TC-301 Teleconverter since the focal length is doubled and the minimum focusing distance is not changed.

AIS 200mm f/4.0 (Introduced 1984, still available) This lens is the same as the AI 200mm f/4.0 IF but in an AIS mount.

MEDICAL NIKKORS

AUTO 200mm f/5.6 (Introduced 1963, discontinued 1984) This lens is equipped with six auxiliary lenses which, when used in varying combinations, will yield ten different reproduction ratios from 1:15 to 3:1. The diaphragm automatically sets itself to yield proper exposure when the film speed and reproduction ratio are set. The flash has a duration of approximately 1/500 of a second with a recycling time of approximately 13 seconds on either AC or the DC battery pack.

120mm f/4 IF (Introduced 1981, still available) This unique lens, which features internal focusing, provides continuously variable reproduction ratios from 1:11 up to 1:1. By adding the 2X close-up attachment (which is included), reproduction ratios up to 2X can be realized. Because focusing is internal, there is no extension in the lens barrel, making the lens well balanced at all magnifications. The aperture sets itself automatically and the silicon controlled rectifier corrects flash output, making correct exposure easy regardless of the magnification. The reproduction ratios can be seen in the viewfinder and/or printed in the lower right hand corner of the film. The flash duration is approximately 1/500 of a second with either AC or the DC battery back.

THE FIRST MOVIE-8 CAMERA WITH NIKKOR ZOOM

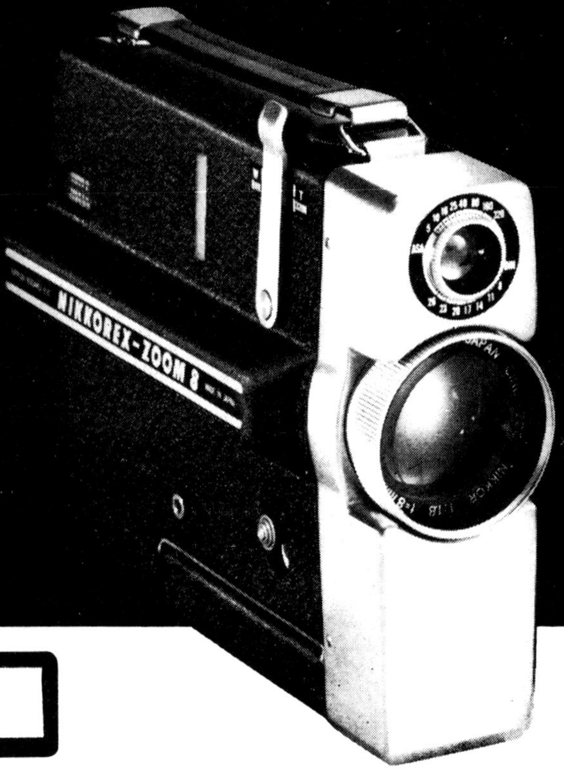

APRIL 1963

Many movie cameras have *zoom,* but only this one has the Nikkor-Zoom, designed to give you *sharp* zoom — *sharp* at 8mm, *sharp* at 32mm, and *sharp* at every focal length in between. The new Nikkorex 8 Zoom with its f1.8 Nikkor lens combines all the advantages of *zoom* versatility with the proven quality and performance of Nikkor optics.

Furthermore, the Nikkorex 8 Zoom is push-button easy to use. A fully automatic CdS electric eye automatically gives you correct exposure with any film from 5 to 400 ASA. And there's no spring to wind. Camera motor runs on 4 penlite batteries, good for up to 25 rolls of film.

A true, thru-the-lens reflex finder shows you the scene exactly as the lens sees it. As you zoom from wide angle to dramatic close-up, you see the effect on the bright finder field just as it will appear on the projection screen. And there's a built-in split-prism rangefinder for critically sharp focus.

What's more you can set exposure manually, if you choose. Meter needle is visible in finder. And there's a cable release for single frame exposures, built-in battery testers and a receptacle jack for the plug-in, remote-control accessory. Camera also accepts pistol-grip and close-up accessory lens.

Smartly styled, and amazingly compact, the new Nikkorex 8 Zoom is a delight to handle. Price is $169.50. See it at your photo dealer. For complete description, write to: Dept. MP-4.

NIKON INCORPORATED • 111 FIFTH AVENUE, NEW YORK 3, NEW YORK • Subsidiary of Ehrenreich Photo-Optical Industries, Inc.

NEW NIKKOREX 8 ZOOM BY NIKON HAS F1.8 NIKKOR LENS WITH 8 THRU 32MM ZOOM, FULLY AUTOMATIC ELECTRIC EYE, REFLEX FINDER, BATTERY-MOTOR DRIVE, PUSH-BUTTON OPERATION

CHAPTER SEVENTEEN

MOTION PICTURE AND VIDEO CAMERAS

NIKKOREX 8 (Introduced 1961, discontinued 1964) This is a very small and simple standard 8mm motion picture camera. It weighs only 22.5 oz. and fits in a pocket; it approximates the size of a paperback novel. It has a fixed focus 10mm f/1.8 Nikkor lens and is driven by 4 AA batteries. Exposure is set automatically with a built-in meter or manually. Identify by "NIKKOREX-8" inscribed on top of the fold-out optical viewfinder.

NIKKOREX 8F (Introduced 1964, discontinued 1966) This camera has the same features as the Nikkorex 8 and is about the same size. The difference is that the 8F accepts an accessory lens which converts the built-in 10mm fixed focal length lens to a zoom lens. In 1964, the additional price for the zoom-conversion accessory lens was "under $30."

NIKKOREX ZOOM 8 (Introduced 1963, discontinued 1966) This is a compact standard 8mm electric motor driven motion picture camera with a 8-32mm f/1.8 Nikkor zoom lens. Exposure can be set manually or automatically via a built-in CdS meter. It uses double-8mm film on a 25 foot spool; the motor is driven by 4 AA batteries which are good for about 20 rolls. Identify by "NIKKOREX-ZOOM 8" inscribed on the side of the reflex viewfinder.

NIKON SUPER ZOOM 8 (Introduced 1967, discontinued 1971) This super 8 film camera has an 8.8mm-45mm f/1.8 power zoom lens which will focus as close as 4 feet. Supplementary close-up lenses permit filming to 15 1/3 inches. Exposure is either automatic TTL or manual. An "instant response diaphragm" activated by an electronic oscillator eliminates lag time when there are light changes. It is an all electric reflex. The lens and film transport are powered by separate motors. There are variable filming speeds of 12, 18 and 24 fps as well as single framing. The finder has a built-in diopter.

NIKON 5X SUPER ZOOM. No information.

NIKON 8X SUPER ZOOM (Introduced 1969, discontinued 1974) Super-8 format movie camera with a 7.5-60mm f/1.8 Nikkor zoom lens. The camera is powered by 4 AA batteries and features variable film speeds and automatic exposure. It has a reflex viewfinder with split-image rangefinder. Identify by "NIKON 8X SUPER ZOOM" inscribed on the left side of the camera.

NIKON R-8 SUPER ZOOM (Introduced 1973, discontinued 1980) Super-8 format movie camera with 7.5-60mm f/1.8 macro 2-speed power zoom with automatic through-the-lens exposure control, automatic fade and dissolve, variable shutter and sound capability. Identify by "R8 SUPER" inscribed on the right side of the body.

NIKON R-10 SUPER ZOOM (Introduced 1973, discontinued 1980) Super-8 format movie camera with 7-70mm f/1.4 macro 2-speed power zoom with automatic through-the-lens exposure control, automatic fade and dissolve, variable shutter and sound capability. Identify by "R10 SUPER" inscribed on the right side of the body.

FEBRUARY 1975

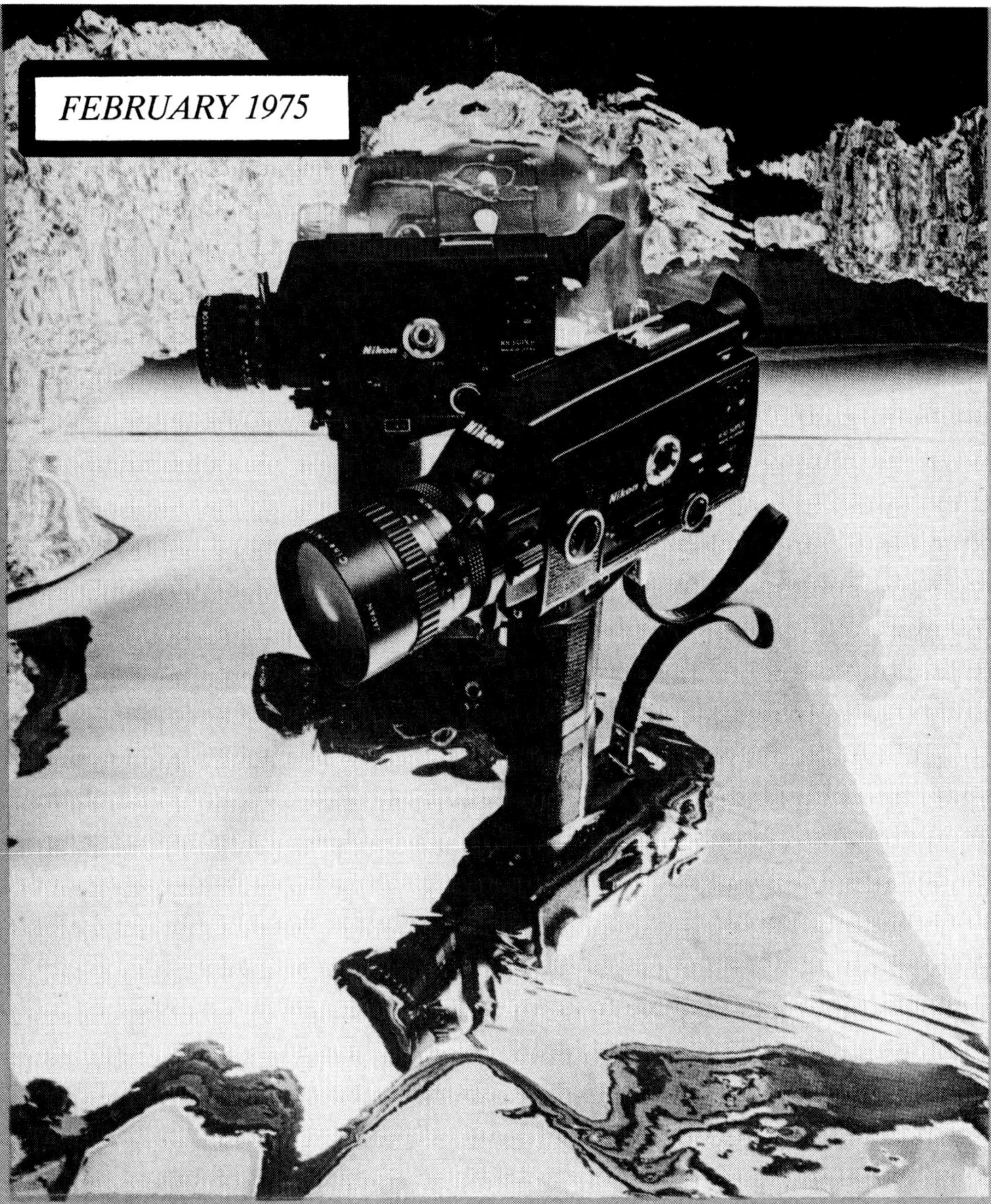

Introducing a new concept in film...

Super-8, with its bigger image, was a breakthrough.

Serious-8, the first Nikon Super-8 cameras, with their legendary Nikkor Zoom lenses came next.

Now, Professional-8. The next major step forward. The new Nikon R8 and R10.

The optics, as you would expect, are exceptional. Your choice of 7.5—60mm f1.8 (8-time) or 7—70mm f1.4 (10-time) zoom lens, resolution, contrast, sheer incredible crispness are beyond description. The result of years of zoom optics experience.

And the features are there, of course. Everything you'd expect, and some little more. Variable speeds to 54 fps. A variable shutter, just as on the finest 16mm and 35mm motion picture cameras. Macro focusing right down to the front surface of the lens, which the best of the big cameras don't have. An accurate reflex finder, single frame with x-synch; sound capability.

Plus fade-ins, fade-outs, lap-dissolves, multi-exposures and reverse filming, automatically, with a single control. For control, and controls, are much of the essence of these tools. For operating convenience, they positively represent new standards of a manufacturer's response to the film maker's needs. You can only appreciate them once you've experienced them.

Professional·8
Nikon R8 & R10

NIKON ACTION-8 VIDEO CAMCORDER MODEL VN-800 (Introduced October 15, 1986, discontinued 1987) One piece 8mm video camera and recorder. Features autofocus, automatic exposure control, a f/1.2 6X power zoom lens with fade and backlight controls. Identify by "8mm VIDEO VN-800" inscribed on the upper left side of the camera.

NIKON ACTION-8 VIDEO CAMCORDER MODEL VN-810 (Introduced ?, discontinued 1988) All of the features of the VN-800 plus a high-speed electronic shutter of 1/500 or 1/1000 and a flying erase head. Identify by "8mm VIDEO VN-810" inscribed on the upper left side of the camera.

NIKON ACTION PRO CAMCORDER MODEL VN-3000 (Introduced April 15, 1988, discontinued 1988) The VN-3000 incorporates all of the features of the VN-810 but utilizes a standard VHS cassette rather than the 8mm. Identify by "VN-3000" inscribed in very small letters on the left side of the camera; it's hard to miss since it is the only Nikon VHS camcorder.

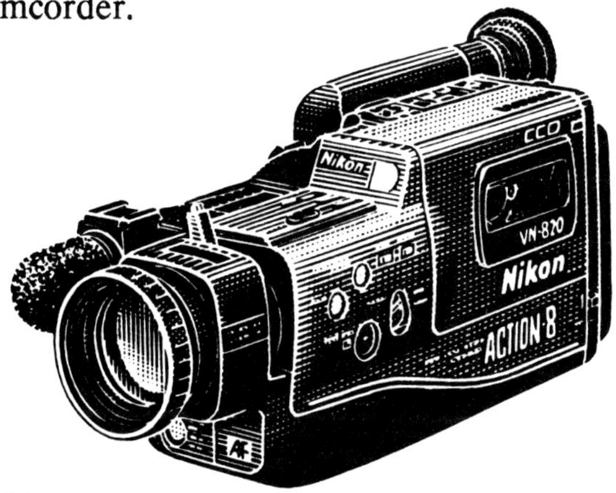

NIKON ACTION-8 VIDEO CAMCORDER MODEL VN-820. (Introduced 1988, discontinued 1988) An 8mm camcorder with 6X power zoom lens with macro capabilities, electronic viewfinder, date/time input and 2-title superimposition. Identify by 'VN-820" inscribed on the left side of the body.

NIKON ACTION-8 VIDEO CAMCORDER MODEL VN-830 (Introduced March 1989, discontinued 1989) This 2.7 pound 8mm camcorder features a 6X power zoom lens with macro capabilities, autofocus and a variable shutter with speeds up to 1/4000th of a second. Identify by "VN-820" inscribed in small letters on the left side of the camera.

NIKON ACTION-8 VIDEO CAMCORDER MODEL VN-840 (Introduced November 1989; discontinued 1990) This 8mm camcorder features an 8X power zoom with macro close-up, autofocus and a variable shutter to 1/4000. It is virtually the same as the VN-830 except for the zoom range. Identify by "VN-840" inscribed in small letters on the left side of the camera.

NIKON ACTION-8 VIDEO CAMCORDER MODEL VN-900 (Introduced 1989, discontinued 1989) Generally the same features as the VN-830 only smaller and lighter, weighing only 2 pounds. Has a manual iris control and a 2-title memory with scroll and reverse. Identify by "VN-900" inscribed on the right side of the body.

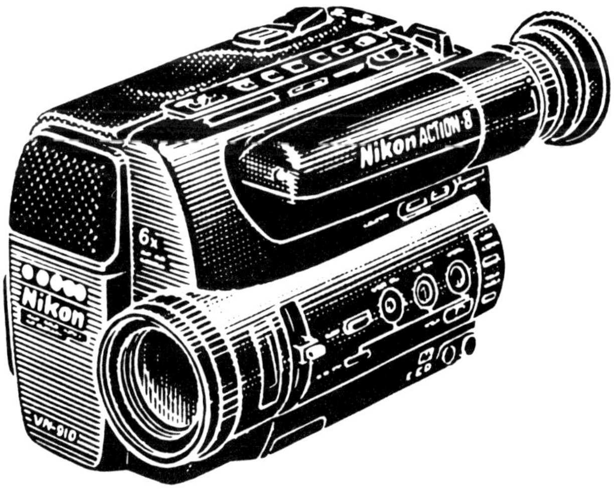

NIKON ACTION-8 VIDEO CAMCORDER MODEL VN-910 (Introduced October 1989, still available) This is Nikon's version of the Sony Handicam. It weighs only 28 oz. and will fit in many pockets. It has a 6X power zoom with macro, variable shutter speeds to 1/4000, TTL autofocusing, an electronic viewfinder and various title superimposition functions. Identify by "VN-910" inscribed on the front.

NIKON ACTION-8 VIDEO CAMCORDER MODEL VN-950 (Introduced May 1989, still available) This is Nikon's entry into the field of 8mm HiBand recording with over 400 lines of horizontal resolution. Has an 8X power zoom lens with macro capabilities, automatic focus and iris control with manual override. Identify by "VN-950" inscribed on the right side of the body.

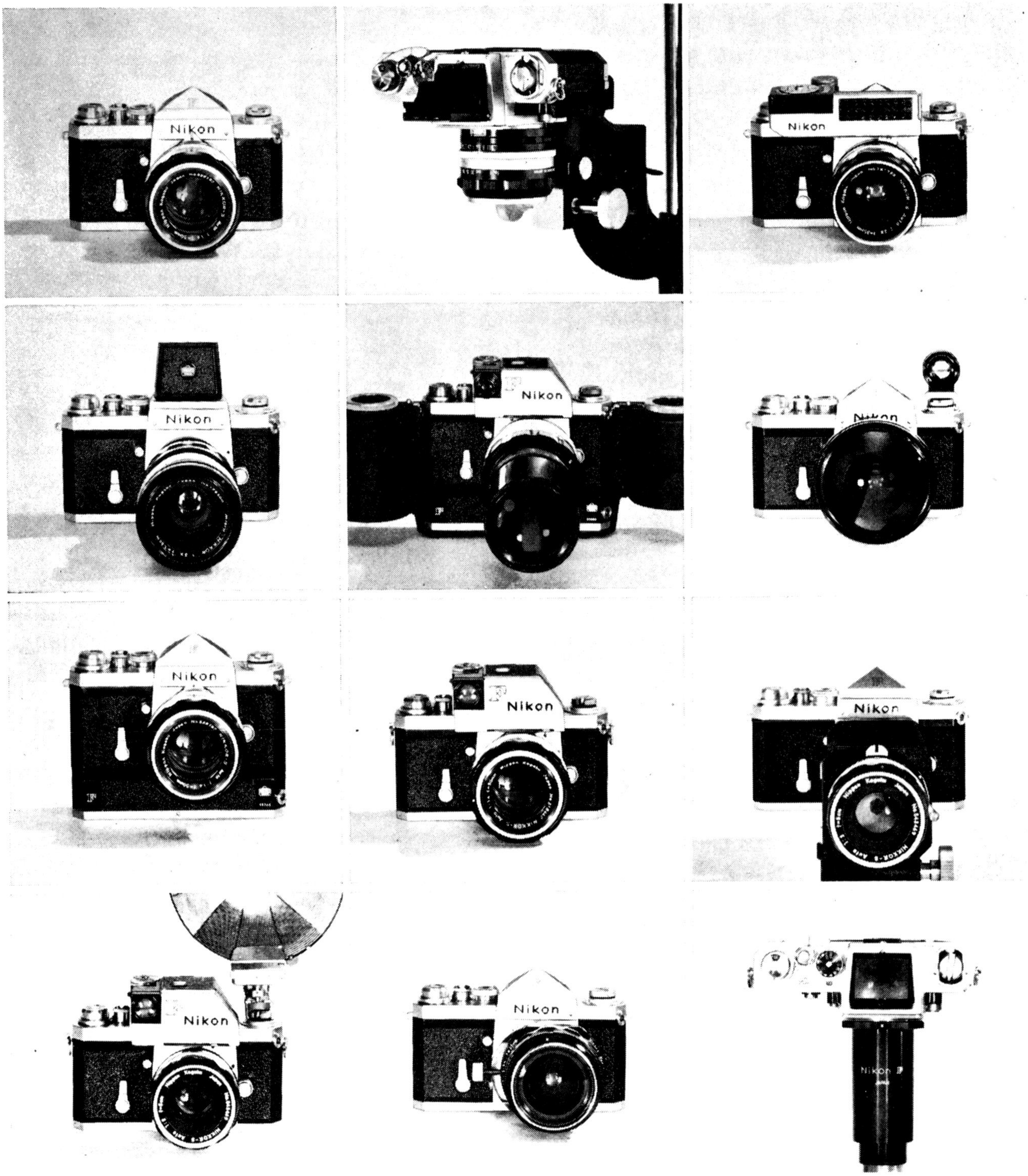

JUNE 1963

there is only one Nikon F

Yet, it appears in an almost infinite variety of shapes — no two alike. With the number of lenses it can draw upon, the manifold accessories and attachments it can bring into use, it is sometimes impossible to tell a Nikon F from its appearance alone. • There are, for example, 21 interchangeable Nikkor lenses for the Nikon F. And there are 3 interchangeable finders which can be used with each of these lenses: standard prism, waist-level, and the Photomic system, combining prism finder *and* coupled meter. • This alone gives you 63 different combinations. Now, consider that you can also use the Electric Motor Drive in each instance — copy accessories, photomicrographic equipment, and the many other available aids and attachments. The number of possible combinations assumes astronomical proportions. • The man with a Nikon F is literally master of all he surveys. There is hardly an assignment he can't tackle, hardly a picture problem he isn't equipped to handle with ease and with confidence, and with complete certainty as to his results. There is only one Nikon F, and it is the most versatile of all 35's. See it at your dealer, or write Dept. PP-6.

Nikon Incorporated, 111 Fifth Ave., N. Y. 3, N. Y., Subsidiary of Ehrenreich Photo-Optical Industries, Inc.

CHAPTER TWENTY

BATTERIES

Since the days of flash powder ended, electricity has been an important part of photography and picture taking equipment. For photographers, this has meant using batteries. When the first Nikon camera was produced, the only piece of equipment needing a battery was the flash gun; all other picture taking functions were mechanical or done by hand. But as time went by, more and more functions have become electronic. And so batteries have become more important.

Today, many Nikon users are essentially out of commission without batteries. Fortunately, Nikon continues to produce a camera - the FM2n - which operates, except for the built-in light meter, without battery power. Many professionals include an FM2n (or an FM or FM2) as a part of their kit.

Just as camera technology has progressed, so has battery technology. Today, there are a number of different types of batteries to choose from. No one type is better than any other; they are just different. The most suitable battery depends on the circumstances.

Each Nikon product should be powered by the type of battery recommended by Nikon. It should be emphasized that this book is a buyers' and sellers' guide, not a users' manual. Each Nikon product comes with printed instructions. Before using any item, photographers are strongly advised to read the instructions very carefully. For those without this necessary information, instruction booklets on almost every current and past Nikon product can be obtained at a nominal cost. For the nearest Nikon facility, see Chapter 1.

Photographers should always try to purchase batteries from a photo dealer. Most dealers only stock batteries which are suitable for cameras and photo accessories. All prudent photographers carry spare batteries in their kit. If, in an emergency situation, batteries cannot be purchased from a photo dealer, care should be taken to buy an <u>exact</u> replacement.

Cameras and accessories use batteries composed of different materials: mercury, silver oxide, alkaline, lithium and nickel cadmium. Each has advantages and disadvantages.

MERCURY. Mercury supplies a relatively steady and almost unchanging power over its total life. These properties result in accurate and reliable exposure when used to power cameras. Also they produce more amperage than others. Mercury cells produce up to 1.4 volts per cell.

SILVER OXIDE. Silver oxide batteries are similar to mercury insofar as producing a steady and unchanging power source. They last longer than alkaline or lithium, but cost more. Silver batteries have approximately a two-year shelf life. They will deliver about two times as many photographs as will alkaline. Silver is the best choice for those who take a large number of pictures on a regular basis.

ALKALINE. One great advantage of alkaline is that AA and AAA cells are available almost anywhere. Also alkaline batteries are relatively inexpensive. Alkaline batteries produce 1.5 volts per cell. Since alkaline batteries have only about a two-year shelf life, care should be taken to purchase from a source with rapid turnover. Alkalines are an economic choice - about half the price of silver - and a good one for those who shoot a moderate amount on a regular basis.

LITHIUM. A big advantage of lithium batteries is that they have a very long shelf life, at least five years. And they lose only about 0.5 percent a year. All batteries are affected by cold, but lithiums function better under cold conditions than do the other types. Lithium batteries tend to recycle more rapidly and, when used in a strobe, may produce up to two times as many flashes. Lithium batteries produce 3 volts per cell. Due to the long shelf life, those who go considerable periods without using the equipment should choose lithium if their equipment offers the choice. But lithiums have a problem: near the end of their life, they slowly loose voltage. Alkalines, on the other hand, maintain voltage until the end. When the voltage is reduced, some functions in some cameras may be affected. If you are using lithiums and you think your camera needs repair, first try it with alkalines.

NICKEL CADMIUM. Called nicads by most photographers, one great advantage of these batteries is that they are rechargeable. Each nicad cell produces 1.2 volts. Even though nicads produce less voltage per cell than do the others, they supply more amperage. Some strobe units are designed for the one amp from an alkaline and may be damaged by the two nicad amps. Read the instructions carefully before making a substitution. The other big advantage of nicads is that they recycle in about half the time of alkalines. The down-side of this is that fully charged nicads will provide approximately one-third fewer flashes than alkalines. With time, nicads lose a lot more energy than do the other types. So they have to be kept charged up. They will lose about half their charge in approximately three months. Nicads are initially more expensive, but they have an indefinite shelf life, if maintained properly, and can be recharged up to 1000 times.

CARBON ZINC. These batteries have the same general characteristics as alkaline, but with a shorter life; when used in a strobe, they produce fewer flashes. Their only advantage is that they are about half the price of alkalines.

CROSS-INDEXED BATTERY TABLE

UPC	Type	EVER	BSTAR	BURG	DURA	RAYO	PANA	VARTA
1131	AK	E91	7524	B15A	MN1500	815	AM3	4006
1138	AK	E95	7520	B13A	MN1300	813	AM1	4020
1334	CZ	412	none	U15	M215	none	015	V72PX
1386	CZ	504	none	none	M504	none	W10E	V74PX
1399	AK	E92	7526	B24A	MN2400	824	AM4	4003
1894	LI	EL223A	none	none	none	none	BR-P2	none
3722	SO	EXP76	none	none	MS76	RS76	G-13	V76PX
4370	MC	EPX625	none	none	PX625	RPX625	H-D	V625PX
4371	MC	EPX13	none	none	PX625	RPX13	HS-D	V13PX
4922	MD	A76	none	none	PX76A	none	LR44	V13GA
4923	MD	A544	none	none	PX28A	none	4LR44	V4034PX
8896	SO	544	none	none	PX28	RPX28	4G-13	V28PX
9173	NC	CH15	none	CD6	NC15	615	P-50AA	501RS
9252	LI	2L76	none	none	DL1/3N	none	none	CR1/3N

Type Code: SO = Silver Oxide, MC = Mercury, LI = Lithium, AK = Alkaline, NC = Nickel Cadmium, CZ = Carbon ZINC, MD = Manganese Dioxide

Brand Code: EVER = Eveready, BSTAR = Bright Star, BURG = Burgess, DURA = Duracell, RAYO = Ray-O-Vac, PANA = Panasonic, VARTA = Varta

NIKON BATTERY GUIDE

Following is a battery guide for Nikon photographic products. The code number is the UPC number which indicates the type of battery recommended. To select a battery by brand, refer to the table on the previous page.

Product	UPC Number(s)
FA, FG, FG-20, FE, FE2, FM, FM2, Nikonos IV-A, V	3722, 4922 or 9252
F2, F2SB, F2A, F2AS, F3	3722, 4922
EL2	8896 or 4923
EM, Nikkormat FT3	3722 or 4922
F Photomic Finder, Nikkormat FT, FTN, FT2 (early) T, TN FTN Photomic Finders	4371 or 4370
N Series, L35AF	1131 or 1399
L135AF, Fun Touch, Tele-Touch Nikkormat EL, ELW, EL2	1399
One Touch	1399 or 1894
MD-2, MD-4, MD-11, MD-12, MD-14, MD-15, AW-1, MD-E	1131
F-250, F-36	1131 or 9173
MB-2	1131 or 9176
SB-E, SB-2, SB-3, SB-4, SB-5, SB-7E, SB-8, SB-8E, SB-9, SB-10, SB-11, SB-12, SB-15, SB-16, SB-17, SB-19, SB-21, SB-22, SB-101, SB-102, F4, F4s	1131
BC-2, BC-3, BC-5	1334
BC-7	1386
SR-2, SM-2	1138

APRIL 1982

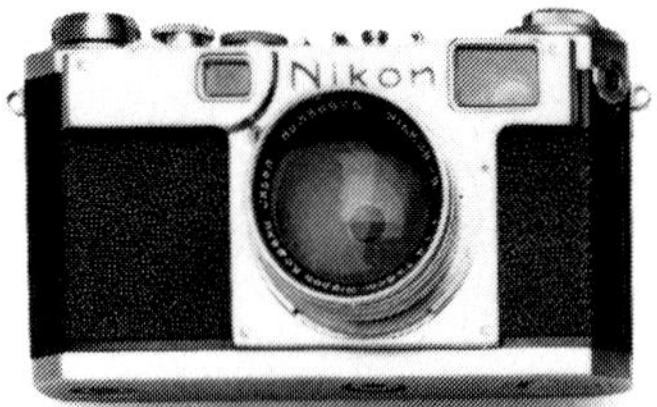

Nikon S2 1954

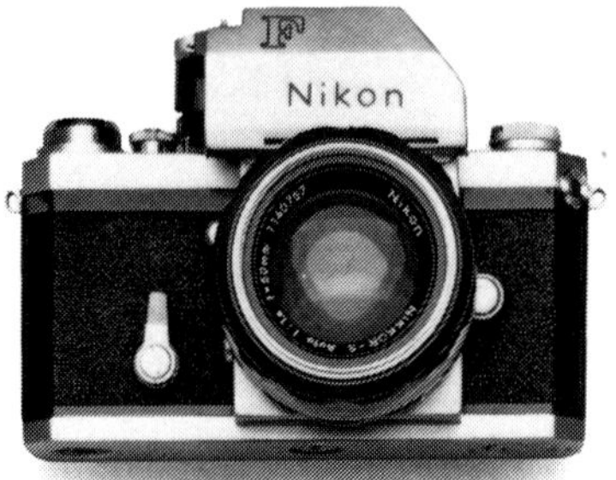

Nikon F Photomic Tn 1967

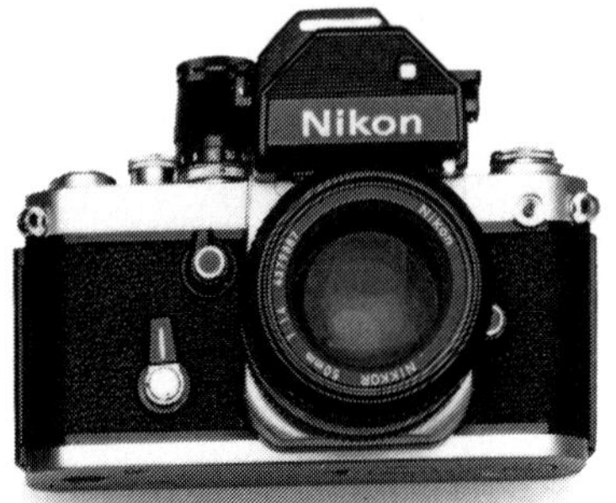

Nikon F2S Photomic 1973

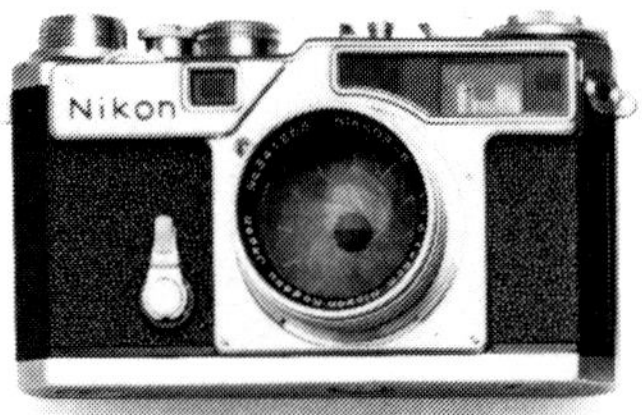

Nikon SP 1957

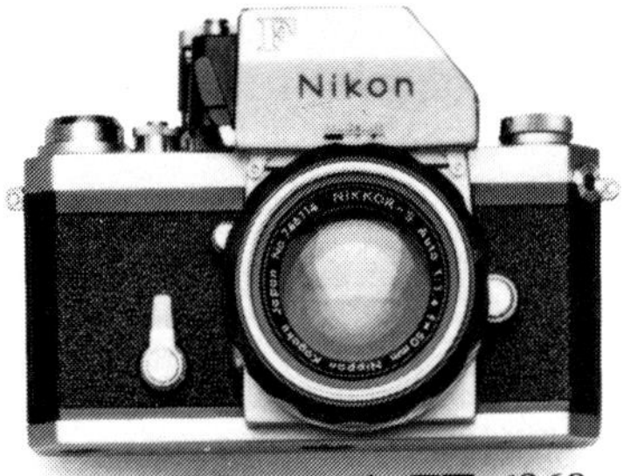

Nikon F Photomic FTn 1968

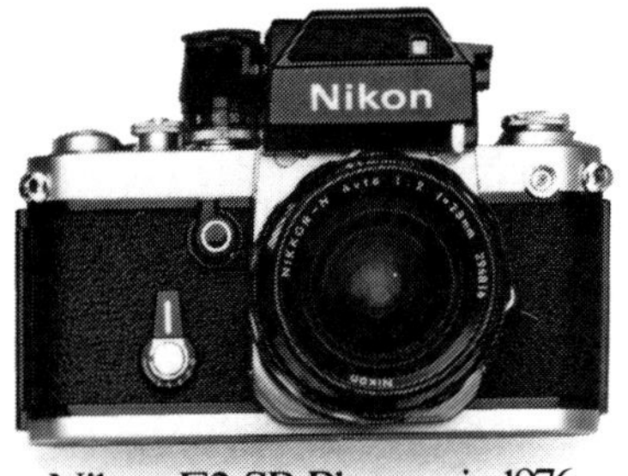

Nikon F2 SB Photomic 1976

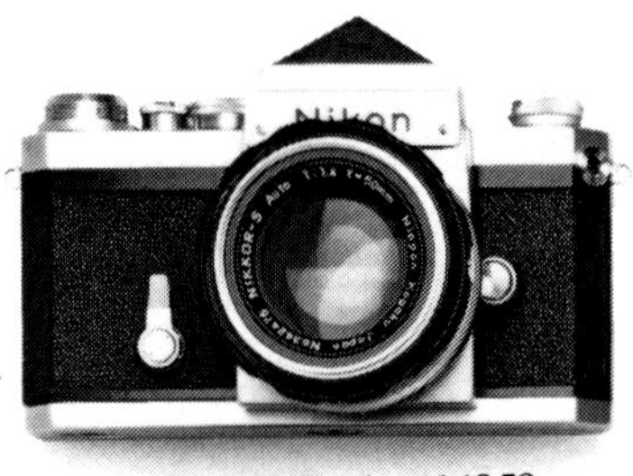

Nikon F Eyelevel 1959

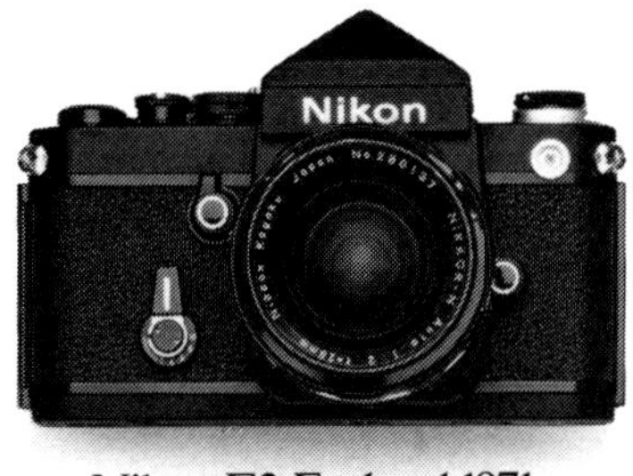

Nikon F2 Eyelevel 1971

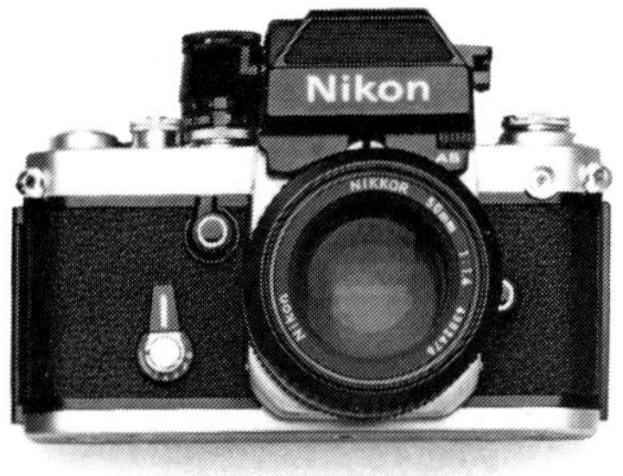

Nikon F2 AS Photomic 1977

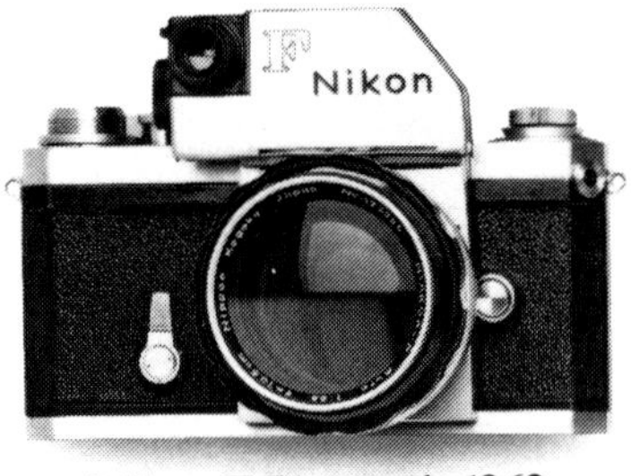

Nikon F Photomic 1962

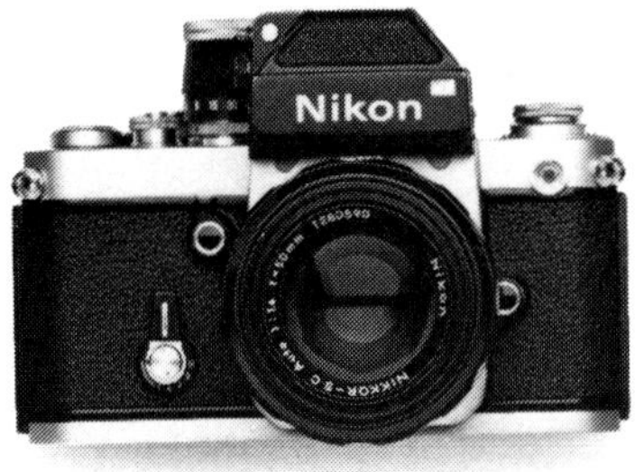

Nikon F2 Photomic 1971

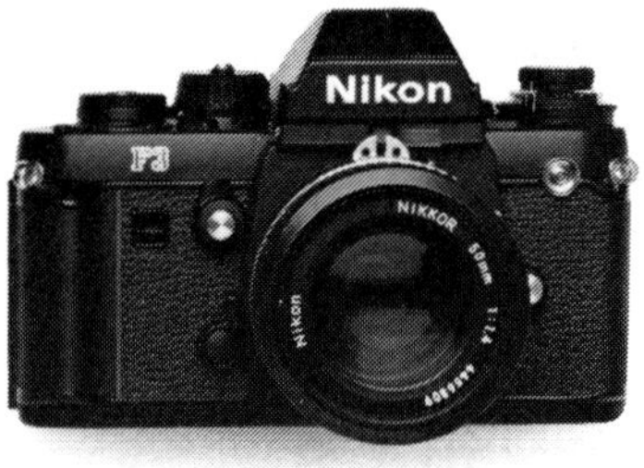

Nikon F3

Nikon. The one company where dedication to making great professional cameras didn't happen overnight.

After decades of making cameras for amateurs, some companies have suddenly come out with cameras they hope professionals will like. As you probably suspect, it takes more than good intentions to create a great professional camera.

Among the qualities that have to be considered in any camera that claims to be professional are: How reliable is the camera? And how rugged is the camera? Qualities, for the most part, that can only be measured by the test of time.

A Nikon, of course, is made by people who have had more success at making professional cameras that have withstood the test of time than anyone else. In fact, more professional photographers own a Nikon than all other 35mm SLR cameras combined. Which is probably why so many amateurs who are serious about photography also prefer to own a Nikon professional camera.

In the eighties that camera is the Nikon F3. The camera that only Nikon's decades of experience could have produced.

Of course, it's when you spend a few moments looking back at what Nikon has done, that you really begin to understand just how far ahead we've really been.

Nikon

We take the world's greatest pictures.™

Battery Selector Chart

ITEM	QUANTITY	TYPE
Cameras		
Nikon F3, F2, F2S, F2SB F2A, F2AS Photomic, FM, FE, FM2, FG, FG-20, EM, FE2, FA, Nikonos V	2	1.5V Silver Oxide or one 3V Lithium
N4004, N8008	4	AA Alkaline
N2000, N2020	4 4	AAA Alkaline (MB-4) AA Alkaline (MB-3)
One-Touch (New), Tele-Touch Deluxe	1	6V Lithium
L35AF & L135AF, One-Touch, Action-Touch, Fun-Touch	2	AA Alkaline
Nikonos IV-A	2	1.5V Silver Oxide
Nikkormat FT2, FT3	2	1.5V Silver Oxide
Nikkormat FT, FTN	1	1.3V Mercury
EL, ELW, EL2	1	6V Silver Oxide
Super 5X, 8X (Motor) (Meter)	4 2	AA Alkaline 1.3V Mercury
R-8 Super Zoom (Motor) (Meter)	6 2	AAgAlkaline 1.3V Mercury
R-10 Super Zoom (Motor)	6	AA Alkaline
DL-1 Photomic Illuminator	1	1.3V Mercury
DB-2 Anti-Cold Battery Pack	2	AA Alkaline
DB-3 External Battery Pack f/MF-12	2	AAA Alkaline
Motor Drives		
F36 Motor (Cordless)	8	AA Alkaline
F250, F36 Motors with Standard Pack	8	C Alkaline
F3 MD-4	8	AA Alkaline or MN-2 NiCad (#125)
F2 MB-1 Battery Pack	10	AA Alkaline or MN-1 NiCad Battery Pair (#38)
F2 MB-2 Battery Pack	8	AA Alkaline
MD-11 & MD-12 Motor	8	AA Alkaline
MD-E	6	AAA Alkaline
MD-14 & MD-15 Motor	8	AA Alkaline
Auto Winder		
Auto-Winder AW-1	6	AA Alkaline
Remote Controls		
Modulite Transmitter	1	9V. Standard Battery
Modulite Receiver	4	AA Alkaline
Wireless Remote Control Transmitter	8	AA Alkaline
Wireless Remote Control Receiver	8	AA Alkaline
Intervalometer MT-1	4	AA Alkaline
Intervalometer MT-2	4	AA Alkaline
Data Backs		
MF-12	2	1.5V Silver Oxide
MF-14	2	1.5V Silver Oxide
MF-15	2	1.5V Silver Oxide
MF-16	2	1.5V Silver Oxide
MF-18	2	1.5V Silver Oxide
MF-19	2	1.5V Silver Oxide

ITEM	QUANTITY	TYPE
EE Control		
EE Aperture Control	1	NiCad Battery DN-1 (#48)
DB-1 Battery Pack f/EE	4	C Cell
Flash Units		
120mm Medical Nikkor Battery Pack (LD-2), SB-21 Macro Speedlight (External Power Pack)	8	AA Alkaline
200mm Medical Nikkor I Battery Pack	4 1	D Alkaline 240V Battery
200mm Medical Nikkor II Battery Pack	8	D Alkaline
Battery Pack f/SB-1	6	D Alkaline
High Voltage Pack f/SB-1	1	510V Battery
Repeating Flash Battery Pack	8	NiCad Battery SN-3 (#294)
BC-7 Flash	1	15V Battery
SB-2 Speedlight	4	AA Alkaline
SB-3 Speedlight	4	AA Alkaline
SB-4 Speedlight	2	AA Alkaline
SB-5 Speedlight	1	NiCad SN-2 (#309)
SB-5 Battery Pack, SD4	1 or 2	480V Battery 240V Batteries
SB-7E Speedlight	4	AA Alkaline
SB-8E Speedlight	4	AA Alkaline
SB-9 Speedlight	2	AA Alkaline
SB-10 Speedlight	4	AA Alkaline
SB-11 Speedlight	8	AA Alkaline
SB-12 Speedlight	4	AA Alkaline
SB-15, 17	4	AA Alkaline
SB-16A, 16B	4	AA Alkaline
SB-14, 140 Battery Pack, SD-7	6	C Cell
SB-20, 22 Speedlight	4	AA Alkaline
SB-23 Speedlight	4	AA Alkaline
SB-E Speedlight	4	AAA Alkaline
SB-19	4	AA Alkaline
SB-21A, SB-21B Macro Speedlight	4	AA Alkaline
DC Power Supply For Ring Lights SR-2, SM-2	8	D Alkaline

Note: AA Zinc Carbon Batteries (1.5V each) may be used instead of AA Alkaline in the above listing.

Note: While both Silver Oxide and Lithium cells will operate some camera models, there is some difference in the performance characteristics of these two battery types. We suggest that you check with your battery supplier to get specific information about the battery you intend to use.

FEBRUARY 1964

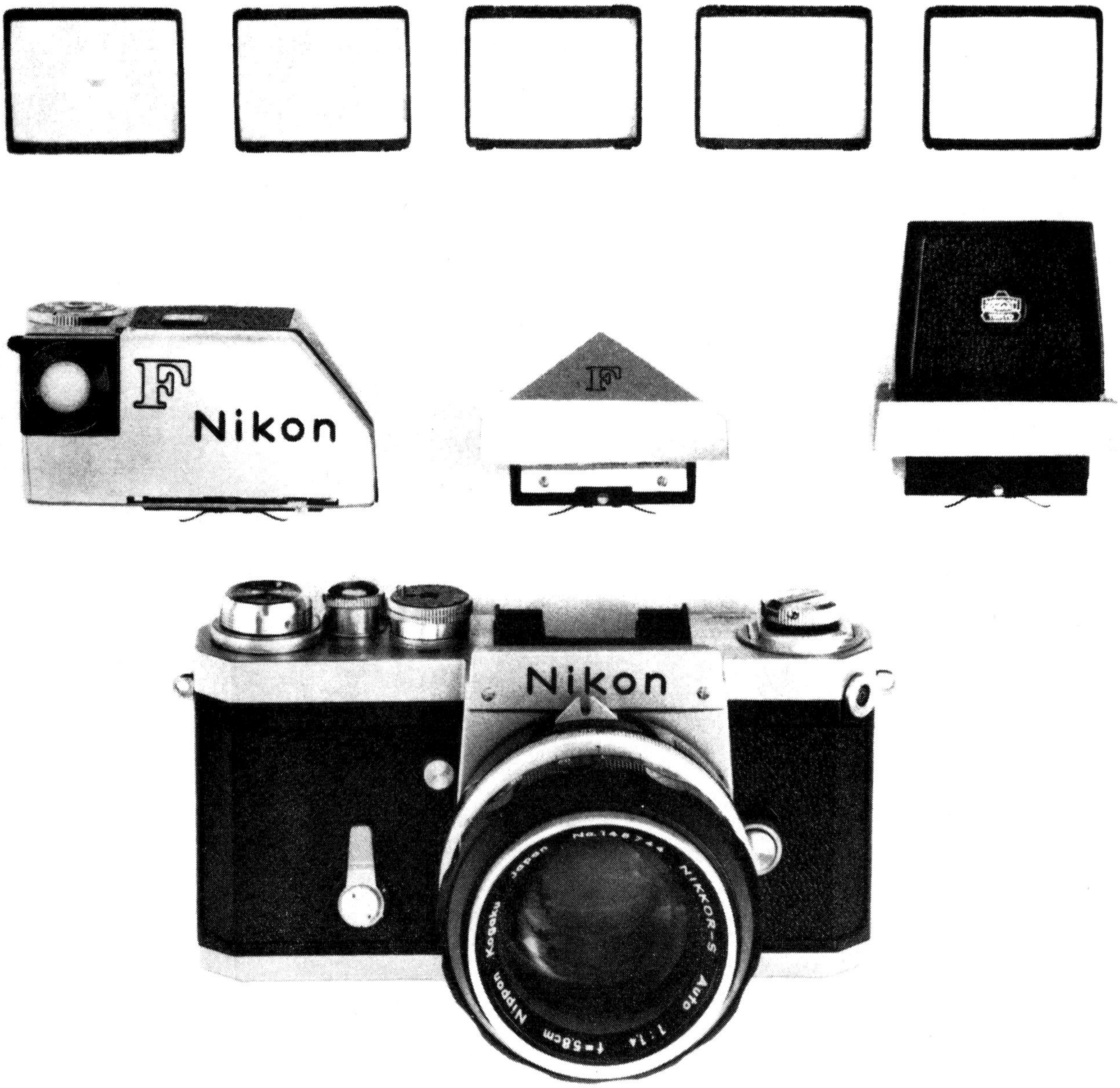

How the finder system helps make the Nikon F most versatile of all 35s.

The Nikon F user enjoys a number of unique advantages. One of the most significant is the interchangeable finder system. He can select any of three finders, and he can interchange viewing screens.

Depending on his choice of finders—standard prism, waist-level, or Photomic prism/meter—he can sight in many ways: conventionally, or with camera upside down above his head, or at right angles to the subject, or from below. And with the Photomic, he also enjoys the advantage of built-in exposure control. Whichever he selects, the finder frames the subject exactly as it will be framed on the film.

The five focusing screens he can choose from each has its own characteristic pattern: the standard Type A has a Fresnel field, matte spot and split-image rangefinder; Type B, Fresnel field and matte spot, but no rangefinder, for long focus lenses; Type C, matte field and clear spot with cross hairs for photomicrography; Type D, all matte, for specialized copy photography; and Type E, Fresnel field, matte spot, and etched vertical and horizontal lines for architectural and other applications requiring accurate image alignment.

The interchangeable finder system is only one example of the meticulous care given to Nikon F design. And it is one of the many facilities that contributes to the inevitable fact that the Nikon F is the most versatile of all 35s. See it at your camera dealer soon. For complete details, write to Dept. PP-2.

EPI NIKON INCORPORATED 111 Fifth Avenue New York 3, N. Y. Subsidiary of Ehrenreich Photo-Optical Industries, Inc.

CHAPTER NINETEEN

DATE AND PRICE INFORMATION

The material in the next chapter (20) lists each 35mm Nikon camera plus lenses and major accessories for 35mm Nikon cameras which have been produced since World War II. Prior to the war, the company's products were, for the most part, inappropriate for a camera data guide.

DATES. Column one indicates the first year each item was available to retail outlets from the US suppliers.

In the years immediately following the war, Nikon products were first imported by the Overseas Finance and Trading Company of San Francisco. Subsequently, distribution was assumed by Ehrenreich Photo-Optical Industries, Inc. on the East Coast of the US. On the West Coast, it was assumed briefly by Farnan & Seeman and then Gary Lehmann Inc. Eventually Ehrenreich and Lehmann merged and took on the name E.P.O.I. Nikon in Japan, who had always had excellent relations with founder Joseph Ehrenreich, purchased E.P.O.I. and changed the name to Nikon Inc. At the same time, Nikon Inc. stopped distributing other lines such as Bronica and thereafter handled Nikon only. It is primarily from their old catalogue pages that the authors have gained information about the early years and the information in the first three columns pertaining to early products.

The second column lists the last year each item was available to dealers. If the date in the second column is that of the current year, the product may still be available. Products listed as currently available are not necessarily continuously supplied by Nikon Inc. to dealers. Nikon Inc. may add or withdraw items anytime during a given year. The information in this publication is as current as possible.

NEW PRICES. The data in column 3 was obtained from printed price lists supplied by the US supplier to US retail dealers appointed by Nikon Inc. Column 3 is the suggested list price. As a consequence of the famous Volkswagen case, the Supreme Court has ruled that suppliers may not dictate retail prices as a condition of a dealership. Very few retail outlets which deal in photographic products sell items at the suggested list price.

RETAIL SALES. Column 4 is a low average price offered by most medium size camera dealers located in metropolitan areas. Prices can vary as much as 10 percent below to 20 percent above those listed. Dealers who have a larger volume often sell some items for as much as ten percent below the listed amount. Smaller dealers often sell at prices above the listed amount. But very few dealers sell at the manufacturer's suggested list price.

The exception is hard-to-get items. These items are usually those which have been recently introduced and an adequate supply has not yet filled the distribution pipeline. So if you can wait a while for a just introduced item, you can usually save money.

While there are a few chains, most camera stores are relatively small operations. But often, large operations such as mail order houses, discount stores, department stores and electronic outlets offer photographic products for sale. Sometimes these organizations offer products at lower prices than those listed in column 4. There are many reasons such companies are able to do this. First of all, it is apparent that some outlets obtain merchandise at less than the lowest published dealer price. This can be accomplished in many ways. Some of these ways can harm the consumer:

1) The "gray market." In this case, items are imported by an entity other than Nikon Inc. from a country where favorable currency exchange rates allow the US dollar to purchase more than in Japan. In other words, Nikon in Japan sells to a supplier or distributor in LaLaLand. The supplier or distributor in LaLaLand then resells to a distributor or dealer in the US. These items may not have a US warranty and the instruction books may be printed in a language other than English. (This in itself is not a big problem, however, since Nikon Inc. sells instruction books at a very modest cost.)

2) Repacks. Some outlets purchase equipment which was used as demonstrators, salesmen's samples or even refurbished rejects. In these instances, Nikon Inc. clearly marks the boxes containing the products and also marks the products in a way discernible only to Nikon and authorized repairmen. These reconditioned items carry a 90 day warranty. Nothing (but the law) prevents an unethical dealer from removing these labels and selling the products as new. To guard against this, examine the warranty card. Make sure the serial number is printed, not hand written. A new product carries a one year warranty while a repack carries only a 90 day warranty.

3) Unauthorized Importation. Small amounts of goods can be carried into the US by frequent travelers and then resold for a profit, but at less than the retail outlet's normal price. This practice circumvents import duties and transportation costs. Smuggled equipment has the same warranty and language problems as does gray market.

4) Float. Some large companies earn more profit moving money than they do moving merchandise. If they can put customers' money to work immediately making interest while, at the same time, stalling deliveries, they profit. The longer they stall, the more they make. Bankcard A.D.C. (automatic data capture) systems draw money immediately from customers' accounts the same day an order is placed. After receiving merchandise from Nikon, outlets normally have 30 days to pay. If they place the Nikon order at a certain time of the month, that can be extended another 15 days. And, of course, payment to Nikon can sometimes be delayed beyond the date actually due. Float should not be confused with back-ordering. Nikon is infamous for back-ordering, so if a mail order is not promptly received, it is not necessarily the fault of the merchant.

MAIL ORDER SALES. Column 5 represents current average low mail order prices for **new** products. If there is no price for an item in this column, none (or too few to average) were offered during the past calendar year.

Many, but not all Nikon products are offered through the mail (or actually UPS in most cases) via advertisements in consumer photographic publications. With the demise of *Modern Photography*, the publication with the most and varied advertisements is *Popular Photography*. In perusing any one issue, one can find a great variety of prices for the same item. The price listed in column 5 was determined by averaging the three lowest. Occasionally, a single mail order price is printed for an amount significantly lower than that listed by the other dealers. In these cases, this single low price was discarded in figuring the price listed in this data book. The reason for this is that when such unique low prices are investigated, they turn out to be typographic errors, mistakes or come-ons. Usually, the lowest obtainable consumer prices are from mail order dealers, most of whom are in New York City.

If you are going to buy an item new, why not then, buy mail-order? One problem is recourse. In most cases, you will be buying from a company in a different state. If you encounter a problem which you might want to resolve in the courts, this recourse may be too expensive. On the other hand, if you buy locally, most states have a "small claims court" where you can represent yourself and the expense is minimal.

Another problem is the warranty. Some items sold by mail order dealers do not have a warranty which will be honored by the Nikon Inc. If the item was purchased on the so-called "gray market," whatever warranty which may accompany it is not valid. In the US, Nikon Inc. only honors a Nikon Inc. warranty. Since gray market products are not imported to the US through the authorized channel, there is no Nikon Inc. warranty. When a gray market product is purchased, it may be packed with a non-Nikon Inc. warranty of one sort or another. The vender may claim this is a valid warranty, but it is NOT. For a warranty to be valid, it must be accompanied by a sales receipt which shows the date of purchase. If an item is presented for warranty repair outside of the US with a non-Nikon Inc. warranty and a receipt from a US dealer, it will not be accepted. So the warranty is not valid anywhere!

Even if the item does have a warranty honored by the US distributor, when you purchase mail order, you have to take care of the matter yourself if there is a problem. When you buy from your local camera dealer, you can return the item to him and he may take care of the details.

When you buy from a local dealer, you can handle an item and usually discuss the purchase with a knowledgeable sales person. You can also usually trade in items if you so choose. A few mail-order dealers accept trades too, but this is an awkward transaction.

When you buy mail order, in spite of what you may be told over the phone, you do not necessarily have any assurance of just when the product will arrive. At a camera store, of course, you walk away with it under your arm. Some mail order companies take orders and accept money for items they do not have in stock. Receiving refunds for items never delivered can be time consuming and troublesome. Occasionally, customers must refer cases to the US Postal Inspector.

The differential between the mail order price and the price at a camera store is not always worth the risk. Those who do purchase mail order are strongly urged to pay only by credit card so that if there is a problem, the credit card company can be prevailed upon to intervene, particularly in the instance of non-delivery.

It is impossible not to mention that sometimes mail-order dealers sell some items at prices less than dealer cost. How can this be? Obviously every retail business has to sell items at amounts greater than cost. Sometimes the answer is the so-called "gray market." In this case, the mail-order dealer has purchased from a source other than Nikon Inc. It has also been reported that some "new" items are actually demonstrators or have been "re-packaged." In the latter case, an item may have been returned for repair; the original item was replaced with a new item and the repaired item is then sold as new.

There are, however, very legitimate mail order dealers and there are many mail order transactions which result in happy customers. If you receive merchandise which has been represented as new with US warranty and you find it questionable, here is what to look for: 1) Missing instruction books and/or warranty certificate. 2) Instruction books printed in a language other than English. 3) Warranty certificates which say "international warranty" instead of "warranted by Nikon Inc." 4) Evidence that a gummed label has been removed from the box. 5) Boxes and/or packaging materials which do not appear factory fresh. 6) Evidence that the item has been used such as scuff marks on a camera base plate or oily smudges on the exit pupil of the viewfinder.

USED PRICES. The last three columns are for used items in conditions "8," "9" and "10." An "8" camera is often called a "user." This means it's not pretty, but everything is in good operating order. There may be considerable brassing and a few dents, but it works. A "9" shows some use, but there are no dents or extensive brassing. A "10" is in mint condition, like new, in other words. Sometimes items which are sold as used include the original packaging, instruction book and guarantee cards. In these cases, one can often expect to pay a premium.

Often items are offered in "excellent + +," "mint -," or some such in-between categories. In these instances, the buyer should interpolate between the columns in this book.

Items offered in conditions less than "8" or "ugly" should be purchased at prices less than those in the USER column.

Remember, the prices in the three used columns are derived from advertising. They are **LOW averages** of offered goods. It is entirely possible that some of these items changed hands at lower prices. It is also very probable that many items are offered and have been sold at prices higher than those listed in this book. Many individuals will negotiate while many dealers will not. <u>Dealers should take note that the prices listed are those for which the items can probably be sold!</u> Obviously a dealer must pay less to acquire an item in order to make a profit.

The prices for these used items assume that the equipment is in good working order. If it is not, it is impossible to establish a price without knowing the cost of repair. Sometimes, it is more expensive to repair an item than the item is worth. And some Nikon equipment can be quite expensive to repair. For some products - the Nikonos I is an example - parts are no longer available from Nikon Inc.

SNOW, SLEET, RAIN OR SAND MEAN NOTHING TO A CAMERA THAT CAN BE USED 160 FEET UNDER WATER

You don't mind getting wet . . . even a little dirty . . . if it means getting a good picture. Trouble is, your camera does. And, so you're forced to pass up some great picture opportunities. Unless you have a Nikonos III, the unique, compact 35 from Nikon that can give you the pictures you want in any weather and any environment.

Designed as an underwater camera requiring no housing, the Nikonos III is waterproof to depths of 160 feet, dust- and dirtproof, corrosion-resistant . . . and rugged beyond belief. It's been bounced off hard roads, frozen in ice, drenched in salt spray . . . and come up shooting every time. Here's a camera you can take out in rain or snow, on a boat, to the beach or into your pool and never worry about it. To clean your Nikonos III, just rinse it in fresh water.

Above all, the Nikonos III is a superbly competent and versatile photographic instrument. You'll love the fast and easy way it handles . . . with oversize controls, an ingenious combination film transport/shutter release lever, and cross-ribbed rubber covering that gives you a secure grip even under water.

The Nikonos III accepts special, interchangeable Nikkor lenses that are exactly what you would expect from Nikkor optics; outstandingly sharp, with superb color quality. The 35mm and 80mm can be used above or below the surface, while the 15mm and 28mm are specifically corrected for underwater photography. The Nikonos system also includes a close-up outfit, underwater flash and meter, filters, and action finders.

Your Nikon dealer can tell you more. He's listed in the Yellow Pages. Or write to Nikon Inc., Dept. N-24, Garden City, New York 11530. Subsidiary of Ehrenreich Photo-Optical Industries, Inc., EPOI (In Canada: Anglophoto Ltd., P.Q.)

DECEMBER 1978

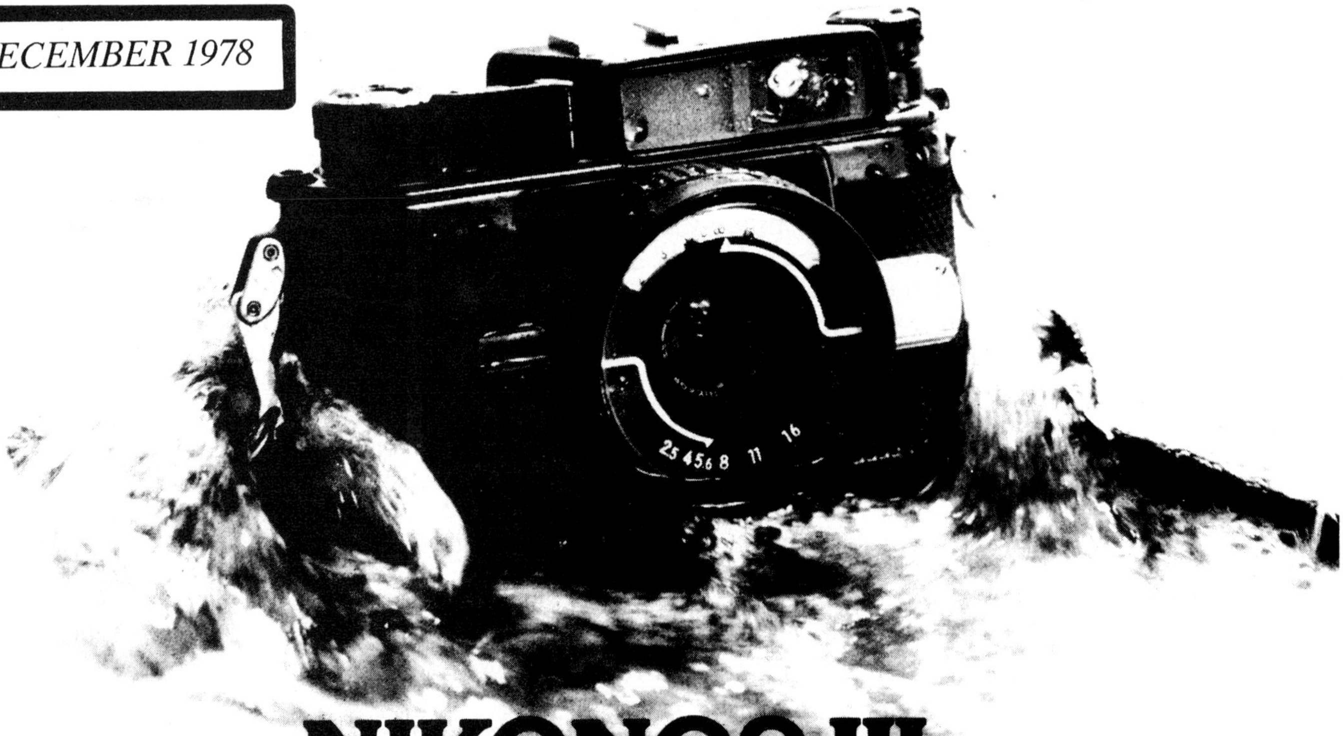

NIKONOS III

The 35mm camera that goes where others can't.

CHAPTER TWENTY

PRICE DATA

Explanation of columns:

1. Column 1 tells the first year the product was available from Nikon Inc. It is possible and even likely that examples of the product were produced in Japan previous to this date. It is also possible that the product was displayed at Photokina and even sold in other countries previous to this date.

2. The second column is the last year the product was available from Nikon Inc. Some retail outlets may have offered the product from stock on hand after this date.

3. MFG LIST. The third column is the list price suggested by the US supplier: in recent years, Nikon, Inc. Virtually every retailer sells products at prices less than the suggested list price. This is the price for the item during its last year of availability (column 2).

4. CAMERA STORE. The fourth column represents the price customers will usually encounter at most camera stores. These figures were determined from a survey of medium size camera dealers in metropolitan areas. They are low average selling prices for new products with the USA warranty. This price is for the item during its last year of availability (column 2).

5. MAIL ORDER. Column 5 is an average of the lowest prices offered by dealers who advertise in national publications, principally *Shutterbug* and *Popular Photography.* They are a **low** average advertised price for new items offered with or without the USA warranty. A zero (0) in this column means too few (or none) were advertised during the past year.

6. USER. The sixth column is the price a diligent buyer is most likely to encounter when purchasing a used item in "user" condition. This level of condition means that the product shows considerable wear including brassing and possibly a few dents, but is in good working order. The figures were derived from a low average of advertised prices.

7. XLNT. The seventh column is the price a diligent buyer is most likely to encounter when purchasing a used item in "excellent" condition. This level of condition means that the product shows some wear, but not much. There may be a slight amount of brassing. The product is in excellent working condition. The figures were derived from a low average of advertised prices.

8. MINT. The eighth column is the price a diligent buyer is most likely to encounter when purchasing a used item in "mint" condition. This level of condition means that the product shows essentially no wear and is without any brassing. It is in "as new" working condition. Instruction books, warranty cards and the original packing materials may be included. The figures were derived from a low average of advertised prices.

Notes: A zero (0) indicates insufficient, unreliable or no data available. Rangefinder cameras are collector items. An insufficient number were advertised, therefore, the prices are estimates based on those which were offered plus data from various collector camera price guides.

RANGEFINDER CAMERAS

	DATES	LIST	STORE	MAIL	USER	XLNT	MINT
I w/lens	48 49	0	0	0	2000	3000	4000
M (w/ lens)	49 50	0	0	0	800	950	1200
S w/lens	51 54	269	269	0	120	150	180
S2 Black w/lens	54 58	319	310	0	175	200	250
S2 Chrome w/lens	54 58	299	299	0	155	205	255
S3 Black w/lens	58 60	205	205	0	475	500	725
S3 Chrome w/lens	58 60	185	185	0	250	325	395
S3 Olympic	58 0	0	0	0	595	800	995
S3M (with S72 motor)	60 61	449	359	0	4100	4500	5000
S4 w/lens	59 0	0	0	0	435	500	645
SP Black w/lens	57 65	275	219	0	450	550	650
SP Chrome w/lens	57 66	245	199	0	395	500	565

SINGLE LENS REFLEXES

	DATES	LIST	STORE	MAIL	USER	XLNT	MINT
EM	79 84	231	180	0	70	90	110
F Black (w/ finder)	59 74	375	316	0	90	110	130
F Chrome (w/ finder)	59 74	355	304	0	70	100	120
F Photomic Black	62 66	275	200	0	130	140	165
F Photomic Chrome	62 66	255	200	0	120	135	150
F Photomic FTN Black	68 74	494	395	0	200	240	260
F Photomic FTN Chrome	68 74	474	370	0	180	225	250
F Photomic T Black	65 66	305	244	0	135	155	180
F Photomic T Chrome	65 66	285	220	0	125	145	170
F Photomic TN Black	67 68	315	252	0	160	210	230
F Photomic TN Chrome	67 68	295	230	0	150	200	220
F2 Black (w/ finder)	71 80	666	519	0	260	360	410
F2 Chrome (w/ finder)	71 80	643	490	0	250	325	400
F2 Photomic Black	71 77	649	430	0	325	360	410
F2 Photomic Chrome	71 77	629	420	0	300	350	400
F2 Titan (Space Model)	76 76	0	0	0	0	0	2750
F2A Photomic Black	77 80	826	637	0	400	430	490
F2A Photomic Chrome	77 80	803	620	0	380	440	530
F2AS Photomic Black	77 80	1025	807	0	450	690	775
F2AS Photomic Chrome	77 80	1002	779	0	400	600	760
F2H (High-Speed)	76 80	2995	2430	0	0	0	0
F2S Photomic Black	73 76	765	602	0	350	400	425
F2S Photomic Chrome	73 76	745	587	0	300	370	400
F2SB Photomic Black	76 77	815	580	0	360	410	460
F2SB Photomic Chrome	76 76	795	563	0	350	400	450
F2T (Titanium)	76 80	707	575	0	900	1000	1300
F3 (w/ finder)	80 83	810	625	600	480	520	525
F3/T (Titanium)	82 90	1595	1290	1190	725	875	1050
F3AF (Autofocus)	83 88	1710	1390	0	600	650	725
F3HP (High-Eye Point)	82 90	1295	900	810	585	600	645
F3P (Professional)	83 90	1709	0	0	850	1000	1200

	DATES	LIST	STORE	MAIL	USER	XLNT	MINT
F4S (w/ finder)	89 90	2428	1980	1795	1500	1600	1650
FA Black	83 88	790	610	520	360	400	430
FA Chrome	83 88	765	590	500	350	395	410
FE Black	78 83	420	320	0	235	260	280
FE Chrome	78 83	399	307	0	230	250	270
FE2 Black	83 88	550	425	0	350	380	440
FE2 Chrome	83 88	530	408	0	340	375	430
FG Black (w/ 50 1.8E)	82 86	453	290	0	170	180	230
FG Chrome (w/ 50 1.8)	82 86	436	280	0	140	160	190
FG-20 (w/ 50 1.8E)	84 86	380	292	0	110	160	165
FM Black	77 83	314	242	0	200	240	270
FM Chrome	77 83	301	232	0	190	210	250
FM2 Black	82 88	545	410	400	275	300	330
FM2 Chrome	82 88	525	390	340	260	290	320
FM2n Black	89 90	545	475	380	310	350	360
FM2n Chrome	89 90	525	462	360	295	325	335
N2000	85 90	440	330	270	195	220	230
N2020	86 88	603	0	330	240	250	300
N4004	87 88	478	350	315	150	220	235
N4004s	89 90	485	390	315	190	225	240
N8008	88 90	858	630	610	425	500	515
Nikk. (Nikon) EL2 Bl.	77 78	582	400	0	210	250	290
Nikk. (Nikon) EL2 Ch.	77 78	562	390	0	200	220	260
Nikkorex 35	60 61	0	0	0	0	0	0
Nikkorex 35 Zoom	63 65	220	176	0	120	150	170
Nikkorex 35-2	62 64	125	99	0	0	0	0
Nikkorex Auto 35	64 66	130	104	0	0	0	0
Nikkorex F	62 65	110	80	0	40	50	60
Nikkormat EL Black	72 76	478	382	0	170	190	210
Nikkormat EL Chrome	72 76	460	368	0	165	170	200
Nikkormat ELW	76 77	500	399	0	200	220	250
Nikkormat FS	65 70	114	90	0	120	140	150
Nikkormat FT Black	65 66	194	155	0	120	170	180
Nikkormat FT Chrome	65 66	184	140	0	115	165	170
Nikkormat FT2 Black	75 77	297	237	0	160	200	210
Nikkormat FT2 Chrome	75 77	287	230	0	150	165	200
Nikkormat FT3 Black	77 78	307	245	0	160	180	200
Nikkormat FT3 Chrome	77 78	307	245	0	150	170	190
Nikkormat FTN Black	67 74	285	220	0	120	145	160
Nikkormat FTN Chrome	67 74	275	220	0	100	130	140

UNDERWATER CAMERA BODIES

	DATES	LIST	STORE	MAIL	USER	XLNT	MINT
Nikonos I	63 67	100	80	0	150	175	190
Nikonos II	68 74	187	149	0	170	190	210
Nikonos III	75 80	359	269	0	180	215	250
Nikonos IV-A	80 84	516	387	0	250	270	300
Nikonos V (Green)	84 90	620	460	380	300	320	340
Nikonos V (Orange)	84 90	620	460	380	300	320	340

LIGHT METERS AND METER PRISMS

	DATES	LIST	STORE	MAIL	USER	XLNT	MINT
Exposure Meter Model 3	63 67	39	32	0	0	0	0
Exposure Meter Model A	60 65	27	24	0	0	0	0
Exposure Meter Model D	63 70	14	12	0	0	0	0
Photomic F	62 66	80	64	0	40	50	60
Photomic F2	71 77	225	180	0	0	0	0
Photomic F2A	77 84	305	240	0	0	0	0
Photomic F2AS	77 84	514	400	0	0	0	0
Photomic F2S	71 76	327	260	0	0	0	0
Photomic F2SB	76 78	489	399	0	0	0	0
Photomic FTN Black	68 74	179	144	0	120	160	180
Photomic FTN Chrome	68 74	173	139	0	100	150	170
Photomic T Black	65 67	112	90	0	45	55	65
Photomic T Chrome	65 67	110	90	0	40	50	60
Photomic TN Black	67 67	122	99	0	55	65	75
Photomic TN Chrome	67 67	120	96	0	50	60	70

POINT & SHOOT CAMERAS

	DATES	LIST	STORE	MAIL	USER	XLNT	MINT
Action Touch	86 90	322	240	175	150	190	200
Fun Touch	87 88	194	150	110	0	0	0
New One Touch	87 88	275	210	170	0	0	0
Nice Touch	84 86	175	135	0	90	100	110
One Touch	83 88	238	183	120	75	90	100
One Touch 100	88 90	210	156	115	90	100	120
Tele Touch	86 88	339	240	190	80	110	120
Tele Touch 300	89 90	243	180	150	0	0	0
Tele Touch 300 Date	89 90	259	200	0	0	0	0
Tele Touch deluxe	88 90	317	240	187	130	140	149
Tele Touch deluxe Date	89 90	323	245	195	140	150	160
Zoom Touch 500	89 90	388	286	295	0	0	0
Zoom Touch 500 Date	89 90	404	311	277	0	0	0

LENSES FOR 35mm CAMERAS

AUTOFOCUS	DATES	LIST	STORE	MAIL	USER	XLNT	MINT
AF 20mm 2.8	88 90	648	500	445	370	400	425
AF 24-50mm 3.3-4.5	88 90	485	375	320	250	290	310
AF 24mm 2.8	86 90	410	316	270	200	225	240
AF 28-85mm 3.5-4.5	86 90	500	386	350	250	275	300
AF 28mm 2.8	86 90	248	191	165	110	130	150
AF 35-105mm 3.5-4.5	86 90	510	394	330	250	300	330
AF 35-135mm 3.5-4.5	86 88	543	370	360	300	320	340
AF 35-135mm 3.5-4.5N	89 90	543	410	400	0	0	0
AF 35-70mm 2.8	88 90	798	616	600	450	460	475
AF 35-70mm 3.3-4.5	86 89	223	175	135	100	110	120
AF 35mm 2.0	88 90	418	323	280	0	0	0
AF 50mm 1.4	86 90	308	237	185	155	170	185
AF 50mm 1.8	86 90	103	80	65	40	45	50
AF 55mm 2.8 Micro	86 89	448	346	340	275	295	310
AF 60mm 2.8 Micro	89 90	494	340	390	0	0	0
AF 70-210mm 4.0	86 87	316	243	245	210	230	240
AF 70-210mm 4.0-5.6	88 90	335	259	235	170	185	195
AF 75-300mm 4.5-5.6	88 90	658	508	490	0	0	0
AF 80-200mm 2.8 ED	88 90	1150	888	925	750	775	800
AF 80mm 2.8	83 88	550	410	0	170	180	190
AF 85mm 1.8	88 90	425	328	295	260	275	290
AF 105mm 2.8 Micro	90 90	0	0	0	0	0	0
AF 180mm 2.8 ED-IF	86 89	845	652	615	550	600	625
AF 180mm 2.8N ED-IF	89 90	925	705	0	0	0	0
AF 200mm 3.5	83 88	1475	1100	600	400	440	500
AF 300mm 2.8 ED-IF	87 88	3880	3252	3260	2400	2600	2700
AF 300mm 2.8N ED-IF	88 90	4520	3673	3350	0	0	0
AF 300mm 4.0 ED-IF	87 90	1155	891	800	0	0	0

AUTOMATIC INDEXING	DATES	LIST	STORE	MAIL	USER	XLNT	MINT
AI 6mm 2.8 Fisheye	77 84	6247	6195	0	0	0	0
AI 8mm 2.8 Fisheye	77 84	1071	868	0	680	700	790
AI 13mm 5.6	77 84	5590	4540	0	0	0	0
AI 15mm 3.5	80 84	1452	1090	0	0	0	0
AI 15mm 5.6	77 79	1646	1330	0	0	0	0
AI 16mm 2.8 Fisheye	79 84	579	434	0	500	550	570
AI 16mm 3.5 Fisheye	77 78	753	611	0	0	0	0
AI 18mm 3.5	82 84	762	571	0	500	600	650
AI 18mm 4.0	77 82	856	660	0	540	580	650
AI 20mm 3.5	79 84	361	270	0	0	0	0
AI 20mm 4.0	77 78	525	388	0	225	250	275
AI 24mm 2.0	78 84	485	370	0	375	400	450
AI 24mm 2.8	77 84	313	243	0	200	220	230
AI 25-50mm 4.0	80 84	762	571	0	250	270	300
AI 28-45mm 4.5	77 79	865	667	0	220	270	300
AI 28mm 2.0	77 84	464	377	0	300	340	360
AI 28mm 2.8	77 84	292	225	0	140	155	210
AI 28mm 3.5	77 84	215	166	0	110	135	160

AUTOMATIC INDEXING	DATES	LIST	STORE	MAIL	USER	XLNT	MINT
AI 35-105mm 3.5-4.5	83 84	324	243	0	0	0	0
AI 35-70mm 3.5	78 84	675	506	0	300	330	345
AI 35mm 1.4	77 84	506	393	0	310	340	390
AI 35mm 2.0	77 84	270	230	0	120	140	200
AI 35mm 2.8	77 84	180	138	0	75	90	125
AI 43-86mm 3.5	77 81	349	250	0	90	120	160
AI 50-135mm 3.5	83 84	540	405	0	0	0	0
AI 50-300mm 4.5	77 80	1953	1460	0	500	555	700
AI 50-300mm 4.5 ED	78 84	1929	1567	0	500	550	775
AI 50mm 1.2	79 84	363	270	0	180	200	220
AI 50mm 1.4	77 84	235	172	0	100	110	130
AI 50mm 1.8	78 84	159	119	0	80	90	100
AI 50mm 2.0	77 78	148	111	0	40	50	75
AI 55mm 1.2	77 78	321	247	0	220	230	250
AI 55mm 2.8 Micro	80 84	264	198	0	0	0	0
AI 55mm 3.5 Micro	77 79	325	212	0	170	175	185
AI 58mm 1.2 NOCT	78 84	1038	778	0	0	0	0
AI 80-200mm 2.8 ED	83 84	2695	2020	0	0	0	0
AI 80-200mm 4.0	82 84	701	525	0	0	0	0
AI 80-200mm 4.5	77 81	954	853	0	250	300	340
AI 85mm 1.4	81 84	625	468	0	0	0	0
AI 85mm 2.0	77 84	292	243	0	115	175	230
AI 105mm 1.8	81 84	521	390	0	0	0	0
AI 105mm 2.5	77 84	271	208	0	150	160	175
AI 105mm 4.0 Micro	77 84	456	385	0	260	300	320
AI 135mm 2.0	77 84	664	498	0	420	440	480
AI 135mm 2.8	77 84	286	265	0	110	140	200
AI 135mm 3.5	77 84	198	149	0	55	75	100
AI 180-600mm 8.0 ED	82 84	4744	3558	0	0	0	0
AI 180mm 2.8	77 81	875	675	0	485	500	520
AI 180mm 2.8 ED	81 84	679	509	0	450	470	500
AI 200-600mm 9.5	82 83	1510	1132	0	0	0	0
AI 200mm 2.0 ED-IF	80 84	2470	1850	0	0	0	0
AI 200mm 4.0	77 84	318	276	0	130	145	210
AI 200mm 4.0 IF Micro	79 84	618	464	0	450	465	485
AI 300mm 2.8 ED-IF	78 84	2695	2021	0	0	0	0
AI 300mm 4.5	77 84	464	385	0	290	300	350
AI 300mm 4.5 ED	77 78	1298	1050	0	500	550	590
AI 300mm 4.5 ED-IF	79 84	865	667	0	500	550	590
AI 360-1200mm 11.0 ED	82 84	7318	5488	0	0	0	0
AI 400mm 3.5 ED-IF	78 84	3153	2364	0	0	0	0
AI 400mm 5.6 ED	77 78	1966	1597	0	900	1000	1200
AI 400mm 5.6 ED-IF	78 84	1510	1132	0	1000	1095	1150
AI 600mm 4.0 ED-IF	79 84	4198	3148	0	0	0	0
AI 600mm 5.6 ED-IF	78 84	3220	2415	0	2850	2900	3100
AI 800mm 8.0 ED-IF	79 84	3614	2710	0	1800	2000	2200
AI 1200mm 11.0 ED-IF	79 84	5020	3765	0	0	0	0

AI SHUTTER/PROGRAM		DATES	LIST	STORE	MAIL	USER	XLNT	MINT
AIS	6mm 2.8 Fisheye	84 90	13580	11030	0	0	0	0
AIS	8mm 2.8 Fisheye	84 90	1865	1515	1100	850	875	900
AIS	13mm 5.6	84 90	11680	9490	0	4900	4950	5000
AIS	15mm 3.5	84 90	2205	1700	1370	1150	1200	1250
AIS	16mm 2.8 Fisheye	84 90	865	700	560	505	555	570
AIS	18mm 3.5	84 90	1290	1000	770	650	680	750
AIS	20mm 2.8	85 90	635	490	425	275	320	350
AIS	20mm 3.5	84 84	361	270	0	280	290	300
AIS	24mm 2.0	84 90	799	616	500	390	410	430
AIS	24mm 2.8	84 90	453	342	290	200	215	250
AIS	25-50mm 4.0	84 85	762	570	0	325	360	390
AIS	28-50mm 3.5	84 86	455	341	0	240	260	290
AIS	28-85mm 3.5-4.5	86 90	638	492	425	325	365	385
AIS	28mm 2.0	84 90	698	538	450	315	335	400
AIS	28mm 2.8	84 90	443	342	280	205	225	250
AIS	28mm 3.5	84 85	215	161	0	110	140	170
AIS	35-105mm 3.5-4.5	84 90	520	402	340	240	260	280
AIS	35-135mm 3.5-4.5	85 89	645	498	400	325	350	380
AIS	35-200mm 3.5-4.	86 90	1015	780	615	450	500	625
AIS	35-70mm 3.3-4.5	85 88	238	187	0	140	150	160
AIS	35-70mm 3.5	84 86	725	543	160	345	365	430
AIS	35mm 1.4	84 90	878	677	525	350	370	500
AIS	35mm 2.0	84 90	410	317	275	180	190	200
AIS	35mm 2.8	84 85	180	135	0	160	170	175
AIS	50-135mm 3.5	84 85	540	405	0	240	270	320
AIS	50-300mm 4.5 ED	85 90	3145	2550	1965	1300	1400	1500
AIS	50mm 1.2	84 90	543	418	340	225	235	275
AIS	50mm 1.4	84 90	373	281	255	135	160	170
AIS	50mm 1.8	84 86	159	119	105	40	70	75
AIS	50mm 1.8N	86 90	118	88	90	50	60	70
AIS	55mm 2.8 Micro	84 90	386	300	250	170	180	250
AIS	58mm 1.2 Noct.	84 90	1755	1355	1250	850	870	890
AIS	80-200mm 2.8 ED	84 86	3525	2640	0	1350	1500	1650
AIS	80-200mm 4.0	84 90	973	751	630	430	460	470
AIS	85mm 1.4	84 90	968	747	580	450	520	550
AIS	85mm 2.0	84 90	415	321	300	160	225	250
AIS	100-300mm 5.6	84 90	645	500	380	305	345	345
AIS	105mm 1.8	84 90	798	616	480	355	400	450
AIS	105mm 2.5	84 90	410	317	265	150	180	195
AIS	105mm 2.8 Micro	84 90	740	571	480	415	425	460
AIS	105mm 4.0 Micro	84 84	456	344	0	320	330	350
AIS	105mm 4.5UV Micro	85 90	3030	2458	2000	0	0	0
AIS	135mm 2.0	85 90	1045	808	620	460	590	620
AIS	135mm 2.8	84 90	410	317	260	150	190	240
AIS	135mm 3.5	84 85	198	148	140	70	75	90
AIS	180-600mm 8.0 ED	84 90	9845	8000	6200	4500	5000	5200
AIS	180mm 2.8 ED	84 89	1035	776	870	580	600	630
AIS	200-400mm 4.0 ED	84 88	6458	4840	4250	3500	4000	4200
AIS	200mm 2.0 ED-IF	84 88	4673	3800	2960	2400	2700	2800
AIS	200mm 2.0N ED-IF	89 90	4673	3500	3300	2400	2650	2895
AIS	200mm 4.0	84 90	463	358	275	200	235	250
AIS	200mm 4.0IF Micro	84 90	945	730	570	535	550	565
AIS	300mm 2.0 ED-IF	84 90	29150	29000	0	0	0	16000

AI SHUTTER/PROGRAM	DATES	LIST	STORE	MAIL	USER	XLNT	MINT
AIS 300mm 2.8 ED-IF	84 89	4195	3400	2995	2800	2825	2850
AIS 300mm 2.8N ED-IF	89 90	4195	3400	0	0	0	0
AIS 300mm 4.5	84 90	730	563	475	365	375	400
AIS 300mm 4.5 ED-IF	84 90	1338	1034	920	740	750	760
AIS 360-1200 11.0 ED	84 84	7318	5940	0	0	0	0
AIS 400mm 2.8 ED-IF	85 90	7595	6170	5275	4100	4200	4300
AIS 400mm 3.5 ED-IF	84 90	4805	3917	3110	2500	2700	2800
AIS 400mm 5.6 ED-IF	84 90	2305	1873	1575	900	1200	1275
AIS 500mm 4.0 ED-IF P	88 90	5200	4225	3600	0	0	0
AIS 600mm 4.0 ED-IF	84 88	7745	6290	0	3900	4200	4500
AIS 600mm 4.0N ED-IF	89 90	7745	6294	4950	0	0	0
AIS 600mm 5.6 ED-IF	84 88	5095	4140	3275	2500	2650	2800
AIS 600mm 5.6N ED-IF	89 90	5095	4140	3500	0	0	0
AIS 800mm 5.6 ED-IF	86 90	6458	5247	4180	0	0	0
AIS 800mm 8.0 ED-IF	84 88	4750	3860	0	2300	2400	2450
AIS 1200mm 11.0 ED-IF	84 88	6295	4900	0	0	0	0

E TYPE	DATES	LIST	STORE	MAIL	USER	XLNT	MINT
E 28mm 2.8	80 86	158	126	125	100	115	125
E 35mm 2.5	79 83	114	91	0	65	70	80
E 36-72mm 3.5	82 84	290	229	0	135	140	145
E 50mm 1.8	79 86	97	75	0	30	40	50
E 70-210mm 4.0	82 86	453	362	300	145	165	180
E 75-150mm 3.5	80 84	316	249	200	125	150	200
E 100mm 2.8	79 80	134	107	112	60	70	90
E 135mm 2.8	81 84	160	128	90	100	110	130

MEDICAL	DATES	LIST	STORE	MAIL	USER	XLNT	MINT
Medical 120mm 4.0 IF	81 90	1655	1324	1000	940	955	970
Medical 200mm 5.6	63 84	970	775	0	275	300	450

NON-AUTOMATIC INDEXING	DATES	LIST	STORE	MAIL	USER	XLNT	MINT
NAI 6mm 5.6 Fisheye	72 77	1355	1101	0	600	650	700
NAI 8mm 2.8 Fisheye	70 77	1175	955	0	0	0	0
NAI 13mm 5.6	76 77	6250	5070	0	0	0	0
NAI 15mm 5.6	73 77	1249	1000	0	650	800	950
NAI 16mm 3.5 Fisheye	73 77	570	460	0	380	400	420
NAI 18mm 4.0	74 77	649	500	0	230	250	300
NAI 20mm 3.5	69 73	320	260	0	200	275	330
NAI 20mm 4.0	74 77	400	308	0	180	190	210
NAI 24mm 2.8	67 77	292	233	0	170	190	225
NAI 28-45mm 4.5	74 77	660	528	0	200	220	240
NAI 28mm 2.0	71 77	460	355	0	300	310	340
NAI 28mm 2.8	74 77	318	245	0	150	175	190
NAI 28mm 3.5	59 77	253	195	0	75	100	150
NAI 35mm 1.4	70 77	495	382	0	200	275	350
NAI 35mm 2.0	65 77	283	217	0	125	145	190

NON-AUTOMATIC INDEXING	DATES	LIST	STORE	MAIL	USER	XLNT	MINT
NAI 35mm 2.8	59 77	205	160	0	65	75	85
NAI 43-86mm 3.5	63 77	300	240	0	70	90	120
NAI 45mm 2.8 GN	69 77	149	115	0	75	90	140
NAI 50-300mm 4.5	65 77	1450	1160	0	400	480	600
NAI 50mm 1.4	63 76	216	168	0	40	65	80
NAI 50mm 2.0	59 76	125	89	0	25	35	50
NAI 55mm 1.2	65 76	318	245	0	110	140	180
NAI 55mm 3.5 Micro	63 77	293	234	0	120	140	175
NAI 58mm 1.4	59 60	155	124	0	90	100	140
NAI 80-200mm 4.5	70 77	705	564	0	275	295	350
NAI 85-250mm 4.0	59 69	512	410	0	200	250	275
NAI 85mm 1.8	64 77	300	230	0	170	190	200
NAI 105mm 2.5	59 77	307	236	0	90	115	125
NAI 105mm 4.0 Micro	74 77	530	424	0	260	280	300
NAI 135mm 2.0	76 77	650	500	0	400	450	500
NAI 135mm 2.8	65 77	320	223	0	70	100	120
NAI 135mm 3.5	59 77	230	177	0	55	65	75
NAI 180-600mm 8.0 ED	74 77	5795	4630	0	0	0	0
NAI 180mm 2.8	70 77	630	486	0	450	490	550
NAI 200-600mm 9.5	63 76	1369	1095	0	500	650	750
NAI 200-600mm 9.5 ED	77 81	1873	1498	0	0	0	0
NAI 200mm 4.0	63 77	325	235	0	90	100	120
NAI 300mm 4.5	64 77	485	373	0	200	250	325
NAI 300mm 4.5 ED	75 77	990	800	0	0	490	0
NAI 360-1200mm 11 ED	74 81	8499	5460	0	0	0	0
NAI 400mm 4.5	66 79	1198	958	0	0	0	0
NAI 400mm 5.6	73 74	1405	1124	0	450	500	550
NAI 400mm 5.6 ED	75 77	1500	1200	0	0	0	0
NAI 600mm 5.6	64 79	1579	1260	0	0	0	0
NAI 600mm 5.6 ED	75 80	2544	2035	0	0	0	2250
NAI 800mm 8.0	64 78	2050	1640	0	0	0	0
NAI 800mm 8.0 ED	75 78	3127	2500	0	0	0	0

NOT METER COUPLED	DATES	LIST	STORE	MAIL	USER	XLNT	MINT
NMC 6.2mm 5.6 Fish	69 69	895	716	0	0	0	0
NMC 6mm 5.6	77 79	1762	1400	0	0	0	0
NMC 6mm 5.6 Fisheye	70 76	1355	1100	0	0	0	0
NMC 7.5mm 5.6 Fish	67 71	512	409	0	0	0	0
NMC 8mm 8.0 Fisheye	63 66	460	368	0	0	0	0
NMC 10mm 5.6	77 81	1585	1268	0	0	0	0
NMC 10mm 5.6 Fisheye	69 76	1215	987	0	0	0	0
NMC 21mm 4.0 Preset	59 67	200	160	0	0	130	0
NMC 105mm 4.0 Bellows	69 76	219	175	0	0	0	0
NMC 105mm 4.0 Preset	59 76	530	424	0	0	0	0
NMC 300mm 2.8 ED	75 77	3000	2400	0	0	0	0
NMC 1200mm 11.0	64 78	2354	1883	0	0	0	0
NMC 1200mm 11.0 ED	75 78	3904	3123	0	0	0	0

PERSPECTIVE CONTROL	DATES	LIST	STORE	MAIL	USER	XLNT	MINT
PC 28mm 3.5	74 90	1245	961	760	595	625	695
PC 35mm 2.8	63 88	815	630	490	360	380	420
PC 35mm 2.8N	89 90	815	424	0	0	0	0

RANGEFINDER	DATES	LIST	STORE	MAIL	USER	XLNT	MINT
RF 21mm 4.0	60 62	200	159	0	0	0	0
RF 25mm 4.0	51 63	160	128	0	0	0	0
RF 28mm 3.5	48 67	125	99	0	0	0	0
RF 35mm 1.8	56 67	161	128	0	0	0	0
RF 35mm 2.5	48 63	120	96	0	0	0	0
RF 35mm 3.5	48 63	95	76	0	0	230	0
RF 50mm 1.1	56 65	300	239	0	0	0	0
RF 50mm 1.4	48 71	123	104	0	70	80	100
RF 50mm 2.0	48 71	80	0	0	0	0	0
RF 50mm 3.5 Micro	63 64	145	116	0	0	0	0
RF 85mm 1.5	51 62	300	249	0	0	0	0
RF 85mm 2.0	48 66	190	149	0	0	130	0
RF 105mm 2.5	48 67	153	129	0	0	0	0
RF 105mm 4.0	60 71	81	65	0	0	0	0
RF 135mm 3.5	48 68	135	110	0	100	120	150

MIRROR	DATES	LIST	STORE	MAIL	USER	XLNT	MINT
Reflex 500mm 5.0	63 69	530	424	0	0	0	0
Reflex 500mm 8.0	69 84	492	393	0	250	300	320
Reflex 500mm 8.0N	84 90	868	670	570	425	450	505
Reflex 1000mm 11.0	65 88	1885	1500	0	700	850	1000
Reflex 1000mm 11.0N	89 90	1885	1532	1100	0	0	0
Reflex 2000mm 11.0	69 88	8775	7020	0	0	0	0

SHORT MOUNT	DATES	LIST	STORE	MAIL	USER	XLNT	MINT
SM 135mm 4.0	61 67	125	100	0	0	0	0
SM 180mm 2.5	55 66	425	340	0	0	0	0
SM 250mm 4.0	55 63	250	200	0	0	0	0
SM 350mm 4.5	58 64	420	336	0	0	0	0
SM 500mm 5.0	55 61	550	440	0	0	0	0
SM 1000mm 6.3	58 65	1750	1440	0	0	0	0

TELECONVERTERS	DATES	LIST	STORE	MAIL	USER	XLNT	MINT
TC- 1	78 81	260	208	0	245	250	255
TC- 2	78 83	520	416	0	0	0	0
TC- 14	79 83	417	333	0	290	300	330
TC- 14A	84 90	323	250	220	180	185	190
TC- 14B	84 90	673	520	435	290	310	350
TC- 14C	86 87	595	476	0	0	0	0
TC- 16A	84 90	435	348	0	190	221	245
TC- 16B	84 90	228	176	160	85	95	110
TC-200	78 83	188	150	0	125	130	135
TC-201	84 90	323	250	210	130	145	155
TC-300	78 83	417	333	325	240	260	280
TC-301	84 90	673	520	410	395	405	420

UNDERWATER	DATES	LIST	STORE	MAIL	USER	XLNT	MINT
UW 15mm 2.8 UW	73 83	986	788	0	0	0	0
UW 15mm 2.8 UW (new)	83 88	1732	1285	0	0	0	0
UW 15mm 2.8N UW	89 90	1736	1400	1100	0	0	0
UW 20mm 2.8 UW	86 90	760	617	485	0	0	0
UW 28mm 2.8 LW	83 88	270	216	0	0	0	0
UW 28mm 3.5 UW	65 90	385	312	250	180	185	200
UW 35mm 2.5	63 90	188	140	125	65	80	100
UW 80mm 4.0	72 90	385	312	260	160	190	220

MOTOR DRIVES FOR NIKON CAMERAS

	DATES	LIST	STORE	MAIL	USER	XLNT	MINT
Auto Winder AW-1	80 84	117	95	0	60	80	100
F-250 (with battery)	0 83	1127	915	0	810	850	900
F-36 (with battery)	0 81	879	700	0	270	290	315
MD- 1 w/battery pack	71 74	630	500	0	300	330	350
MD- 2 w/battery pack	74 84	939	750	620	375	420	450
MD- 3 w/battery pack	78 84	414	330	0	250	300	310
MD- 4	80 90	485	395	330	250	275	300
MD-11	77 79	292	230	0	150	160	185
MD-12	80 90	398	324	250	170	180	225
MD-14	82 86	200	160	0	110	130	150
MD-15	84 88	295	235	0	170	250	280
MD-E	80 86	116	93	0	60	95	100
S-36 (for SP or S3)	57 66	230	184	0	200	250	350

BACKS FOR NIKON 35mm BODIES

	DATES	LIST	STORE	MAIL	USER	XLNT	MINT
MF- 1 250X magazine	74 84	226	180	200	270	280	300
MF- 2 800X magazine	74 84	5131	4160	0	0	0	0
MF- 3	74 84	110	90	0	60	75	80
MF- 4 250X magazine	82 90	1135	899	700	600	660	690
MF- 6	80 84	81	65	0	50	55	60
MF- 6B	84 90	120	96	70	40	50	60
MF-12 data	82 84	175	140	0	55	65	95
MF-14 date	82 90	215	175	135	45	85	120
MF-15 data	82 86	175	140	0	65	80	90
MF-16	83 90	213	174	150	70	90	125
MF-17 250X magazine	83 90	4550	3690	0	0	0	0
MF-18 date	85 90	351	280	290	0	0	0
MF-19 data	85 90	225	184	145	100	110	120
MF-20 data	88 90	94	78	75	50	60	65
MF-21	88 90	225	188	190	125	135	150
MF-22	88 90	170	139	135	110	125	130
MF-23	88 90	600	488	490	395	425	455
MF-24 250X magazine F4	89 90	4200	4100	4000	0	0	0
Speed Magny 100	66 74	490	450	0	280	320	335
Speed Magny 100-2	72 75	600	540	0	400	420	435
Speed Magny 45	67 74	490	450	0	0	0	0
Speed Magny 45-2	72 78	710	639	0	0	0	0
Speed Magny 45-3	82 86	1925	1560	0	0	0	0
Speed Magny RF	69 78	750	675	0	0	0	0

FLASH AND STROBE UNITS

	DATES	LIST	STORE	MAIL	USER	XLNT	MINT
BC-1	0 0	0	0	0	0	0	0
BC-2	0 0	0	0	0	0	0	0
BC-3	0 60	35	28	0	0	0	0
BC-4	0 0	0	0	0	0	0	0
BC-5	0 66	30	24	0	0	0	0
BC-6	0 66	11	10	0	0	0	0
BC-7	67 83	40	32	0	0	0	30
Repeating AC power	69 75	900	720	0	0	0	0
Repeating battery pwr	69 75	645	516	0	0	0	0
SB- 1	69 73	200	160	0	40	50	60
SB- 2	77 77	130	104	0	40	50	60
SB- 3	77 77	125	100	0	0	0	0
SB- 4	77 78	80	64	0	0	0	0
SB- 5	77 81	712	569	0	230	250	260
SB- 6	78 90	2350	1910	0	0	0	0
SB- 7E	78 78	135	99	0	40	50	60
SB- 8E	78 78	135	56	0	15	20	30
SB- 9	77 79	65	30	0	20	25	30

	DATES	LIST	STORE	MAIL	USER	XLNT	MINT
SB- 10	78 84	105	78	0	40	50	60
SB- 11	80 90	435	348	245	170	200	220
SB- 12	80 83	145	116	85	45	60	80
SB- 14	82 90	550	440	350	240	260	290
SB- 15	82 87	135	108	0	95	120	130
SB- 16A	83 90	355	275	230	140	170	185
SB- 16B	83 90	335	260	225	150	180	190
SB- 17	83 90	220	170	135	65	115	120
SB- 19	84 87	80	64	60	30	40	50
SB- 20 AF	86 90	255	196	160	80	95	110
SB- 21A (Macro) F3	86 90	525	406	335	260	280	300
SB- 21B (Macro) ISO	86 90	500	386	340	220	230	250
SB- 22 AF	87 90	168	130	100	70	80	100
SB- 23 AF	88 90	129	100	89	60	70	80
SB- 24 AF	88 90	370	288	255	200	250	275
SB-101 (underwater)	80 84	469	375	0	0	0	0
SB-102 (underwater)	85 90	1105	880	750	500	550	600
SB-103 (underwater)	85 90	588	470	420	240	260	290
SB-140	86 90	638	510	400	0	0	0
SB-E	79 86	60	48	29	20	22	37
SM-1	71 73	120	96	0	0	0	0
SM-2	75 88	325	260	0	0	0	0
SR-1	71 73	110	88	0	0	0	0
SR-2	75 88	275	220	0	0	0	0
Underwater Flash Gun	65 74	136	108	0	0	0	0
Underwater Flash Ni II	75 85	190	152	0	0	0	0
Underwater Flash NiIII	75 85	235	188	0	0	0	0

MOVIE AND VIDEO CAMERAS

	DATES	LIST	STORE	MAIL	USER	XLNT	MINT
5X Super Zoom	0 0	0	0	0	0	0	0
8X Super Zoom	69 73	400	320	0	0	0	0
Nikkorex 8	61 63	80	65	0	0	0	0
Nikkorex 8 Zoom	63 65	170	136	0	0	0	0
Nikkorex 8F	64 65	90	72	0	0	0	0
R- 8 Super Zoom	73 79	800	400	0	0	0	0
R-10 Super Zoom	73 79	1000	500	0	0	0	0
Super Zoom 8	67 70	250	200	0	0	0	0
VN- 800 Camcorder	86 87	1849	1495	0	0	0	0
VN- 810 Camcorder	87 88	1810	1495	0	0	0	0
VN- 820 Camcorder	88 88	1700	1195	0	0	0	0
VN- 830 Camcorder	89 89	1300	995	850	0	0	0
VN- 840 Camcorder	89 90	1400	995	995	0	0	0
VN- 900 Camcorder	89 89	1850	1495	1495	0	0	0
VN- 910 Camcorder	89 90	1500	1295	1300	0	0	0
VN- 950 Camcorder	89 90	2200	1995	2000	0	0	0
VN-3000 VHS Camcorder	88 88	1650	1395	0	0	0	0

POSTSCRIPT

Much of the information in this book was developed from data derived from a collection of consecutive Nikon USA price lists. Usually, the company sends a new price list around the beginning of each year to all authorized dealers. In 1990, however, by the time this book went to press, no new price list had been issued. The authors have been told there probably will not be one until early summer. The significance of this is that, in all likelihood, there will be no price increases.

The Nikon line of products is so vast that one book cannot list every item. In this volume, the authors intentionally omitted binoculars, large format lenses and close-up accessories for the rangefinder camera series. Also small items such as filters were left out. Nikon made many special items for military and space applications, but usually they are modified versions of stock products.

One camera that deserves mention is the 25th Anniversary edition of the Nikon F2. It came in a wooden box and the camera bore a special inscription plate. While possibly collectible, other than the plate, the camera is the same as any other F2. The plate was glued on in the US. It does not appear on any of the price lists the authors have seen.

Some interesting facts and trends were discovered during the compilation of the price data. Beginning in 1989, data was entered into a computer. After recording price data from monthly magazines, prices that were extremely high or extremely low were discarded on the basis that these were probably errors. The result was excellent samples of prices for most Nikon products.

Two major trends were obvious. First, the prices for used Nikon products are increasing. From August 1989 to March 1990, the prices have increased an average of 9 percent. Some products decreased during this time span, but they were exceptions. Key items like the FA, plus the FM and FE series pulled the average up. Second, the price differences from various sources seem to be narrowing. Retailers are selling for less and many mail-order prices are proportionately higher.

Other interesting facts that emerged concerned price variations. In the same issue of *Shutterbug*, some advertisers will ask more for a used item than another will offer it new! After observing this phenomenon a number of times, one of the authors called some of these sellers and was told the used items had already been sold, usually at the asking price.

Finally, the authors would like to solicit your help in obtaining data for future editions. In some cases, the authors have been unable to obtain information regarding certain items. Nikon, Inc. kept old files in the basement of their New York offices. Unfortunately, the basement was flooded and some records have been destroyed.

If any readers can shed light on these matters, the authors would be most appreciative and will include the information in the next edition together with credit where credit is due. Price information is needed for the following products: Rangefinder models I, M, S3 Olympic, S4; Nikkorex 35; Flash guns BC-1, BC-2, BC-4; 5X Super Zoom 8mm camera. Any data would be appreciated such as instruction books, brochures, ads or whatever.

Pre-1960 price lists are needed. Additionally, the authors would like to verify their copies of sixties price lists. Secondary sources such as catalogs and advertisements will help too. Please send Xerox copies. Don't send original materials in case of loss in the mail.

Please mail materials to Paul Comon and Art Evans, 800 S. Pacific Coast Highway, Suite 8332, Redondo Beach, CA 90277.